THE HEART OF THE GOSPEL

The Heart of the Gospel

SERMONS ON THE LIFE-CHANGING POWER OF THE GOOD NEWS

A. T. PIERSON

Grand Rapids, MI 49501

The Heart of the Gospel: Sermons on the Life-Changing Power of the Good News by A. T. Pierson

Published in 1996 by Kregel Publications, a division of Kregel, Inc., P. O. Box 2607, Grand Rapids, MI 49501. Kregel Publications provides trusted, biblical publications for Christian growth and service. Your comments and suggestions are valued.

Cover design: Alan G. Hartman

Library of Congress Cataloging-in-Publication Data
Pierson, A. T. (Arthur Tappan), 1837–1911.
 [Gospel—Its heart, heights, and hope]
 The Heart of the Gospel: sermons on the life-changing power of the good news / A. T. Pierson.
   p. cm.
 Originally published: The Gospel—Its Heart, Heights and Hope, Grand Rapids, Mich.: Baker Book House, 1978.
 1. Presbyterian Church—Sermons. 2. Sermons, American. I. Title.
BX9178.P55G67   1996   252'.051—dc20   95-38172
                                        CIP

ISBN 0-8254-2475-5

1 2 3 4 5 printing / year 00 99 98 97 96

Printed in the United States of America

Dedication

To the Memory of
Charles Haddon Spurgeon

That valiant soldier of the cross, who for forty years wielded with such power the sword of the Spirit, which is the word of God, and bravely bore the banner of the cross until it fell from his dying grasp, this volume of sermons, which represents a humble effort to perpetuate his testimony to the same old Gospel is most lovingly dedicated.

Contents

Foreword 9
Note to Part One 11
Note to Part Two 12
Note to Part Two 13

PART ONE • THE HEART OF THE GOSPEL

1. The Lesson of Pentecost 17
2. The Heart of the Gospel 35
3. Sin Compels Separation 52
4. The Mystery of Godliness 69
5. The Privileges of Saints 86
6. The Individuality of Grace 104
7. Life by Believing 117
8. Believing and Knowing 134
9. The Mountaintop of Prayer 152
10. The Perfect Peace 167
11. The New Birth, No Marvel 184
12. The Riches of Grace 204

PART TWO • THE HEIGHTS OF THE GOSPEL

1. The Three Determining Wills 224
2. The Secret of Overcoming Satan 242
3. Sin's Dominion Destroyed 260
4. The Security of the Saint 277
5. The Present Rest of Believers 295
6. The Christian's Crown Jewels 314
7. The Transformed Temper 329

8. The Height of Transfiguration 344
9. Awaking, Arming, Acting 360
10. Appointed and Anointed for Service 380
11. Renunciations and Compensations 396
12. Duty, a Delight 413

PART THREE • THE HOPES OF THE GOSPEL

1. The Perfection of the Law; or, No Hope in Legal Obedience 433
2. The Five Revelations; or, The Hope of Justification 452
3. The Vision of the Candelabra; or, Hope in Divine Power 467
4. The Eight Beatitudes; or, The Hope of Blessedness 484
5. The Vicarious Sufferer; or, Hope in the Cross ... 503
6. Knowledge and Duty; or, Hope in Obedience to God 517
7. The Message to Sorrowing Souls; or, Hope in Trouble 535
8. Preservation and Presentation; or, The Hope of Consummation 554
9. The Attestation of the Son of God; or, Hope Through Christ's Resurrection 570
10. The Mystery of the Resurrection; or, Hope of the Rising of the Dead 584
11. The Christian's Inventory; or, The Hope of the Inheritance 600
12. The Sum of the Gospel; or, The Hope of Intercession 616

Foreword

Arthur Tappan Pierson (1837-1911) was a man with a rich and varied ministry. Pierson helped to organize the famous Student Volunteer Movement, and for thirteen years edited *The Missionary Review of the World*. He was also involved with the deeper-life movement, particularly the ministry at English Keswick. He is one of the few American preachers to speak repeatedly at this famous conference.

But Dr. Pierson was also a pastor. He trained for the ministry and graduated in 1860 from Union Seminary in New York City. His first church was The First Congregational, in Binghamton, New York, and in 1863 he moved to the First Presbyterian Church in Waterford, New York. From 1869 to 1882 he served the renowned Fort Street Church of Detroit, and from 1883 to 1889 he pastored the Bethany Church of Philadelphia.

In 1889, Pierson went on a missionary preaching tour to Great Britain. He caught the eye and ear of Charles Haddon Spurgeon, who was ill, and looking for a capable pulpiteer to assist him. When Spurgeon died in 1892, Pierson pastored the Metropolitan Tabernacle for two years. He was good for the church—and apparently the church was good for him, for in 1896 he was baptized by immersion! During 1902 and 1903 he served Christ Church, Westminster Bridge Road, London.

Foreword

Today we know A. T. Pierson primarily as a writer. While his missionary books are still helpful and inspiring, it is to his Bible studies and sermons that we turn, not forgetting, of course, his biography of George Müller. Pierson served as a consulting editor for the original Scofield Bible and also wrote for the original series, *The Fundamentals*. His books are doctrinal and devotional, but the heart of the soul-winner and missionary always breaks through.

Pierson is practical. He is not interested in merely sharing the truth; he wants the truth to grip us and reveal itself in daily practice. He was not unlike his good friend D. L. Moody, who often said, "Every Bible should be bound in shoe-leather!" A great defender of the inspiration of the Bible, Pierson stood as a champion of orthodoxy at a time when science and higher criticism were attacking the Word of God.

It is difficult to know which Pierson book to read first. *Keys to the Word* is a favorite, as is *The Bible and Spiritual Life*. I rejoice that three of his books on the gospel have now been combined into this beautiful reprint volume, *The Gospel: Its Heart, Its Heights, Its Hopes*. These messages of A. T. Pierson will warm your heart and instruct your mind. Of course, Pierson's purpose is to stir your will so that the living and the sharing of the gospel will motivate your life.

If this is your first introduction to A. T. Pierson, I as sure this book will prompt you to look for his other titles. If you are a confirmed Pierson fan, you will, with me, thank the Lord that these timeless messages are now available again.

Warren W. Wiersbe
Chicago, Illinois 1978

Note to Part One

This book aspires to no pre-eminence as furnishing homiletic models.

Twelve sermons are here put in print which were preached in the Metropolitan Tabernacle, London, in the autumn of 1891 while Pastor C. H. Spurgeon was seeking recovered health at Mentone. They were never written, even in part, and are reproduced almost verbatim.

If any interest invests them, it is almost wholly circumstantial owing to the unique conditions under which they were spoken. Many and marked as are their defects, it pleased God in a remarkable degree to use them both to convert sinners and confirm saints.

There was a call for their publication and it was so general that it was thought best not to disregard it. It is devoutly hoped that He, for Whose sake they were prepared and preached, may have even yet some further errand for them to accomplish. With this prayer, they are sent forth in His name.

Arthur T. Pierson

Metropolitan Tabernacle
London, 1892

Note to Part Two

The sermons embraced in this volume were selected simply because they bear upon one topic which it was my special desire to present with more than usual fullness and clearness, namely, the privilege and delight which belong to a true disciple.

No firmer persuasion possesses my own mind than this—that very few, even among the saints, apprehend or appreciate the honours, dignities, and rewards which are the heritage of a child of God, even in this life. And, as in a previous series of discourses, we sought to uncover the heart of the Gospel, so in this series we have sought to get up to the heights of the Gospel, to climb the delectable mountains where the present privileges of the saints are both seen and enjoyed, and from which the towers and turrets of the celestial city are more plainly visible.

Arthur T. Pierson

Metropolitan Tabernacle
London, 1893

Note to Part Three

The apostle Paul reminds us that "we are saved by hope." Nothing has a more refining, purifying, exalting influence on character than holy expectations based on divine promises. Hope is the echo of the soul's noblest desires, and like any other echo, it answers you with increasing delicacy and ethereal tenderness of tone, losing more and more all coarseness and carnality.

This volume of sermons delivered in the Metropolitan Tabernacle groups together twelve discourses whose common center of unity is found in the various aspects of the hopes which they present and to which they appeal.

The memory of the blessed years during which it was my privilege to minister to the beloved congregation in the Tabernacle makes the preservation and publication of these familiar addresses doubly pleasant. And the hope that, after life's trials and conflicts, we may all find our mutual compensation and consummation in the presence of our blessed Lord will be the inspiration of the time to come.

Meanwhile, may our eyes be fixed on Him who is our hope. And, girding up the loins of our mind and being sober, let us hope to the end for the grace which is to be brought unto us at the revelation of Jesus Christ.

Arthur T. Pierson

London, 1896

PART ONE

The Heart of the Gospel

SERMON ONE

The Lesson of Pentecost

"Therefore came I unto you without gainsaying, as soon as I was sent for. I ask, therefore, for what intent ye have sent for me."—ACTS x. 29

THERE was a little Pentecost that day in Cæsarea. It is a great mistake to suppose that the first Pentecost at Jerusalem was the end of blessing; it was only the beginning. There are some who tell us that we should not pray that the Holy Ghost may "descend" upon us, because the Holy Ghost has already come down once for all, and he cannot be expected to come down again. Is there not here, possibly, a grave mistake? It will be observed that the Holy Spirit, who descended upon the disciples on the Day of Pentecost in Jerusalem, was also "received" by Samaritan converts, and likewise "fell on all those that heard the Word" that day in Cæsarea; and the same Holy Ghost came down also upon the disciples in Ephesus who had not before "heard whether there were a Holy Ghost or no." Now, if the Spirit of God could come down thrice in Apostolic days after the Pentecost at Jerusalem, why may the Holy Ghost not "come down" again this morning upon us who are here assembled.

There is a distinction between the work of the Holy Spirit in the conversion and sanctification of a human soul, and the work of the same Spirit *upon* us as the servants that have already received his power *within*. Those little prepositions, "in" or "within," and "on" or "upon," seem to be always used in the New Testament, and, indeed, in the whole Bible, with very great discrimination. The first two prepositions refer to that work of the Holy Ghost which is *permanent* in the soul of a child of God; but the other prepositions, "on" and "upon," refer to the *temporary* influence of the Spirit in bestowing the special endowment of power upon us during the period of our service. So that, while we may not expect or pray that the Holy Ghost will come down again in the sense of saving and sanctifying power within us, since he already dwells there, we may expect that he will come down in the sense of power for service, a new anointing for the tongue of the minister of Christ, and a new anointing for the ear of the hearer. Let us seek to get hold of this thought at this time, for it is the key of whatever work I seek to do among you in the name of the Lord. I regard the Pentecost at Jerusalem as the type and the prophecy of Pentecosts all through the history of the church of God. That was a kind of "firstfruits"—a little gathered out of the harvest field—a specimen and a prophecy of the harvest that was to come, and not as ripe and fully developed as the whole harvest would be when it was perfectly matured. So, in this sense, we are justified in looking for other Pentecosts in history that shall not only be like the first Pentecost at Jerusalem, but greater than that in results, as that was greater in results than any work of the Spirit that went before.

If intelligent disciples were asked what is the greatest

lack in the church of God to-day, I am sure the answer would be—the greatest lack is the loss of the power of the Holy Ghost. It is not so much a lack of ministers; some of them, doubtless, might as well not be ministers at all. It is not a lack of learning, for we have many learned ministers; and I have sometimes thought that a little of their learning might be dropped out without any damage. It is not a lack of churches, we have hundreds and thousands of them. Nor is it a lack of members, for we could drop a few out of our rolls without any harm to the church of God. What, then, is the lack? Why, it is the absence of spiritual power; the loss of that anointing of the Holy Ghost that makes the tongue of the minister of Jesus Christ most of all learned in the school of the grace of God. It is the lack of converting and sanctifying power attending the Word. In brief, it is the lack of the Spirit's gracious influences coming down like rain from above.

Now let us notice again that the laws of power are fixed laws. There are certain great powers of the universe that we call by the name of "forces." For instance, there is gravitation, the tendency of a falling body towards a centre. There is electricity; there is steam; there are light and heat; there are adhesion and cohesion. All these are powers in the natural world; and they all obey laws, that is, they move within certain limits on a fixed track, just as much as a train of railway carriages moves on its double lines of steel; and you can never utilize the power, off its track, any more than you can have an engine moving properly and effectively if it does not move on those steel rails.

There is one great law that pervades the universe of God; and I would emphasize that law by repetition, that you may write it down on the tablets of your memory, namely, that *whenever you obey the law of the power, the power obeys you:* but that whenever you disregard the law of the power, the power refuses to obey and serve you; and may sometimes not only oppose and defeat you, but absolutely destroy you. If you get into proper relations to the fire you are warmed and filled with its glow; but if you get into wrong relations to the fire, it burns and blisters and consumes you. If you get into right relations with steam you may harness the steam to your carriages on the land, or to your vessels on the deep, and they will bear you in safety to other parts; but if you disobey the law of the steam it not only refuses to serve you, but explodes with tremendous violence and tears you limb from limb. Just so about electricity; just so as to magnetism, and all other natural powers in the universe. Now, let it be reverently said, the Holy Ghost is the greatest of all the powers of the universe. The Holy Ghost acts according to the laws of his own power; and if you will obey those laws he will serve you, but if you transgress the laws by which that Power of God is evermore guided in his ministry among the saints, he will refuse to bless you. (Acts v. 32.)

This introduction is necessary that we should get to the doorway of this great theme. Here we have power from heaven falling upon all those that heard the Word, so that they were immediately brought to the saving knowledge of Jesus Christ, and were baptized into the company of the faithful. So seldom do we behold any such manifestations of the Holy Ghost in our modern assemblies that we might almost say that such power has been withdrawn from the church at large, at least in great manifestations, and it is only here and there, and now and then, that the Spirit of God is exhibited after the manner of the original Pentecost.

The Lesson of Pentecost

The vital question arises—What are the laws or conditions of this divine power? What is the track along which the Spirit of God moves when he bears such blessing to the souls of men? It will repay us richly if, at the outset of this brief period of service among you, having asked what is your intent in sending for me, we all, as spiritually-minded disciples, seek an answer according to the Word to that other question concerning the conditions of blessing.

Let us, looking at this incident, see what were the conditions of this power as here illustrated. God is the same: he never changes. It is man that changes. Suppose you have a fixed object here, and you move around it, the object does not change; it is in the same place and plane; it preserves the same attitude and position; but you change your position, and, therefore, your relative position with regard to the object. Now God is the one great fixed Being of the universe. He is eternally and unchangeably the same; and if he appears different, and is relatively different to us at different times, it is because of our different attitude and position with respect to him; so that if we can find out the conditions of power in this tenth chapter of the Acts of the Apostles, and can reproduce those conditions this very day in this Tabernacle of God, we have reason to expect such a manifestation of the Holy Ghost as they had in the house of Cornelius the centurion. May the Lord, therefore, guide us as we explore this great question, and show us the obvious conditions of the Holy Spirit's power! We must not only examine these conditions, but must carefully keep out any other admixture if we want this power. In chemistry, when you try to analyze certain substances, if you introduce some foreign matter, whether it combines with the rest or not, you may neutralize the effect of the other substances. Now, if we mingle with these conditions of power some foreign element, as it were, we might neutralize the power, or prevent its exercise. So let us be very careful and follow the lead of the Scriptures and of the Spirit of God.

I. In the first place we have here a messenger with a message and a prepared mind and heart.

There was a *messenger*. Mark who he was. Peter, a man, a very frail man, who dared not stand up before a maid and say—"I am Jesus' follower," but three times—and the second and third time with increasing emphasis of oath and blasphemy—declared that he did not know the man. The messenger was Peter.

Why not an angel? There is an angel in the narrative. In the beginning of this chapter we read that an angel appeared to Cornelius. Why should not that angel have told the centurion about the way of salvation? He was there; Peter was in Joppa; at least a day and a half's journey from Cæsarea. Why take those three days to send men to Joppa, to lodge over-night and bring back Peter with them, when the angel of God was there on the spot, and could have taught Cornelius "words whereby he and his house might be saved"? Although the angel came into that house, there was a limit to angelic ministry. All he was permitted to say was, "Send to Joppa, and call for Simon, whose surname is Peter"—the very disciple that denied his Lord— "and *he* shall tell thee words whereby thou and thy house shall be saved." Do you not suppose that the angel would have been glad to have told the good tidings to Cornelius? But the Lord would not allow it. I say that advisedly, because, whenever an angel appears in the New Testament, he is never permitted to tell the story of redeeming love.

The Lesson of Pentecost

In the eighth chapter of the Acts, we read that the angel said to Philip, " Go and join thyself to the chariot of the eunuch." Why did he not go himself? Again, in the twenty-seventh chapter, we find that the angel appeared to Paul in a vision of the night, and said, " God hath given thee all them that sail with thee." Why did not the angel appear to the crew and make that same announcement?

> " Never did angels taste above
> Redeeming grace and dying love."

The Lord wants *testimony*, and hence *witnesses;* and because the angels never sinned and never fell, and so were never saved by Jesus Christ, God crowds the angels back, and thrusts you and me forward. However poor a preacher, I can preach the gospel better than Gabriel can, because Gabriel cannot say what I can say, " I am a sinner saved by grace." So any believer may preach better than he. And Peter could preach better, for the very fact that he had denied his Lord, and been forgiven for his denial; the poor backslider could preach better to other backsliders because he had had that experience. So the Lord says, " When thou art converted "—or brought back to the way of duty—"strengthen thy brethren," that are liable to fall in the same way that you fell. The Lord wants witnesses. What is a witness? That Saxon word " Witan," from which the word " witness " comes, means *to know*. If you only know, and have a tongue with which to tell what you know, the Lord says, " You can be my witness "; and if you know never so much, but know not what it is to be saved by grace, God will not have you for a witness. You could not witness if He would, for you have nothing to witness. And one reason why so few, even of disciples, appear to have any real witness for God is because they know so little about the Lord themselves. Our knowledge limits our testimony. A herald is the mouth of a message, but a witness is the mouth of an experience. Lord, give us not only the message, but the experience, that we may be true witnesses for thee!

Peter had a mind prepared to deliver his message. Peter was a kind of ecclesiastical aristocrat. He felt that all people, outside those Jews to whom he belonged, were a kind of barbarians, just as Thales, the wisest and best of the Greeks, thought of all people outside Greece. In other words, Peter had what we sometimes call *caste*. You know what the caste spirit is. "The Jews had no dealings with the Samaritans," as the woman of Samaria said to Jesus. "No dealings": that meant that a Jew would not show a lost traveller his way, or point him to a spring when he was athirst, if he was a Samaritan. That is the caste spirit on the broadest scale. Peter was an aristocrat; and it became necessary that God should take his aristocracy out of him, and break his caste spirit, before he could go and preach the gospel to these Gentile Romans in the palace of the Cæsars. A sheet was let down from heaven by four corners, and in it were all manner of four-footed beasts of the earth, wild beasts, reptiles, and fowls of the air; and Peter was told to "rise, kill, and eat." But he said, "Not so, Lord; I am a Jew, and nothing that is common or unclean ever entered my mouth." The Lord said thrice, in order that he might learn the lesson: "What God hath cleansed that call not thou common." Did you ever see anything of this kind of churchly aristocracy and caste spirit in our own day? Did you ever see any of those high-minded people who look down with scorn and contempt on what they call "the working classes," "the masses," or the "outcasts," or "the people in the slums"? We can never preach the gospel with power until we get over the caste spirit. Let me say to every Christian worker in this great congregation, if you do not get cured of your spiritual aristocracy, God never will give you the power of the Holy Ghost in reaching souls. Peter could not go down to that household in Cæsarea and preach the gospel with power to them until he had learned that any man, woman, or child in the wide world to whom God sends the message of his gospel is, before God, on an equality of right and privilege with the proudest nobles of the earth.

II. We turn from the messenger with his message and his prepared mind to the *people who heard the message*. In the first place, there were none of the ordinary conditions associated with power. There may be thousands of people in this Tabernacle this morning, and we are wont to connect power with a multitude; but here was a Pentecost when there was just a handful of the people gathered together, the kinsmen and near friends of Cornelius. Yet there was in one respect a greater display perhaps than on the day of Pentecost. We are not told that at the Pentecost in Jerusalem all those that heard the Word were converted; but we are told here that the Holy Ghost fell on "all those that heard the Word"—the men, women, and children gathered together there—every one of them received the gift of the Holy Ghost.

Then notice, again, that these hearers had also a prepared mind for the message. That is especially important. When Peter came in, Cornelius said to him, "Now, we are all here present before God to hear all things that are commanded thee of God." Was there ever another minister of Jesus Christ who had an audience that addressed him in that fashion? Suppose I should hear from this great assembly to-day in this Tabernacle one unanimous voice, " Here we are all present before God to hear all things that are commanded thee of God." It would not be possible even for so weak and unworthy a messenger to preach gospel tidings without power, if you would all give such audience as that! Did it ever occur to you what a contribution a hearer makes to the eloquence of the preacher? .A great deal is said and written about power in the pulpit, but we do not hear much about power in the pew. Mr. Gladstone says that eloquence is the pouring back on the audience in a flood what the speaker first gets from the audience in vapour. A beautiful definition of eloquence! The sun draws water from the little pools; from the open cup of every little flower that holds the dew there goes up vapour. It arises into the upper atmosphere where it is colder, and the vapour is condensed first into clouds, and then into rain; and then it comes down in a flood on the dry and thirsty earth. So the preacher of the gospel, when he speaks with power, draws from the hearts of the hearers, whom he addresses, the dewdrops, which come to him as in vapour, and he condenses the vapour and pours it back upon them in a flood of sacred eloquence. So many a minister who does not know whence his power comes owes it to praying, sympathetic, loving hearers. Charles H. Spurgeon owes to this people under God much of the inspiration of his ministry. I remember when I preached here incidentally on the 7th December, 1889, I was met beforehand by these dear brethren that surround me on this platform, and one who is no more with us but is in the glory, and there for twenty minutes they besought God in prayer that he would help me in preaching the gospel to this people; and I felt the sense of being divinely uplifted and upborne by those prayers. A man cannot help preaching a good sermon when the people are thus praying for him, and when their hearts are open to receive the Word, and they can say in the presence of God, "Here we are before the Lord, all waiting to hear whatever is commanded thee of God." How different the conditions when people come together, with critical and itching ears, demanding of the minister that he should say only what their prejudices or prepossessions incline them to hear; who want "smooth things" delicately said, not the sword of the Spirit sharp on the edge and piercing on the point; who like to hear something in place of the gospel, some discourse on good roads, or good laws, or good magistrates, or sanitary regulations, or the Czar of Russia, the Sultan of Turkey, or some such theme, instead of the precious Gospel! Even a mighty man of God has little power in a congregation whose hearts and minds are not ready for the reception of the truth. For observe God never forces the citadel of a human heart. May I repeat that? *God never forces the citadel of a human heart.* He will stand and knock, but there must be a hand within that opens, there must be a receptive mind and an obedient will, or God enters not to take possession.

Notice another thing: these hearers, few in number as they were, who had their hearts and their minds prepared for the Word of God, had introduced into their little assembly nothing, the nature of which was calculated to *divert attention from the truth* of the living God. There was simply a room in the house of Cornelius. They came for one purpose—to hear what Peter had to say in God's name. There seems nothing to divert or distract their minds, or hinder the power of the Spirit. Can you not understand why there is so little power in some churches of God to-day? You go into one assembly, for instance, and find, instead of the primitive apostolic praise in which the whole congregation join, an operatic quartette choir, with perhaps a very costly organ, with star singers, such as you hear in the concert hall, singing without spirit and without understanding, having no sympathy with what they sing, and simply conducting a performance in the name of worship. You go into another congregation where the minister delivers an essay, or oration, or lecture, and it would take ten thousand such, condensed and boiled down, to give you one single drop of gospel essence. The Holy Ghost never tolerates idols in his courts. If you will import into the place of worship that which takes the place of Almighty God, his praise, prayer, message of the gospel, and the single mind that looks to him for a blessing, you forfeit the blessing because you do not obey the law of the power. I owe it, as a tribute to the work of God in the Tabernacle, to say that I believe the success of this great church is owing to nothing more than to this, that the man who preaches the gospel here never preached anything else for forty years. Moreover every time a hymn is sung the people sing, and even if the rear part of the congregation chases the fore part of the congregation in a vain attempt to keep up in time, the question is how do these mingling voices salute the ears of the Lord God of hosts. If such singing offends the canons of art it does not violate the beauty of holiness; if you do transgress the laws of what some cultivated people call "æsthetics," you do not transgress the laws of the power of the Holy Ghost; and so important is this testimony to simple worship, that it were better that some calamity happen

The Lesson of Pentecost 29

to this Tabernacle itself than that it should ever be perverted to an unsanctified, a secularized art.

If we really desire to keep out of divine worship everything that turns attention from God, or hinders the power of the Holy Ghost, we are divinely taught what to do. Moses, on behalf of God, gave the Israelites a command that they should not lift up the tool of iron on his altar, but that they should worship with an altar of unhewn stone. And so even the altar of burnt sacrifice, put into the Temple courts by Solomon, was extremely simple in its whole construction. Ahaz, that idolatrous king, looked on that altar, and said, "This is very bald, this is a very bare kind of worship"; and when he went to Damascus and saw there one of the carved altars of Assyria, he said, "I will displace the plain brazen altar of sacrifice in the Temple courts, and will have this beautiful æsthetic altar of Damascus in its place." So he brought it and put it there, and crowded God's plainer altar to one side. But remember this, the Holy Ghost left the holiest place when the Damascus altar came into the courts of the Temple. I can take you to-day into more than one nominal place for the worship of God where such a Damascus altar is found with its secular and profane art in place of the unhewn altar of God, and you may penetrate to the innermost recesses of those churches, and the pillar of cloud and fire is not there, and the Shekinah of glory does not there shine. And I can take you on the western prairies of America to a little log hut that is used as a place of worship, where nothing but the gospel is preached, and nothing but the praise of God is sung, and where prayer arises from stammering lips into the ears of the Lord God, and I will show you a congregation where the Lord adds "daily to the church such as shall be saved." The church of God is doing the maddest thing that the church of God could do—trying to make up for the lack of the Holy Ghost by the presence of a worldly fashion, art, architecture, furniture, garniture, and secular influence, and she can never make up for that lack by any such substitutes. An angel came down at a certain season and troubled the pool of Bethesda, and, after the troubling of the waters, whoever first stepped in was made whole of whatsoever disease he had. Now, suppose the angel had not troubled the pool, and that the Jerusalemites, anxious that the healing properties should still be found in the water, had called all the quack doctors of Jerusalem together, and had said, "Now, drug these waters. Pour in your medicine, and let us make up for the absence of the angel by the presence of your drugs!" That is what the church of God does, when, instead of waiting for God's angel to come down and trouble her pool, or when the angel refuses to come because idols are found in God's courts, the doctors of the world are called in to drug the waters, and make them healing waters; but it is all in vain.

My fellow disciples, you have called a very frail man from the other side of the sea to preach for a little season to you the gospel of the grace of God. I do not know anything but Jesus Christ, and I want to know nothing else. Now the question is, for what intent have ye sent for me? Let me ask you three questions, and answer them in your own hearts: first, are you *prepared* for a blessing yourselves? secondly, are you *expecting* a blessing yourselves? and thirdly, are you *depending upon the Holy Ghost*, and on him alone, for the blessing?

A story is told about Mr. Spurgeon—and I have no doubt

of its truth—that one Sabbath morning after the service was over, and the people came forward to shake hands with this beloved man of God, one young minister of the gospel came and said to him, " Mr. Spurgeon, I should like to ask you a personal question." " Well, what is it ? " " I am a minister of Christ, and I have been preaching for several years, but I have not had much fruits of my preaching. Yet I believe I preach the truth in a right spirit, but the Lord does not give me souls." "Well," said Mr. Spurgeon, "you do not expect that every time you preach the gospel the Holy Ghost is coming down upon the people to turn some soul to Jesus Christ, do you ? " " Why, of course not." " *Well, that is just what I thought,*" said Mr. Spurgeon ; "according to your faith be it unto you." Do you expect a blessing? then you will prepare your heart for it. May I say that I expect a blessing ? I never would have come those three thousand miles across the stormy Atlantic, and have left all the work in America that was at my hands, to preach in this Tabernacle, had I not been confident that God called me, and meant, through this poor ministry of mine, to second the glorious testimony of Pastor Spurgeon, and that I should come to a prepared people. And I want solemnly to say that, if we do not have a blessing, it will be our own fault ; for God is great and rich in mercy, and the Holy Ghost is even now hovering over this assembly like a dove at a window ; and if we will open the window the Holy Dove will come in.

There are some unsaved souls here this morning : may I say one closing word to you ? What is the reason you are not saved ? If there is one of you that has come here to hear whatever is commanded of God for your soul, and you will at this moment open your hearts to the incoming of His message, you will go out of this place saved. Let us try the sacred experiment. I will read, as the conclusion of this address, Peter's sermon on that day in Cornelius's house: and so we will have the same message in prayerful dependence upon the same Spirit; and, while I read these few words, let all of you that love Jesus Christ, and are his disciples, in your hearts send up prayer to God that every unconverted soul in this house may hear these words whereby such hearers may get a present salvation.

"God anointed Jesus of Nazareth with the Holy Ghost and with power: who went about doing good, and healing all that were oppressed of the devil; for God was with him. And we are witnesses of all things which he did both in the land of the Jews, and in Jerusalem; whom they slew and hanged on a tree: him God raised up the third day, and shewed him openly; not to all the people, but unto witnesses chosen before of God, even to those, who did eat and drink with him after he rose from the dead. And he commanded us to preach unto the people, and to testify that it is he which was ordained of God to be the judge of quick and dead. To him give all the prophets witness, that through his name whosoever believeth in him shall receive remission of sins.

"While Peter yet spake these words, the Holy Ghost fell on all them which heard the word." In the eleventh chapter, at the fifteenth verse, he tells us, "*As I began to speak* the Holy Ghost fell on them as on us at the beginning." That is to say, Peter never finished that sermon. He got far enough to declare the conditions of salvation, and the Holy Ghost—may I say it with reverence!— was so divinely impatient to bless those hearers that he would wait no longer. He crowded Peter aside, as though he would say to him, "You have said enough : the gospel is given to these people," and immediately "the Holy Ghost fell on them that heard the word. Now the same gospel is preached in your ears. How simple it is to receive it!

In the Jerry McAuley mission in New York, at 316, Water Street, there is a man who has been for years conducting with great success this mission among the outcast drunkards and thieves of that degraded portion of the city. I heard him tell the story of his own dissipation, how he went from an occasional wine-bibber down to an habitual drunkard, and then, as a hopeless sot, frequenting the lowest class of drinking-houses till, having no more money, he was kicked out of doors. One night he found his way into a low haunt, where they simply tolerated him because the rest of them were so drunk that they could not eject him from the premises. He sat on an empty whiskey barrel in the corner of that drink-shop. The curse of twenty years of dissipation was so telling upon him that he felt as though he were dying ; and he thought of what he had heard years before, "Come unto me, all ye that labour and are heavy laden, and I will give you rest." He had not enough sobriety to conduct a process of thought or of reason ; he could not pray intelligently, for he could not put incoherent and babbling words into prayer ; but he thought to himself, " I have heard it said, if one will only look to Jesus, he is so desirous to save a poor sinner, that he will take the look for a prayer"; and he yearned to look towards Jesus, but thought, " Where shall I find him ? " He felt himself falling from the hogshead to the floor, and he said, "*I will fall towards the cross*"; and that fall towards the cross saved him ! My friend, if you get so much willingness in your heart this morning to be saved, as that if you were falling you would fall towards the cross, then there is salvation for you; and now, just now, in your heart say unto the blessed Saviour, "I do open my heart, and take thee in as my Redeemer from the curse and condemnation of my sin!"

SERMON TWO

The Heart of the Gospel

"For God so loved the world, that he gave his only begotten Son, that whosoever believeth in him should not perish, but have everlasting life."—JOHN iii. 16

THERE is one text in the New Testament that has been preached from oftener than any other in the Bible. It has been the foundation of great revivals of religion, like that among the Tahitians; or that among the Telugus in India, where two thousand two hundred and twenty-two people were baptized in one day, nearly five thousand people in thirty days, and ten thousand people within ten months; and where, even during the year drawing to its close, nearly ten thousand more souls have been baptized. It is a wonderful text. Luther called it one of "the little gospels." It is this (John iii. 16) :—" For God so loved the world, that he gave his only begotten Son, that whosoever believeth in him should not perish, but have everlasting life."

You will naturally wonder what there is in that old text that is new. I have found something that was very new to me, and which also may be to you. I suppose that I had read that verse tens of thousands of times, and yet, a little while ago, as I was led to preach upon that text, I sought of the Lord a clearer view of it, that I might glorify him, by bringing forth out of his treasure things new and old. After reading these familiar words over, perhaps a hundred times, prayerfully asking for new light and insight, there suddenly came to me this absolutely new discovery, as though one, looking up into the heavens, should see a cloud swept away from before the stars, and a new constellation revealed. It flashed on my thought that there are *ten words* in the verse that are quite prominent words, such as " God," " loved," " world," "whosoever," and so on. Then a little more close and careful search showed those words in a hitherto undiscovered mutual relation : *the ten words were in five pairs.* There is one pair of words that has to do with the two persons of the Godhead—God the Father, and God the Son. There is a second pair of words that has to do with the expression of the Father's attitude or posture towards this world—he "loved," and he "gave." Then there is a third pair of words that refers to the objects of the divine love—" world," and " whosoever." Then there is a fourth pair of words that shows us what the attitude of man ought to be when God's love and gift come to his knowledge—"believe " and " have." Then the last pair of words points us to the extremes of human destiny : the result of rejection, and the result of acceptance— " perish " and " life."

Often as I had read this "gospel in a sentence," I had never seen before that singular relation borne by the main words in the sentence ; and, so far as I know, nobody else had seen it before ; for it is one of the beautiful privileges about the study of the precious word of God that the humblest believer who asks the grace of God and the guidance of the Holy Spirit in studying the holy Scriptures, may make a discovery for himself that nobody has ever made before, or if so, without his knowledge; so that it is still his own discovery.

Let us look at this text in the light of this fresh arrangement of the thoughts which it contains. To my mind, it is one of the most remarkable discoveries that it has ever been permitted me to make in the study and exploration of the hidden treasures of the Word of God.

In the first place, " *God* so loved the world, that he gave his only begotten *Son*." There are two of the persons of the Godhead. Many persons are troubled about the relation of the Father to the Son, and of the Son to the Father. They cannot exactly see how Jesus Christ can be equal with God if he is God's Son; and they cannot see how he can be as glorious as the Father, and how he can be entitled to the same honour and homage and worship as the Father if he proceeds forth from the Father, and comes into the world. But let us seek a simple illustration. It is said, in the introduction of this Gospel according to John, " In the beginning was the Word, and the Word was with God, and the Word was God." What is a word? It is the expression of a thought that lies in the mind. The thought is not visible, the thought is not audible; but, when it takes the form of a spoken word or a written word, that thought that was invisible in the mind, that you could not see, or hear, or know about in any other way, comes to your eye on the printed page, or to your ear through the voice of the speaker. And so my invisible thoughts are coming to you now through these audible words. The word is so connected with the thought that it is the expression of the thought. The thought is the word invisible: the word is the thought visible. Now Jesus Christ was the invisible thought of God put into a form in which you could see it and hear it ; and just as the word and the thought are so connected that if you understand the word you understand the thought, and if you understand the thought you understand the word; and as the word would have no meaning without the thought, and the thought no expression without the word, so Jesus Christ helps us to understand the Father, and the Father could not make himself perfectly known to us except through the Son. But, again, we are told that Christ is "the Light of the world." Suppose I should say, " In the beginning was the light, and the light was with the sun, and the light was the sun." The sun sends forth the light, and the light proceeds from the sun ; yet the light and the sun are the same in nature and the same in essence, and the glory of the sun is the glory of the light, and the glory of the light is the glory of the sun ; and although the light goes forth from the sun, it is equal with the sun, shares the same glory, and is entitled to the same valuation. We cannot think of the one without the other.

In this text not a word is said about the love of the Son for sinners, nor a word about the Son's offering of himself for the salvation of men. What is the common, old-fashioned notion that we sometimes find cropping out even in the conceptions of Christian people, as well as unbelievers, in these days ? Many think of the Father as representing justice, and of the Son as representing mercy. They imagine the Son as coming between the wrath of the Father and the guilty sinner. It is very much like the story of Pocahontas, the daughter of an Indian chief, who came between the executioner and Captain Smith, when the executioner was standing with his club uplifted, ready to strike the fatal blow on the head of his victim. The notion of a great many people is that God the Father is all wrath, and that we can never look at God or think of God, and that God never can look at us or think of us, except with a kind of mutual abhorrence and antagonism; and that so Jesus Christ incarnates the principle of love, and comes in between the angry God and the sinner. That is a very shallow notion indeed. Have you never got hold of the idea that the Father is just as much interested in you as the Son is, and that the Father loves you just as much as the Son does? Look at this verse. It puts all the glory of the love and the sacrifice upon the Father : " *God so loved* the world *that he gave* his only begotten Son." He puts it thus that you and I may understand that our notion of the Son is our notion of the Father. When Philip said, "Lord, show us the Father, and it sufficeth us," Jesus answered, " Have I been so long time with you, and yet hast thou not known me, Philip? he that hath seen me hath seen the Father ; and how sayest thou then, Shew us the Father ?"

Do you not understand my thought if you understand my word? And if my word is the right expression of my thought, how absurd it would be for somebody to say, "I understand his word well enongh, but I wish that I could understand his thought". My word, being human, may not always properly express my thought ; but with God the Word is the perfect expression of the thought ; and so if you have understood the word you have understood the thought : and if you have understood the thought you have understood the word. If you have seen the Son, you have seen the Father. If the love of the Son has touched you, the love of the Father has touched you. If you worship the Son, you worship the Father. If you obey the Son, you obey the Father ; so that you need not be troubled about your feelings toward the Father, and say, as many a person has said to me, " I wish that I could feel towards God the Father as I feel towards Jesus. I wish that I could have those views of God the Father that I have of Jesus. I wish that I could have the freedom with the Father that I have with the Son."

Now, dismiss all that kind of trouble and perplexity from your mind ; for as you think of the Son you think of the Father ; as you love the Son, you love the Father ; as you pray to the Son, you pray to the Father ; and as you obey and serve the Son, you obey and serve the Father. The Son thinks of you just as the Father does, and the Father thinks of you just as the Son does."

> " So near, so very near to God,
> Nearer I cannot be ;
> For in the person of his Son
> I am as near as he.
>
> So dear, so very dear to God,
> Dearer I cannot be ;
> For the love wherewith he loves the Son
> Is the love he bears to me."

The second pair of words is " loved " and " gave." He loved and gave. I have no desire to enter into nice distinctions, but with the simplicity of a little child approach this heart of the gospel. And yet a child will understand that when we use the word " love," we sometimes mean one thing and sometimes another. For instance, suppose that you should try to get some poor criminal out of prison—a miserable, filthy, degraded, defiled man. Somebody asks you why you do it, and you say that you *love* him. Now, that would not be taken to mean the same kind of love as you bear your mother. Those are very different loves— the love that you bear to your mother and the love that you bear to some vile criminal. The word "love" has a different meaning in different cases. The apostle John says, "We love him because he first loved us." Was not the love of God to us something different from the love that we bear to him? I love God because I know him to be the most beautiful, the most wise, the most glorious, the most fatherly, the most tender, the most pitiful, the most gracious being in the universe. Why did he love me? Because he saw that I was beautiful and truthful, and lovely, and honest, and honourable? Not so, says the apostle. "When we were enemies he loved us, and he commendeth his love toward us in that while we were yet sinners Christ died for us." So there are two kinds of love. We call them the love of complacence and the love of benevolence. Complacence means a feeling of pleasure. You love a beautiful person, a lovely character, because you see something in the person and in the character that draws out your love. But that is not the kind of love that we call the love of benevolence, for such love is bestowed on people in whom we do not see anything beautiful or lovely. We love them for the sake of the good that we may do them, and for the sake of the beautiful character that, by grace, we may help to develop in them. So, therefore, the love of complacence is intensive, but the love of benevolence is extensive; the love of complacency is partial, the love of benevolence is impartial; the love of complacency is exclusive and select, the love of benevolence is inclusive and universal. The love of complacence is a kind of selfish love, but the love of benevolence is a generous love. The love of complacency may be an involuntary love: we see the qualities that attract affection, and we love unconsciously and involuntarily; but the love of benevolence is voluntarily exercised. The love of complacence has to do with comparatively few of the people whom we know; the love of benevolence takes in the whole world, and hundreds and thousands of people whom we do not know, and never saw, but whom, for the sake of Jesus, we love.

Have you fixed that in your thought? The kind of love, then, that God had for us was the love of benevolence—extensive, inclusive, impartial, universal, self-denying, self-forgetting, voluntary.

Now, it is the characteristic of *that* kind of love that *it gives*. We call it the love of benevolence, and "benevolence is another word for "giving"; and such love keeps nothing, but gives every thing that it has, and gives to everybody. Of course, if God loved us after that sort he had to give. He could not so love if he did not give, any more than the sun could be the sun without shining, or a spring of water could be a spring without flowing out into a stream. And so these words, "loved" and "gave," naturally go together. You could not have the one without the other. There could not be this wonderful giving without this wonderful loving; and there could not be this wonderful loving without this wonderful giving.

Now let us look at the third pair of words—" world " and " whosoever."

It need not be said that those are both *universal terms*. " World " is the most universal term that we have in the language. For instance, we sometimes mean by it the whole earth on which we dwell; sometimes the whole human family that dwells on the earth; and sometimes the world-age, or whole period during which the whole family of man occupies the sphere. That is the word that God uses to indicate the objects of his love. But there is always danger of our losing sight of ourselves in a multitude of people. In the great mass individuals are lost, and it becomes to us simply a countless throng. But when God looks at us, he never forgets each individual. Every one of you to-night stands out just as plainly before the Lord as though you were the only man, woman, or child on earth. So God adds here another word, "whosoever," that is also universal, but with this difference between the two: "world" is collectively universal, that is, it takes all men in the mass; "whosoever" is distributively universal, that is, it takes everyone out of the mass, and holds him up separately before the Lord. If this precious text only said, "God so loved the world, that he gave his only begotten Son," one might say, "Oh, he never thought of me. He had a kind of general love to the whole world, but he never thought of me." But when God uses that all-embracing word "whosoever," that must mean you and me; for whatever my name or yours may be, our name is "whosoever," is it not? John Newton used to say that it was a great deal better for him that this verse had the word "whosoever" in it than the words "John Newton"; "for," he said, "if I read 'God so loved the world, that he gave his only begotten Son, that when John Newton believed he should have everlasting life,' I should say, perhaps, there is some other John Newton; but 'whosoever' means this John Newton and the other John Newton, and everybody else, whatever his name may be." Blessed be the Lord! He would not have us forget that he thought of each one of us, and so he said, "whosoever." You notice the same thing in the great commission, "Go ye into all the world" (collectively universal) "and preach the gospel to every creature" (distributively universal).

Before I leave this pair of words, let me illustrate what a precious term this word "whosoever" is. It reminds me of the great gates of this Tabernacle, that spring open to let in poor souls that want to hear the gospel. This word "whosoever" is the wide gateway to salvation, and lets in any poor sinner who seeks to find for himself a suffering but reigning Saviour.

In the South Seas, in the beginning of the present century, was a man of the name of Hunt, who had gone to preach the gospel to the inhabitants of Tahiti. The missionaries had laboured there for about fourteen or fifteen years, but had not, as yet, a single convert. Desolating wars were then spreading across the island of Tahiti and the neighbouring islands. The most awful idolatry, sensuality, ignorance, and brutality, with everything else that was horrible, prevailed; and the Word of God seemed to have made no impression upon those awfully degraded islanders. A translation of the gospel according to John had just been completed, and Mr. Hunt, before it was printed, read, from the manuscript translation, the third chapter; and, as he read on, he reached this sixteenth verse, and, in the Tahitian language, gave those poor idolaters this compact little gospel: "God so loved the world, that he gave his only begotten Son, that whosoever believeth in him should not perish, but have everlasting life."

A chief stepped out from the rest (Pomare II.), and said, "Would you read that again, Mr. Hunt?" Mr. Hunt read it again. "Would you read that once more?" and he read it once more. "Ah!" said the man "that may be true of you white folks, but it is not true of us down here in these islands. The gods have no such love as that for us." Mr. Hunt stopped in his reading, and he took that one word "whosoever," and by it showed that poor chief that God's gospel message meant *him;* that it could not mean one man or woman any more than another. Mr. Hunt was expounding this wonderful truth, when Pomare II. said, "Well, then, if that is the case, your book shall be my book, and your God shall be my God, and your people shall be my people, and your heaven shall be my home. We, down on the island of Tahiti, never heard of any God that loved us and loved everybody in that way." And that first convert is now the leader of a host, numbering nearly a million, in the South Seas. Reference has already been made to the fact that this was the great text that Dr. Clough found so blessed among the Telugus. When the great famine came on, in 1877, and the missionaries were trying to distribute relief among the people, Dr. Clough, who was a civil engineer, took a contract to complete the Buckingham Canal, and he got the famishing people to come in gangs of four thousand or five thousand. Then, after the day's work was over, he would tell them the simple story of redemption. He had not yet learned the Telugu language sufficiently to make himself well understood in it, but he had done this : he had committed to memory John iii. 16 in the Telugu tongue. And when, in talking to his people, he got "stuck," he would fall back on John iii. 16. What a blessed thing to be able at least to repeat that ! Then he would add other verses, day by day, to his little store of committed texts, until he had a sermon, about half-an-hour long, composed of a string of texts, like precious pearls. I have sometimes thought that I would rather have heard that than many modern sermons. So, once again the great text that God used for bringing souls to Christ was still Luther's little gospel : " God so loved the world that he gave his only begotten Son, that whosoever believeth in him should not perish, but have everlasting life."

Now we come to the fourth pair of words, "believe" and "have." You will see how important these words are. If God so loved that he gave, what is necessary on the part of man? Only this, that he should *take* and *have*. That is very plain. If God loved you and the whole world, and gave you all that he had to give, all that remains for anybody to do is so to appreciate the love of God as to take the gift that God bestows, and so to have the gift that he takes. *Believing is receiving.* John, at the beginning of this gospel, tells us in what sense he is going to use the word "believe." That word occurs forty-four times in the gospel according to John, which is the great gospel of "believing." You do not find the word "repent" in it once, but it is constantly repeating believing, believing, believing, and having life. In the twelfth and thirteenth verses of the first chapter, we read: "To as many as *received* him, to them gave he power to become the sons of God," even to them that *believe* on his name." "To as many as *received,* even to those that *believed.*" That little word "even" indicates that to *believe* is equivalent to *receive.* You may, in any one of those forty-four instances in this gospel, put the word "receive" in the place of the word "believe," and still make good sense. For example: "God so loved the world that he gave his only begotten Son, that whosoever received him might have everlasting life."

You *have* what you *take,* do you not? It is a very simple thing to take what is given to you, and so to have it. That is, practically, *all there is in faith.* We may make faith obscure by talking too much about it, leading others to infer that there is in it some obscurity or mystery. Faith is very simple : it is taking the eternal life that is offered to you in Christ. If you can put forth your hand and receive a gift, you are able to put forth your will and receive the gift of God, even Jesus Christ, as your Saviour. I heard of an old lady, who was starting on a railway journey from an American station, out of which many trains move, although in different directions. Not having travelled much on the rail cars, she got confused. The old lady I speak of was going up to Bay City, Michigan, and she was afraid that she was, perhaps, on the wrong train. She reached over, and showed her ticket to somebody in the seat immediately in front of her, and said, " I want to go to Bay City. Is this the right train ? " " Yes madam." Still, she was not quite at ease, for she thought that perhaps this fellow-passenger might have got into the wrong train too ; so she stepped across the aisle of the car, and showed her ticket to another person, and was again told, " Yes, madam, this is the right train." But still the old lady was a little uncertain. In a few moments in came the conductor, or, as you call him, the guard ; and she saw on his cap the conductor's ribbon, and she beckoned to him, and said, " I want to go to Bay City ; is this the right train ? " " Yes, madam, this is the right train." And now she settled back in her seat, and was asleep before the train moved. That illustrates the simplicity of taking God at his word. She did nothing but just receive the testimony of that conductor. That is all ; but that is faith. The Lord Jesus Christ says to you, " I love you ; I died for you. Do you believe ? Will you receive the salvation that I bought for you with my own blood ? " You need do no work ; not even so much as to get up and turn round. You need not go and ask your fellow-man across the church aisle, there, whether he has believed, and received, and been saved. All that you need to do is with all your heart to say, " Dear Lord, I do take this salvation that thou hast bought for me, and brought to me." Simple, is it not? Yes, very simple : yet such receiving it is the soul of faith.

And what is assurance but consciously *having* what you *take ?* Somebody comes and offers me, to-night, some freewill offering. It costs me nothing. All that I have to do is to take what is given to me, and have it for my own. Faith is the *taking*, and the assurance is the conscious *having;* and that is all that I know about it.

There remains another pair of words. Would to God that I might impress the meaning of those terms, " perish " and " everlasting life " ! What does " perish " mean, and what does " life " mean ? When the prodigal son went into the far country, and had wasted his substance in riotous living, he came to himself ; and he came back to his father, and he said, " Father, I have sinned." And the father said, " This my son was dead, and is alive again. He was lost, and is found." A son that is lost to his father is dead to his father, and a son that is found by his father is alive to his father. God said to Adam, " In the day that thou eatest of the forbidden fruit, thou shalt surely die." It did not mean that Adam should that day die, physically. It meant something worse than that. He *died to God* when he ate. One proof that he died to God when he ate that forbidden fruit is that, when the Lord God came down to walk in the garden as the companion of Adam in the cool of the day, our first parents shrank from the presence of the Lord, and hid behind the trees of the garden, when they heard his footsteps and the sound of his voice. They were dead to sympathy towards God, dead to love towards God, dead to

The Heart of the Gospel

pleasure in God: and so they tried to get out of the way of God—as if it were possible to put a veil between them and him. How do you know you are dead to God? You want to get out of his way. You do not love the things that God loves; you would like to be independent of God's rule. You would like, if possible, to get into some corner of the universe where there is no God. You are like the men in America who went across to California, when the golden gates of that country were first opened, that they might enrich themselves. They tried to do without God, and there was a horrible state of sensuality and criminality there; and though there were, nominally, Christian families, and even Christian churches, these gold-seekers had left God on the other side of the Rocky Mountains, if not still further off, on the other side of the Alleghanies. They sought to get where there was no sanctuary, Bible, or family altar, and no restraint of Christian government, or recognition of a God above. The Psalmist twice says, "The fool hath said in his heart, there is no God"; and if you leave out the italicized words, which are not in the original, it reads like this: "The fool hath said in his heart,—No God!" That is, "I wish that there were no God." The impious man hates God. It is an uncomfortable thing for him to think that there is a Sovereign of all the earth who will judge all the works done in the body. It is uncomfortable to think that beyond the grave there lie the great assizes of the judgment day, and that one is unprepared to go into that judgment, and meet the judge. And so people try to make up their minds that there is no hereafter or judgment, and that there is no God. It is a sign that you are "dead" when you would like that there should be no God, and you do not want God to have any rule over you. And what is the sign that you are alive? You come to yourself, and then you come to the Father? You would not have God out of the universe if, by a stroke of the hand, you could annihilate him. You would not have the judgment-seat out of the universe, for that is the place where all wrongs are righted. You would not have heaven blotted out, for that is where

> The quenched lamps of hope are all re-lighted,
> And the golden links of love are re-united;

and where there shall be no more sin, nor sorrow, nor sighing, nor tears; and where every shadow shall flee away. Paul says that the "woman who lives in pleasure is dead while she liveth." That is to say that, while she exists, she is so wrapped up in fashion, in ornaments, in the plaiting of the hair, and the putting on of gold and of gorgeous apparel —living for this world and her own indulgence, that she is dead to the things that are alone worth living for, and that take hold of the invisible, divine, and eternal.

Now, let us once more hear the word of the living God. God so loved you that he gave the best that he had to give, and all that he had to give; and while he gave to the whole world, he singled you out as the object of his love, and said, "whosoever"—"every creature." And now that that gift is given to you, and there is no more to be given, God can do no more. He does not ask you to pay the one-thousandth part of a farthing for the priceless values represented in the Son of God. All that God can do now is to say to you that the very fact that you reject his dear Son is a proof that you are spiritually dead. Even though you dispute the fact, you are dead; as a deaf man may not understand how deaf he is, and a blind man may not understand the glories of sight, so a dead man cannot understand the energies of the living. And so the very fact that you think that you

The Heart of the Gospel

are not dead is another proof that you are. You have no sensibility even to the fact that you are spiritually without life. God comes and says, " Come back to me, my prodigal and wandering son. You shall have the robe ; you shall have the ring ; you shall have the shoes. I will give them all to you with the absoluteness of an infinite love, and you shall take them, and have them because you take them." Just the moment that you turn toward God, and say, "My Father, I take the robe and the ring, and the shoes, and the place of a restored son in the Father's house," you will live again ; for you recognize your Father, and yourself as his son. You recognize his right to command, and your duty to obey. You recognize that the only place for a son is the home and the heart of his father. That is the proof that you are once more alive.

" Tell me how long it would take to change from death unto life ? " Just as long, and no longer, as it takes you to turn round. Your back has been on God. You turn, and your face is toward him. It will take no longer for a sinner to become a living son of God than that. Just put your heart into your acceptance of Jesus. Cast your whole will into the acceptance of the Fatherhood of God, renounce your sin and your rebellion, and take the salvation that is given to you as freely as the sun gives its light, or the spring gives its stream ; and before you turn round to go out of that church door, you may have this salvation, and perhaps enjoy in yourself the consciousness that you are saved !

SERMON THREE

Sin Compels Separation

"Depart from me, for I am a sinful man, O Lord."—LUKE v. 8

HERE is a very remarkable confession, and a very remarkable prayer. The confession is, "I am a sinful man, O Lord." The prayer is, "Depart from me." The confession would not be so very remarkable in itself, if it were not evidently the expression of a deep sense of sin. That is very rare in these days. It is told of Nelson, at Trafalgar, that, when he received his death wound, he sent for the chaplain, and he said, "Chaplain, they tell me that I have got to die; but really, I do not know that I have been a very great sinner." And while there are many people in this world who are ready to confess that they are sinners, the confession is sometimes nothing more than a kind of veil to hide their self-righteousness. They do not mean it. They have no sense of sin. One morning in the year 1878, while I was sitting in my study in Detroit in Michigan, just after my breakfast, I heard a knock at the door, and I said, "Come in," and a man about thirty years of age opened the door. I saw that he had been violently weeping, and he said, "May I come in, sir?" I said, "Yes, indeed you may. Can I do anything for you?" "Well, sir," said he, "I do not know, but I am a great sinner, and I want a Saviour."

Sin Compels Separation

Said I, "Come right in, my friend. You are just the man that I have been looking for, for about ten years,"—a man, deeply afflicted with a sense of his sin, and deeply desirous of finding a Saviour from his sin. That is the man I wanted to see then, and that is the man I want to see now; and if there were enough of such to take up the time till to-morrow morning, who would not gladly stay here and talk with such, and point them to Jesus? How many pastors there are all through Great Britain, as in America, who are thus yearning to find some souls oppressed with a sense of guilt, and desirous to find a salvation from sin.

Simon Peter, on this occasion if never before, had a deep sense of his own sin, and so that confession was wrung out of him—"I am a sinful man, O Lord"; and it was accompanied by an involuntary prayer, "Depart from me," for he felt that, as a sinner, he was unfit to associate with such a Saviour.

Why is it that there are so few people in these days that seem to have any deep sense of sin? I am speaking, now, of the unsaved, those that are not disciples of Jesus Christ.

Because, in the first place, there is very little *right thinking about sin* itself. If you ask a man whether he is a sinner, he understands you to mean by that a great, a flagrant, an outbreaking transgressor. If you tell him that he is a great sinner in the sight of God, he thinks perhaps that you mean to accuse him of being a blasphemer, a perjurer, a thief, an adulterer, a murderer. Without any of these outbreaking forms of sin there may be a deep and damning hatred of God in the human soul. There are many diseases that have no corresponding outward symptom. A man fell through a hatchway and was taken up dead, and there was not an outward sign on his body, that one could perceive, of the fatal injury. It was the shock that killed him, and yet there was no appearance of his having come to his death by any such violence. It is said that in the great plague that devastated London a long time ago, if there appeared in the cheek just one little round red spot it was the sign of death, and death came very rapidly. That single symptom was the sign of approaching dissolution. Sin may not break out in violent trampling on the ten commandments; but Almighty God, looking with omniscient eye beneath the veil of outward propriety, and even morality, sees lurking in souls the desperate and deadly hatred of himself.

Then again, there is a large bulk of sins, which some of us never even think of, and which may be called *sins of omission*, that is, things that are left undone; for sin includes not merely what is done contrary to the will of God, but what we fail to do which is in accordance with his blessed will—laws unkept, commands disregarded, paths of duty never walked in. What about all that class of sins included under those sins of omission?

Did you ever notice this fact—that three of the greatest arraignments in the whole word of God on the subject of sin have to do with what is *not done?* For instance, when Jesus Christ, in the sixteenth chapter of John, speaks of the coming of the Holy Spirit and of his work in the sinner's soul, he says, "He shall convince of sin because they believe not on me." *Not believing.* In the great vision of judgment in the twenty-fifth chapter of Matthew, when the King sits on the throne of his glory, those that go away into everlasting punishment are addressed by him in these words, "I was hungry, and ye gave me no meat; a stranger, and ye took me not in;

Sin Compels Separation 55

naked, and ye clothed me not; sick and in prison, and ye visited me not. Inasmuch as ye *did it not* unto one of the least of these my brethren, ye did it not to me." *Not doing:* not something done, but something not done. And, when Paul writes to the Corinthians, as he comes to the end of his epistle, he crowds aside the amanuensis, and he takes up the pen in his own hands, and in large characters he writes, "The salutation of me Paul, with mine own hand. If any man *love not* the Lord Jesus Christ let him be anathema." Not "If any man hate"; not "If any man persecute"; not "If any man blaspheme the Lord Jesus Christ"; but "If any man *love not* the Lord Jesus Christ." Believing not, doing not, loving not—these are the three arraignments of God upon which is based the punishment of the sinner, even his everlasting exclusion from the presence, glory, and power of the Lord.

Again, we have not a *right perception* of sin. We are like people born blind that have not the proper sense of sight, or like people born deaf that have not the proper sense of hearing, or like people born without proper feeling or sensibility, so that they do not perceive as men perceive that have proper eyes, and proper ears, and proper organs. And what is more than that, we become more and more callous about sin *by familiarity* with it. Workmen know that if they continue to use an instrument or an implement or a tool of trade in one hand habitually, that hand becomes callous, hardened by its use, so that the tenderness of the palm is injured. And so you may injure the sensitive surface of your conscience.

> "Vice is a monster of so frightful mien,
> As to be hated needs but to be seen;
> Yet seen too oft, familiar with her face,
> We first endure, then pity, then embrace."

Our conscience is like an alarm clock, which rings out its alarm early in the morning, and if you go to sleep again and disregard it, the next morning when it rings you hear it less plainly; and the next morning it still less effectively disturbs your sleep, until, by-and-by, you can sleep through the noise and never hear it. Disregard the voice of conscience, and to-morrow it will speak more feebly, less clearly. Disregard it still, and the next time it will be a little more faint, a little less clear, until, by-and-by, you can go on in the sleep of sin and scarcely ever hear its remonstrance. And so you learn not to perceive the sin that you are committing, by becoming accustomed to it. It ceases to affect your sensibilities.

Then again, there is a *power in sin to deceive* a man. Remember what the Word of God itself says, "If we say that we have no sin, we deceive ourselves and the truth is not in us." Yes, the heart makes the theology. Why do men like to believe that they are not sinners? Because it makes them uncomfortable to think that they are. A man, perhaps, has about him some fatal disease, and he wants, if possible, to persuade himself that the difficulty is not so serious, and all the urgency and importunity of a friendly physician, advising him to take care of the disease while it is possible, perhaps, to alleviate its symptoms or lengthen his life, does not affect him. He tries to make himself believe that, after all, his case is not a dangerous one. That is the way in which men deal with the subject of sin. They have not a right conception of sin, they have not a clear perception of sin, and sin is itself a cherished deception. Just as an insane man persuades himself that he is sane, and thinks that he is sound in mind, and that everybody round about him is crazy; so a sinner disputes his own sin, and it is part of the madness that is in the hearts of the sons of men while they live, that they persuade themselves that they are not sinners, even against the verdict of God.

How can we get free from this wrong conception, lack of perception, and snare of deception with regard to sin and its nature? How can we come to know that we are sinners, and to see ourselves somewhat as God sees us?

In the first place, we must *receive God's verdict* concerning us. Here is a blind man: he is approaching the edge of a precipice, but he does not see the precipice, and so far perhaps he is not responsible if he falls off, inasmuch as he does not perceive his danger. But suppose that I, who do see his danger, come up, and put my hand on his shoulder, and say, "My friend, ten feet in front of you there is a precipice, and if you keep on walking in the direction in which you are now going, you will go over, and be dashed into pieces." If after that warning he does so, he does it at his own responsibility. It is a case of suicide, for, though he did not see the danger, I did, and I warned him. Now, perhaps you do not see your sin, but God tells you what he thinks of it, and all that you have to do is to take God's verdict concerning yourself. Let the eyes of God become eyes to you to see yourself, and let the ears of God become ears to you to hear your danger, and let the sensibilities of God become sensibilities to you to perceive the guilt and peril in which you are, and then you will come to know yourself somewhat as God knows you.

If you will take the Bible testimony you will see what God thinks of men. It is a fearfully solemn thing to get God's verdict. In the days of Noah the Lord said, "Every imagination of the thought of man's heart is only evil continually, and the whole earth is corrupt before me and filled with violence." In the days of Solomon God looked down from heaven upon the children of men to see if there were any that did understand and seek after God, and he said, "They are altogether become filthy; they are all gone out of the way. There is not one that doeth good, no not one." And in the days of the apostle Paul, when Paul wrote the third chapter of the Epistle to the Romans, what does he say? "There is none righteous, no, not one. There is none that feareth and seeketh after God. The poison of asps is under their lips; their mouth is full of bitterness; their feet make haste to shed innocent blood. Destruction and misery are in their ways, and the way of peace they have not known, and there is no fear of God before their eyes." And when Paul frames this terrible arraignment of the natural and unsaved man, he draws threads for the woof and the warp from the most terrible statements of the entire Old Testament. He selects out of the whole Word of God, as then possessed, these awful expressions of the natural man and the unsaved man, and he weaves them together and says, "That is God's opinion of men."

Once more, in order to come to the sense of my sin it is necessary that I should set up alongside of myself *God's perfect standard* of truth and life, and duty and conduct. One of the common things that men do—and it is a piece of folly and of wickedness—is to compare themselves among themselves, and measure themselves by themselves. Suppose that a carpenter should desire to plane the edge of a board straight. Would he put alongside of that board another crooked board to guide his plane by? If so, he would simply perpetuate imperfection. No, he puts a

Sin Compels Separation

straight-edge alongside of his board, and marks it accordingly, and so he planes it straight. If a mason, building a wall, "sights" the wall that he is building by another wall that, perhaps, leans from the perpendicular or inclines from the horizontal, he will construct his own wall inclining and leaning. In all the arts—the mechanical arts and the fine arts—we have to employ, as near as possible, a perfect standard. We use the plane, the square, the level, the plumb-line, and by these approximations to perfection we are enabled to bring our work itself into an approximation to perfection. If a man takes a standard that is far below perfection he will only make more imperfect work, like the standard that he follows.

God has given us, in his precious Word, a perfect standard of doctrine and of deportment, in the Lord Jesus Christ; and, if ever you are tempted to think that you are not a sinner, set up your character and your conduct beside that of Jesus, and see how far you come short of the standard of perfection; and then you may be able to see why it is that God counts you to be even a great sinner. If you drop a clean white piece of linen on the freshly fallen snow, the linen looks unclean, because there is nothing so white in the universe as the fresh snow from heaven. If you put an oil lamp in front of an electric light, that which was before casting light now casts only a shadow, for the flame of the oil light becomes only an obstacle to the shining of the brighter electric flame. And if the fairest human life be put in the burning focus of the light of the life of Jesus Christ, that fair life will appear but as a shadow in comparison with the intenser lustre of the radiant God-Man.

This train of thought is the natural introduction to

the true understanding of the text. Why was it that Peter came to be so oppressed with a sense of sin, when Christ had performed this miracle? He had toiled all night in the Lake of Galilee, and had taken no fish. Jesus said, 'Let down your nets for a draught"; and so great was now the draught of fishes that the nets began to break, and Simon Peter and his companions had to beckon to their partners in the other ship, James and John, to come and help them to draw the fish to the land.

There was nothing in this miracle that was calculated to call Peter's attention to the moral attributes of Jesus. There was nothing in it to suggest holiness. It might suggest omniscience, that Jesus Christ saw the fish gathered in that place. It might suggest omnipotence, that he gathered the fish into that place. But it did not suggest moral attributes. But, when Peter thought of omnipotence or omniscience, he thought of God, and so, he thought of holiness; for, in connection with the Divine Being, the Jew thought of holiness first of all, and the whole ritual of the old economy and all the prohibitions about the tabernacle were intended to impress the idea of God's purity—that he was of purer eyes than to behold evil, and could not look upon sin. And so when Peter was reminded of the power or knowledge of this Being who was beside him—for it was evidently the power or knowledge of God—he thought of the moral character of God, and especially the divine holiness, and so he thought of his own sin in comparison; and this drew from him the confession, "I am a sinful man, O Lord," and it wrung from him the prayer, "Depart from me."

And now, naturally, the thought is suggested that conscious sin brings conscious sense of separation. If, by any means, the conviction of sin be produced in a human soul, the immediate effect is that there is the consciousness of ill-desert : "I deserve to be separated from all holy beings." It is impossible to have the sense of sin awakened in you without there coming at once into your mind the thought, "I am unfit to be associated with those who are holy, and especially with a holy God"; and so, just as surely as you come to the conclusion that you are a sinner, just so surely will you come to the conclusion that you ought to depart from God, or that God ought to depart from you. This is a very solemn thought, and it is a key to many great mysteries.

An illustration may be drawn from old Greek fables which may be very helpful in understanding this subject. There was a strange being called the Lamia. It was said that by nature it was a serpent, but had power to assume the beautiful form of a seductive woman, and then walked through the groves and avenues to seduce unwary youths to follow her, that she might eat them or suck their blood. The Greeks held a philosopher to be the representative of all that was most beautiful and pure in character; and the old story says that one of these Lamiæ that had taken a beautiful female form suddenly confronted the eyes of one of Greece's purest philosophers. He stood with folded arms, and looked at her with intent and fixed gaze—looked at her as though he read through her deceptive form the secrets of her being; and beneath his pure glance she began to tremble and cringe and shrink away, until she turned into the loathsome reptile that she was, and drew her length along the ground in slime. And so is iniquity stripped of all its disguises before the eye of infinite purity. When God looks upon man, man forgets his self-righteous plea; he forgets the morality in which he has been confident; he forgets the outward propriety in which he has taken refuge; and, giving up all these disguises, he sees himself in God's sight to be a child of the devil and shrinks away before the face of God.

Through the Old Testament and the New you will find one continuous and unchanging testimony on this subject. When, in Eden, Adam and Eve ate the forbidden fruit, and God came down to walk and talk with them in the garden in the cool of the day, as was his custom, to hold fellowship with his human children, they hid behind the trees of the garden, afraid to look upon God. The very presence of God flashed remonstrance in their faces, and made it impossible for them to hold communion with the Holy One. When Moses stood before the burning bush that burned and was not consumed, he turned aside, for we are told that he was afraid to look upon God. When the bright and Holy One appeared to Daniel, as we read in the tenth chapter of his prophecy, and Daniel looked on those eyes that flashed fire, and on those feet that were as burnished brass, and heard that voice as the sound of many waters, he tells us, "Then my comeliness was turned into corruption, and there remained no strength in me." Daniel stood as high above the men of Babylon as the image on the plain of Dura rose above the plain, and yet, when he looked on the holiness of God, even the things on which he had prided himself,—his beauty of person or beauty of conduct, the very propriety of demeanour or excellence of character,—his very comeliness was turned into corruption, and he retained no more strength.

And when even the beloved disciple who leaned on the breast of Jesus at supper beheld, as we read in the Book of

Sin Compels Separation

Revelation, the same vision of the Holy One, he fell at his feet as dead. Ah! you and I can never stand the vision of the holy God till we become partners of the divine nature in Jesus. Then, like the eagle, we can soar up into the heaven, and, with undimmed eye, look at the Sun of Righteousness in the splendour of his noontide glory.

Let me add a few words of practical application.

We have here a key that unlocks many of the mysteries of the future state. The world is full of people who dispute the great Bible doctrine which, I praise God, has never been denied or disputed in this place—the punishment of the finally ungodly and the impenitent with "everlasting destruction from the presence of the Lord and the glory of his power." There is every method taken to get rid of this unpleasant doctrine. Some boldly deny it. Others try to inculcate a doctrine of restoration—some method of universal salvation, some atonement for sin in a kind of purgatory, with deliverance from purgatorial pains and hell fires after the period of purgation has passed by. But I pray you consider, just for a moment, whether there be not in the human soul a revelation that goes side by side with the revelation in the Word of God. Are there not materials in the human soul which, out of themselves, could build a hell if there were no hell revealed? The brothers of Joseph stood before him in the palace of the Pharaohs, and as yet Joseph had not revealed himself to them, and they did not know that it was Joseph. No voice spoke to them from above. God did not accuse them. No man arraigned them for guilt in selling their brother into Egypt. But observe this: "They said among themselves, We are verily guilty concerning our brother, in that we saw the anguish of his soul when he besought us, and we would not hear. Therefore is this distress come upon us."

What were the elements of this self-accusation? First, *memory*—"We saw the anguish of his soul," twenty years ago, when he was put in that pit, and "he besought us, and we would not hear." He asked to be taken back to his father and his father's home, and not to have that awful fraud, of the coat dipped in the blood of a kid, imposed on his father in his old age. "We saw the anguish of his soul when he besought us, and we would not hear." Then, in the second place, there was *conscience:* "We are verily guilty concerning our brother." And then, *reason:* "Therefore is this distress come upon us." If you should go into the next world with your memory and your conscience and your reason uncleansed by the power of the blood of Christ, those three elements that you possess in your own constitution would build a hell for you in any part of the universe of God. I want you to feel the greatness and the awfulness of this truth. It can give a preacher no pleasure to declare such awful truths. But Jesus Christ came into this world to save sinners, and not to save anybody else but sinners; and if you do not feel that you are a sinner he has no mission to save you. And I am especially desirous, at the outset of this temporary ministry, that I shall have help of God to produce a conviction of sin in souls that have never been convinced of sin; for if you find truly convicted sinners, you will shortly find also conscious saints. There are the elements of self-condemnation in any man who has got a memory and a conscience and a reason. There is a law of affinity, in accordance with which every man, when he goes out of this world, goes to his own place, just as Judas did.

Yes, Judas went to his own place. Notice, that first, every man has his own place in this world and in the next.

Second, every man makes his own place in this world and in the next.

Third, every man finds his own place in this world and in the next.

Fourth, every man feels that it is his own place when he gets there.

Suppose that I take filings of various metals and sprinkle them in front of me, and I pass through them a magnet. The magnet takes up all the filings of iron and steel, and rejects the brass, and even the silver and the gold. Why? Because there is a magnetic affinity between the magnet and the steel and iron. Suppose I take various substances, and put them in a phial together, and shake them up violently, and then set the phial down. If there are substances in that phial that are alike and have affinity for each other, they will combine, but otherwise they will refuse to combine, just as oil and water do. That is chemical affinity. And just as there is magnetic and chemical affinity, so there is moral and spiritual affinity among souls. Every man goes to his own place—the place to which, by his own sin or his own regenerate character he belongs. And there is only one place that you can go to, and that is where you by affinity belong. When you are let go by death you will go to your own company. There was a holy man in New England in America, who being asked, when he was dying, "Are you going to heaven?" looked up and said, "Where else could I go?" It was not pride, it was not vain-glory, it was not self-confidence, but it was the knowledge that Jesus was his Saviour, and his whole soul longed after Jesus, and he knew that, when the bars of his cage were broken, he would mount like a freed bird, to see the face of his Lord and make his rest in his presence.

> "Rivers to the ocean run,
> Nor stay in all their course,
> Fire ascending seeks the sun,
> Both speed them to their source,
>
> So a soul that's born of God
> Pants to view his glorious face,
> Upward tends to his abode,
> To rest in his embrace."

If you love God, if you believe in Christ, if you are a partaker of the divine nature, all the demons in hell could not stand between you and the throne of God when you are released from this mortal body. And if you have not sympathy with God, and do not love him, and hate his rule, and have yet an unpardoned sinful nature, all the angels of God could not escort you to his throne. You would go the other way by the force of your own inherent gravitation, towards Satan and towards sin.

Now, once more. As I have tried to show you that self-condemnation makes it impossible that you should dwell with God if you are not like him, and that your affinities make it impossible that you should seek the society of God if you do not sympathize with his nature, so let me add that the glory of God would turn heaven into hell if you had not the nature of a child of God. Did you ever read that tale in old Roman history about Regulus, the Roman senator, being taken captive by the Carthaginians in one of the Punic wars? Carthage sent him to Rome with humiliating terms of peace, and he agreed that if he did not effect the peace with the Romans, he would go back

Sin Compels Separation 67

and put himself under the control of the Carthaginians, and submit to their punishment. Well, when that noble senator rose before the senators of Rome and presented the terms of peace, he advised them to reject the same. He said, " I would not have my country humiliated even for the sake of her peace or of my own safety. I will go back and submit myself to Carthage, but let not Rome submit to peace on these conditions." He went back, and what did the Carthaginians do with him? They inflicted on him the most awful torture that was known in ancient times. They cut off his eyelids; they bound him with his back to the earth and his face to the heavens; and from the time that the sun rose in the morning till the time that the god of day sank behind the hills in the evening, those eyes had to bear the unclouded blaze of sunshine, until the very powers of vision were paralyzed and the eyes were hopelessly blinded. You sometimes talk of going to heaven when as yet you are unsaved, having never been washed in the blood of Jesus Christ, and baptized into his spirit. In the case of Regulus the elements of this awful torture were just these—*an open eye* and *a pure glory?* What if the torture of the lost should consist in simply being compelled to face the glory of the infinitely holy God, without any likeness to him or sympathy with his nature!

I beseech you, do not deceive yourselves. There are just two places where you can find out that you are a sinner. One is at the throne of grace on earth: the other is at the throne of glory in the hereafter. If you go into your secret place and shut the door; if you bow down on your knees before the face of Almighty God, and say, like the little Highland maid, " O Lord, show me myself," he will open the eyes of your understanding, and he will show what a sinner you are. In the first revelation of your own unfitness to dwell with him you may, like Peter, be tempted to cry out, "O Lord, I am a sinful man. Depart from me." But the Lord, like Joseph when he drew toward his conscience-smitten brethren, and said, "Come near to me, I pray you," will throw his arms of mercy and love about you, and will say to you, "I will not depart from thee; neither shalt thou depart from me," for it was to save just such penitent sinners as thou art that Jesus died and rose again.

But if you hide from yourself the fact of your sin and guilt, and try to persuade yourself that you are safe while you are unsaved; if you first learn, at the great white throne of glory above, what a sinner you are, you will then and there be speechless, and the King on the throne shall say, "Depart from me, all ye workers of iniquity."

SERMON FOUR

The Mystery of Godliness

"But if I tarry long, that thou mayest know how thou oughtest to behave thyself in the house of God, which is the church of the living God, the pillar and ground of the truth. And without controversy great is the mystery of godliness: God was manifest in the flesh, justified in the Spirit, seen of angels, preached unto the Gentiles, believed on in the world, received up into glory."—1 TIMOTHY III. 15, 16

THE punctuation of our English Bible is not assured by divine inspiration, inasmuch as there are no punctuation points, properly so called, in the original Scriptures. The punctuation is the device of the translators in hope to make plainer to the ordinary reader what is the meaning. These two verses present us an example of disputed punctuation. Bengel, the author of the Gnomon of the New Testament, remarks that not until the sixteenth century were the words, "pillar and ground of the truth," ever referred to the church of God, but always to the doctrine which follows; and it seems that the better punctuation of these two verses concludes the fifteenth verse with the words, "living God." "These things write I unto thee, hoping to come unto thee shortly, but if I tarry long, that thou mayest know how thou oughtest to behave thyself in the house of God, which is the church of the living God." And then a new sentence should begin : " The pillar and ground of the truth, and, without controversy, great, is the mystery of godliness." This would refer the words " pillar and ground of the truth" to the great doctrine which follows, which embraces the whole system of "piety" or gospel truth which centres in the incarnation of our blessed Lord Jesus Christ.

There is much reason to believe, likewise, that this is a portion of an original apostles' creed, older by far than the oldest confession of faith known to the church of Christ. In those early days of the apostolic church, when they had, as yet, no written Scriptures of the New Testament, and no formulæ or confessions of faith, it was very desirable, if not necessary, that there should be brief expressions of great Christian doctrine, or fact, which could be so arranged as to be readily committed to memory, and which were doubtless recited either as hymns or as confessions among early disciples. There are seven cases in the New Testament in which these fragments of some original confession seem to be found, and they are generally introduced by some such expression as "This is a faithful saying"; that is, "This is a saying which is full of the faith, or expresses the faith." And if you will examine into those seven cases, you will find, in every instance, some great, some central truth of redemption, set before us. For example, in the ninth verse of the fourth chapter, we have one of these faithful sayings which the apostle declares to be "worthy of all acceptation," namely, that "godliness is profitable unto all things, having promise of the life that now is, and of the life that is to come. For therefore we both labour and suffer reproach, because we trust in the living God, who is the Saviour of all men, specially of those that believe."

The Mystery of Godliness 71

The conviction that this text is a fragment of some orignial confession of faith, is confirmed by the poetic form in which it appears. The ancient Hebrews used very largely what we call parallelism, a rhythm and a rhyme of thought rather than a rhythm and a rhyme of words; as, for instance, in the Book of the Proverbs : " A wise son maketh a glad father, but a foolish son is the heaviness of his mother," where it is the sentiment in the two clauses that corresponds, rather than mere rhyme or rhythm or metre ; and so here you have this same poetic construction. And you will observe that there are three couplets here, each consisting, of course, of two members—

> " God was made manifest in the flesh :
> Justified in the Spirit."
>
> " Seen of angels :
> Preached among the nations."
>
> " Believed on in the world :
> Received up into glory."

There is a concession of the fact that this is a mystery, without controversy great. We may as well concede the mystery where even the Holy Ghost does not dispute it. It is said, sometimes, that the Bible is full of mysteries, and men make it an excuse for not receiving the truths of the Word of God because they are mysterious ; but one of the marks that the Bible is the Word of God is found in the presence of these same mysteries. " What man knoweth the things of man save the spirit of man which is in him ? Even so the things of God knoweth no man but the Spirit of God," says Paul, in the second chapter of first Corinthians. And what is the idea ? The ability perfectly to understand the work or workmanship of any man implies in me or in you an equality with that man. Here is a watch, a very dainty and delicate and intricate machine or piece of mechanism. Now, if you can understand every part of that watch, why every jewel is in its place, why certain materials are used in it, and why everything is in the form and in the place which it occupies,—if every detail of the construction of that watch is understood by you, then, if you had the time, and the implements, and the materials, you could make another watch like unto it. The ability absolutely to understand God, implies an equality with God. Because he is as far above us as the heaven is higher than the earth, therefore are his thoughts far beyond the reach of our thoughts, and we can no more take God into our comprehension, than the very smallest flower-cup, that a drop of dew fills, could take in the vastness of the ocean. One of the seals of God upon his word is inscrutable mystery. It is true that the mystery never concerns questions of duty, but always concerns questions of a speculative rather than a practical character. There are secret things that belong unto the Lord our God, but all the things of his law belong to the revealed things that are for the practical guidance of ourselves and our children. And because there never was another being, and never will be another being, like the God-Man, who was not simply God in man, or man in God, but a unique person, the God-Man, two natures in one person—because we have never had before, and shall never have again, another being like him, and so cannot become familiar with, and by familiar contact accustomed to, the fact of such a person—he must always remain an inscrutable mystery. Let us concede it, and confess it, and abandon all idea that we shall, by our philosophy, ever fathom the depth of it.

Then, again, besides the obvious mystery of the incarnation, it is here declared to be the pillar and prop of the truth. The first word indicates that it is *central*, and the other word indicates that it is *vital*. If you took away the pillars of this house, these galleries would fall immediately upon the floor below. When Samson put his arms about the pillars of Dagon's temple, and withdrew them from their standing-place, the whole building came down upon the heads of the worshippers. This great doctrine embodied in this confession, is both central in the system of doctrine, and vital to the doctrine itself. Just as soon as a man begins to doubt that Jesus Christ was God manifest in the flesh, look out for his creed. His whole system of theology is doomed to tumble down and bury him beneath its ruins. He begins by this departure from truth, but all other departures from truth will logically follow; for if you take away the central and vital pillar and prop of the whole redemptive scheme, you have no longer the doctrine that is according to godliness.

This, which is thus a mysterious doctrine and a central doctrine, is also a very comprehensive doctrine. Suppose that we examine these three couplets:

"God was made manifest in the flesh :
Justified in the Spirit.

Seen of angels:
Preached among the Gentiles.

Believed on in the world :
Received up into glory."

This statement of this great doctrine covers everything from Christ's birth in the inn, at Bethlehem, to his ascension and assumption of the throne of the universe at the right hand of the Father. There is nothing that concerns his career, from the manger to the throne, from birth to resurrection and ascension—glory, that is not involved in this brief confession of faith.

This somewhat lengthy introduction is needful to clear the way for the application of this theme. And to make it so simple and easy of apprehension, that even a child may be able to get at the vital truth of it, allow me to say that these three couplets may serve to answer three practical questions : First, *who was he?* second, *why was he?* and third, *where is he?*

I. First, Who was he? It is declared, in the first of these couplets, that he was—

> " God manifest in the flesh,
> Justified in the Spirit."

Here our attention is called to the fact that he was man on the one side, and God on the other—God in man, man in God, the God-Man.

His humanity was the more manifest thing, though " God was manifest in the flesh." We use the word " manifest " oftentimes of that which is very clear, very obvious, and very unmistakable; but not in that sense are we to understand the word " manifest " in this text. The fact is that Jesus Christ was *veiled* in the flesh rather than revealed in the flesh. The flesh was the form which God took for manifestation; but the flesh actually became an obscuring medium. It was his humanity that impressed men, and not his divinity. Even his disciples who walked with him closely for three years, seem to have had doubts of his divinity to the very last, because that which impressed them most, and which was most apparent, was his humanity, and not the divine nature that dwelt in him. As Van Oosterzee finely says, Jesus Christ came in the garments of our humanity, and it was only now and then, when this robe of his humanity was swept aside, as the mantle of some general-in-chief is sometimes swept aside when he is reviewing the troops of a great army, that you might at times discover the imperial star of universal royalty shining and glittering upon his breast. Jesus Christ lived among men as a man. He seemed to be a man, though the greatest and grandest of men; and, because his humanity was manifest rather than his divinity, it became necessary that he should be justified in the Spirit ; that is to say, that by the Holy Ghost dwelling within him and working through him, it should be manifest that he was more than man—that he was God.

How was he justified in the Spirit ?

In the first place, long before he came on earth, the Spirit justified him in advance as the Son of God and the Messiah of men, by the wonderful utterances of prophecy. Three hundred and thirty-three distinct predictions about our Lord and Saviour are found between Genesis and Malachi, entering into the minutest details of prediction, telling when he should be born, and where he should be born, and under what circumstances, and outlining all the great facts of his life, death, resurrection and ascension. And the whole canon of the Old Testament Scriptures closed four hundred years before Christ appeared on the earth, and the collected body of Old Testament Scriptures was in the hands of the Jews at least two hundred years before Christ was born.

This prophetic argument is a mighty argument, both for the divinity of Christ and for the inspiration of the Word of God. We may compare the Holy Ghost and prophets of old to a body of artists completing a picture. At first, in the third chapter of Genesis, is a simple outline, on a broad scale, without colouring, of him who, as the seed of the woman, was to bruise the serpent's head. Then came the fuller prophecies of the period of Moses and the period of David, and the period of the prophets, the earlier and the later; and each prophet, as he comes to the great canvas on which the Holy Ghost had outlined the person and work of Jesus Christ, adds a new feature—here and there a touch of drawing, or a touch of colour, until, when Malachi lays down his pen, there stands a complete and majestic portrait of the coming Messiah, like the perfect picture of some great hero of the future. And then, when the evangelists take up their pens to write the simple story of Christ's life and death and resurrection and ascension, you find that the picture from the evangelists exactly corresponds to the picture from the prophets. The portrait of the future Messiah, made by the prophets under the guidance of the Holy Spirit, is the picture of the Messiah who has already come, as furnished by the evangelists in the New Testament. Nay, you may take the prophetic portrait, and put it over the portrait by the evangelists, and find that the lines of the features exactly correspond throughout. That is the way that in advance the Spirit justified the coming Messiah as one that was to be the Son of God, the mighty worker, the everlasting Lord.

Then, when Christ came, the Spirit justified him by works such as man never wrought, and words such as man never spoke. A great deal has been said in these days about the miracles of Jesus Christ. Often we forget that these were not simply miracles of wisdom, or miracles of power; but they were, above all, miracles of love, miracles of benevolence, unselfish ministry to the wants of men; and how blind, therefore, and how hard, must have been the whole nature of those who said, " He worketh miracles and casteth out devils through Beelzebub, the prince of the devils." Even though Satan might have had the mightiest power

The Mystery of Godliness

among men, can you imagine him using that power in works of mercy and love, and healing and recovery? There were never such words of wisdom as Jesus spoke; and there were never such works of mercy and love, as well as power and wisdom, as he wrought. And so the Holy Ghost testified to him during his life.

And then came the greatest of all the Spirit's testimonies ; for Paul says, in the fourth verse of the first chapter of the Epistle to the Romans, that He was " declared to be the Son of God with power "—that is with especial power— " by the resurrection from the dead." Where all men cease to exercise activity and influence, there the ministry of Jesus Christ practically began the period of its greatest power. Men go into the grave, and we put up by their sepulchres in our cemeteries the broken pillar, the quenched fire, and the plucked flower, as the symbols to express the idea that life has been broken off, and light has been put out, and hope has been blasted. But when you come to the sepulchre of Jesus Christ, there the pillar receives its crown and its capital: there the fire just begins to burn in its celestial glory: there the flower bursts into the fulness of its bloom. The Holy Ghost declared the Son of God to be the Son of God, with power, when he raised him from the dead, so that he broke the bonds of death, and burst the bars of the tomb, and when, on the third day, he came forth in open triumph over death and " him that hath the power of death, that is the devil."

And we must make more of the resurrection of Jesus Christ. Paul says, in the fifteenth chapter of 1 Corinthians, " If Christ be not risen, your faith is vain and our preaching vain, and ye are yet in your sins." We sometimes say that Jesus Christ, by his death, delivers us from the wrath to come. I am not sure that that is an exact and full statement. We are told in the Epistle to the Romans that he was delivered over for our offences, but raised again for our justification. If he had not been raised, the penalty of death would still have been upon him as upon a transgressor of the law. There would have been no sign that his mediation for man was accepted by the Father; but when he rose from the dead, and came forth from his prison in the grave, as man's substitute accepted by God and walking in the universe like a free man, it was evident that God had accepted his sacrifice and his substitution, and that man in him was delivered from his offences.

II. Now, let us examine the second of these couplets: "Seen of angels"—or messengers, which the word means—"preached among the nations." This answers the question, "Why was Jesus Christ? Why was all this manifestation of God in the flesh and justification of the Godhead in him by the Spirit? This couplet answers. Inasmuch as Christ's death for our sins, and resurrection for our justification, were necessary to the salvation of mankind, it was necessary also that he should be preached among the Gentiles as the world's Saviour. I think that the first part of this second couplet includes, in the word "messengers", not only angels, but men. His resurrection must be made an established fact beyond any reasonable doubt; and so Paul, in the fifteenth chapter of 1 Corinthians, gives us an account of the various appearances of Christ after he was risen from the dead, enumerating them in order, and closing with the appearance to himself, to whom Christ appeared as to one born out of due time; and he tells us that He was seen by about five hundred brethren at once, of whom the greater part remained at the time that he was writing, though some had fallen asleep. You perceive with what infinite pains God made clear the fact that Jesus Christ had risen from the dead, so that there is no fact of all history that is more abundantly affirmed and confirmed by many and various witnesses than the fact of Christ's resurrection. For forty days he continued with the disciples, eating and drinking with them after he was risen from the dead, and instructing them in the matters pertaining to his kingdom. The theory that Christ simply appeared to the disciples like a phantom, or a ghost, or an illusion, will not hold for a moment; for ghosts and phantoms do not discourse about spiritual mysteries, and do not eat and drink and continue to accompany people intelligently in converse with them for forty days. I say again, there is no event of all history more abundantly established by many infallible proofs than the resurrection of Jesus Christ from the dead.

And so he was preached among the Gentiles, or nations, as the world's Saviour. We take up the witness of these great facts from those who, before us, have taken the testimony of those that preceded them; and so there is an apostolic succession, of the truest and grandest sort, that reaches back, through generations of believers, and ages of church history, to the time when the disciples, who themselves met Christ repeatedly after his resurrection, gave their witness to this great fact.

III. Now, we come to the third couplet. Where is he?

" Believed on in the world :
Received up into glory."

I want this to be the climax of this text and of this discourse; and may God help me, first of all, to speak in his name, and then help you to hear and heed this testimony of the precious Word of God.

> " Believed on in the world:
> Received up into glory,"

or "caught up into glory." Christ is here and he is also there. He is here, because he is in every believer's heart; he is there, because he is exalted at the right hand of God to be a Prince and a Saviour. And let us not fail to notice that Jesus Christ is not only in the whole body of believers, but he is in every believing soul. We sometimes lose sight of what may be called the individuality of redemption, by referring all the wonderful things said about Jesus, and his indwelling by the Spirit, to the collective body of disciples. He is not only in the great body of believers—the church—but he is in the body of everyone who believes. Paul and Peter say not only that we are stones in a temple and are built up into one spiritual house, but Paul asks, " Know ye not that your body is the temple of the Holy Ghost ? "—not the Body of Christ, not the whole body of believers, but "*your body* is the temple of the Holy Ghost, and the Spirit dwelleth in you." And what does Jesus Christ say in that magnificent promise in the twenty-third verse of the fourteenth of John ? " If any man love me he will keep my words, and my Father will love him, and we will come *unto him* and *make our abode with him.*" "With *him* "; that is to say, with every individual believer. If you love and obey Christ, if your heart goes out to him in holy reverence and supreme obedience, if you open all the avenues of your nature to the entering in of the Son of God by his Word and by his Spirit, he and the Father, as well as the Holy Ghost—the triune God—come down from the high and holy place which they inhabit, and in your humble and contrite heart make their personal dwelling. There is not a man, a woman, a child, who believes in Jesus Christ, who is not a temple of the Holy Ghost. And, as God looks down upon such believers he values you more, individually, as his temple than the most magnificent cathedral ever erected. St. Paul's and Westminster Abbey, and the cathedrals of Cologne and Strasburg, Florence and Milan, and St. Peter's at Rome—all these costly and sumptuous buildings are as nothing to him, who more prizes a humble, contrite, believing soul as his abode than the stateliest of all temples erected from the foundation of the world. And he would have you to appreciate this fact, and with deep thanksgiving to recognize it; that, if you in your heart worship and obey your Master and Lord, he is in your heart as an indwelling power and presence. Each of you can, therefore, test this gospel for yourself. You need not be at the mercy of other people and their testimony. Go into your secret place, commune with your Father who is in heaven, through Jesus Christ your Lord, and, by the power of the Holy Ghost, let God unfold to you his presence and his power within you. That is the standing miracle of the ages. That is the personal and perpetual testimony unto God. That is the great apologetic of Christianity. That is the whole system of "evidences" concentrated in a believing soul—the portable evidence of Christianity.

I have but one more of these phrases to consider, and that lifts us to the highest heaven of praise and glory and adoring worship. "Caught up into glory." What does that mean? Let us not refer this to Christ's resurrection. It refers to a grander event—the event of his ascension! We make far too little of this glorious fact—our Lord's ascension. His incarnation was wonderful; his temptation in the desert was wonderful; his passion in Gethsemane was wonderful; his death on the cross was wonderful; his resurrection from the grave was stupendous: but his ascension overtops them all in majesty, divinity, power, and glory. And, because the ascension of our Lord is so little thought of, even by ministers of Christ and believing disciples, I pray God that I may speak as becomes this august theme in these closing words.

Now, what is it that constitutes the ascension of Christ —his rapture into the glory—as, thus far, the consummation of all the wonders of redemption?

Let me say very briefly that, ever since Jesus Christ came into this world, there has been a deadly conflict going on between the prince of darkness and the Prince of Light, between the prince of this world and the Prince of the Kingdom of God. We cannot stop now to trace the successive stages of this conflict. Every time that the devil met Jesus Christ in deadly encounter it was more desperate and more daring on his part, and his defeat more terrible and overwhelming; for Jesus Christ not only overcame him in every instance, but with more and more overwhelming victory.

When Christ ascended up on high, if there ever was an occasion when Satan would have desired to prevent such a consummation, it was then; for remember that, when Jesus Christ came down in the incarnation, he brought God down to man; but when he ascended, he bore man up to God. If Satan would fain have prevented God coming down to man, how much more would he have prevented man ascending to God! Remember, he tempted Adam in the garden, and the slime of the serpent has been over all human powers and pleasures ever since. The fairest flowers of Eden may remain among us, but they are wilted and withered. The paths of paradise may be dimly seen, but they are covered with the tracks of the serpent. But, mark the stupendous mystery! the very humanity that in the first Adam had fallen was, in the ascension, mounting to the throne of glory! The very humanity that Satan had trod down in the dust of wreck and ruin in Eden, was, in the second Adam, mounting above all principalities and powers and dominions and every name that is named, and ascending the steps of the throne of the universe to sit down with God in the equality of his imperial reign. And, when that cloud hid from the disciples' eyes the ascending Saviour, who can tell what conflict between the prince of the power of the air and the ascending Christ, that cloud may also have hidden from mortal eye? I think I see in the Word of God some indications of this conflict, not only in the passage already quoted, but in that found in the fourth chapter of the Epistle to the Ephesians: "When he ascended up on high he led captivity captive and gave gifts unto men." It needs but the smallest acquaintance with ancient history to understand this language. It is drawn from the customs of great generals, when they had accomplished a wonderful victory; they entered the city of Rome, in triumphal procession, with captives behind them laden with golden chains; and it sometimes occurred that the very generals that had defeated the Roman army, were themselves in turn defeated, and brought in chains to Rome to be sacrificed. Now, Jesus Christ at the grave had been triumphed over, for a time, by the power of Satan, the great destroyer; and then, when he broke the bands of death asunder, and triumphed over Satan, he in turn trod him down in awful defeat; and now the very Satan that had triumphed over Christ at the grave, and made him his captive for a time, he was leading, as in chains, up into the very presence of the august God. The ascension was Christ's triumphal procession, when a multitude of captives, the devil at the head, and all the demons that were associated with him in his work of darkness, were in chains, brought low, and the great General-in-Chief, the imperial Captain of our salvation, with his white plume waving, mounted to the throne of God, holding all these fallen angels captive in his train. Then, like an ancient general in his triumphal procession, he distributed his largess of gifts to men; and, as he led Satan and his bands captive, he flung down from the portals of heaven the golden coin of the kingdom, in the gift of the Holy Ghost. And so you and I are enriched to-day by this celestial currency, because the largess of his ascension triumph has been rained down upon us.

I think I begin to understand something of what the twenty-second and twenty-third and twenty-fourth Psalms mean. The twenty-second Psalm is the psalm of his death. The twenty-third Psalm is the psalm of his burial. The twenty-fourth Psalm is the psalm of his ascension, and it closes with this magnificent challenge: "Lift up your heads, O ye gates; and be ye lift up, ye everlasting doors; and the King of glory shall come in. Who is this King of glory? The Lord strong and mighty, the Lord mighty in battle. Lift up your heads, O ye gates; even lift them up, ye everlasting doors; and the King of glory shall come in. Who is this king of glory? The Lord of hosts, he is the King of glory." It is the appeal to the heavenly gates to unfold on their golden hinges, and let the King of glory, mighty over all foes, enter and take final possession of his throne.

There may be some, even in this audience of believers,

who have never admitted the King of glory into the innermost recesses of the heart, and I entreat you in the name of our ascended and glorified Saviour, to speak to your own hearts this day, and say, Lift up your heads, O gates of my soul; even be lifted up, ye doors of my heart; and let the King of glory come in. Who is the King of glory? The Lord strong and mighty to overcome the power of your sin, as he has overcome already its penalty, and then to banish the presence of sin by-and-by. Lift up your heads, O ye gates of my soul, and be ye lift up, ye doors of my heart. Let the King of glory come in. Who is this King of glory? The Lord of hosts, he is the King of glory!

I am sure that, with me, you would all like to give expression to the rapture of your own hearts in adoring worship to this King, by singing the two familiar verses that begin and close one of our sweetest hymns. And as we rise and sing these two verses, let every voice join. And you that have never believed in Jesus and taken him as your Saviour, let your heart's adoration go out in these verses and hail Him as your Crowned King!

> "All hail the power of Jesu's name!
> Let angels prostrate fall;
> Bring forth the royal diadem,
> And crown him Lord of all!
>
> Oh, that with yonder sacred throng
> We at his feet may fall:
> We'll join the everlasting song,
> And crown him Lord of all!"

SERMON FIVE

The Privileges of Saints

"The Spirit itself beareth witness with our spirit, that we are the children of God : And if children, then heirs ; heirs of God, and joint-heirs with Christ ; if so be that we suffer with him, that we may be also glorified together."—ROMANS VIII. 16, 17

ONE of the highest privileges of a preacher of the gospel is to search into the riches of the grace of God, as found in the eighth chapter of Romans. We shall take a survey of the entire chapter; for I design to call attention to the line of thought which runs through it. The sixteenth and seventeenth verses give us the pivotal point of this glorious gospel message.

"The Spirit itself beareth witness with our spirit, that we are the children of God : and if children, then heirs ; heirs of God, and joint-heirs with Christ."

This eighth chapter of the Epistle to the Romans is one of the mountain tops of the New Testament. It is the grandest thing that the apostle Paul ever wrote, if we may compare one utterance of the inspiring Spirit with another. If Paul had never written anything else but this chapter, he has here given us a continent of thought, as broad as the grace of God ; and we might spend eternity

The Privileges of Saints

in studying that chapter, and still feel that we had touched but the borders of this wondrous theme.

The verses selected as the text form the exact centre of the whole epistle. If we leave out the epilogue—the salutations at the close—taking the argument of the epistle from the first chapter to the last, the exact verbal centre is the sixteenth and seventeenth verses of this chapter; and the logical centre of the whole argument is in these words, " We are children of God; and if children, then heirs."

The two words—"children," "heirs"—naturally suggest the whole train of our thought. It is well, in all preaching, to avoid preconceptions of our own, so as to follow the thought of God; and praying that the Spirit himself may guide our thoughts, let us first settle for a little while, like a bee on a flower, and consider the word " children," and then going from flower to flower like the same bee, find a little more of the honey that is in the word " heirs." For the word " child " expresses the simple idea of being born of God, belonging to him; but the word " heir " suggests the idea of being one in a family of children that come together into the inheritance of an estate. And so the word " child " represents the position of a child as such; and the word " heir " suggests the position of a child in the family, as a member of that family. In this chapter, there are twelve great thoughts that have to do with the sons of God, six of them referring to the child life, and six of them referring to the family life.

I. First of all, how does Paul get to the eighth of Romans? How does he get to the point in the argument where we have now met him? All these previous seven chapters are taken up in describing the condition of a soul that has not yet found perfect rest and satisfaction in God. The first chapters especially exhibit the fact that all mankind are in a state of sin and misery, and can find no hope except in Christ. There are three words in these previous chapters that express the condition of a soul up to the time when he becomes a child of God; "condemned," "enslaved," "dead;" condemned by the law; enslaved, or sold as a slave under sin; and dead in trespasses and sins. If we are to be children of God, we must manifestly get out of this threefold state; and so the apostle begins this chapter by reminding us that a child of God is no longer condemned, is no longer enslaved, and is no longer dead. He says, "There is therefore now *no condemnation,*" no longer condemned; "the law of the *spirit of life,*" no longer dead, "hath made me *free,*" no longer enslaved. So we cannot open this chapter without seeing that the condemned, the enslaved, and the dead one has come to be justified and free and alive unto God in Jesus Christ. That is the starting-point; and if that is the starting-point, what must the goal be?

1. As I have said, six of these thoughts have to do with the child as a child; and the first of them is this—the *spiritual life.* "The law of the spirit of life in Christ Jesus." Every child begins by being alive. The breath of life, which the new-born babe first inspires, marks the entrance upon its existence. How beautifully we are taught here that the first sign that we are children of God is that we have spiritual life! The word "spirit" means breath, because there is no symbol that represents the idea so beautifully as that the Spirit of God is the breath of God. When God created man out of the dust of the ground he breathed

into his nostrils the spirit, or breath of lives —it is plural—, not only animal life and soul life, but spirit life, breathed into man as his image ; and when man sinned, he lost the spiritual life. Made, at first, body, soul, and spirit—a house of three parts : basement, which is the body ; intermediate story, which is the soul, with its various faculties of intellect and heart ; but, above that all, the upper story with windows that look out on heaven, and through which man had communion with God. When man sinned, that upper story became a "death-chamber," and so it remained until Jesus Christ came and breathed on his disciples, and said, "Receive ye the Holy Spirit"—the breath of God, again. Now the little child of God begins by thus breathing, and the Spirit is represented as being the element in which the child of God lives. We read in this chapter that ye are "in the Spirit if so be that the Spirit of God dwell in you." Some say, " I do not understand that : how can I be in the Spirit, and the Spirit in me?" But there is no contradiction. If you go down to the seashore and dip a pitcher in the waves, the water is in the pitcher, and the pitcher is in the water. We call the air the element of the bird, because the bird lives in the air ; but while the bird is in the air, the air is in the bird. We call the element of the fish water, because the fish is in the water, and the water is in the fish. And the Holy Ghost is the element of the Christian disciple, because he is in the Holy Ghost, and the Holy Ghost is in him. And so Jude says, "Praying in the Holy Ghost." When you pray truly, you are like a man in the atmosphere, which he is breathing in and breathing out ; and when you pray to God you are first in-breathing the Spirit, and then out-breathing the Spirit in prayer to God. And so the Spirit of God is the breath of your life that you constantly inspire and expire. You are living in the Spirit; the Spirit is living in you.

2. The second sign of a child of God is the *spiritual mind*. We read here that the "carnal mind is enmity against God; it is not subject to the law of God, neither indeed can be." But we read also that, "They that are after the Spirit mind the things of the Spirit," and "to be spiritually minded is life and peace." That means that, if you have the Spirit of life in you, you will have the mind of the Spirit in you too. That is to say that, as a living child begins to think, to be conscious, to exercise the powers of the mind that God has given him, so the child of God will begin to exercise and develop the mind of the Spirit that has been given him in his regeneration. What is the "mind of the Spirit"?; and what is it to be carnally minded? To be carnally minded is to turn your eyes downwards, and to be spiritually minded is to turn your eyes upwards. To be carnally minded is to think about earth and earthly things, and labour for them, and desire them, and strive to accumulate earthly wealth and enjoy earthly pleasure, and shut out the things of God from your sight. To be "spiritually minded" is to turn your eyes away from earth, to give yourself wholly up to God, and to be filled with a desire after God, and holiness, and heaven. You may write over this eighth chapter of Romans three very similar words, and they will explain that "spiritual mind." They are the words, "reference," "deference," and "preference." That is to say, a child of God who is spiritually minded lives with supreme reference to God, with supreme deference to the will of God, and with supreme preference for the approbation of God.

3. The third thing about the child of God is his *spiritual*

walk. Of course, we can pass over these thoughts only in a hasty way, depending upon a congregation of true disciples to take these suggestions and outlines and make them the basis of their own studies. If you do not follow up, like the Bereans, whatever you hear, by searching the Scriptures daily, to see whether and how far these things are so, you lose, after all, the greatest part of the inspiration and real instruction of preaching. What, then, is the next thing about the child of God? We are taught that, being led by the Spirit, he walks in the Spirit. A little child, born into a family, not only breathes, and gives evidence of having a mind, but he soon begins to walk, under the leadership of those that are older. You take hold of both hands at first, and help the child to learn to stand and take a step; and then you lead by one hand, and then, by-and-by, just by the tips of the fingers, so that the child feels that he has a support, though he has not : and so he learns to walk alone. So, in this chapter, we are taught that the Spirit of God takes the little child of God, and leads him along so that he learns first to stand in Jesus, and then to walk in Jesus. What is it to walk? To walk in God is to make progress, though I am afraid some of us do not walk very fast, and do not learn to walk very soon. There are three words in the New Testament that cover our whole experience as disciples : " stand," " walk," " sit." The word " stand " represents the position I get into in Christ the moment I believe. I come to him, and put my foot on the solid standing-place, my justification in Jesus Christ. Before, I was on quicksands or in the mire; now I get my feet on the immovable rock. What is walking? That is making progress after I have learned to stand; making progress in daily sanctification nearer and nearer to my

Father's house, my Father's heart, and my Father's image. And what is it to sit? It is to get past both the standing and the walking, and take my place with Jesus Christ on his throne in heaven, made perfect in holiness according to the image of God. But, before he can sit down with Christ above, the little child must learn to walk after the Spirit of God in the ways of God. We never ought to be satisfied if we do not take steps toward God every day of our lives.

4. Then the next thing is *spiritual talk*. We expect the child to learn not only to walk, but to talk. And there are common words, used by children when they begin to use the organs of speech. Did you ever think whence came the words " papa " and " mamma " ? Most words we can trace to an etymological source : we can find in the study of language and grammar the roots from which they came ; but you can find no etymological source for " papa " and " mamma." They come from the grammar of nature, the etymology of nature. When a child begins to talk, he uses the simplest consonants and the simplest vowels; and because he knows how to make but one syllable, he repeats the syllable. And so he says, " papa " and " mamma." God gives us the spirit of adoption, and we cry, " Ab-ba." That is the Aramaic for " Papa." It is the two simplest syllables repeated, Ab-ba. The spirit of adoption comes into the child of God, and teaches him to look up into the Father's face, and say, " Papa, papa ! "

When one can walk and talk, he has access or approach to the Father. In this chapter we are told that the Spirit who leads us, and teaches us to say " Father," also teaches us to pray—" maketh intercession for us with groanings that cannot be uttered." The family affords us a homely illustration. A father goes away to his business, and comes home at night. His little boy has something to ask of him, and is a little timid about it; he does not exactly know how to put it, but he wants something. His mother says, "Now, when father comes home to-night you shall go and ask him yourself," and the child is all in a state of excitement. When the father comes home the mother takes the boy by the hand, and leads him up to his father; and if he is a little timid, she says, "Don't be afraid; he is your father; ask him for whatever you want." And if he tries to ask something, and does not get it out with clearness, she says, "Father, this is what he wants to say to you," and puts it in her own language. This precious eighth of Romans gives us some such picture of God's family life. The Spirit of God takes the little child of God, and leads him along to the Father; and then, as he approaches, and is a little timid, the Spirit of God whispers to him—just like a mother—"Now, do not be afraid, he is your Father"—witnessing with our spirit that we are the children of God—and teaching us to say, "Abba,—Father." Then as we go to God, and try to put before him our request, and do not exactly know how, the Spirit takes up the imperfect prayer and says, "Father, this is what the child wants," and so interprets our desires in his own dialect in the Father's ears. I have got down into this blessed chapter for days at a time, like a sponge asoak in a bowl, to absorb something of this wonderful revelation of the love of God to his dear children.

5. What is the next thing? *Spiritual Growth*. God does not want us always to be children; he would have us get out of our infancy and minority and be full-grown; not always remaining "children, carried about

with every wind of doctrine," but growing up "into the measure of the stature of the fulness of Christ." Growth is a two-fold process; there is effluent and affluent action, excretion and secretion, adding to and throwing off. So with the child of God. Two things are taught in this chapter as to growth. "If ye through the Spirit do mortify the deeds of the body, ye shall live." Now what is mortification? Throwing off that which is dead. And then, on the other hand, we are taught that we must be led of the Spirit, and instructed and guided by the Spirit, and so become more and more like God, conformed to his image: that is the other side of growth. Mortification on the one side, sanctification on the other; throwing off what is old and dead on the one hand, taking on what is new and living on the other; taking food into us, becoming built up by it; and casting out the waste—the refuse and poison of evil. The child of God thus grows by the daily mortifying of the deeds of the body, and the daily vivifying of the Spirit through Christ Jesus: the daily putting off the old man of sin, the daily putting on of the "new man, which after God is created in righteousness and true holiness." We make another great mistake if one day passes without a new mortification of the old deeds of the flesh, without a new putting on of Christ Jesus by the sanctification of the Spirit.

6. So the child comes at last to what is called in the chapter before us "*adoption*." That word "adoption" here means "majority." I used to stumble at that word "adoption." People adopt children when they have none of their own by nature; but as the Lord begets children in his own likeness by the natural process of regeneration, he does not need to adopt them. Adoption does not here

The Privileges of Saints

mean taking into the family a child that is not born into the family, but is somebody else's child. "Adoption" means here attaining "majority." In the Latin language the word "adoptio" referred to the declaration of a son's majority. When a young man attained the legal age, his father took him into the Forum, and from the Bema, or platform, said to the citizens, "This is my son; he has now come to full age; he inherits my name, my property, my social position." Then he took off the toga prætexta—the boy toga or coat—and put on the toga virilis, the manly toga, the coat of a man; he <u>invested him</u>, in the presence of the citizens, with the sign of full manhood, and said, "This is my son." Paul seems to refer to this :—"I reckon that the sufferings of this present time are not worthy to be compared with the glory which shall be revealed in us. For the earnest expectation of the creature waiteth for the manifestation of the sons of God. . . The whole creation groaneth and travaileth in pain together until now . . . waiting for the *adoption, to wit, the redemption of our body.*" In your minority you are but children; when you come to your majority you are full-grown sons. There is a day of revelation coming, of manifestation, when God shall take you as his child and set you on the Forum of the universe, and he shall, before that universe, say, "Bear witness, this is my son: in Christ he is the joint-heir of my name, of my nature, of my dignity, of my possessions, of my throne." And then we shall lay aside the body of our humiliation, the toga that we wore when we were minors; and put on the body of our glory, which is the garment we shall wear when we get to our majority; and this new investment of the redeemed son of God in the presence of the universe is ADOPTION.

II. Now let us turn to consider, for a few moments, the *family life* indicated in this epistle. The child of God is also a member of a family. There are also six thoughts that have to do with this.

1. The first of these great thoughts about the family life is *conformity to one likeness*. In human families we find that what is called "heredity" sometimes takes strange freaks. Here is a child that does not look like either the father or mother; you have to go back to the grandfather, to the grandmother, or to the great grandparents, before you find the type of likeness which that child inherits. It may be so in human families, but it is not so in God's family. There are no such freaks there. Every child of God, born into God's family by regeneration, receives the likeness of God, is conformed to the image of God's dear Son, so that the Son stands as the "first-born among many brethren," all bearing the same likeness. That is the first peculiarity of the child as a member of the family, that he looks like the Father, and like all other true members of the family—there is a likeness to God, a conformity to the image of his dear Son, the spiritual heredity in which we inherit, first of all, the nature of God.

2. Secondly, *harmony with the family*. We know that "all things work together for good to them that love God, to them who are the called according to his purpose." Ah, sinner! do you know that you are not in God's harmony? But the moment you come into this blessed harmony you are like a stray planet that again wheels into its orbit round the sun; nothing can harm you if you are a member of the family of God. You know that in a well-regulated family there is this peculiarity: there is not a child that is not thought of, and there is not a need of any child that is not

thought of. He may be a life-long cripple, but he is always remembered, morning, noon, and night, and every hour; and just so God never forgets one of his children. You may be never so obscure in human eyes, you may live down in the lowest slums—God never forgets you. There is no need that he overlooks; there is no cry, or upward glance of your eye, that he does not hear or see. You are in God's harmony, and all things work together for your good, even the things that seem to be working together for your harm.

3. And so this family life insures *each child's security*. We are not always secure under our human father's roof: lightning may strike the house, or earthquake may rock it; disease and death may enter into it, and famine, and all kinds of calamity; but there is no want of security in our Father's family. His divine arms are beneath us, they hold us up; and his precious wings are over us, and they are the roof under which we hide and abide. There can no evil befall us if we are children of God : " If God be for us, who can be against us?" is the apostle's fond exclamation.

And not only is there such security as this; but there is no separation. This chapter opens with "no condemnation to them that are in Christ Jesus," and ends with no separation from the love of God, which is in Christ Jesus our Lord. So we are absolutely secure. We have conformity to his image, we have harmony with his laws and with his family life, and we have absolute security under his blessed care and provision and protection, and no possible separation.

4. Then the next thing about the family of God is *family discipline*. Discipline includes two things—education and correction. I am afraid that in some of our modern

families the element of correction is very largely left out, and that one reason why children in these days do not obey their parents, either in the Lord or out of the Lord, is because they are not compelled to. The rod has been broken asunder, or put into the fire, and we lack the persuading influence of chastisement. Our blessed Lord teaches us in the Word of God, and especially in this chapter, that every child of God is to be led by the Spirit, taught, instructed by the Spirit; and is also to be corrected—"the sufferings of this present world are not worthy to be compared with the glory which shall be revealed in us." My fellow-disciples, have you ever risen to that spiritual height where you are so anxious to be like God that you can say to him these three words, "Take me, break me, make me"? Sometimes God cannot make us until he breaks us first. I saw, a while ago, a golden cup, that had been made out of old gold coins. They had lost the image and superscription originally upon them, and had been put into the melting-pot and wrought into a new and beautiful vessel. Sometimes God takes poor sinners that have got the image and superscription of God rubbed off them in a world of sin; he takes them and breaks them all to pieces, and melts them all up, and then he makes a vessel unto honour out of them. If you want to be made into a vessel of honour you must expect to be broken in pieces first. How beautifully Peter, in the beginning of that first epistle, says, speaking of the "trial of your faith," that it is " much more precious than of gold that perisheth, though it be tried with fire," and that the object of such trial is, that it "might be found unto *praise*, and *honour*, and *glory* at the appearing of Jesus Christ"! Take the figure I have just been using: a goldsmith wants to make a chalice for a king's table. He first takes the metal, and refines it, till he gets all the dross out of it, and then he stamps it approved : that is *praise ;* then he moulds it for the honourable purposes to which it is destined, till it takes the shape he designs : that is *honour;* then he takes the graving tool and the polishing instrument, and covers it all over with inscriptions and ornamental devices, and makes it glow like the sun, and sets it round with gems, until it flashes back the many colours of the rainbow : that is *glory*. So the Lord takes you, and puts you into his crucible, refines away your dross, and puts on you the mark of approval : that is praise, or approbation. Then he makes you into a vessel of honourable character, for his purpose : that is honour. Then he grinds you on the wheel of affliction, and finishes you with his polishing instrument and his graving tools, until you are complete with the glorious likeness of his dear Son : and that is glory.

5. Now, another feature of family life : " the *glorious liberty* of the children of God." Some people have a curious idea about liberty ; they think that it implies the absence of law. Why, the fact is, liberty implies the presence of law. If you took all law away from this community what sort of a city would London be ? I should want to get out of it to-morrow morning early; so would you. It is the very presence of law, and obedience to law, that constitute liberty. And what is more wonderful than that is, that the more you obey the law, the less you know about the law. If you are not stealing, if you are not murdering, if you are not doing anything opposed to the law of this country, you have practically no personal knowledge of law at all. The law sits easily upon you, like a well-fitting garment; but the moment you begin to disobey, the law lays its strong hand on you, and the easy-fitting garment becomes a

strait-jacket. Let us understand that it is so as to the law of God. Paul says, like a philosopher, "The law was not made for the righteous man, but for the lawless and the disobedient." I suppose that Gabriel has no idea of law, because he has never thought of doing a thing that is contrary to the will of God; but just as soon as the angels sinned, and left their first estate, they found there was law, and a terrible law, that held them in its bonds and sunk them down to the depths of perdition. True saints, the more they love to do God's will, the less do they think about God's commands. If you will obey God absolutely in every thing possible, you will forget all about law, and there will be for you no law at all; it will be your delight to do the will of God.

6. The last of these blessed thoughts about family life is the *legacy of heirs*. We are heirs, and notice *of what we are heirs*. There are only four things that I can now mention in the wonderful estate that is waiting for a child of God, for you can never make out the full catalogue of that estate. You may say as Paul did, "All things are yours"—he began the catalogue—"whether Paul, or Apollos, or Cephas"; but he got discouraged, and he used one great word, and said, "and the world." That would not express it all. There is a great deal more than the world, so he added "Life": that would not do; "and death." That is not enough. He added, "Things present:" that is not enough. He said, "Things to come." And even then he could not express all. He had to go back where he began, and he said, "ALL THINGS ARE YOURS." So, do not attempt to catalogue your inheritance, my brother. You never can do it. But I can tell you four things about the inheritance which are very wonderful. In the first place, you are going

to have a soul that has no sin left in it. In the second place you are going to have a body made like to Christ's glorious body. In the third place, you are going to have a home in which the slime of the serpent is no more to be seen, and where there are no more tears; and in the last place you are going to have what is greater than all—what includes all—God himself. Did you ever think of that? We talk about being heirs. According to the human law, a person enters upon the inheritance of another only after the party is dead. The testament has no force while the testator liveth. How can God make you his heirs, since God never dies? Inasmuch as he never dies, he includes himself in your inheritance. He says, " You shall have me, and everything else, in me; you shall have a sinless soul, because you are partakers of my nature; you shall have a resurrection body, because you are like unto my glorious Son, who represents a redeemed humanity; you shall have this heavenly home, because that is where I live, and I am the centre of its glorious attractions." Believers, you are not heirs of God's universe only, but you are heirs of God. Yes, you are " heirs of God, and joint-heirs with Christ." Think of that! The Lord Jesus Christ has nothing that you are not going to have and share with him. " A joint-heir with Jesus Christ." Not that he is going to get the first and main part, and you the subordinate one. Nay, it is not even half and half, for the inheritance is not divided. He has all, and you have all: and so with every other believer—all there is to have belongs to each.

One word in conclusion. Ought we not to be ashamed of ourselves when we go about with our heads bowed down like a bulrush, looking as though we had no friend and no joy? Let the men of grace show that they

and that
>   " Have found
>   Glory begun below,"
>
>   " Celestial fruits on earthly ground,
>   From faith and hope may grow."

We have not attained to our majority yet; but, blessed be God! we have the earnest and the foretaste of our heavenly inheritance. It is my privilege, like a child that has not his full property yet, to get the interest of that property paid all the time up to the point of majority. I am tired of this talk about cross-bearing, as if that was the whole of the Christian's life. Why, there is a great deal more of the crown in it than there is of the cross; and if we could only persuade poor sinners that this coming to Jesus Christ is not all bearing of burdens, is not all carrying a cross, is not all feeling restrained in our desires and impulses and inclinations, but is being filled with God Himself, might we not lead them to Jesus Christ?

There is a myth about the birds, that when they were first created they had no wings; and the story is, that God made the wings, put them down before the birds, and said, " Now come and take the burdens up and bear them." The birds had beautiful plumage and voices; they could sing and shine, but they could not soar; but they took up their wings with their beaks and laid them upon their shoulders, and at first they seemed to be a heavy load, and rather difficult to bear. But, as they cheerfully and patiently bore them, and folded them over their hearts, lo! the wings grew fast, and that which they once bore, now bore them. The burdens became pinions, and the weights became wings. We are the wingless birds, and our duties are the pinions; and when at first we assume them, they seem loads; but if we cheerfully bear them, going after Jesus, the burdens change to pinions, and we, who once thought we were nothing but servants bearing loads, find that we are sons and heirs of God, free to mount up with wings as eagles, running without being weary, walking without being faint. Into just such a blessed inheritance as this, God invites you all upon the simple, single condition of a penitent and believing acceptance of his dear Son!

Sermon Six

The Individuality of Grace

"I am crucified with Christ: nevertheless I live; yet not I, but Christ liveth in me: and the life which I now live in the flesh I live by the faith of the Son of God, who loved me, and gave himself for me."
—GALATIANS ii. 20

STANDING in front of this Table of our Lord, around which is gathered probably as large an assembly of believers as ever met about his Table, vast numbers of disciples coming to give testimony to him, my mind has, very naturally, been drawn to those precious words in the second chapter and twentieth verse of the Epistle to the Galatians:

"He loved me, and gave himself for me."

This passage of Scripture is the counterpart to that little gospel of John iii. 16: "God so loved the world, that he gave his only begotten Son." Nothing is said in that verse about the *love of Jesus* for sinners, or about Jesus *giving himself;* it is God's love and God's gift. But if you put this verse alongside of that, it is like bringing one hand to another in close embrace; you have the two apposite texts that fit together and give us the whole gospel. God loved the world, and gave his only son; Jesus loved me, and gave himself for me.

The Individuality of Grace

We shall naturally look at two things in this text: first, what it says about *Jesus;* second, what it says about *me*.

He *loved* and *gave himself*. Was there ever such love as that? Angels stand and look down into the depths of that love, but even an angel's sounding line cannot reach to the bottom of it. They stand amazed. The intelligence of a cherub and the love of a seraph blended together still confess this love unsearchable and unspeakable. Love that was intense, that was impartial, that was universal, that was unselfish, self-forgetting, self-renouncing, and self-abandoning; love that was towards sinners and enemies; love that could pray, even on the Cross, while hanging by pierced hands and pierced feet: "Father, forgive them; for they know not what they do." Such was that love!

There is something about the love of Jesus Christ that forbids not only description, but imitation. We can only now and then reflect a single beam from this Sun of Righteousness when we catch the inspiration of its unselfishness. We have been accustomed to say that a mother's love can never be counterfeited, but how much more the Saviour's love! I remember during the late American War there was a young soldier that was wounded very seriously, and very nigh fatally. He was borne to the hospital, and rapidly became delirious; but before that he had given the attending surgeon the name and address of his parents. The surgeon, fearing that the worst was near at hand, sent a telegraphic message to his mother, who lived not a great way off. She took the next train and came immediately down to where her son lay in this delirious state. The surgeon met her at the door of the hospital, and he said, "Madam, you must not go in. Your son is hanging between life and death; the least excitement, even the excitement of meeting you, might turn the scale and prove fatal. You must not go in;" and there that mother stood in the vestibule of the hospital and looked through the door at her son lying on the cot, and for two or three hours of mortal agony, such as a mother only could experience, she yearned to go and sit by his bedside. Finally, she could no longer endure it, and she beckoned to the surgeon, and said, "Doctor, just let me go and take that nurse's place. I won't say a word to him; I won't let him know that I am his mother; I will not even call him by name or put a kiss upon his brow, but I must go and sit by him; I shall die if I stay here." "Well," said the doctor, "Madam, you may go if you will solemnly promise me that you will not let him know who you are." She promised. She went in and took the nurse's place. The poor boy was lying with his face towards the wall; by-and-by, in the fever of delirium, he turned round for a moment and groaned; and then as he turned back again towards the wall, she reached out her hand and laid it on the fevered brow. "Why," he said, "nurse, that is *just like my mother's hand.*" If it is impossible to counterfeit a mother's love, who shall counterfeit a Saviour's! Everything about it, all the tenderness of his ministry,—the precious words he spoke to such women as the woman of Samaria at the well, to the woman who was a sinner, in the house of Simon the leper, when she washed his feet with her tears and wiped them with the hairs of her head,—all the marvellous majesty and mercy of that ministry defy competition, defy counterfeiting, almost defy imitation. And when Jesus speaks it is the Father's voice, it is the voice of God; when he touches us, it is the touch of God.

And such love impelled him to *give himself* for us; yes,

The Individuality of Grace 107

for *me,* for me, for me. You know what that self-giving meant. You know what it meant for Jesus Christ to lay aside the mantle of his imperial glory to come down to earth, take the form of a servant, and in the form of a servant accept the destiny of a malefactor and a slave, and be crucified between thieves, be mocked and jeered at, spit upon and scourged, insulted and outraged, to die as a criminal, and be buried as a pauper in the sepulchre that was extended to him as a charity. But the thing that I especially call your attention to, is the fact that he gave himself for you, *for me.* This idea of substitution runs through the entire Scripture. The blood is everywhere on the Bible; you cannot find a page that is not blood-red; and all the events of Old Testament history and the rites and the ceremonies, and even the Biblical characters, are like pearls that are strung upon a crimson cord, and the cord unites them all, and makes one necklet of grace. In the twelfth of Exodus you read the story of the Passover, the blood sprinkled on the right hand and on the left hand, and on the upper door-post—not on the threshold, because God would not have the blood trampled on as a profane thing—and the children of Israel, hiding behind this blood-stained doorway, and then going out through the blood-stained doorway, as though to indicate that behind the blood was safety, and when the blood was around them, there was deliverance. Then you read the sixteenth of Leviticus and study the great Day of Atonement; the two kids that were so like each other that they had to be distinguished, as we are told by Edersheim, by a scarlet cord or a scarlet ribbon tied round the neck of the scapegoat, or the goat Azazel, the goat of removal. One kid slain, in order to express the idea that without shedding of blood there is no remission of sins; and the other standing while Aaron laid his hands heavily upon its head and confessed his own sins and the sins of the people, and then that goat, led away by the hand of a man into the wilderness, where it would never find its way back to the camp to bring the sins of the people before their eyes again. How beautifully that double picture represents Jesus bearing off our sins as the Lamb of God to the Cross, and dying for them, and then, as the scapegoat on whose head the sins were laid, bearing them away from the face of God as into some uninhabited wilderness where they never would be brought back to the thought of God, and need not even be brought back to the thought of God's forgiven redeemed people. And so all through the Word of God there runs this idea of substitution, sacrifice for sin. "In the day thou eatest thereof thou shalt surely die," said God to Adam when he was in the Garden of Eden; and when sin came into this world life was forfeited, and the only way to save man was to have some other life given for the forfeited life. And because "the blood is the life," the shedding of blood represented the giving of the sacrificial life for the forfeited life of the sinner. That key will unlock all the mysteries of the redemptive scheme in the Old and in the New Testaments alike.

Jesus Christ voluntarily *gave himself* a substitute for the sinner. There are many who say that this was not possible! That it is not *just* that one man should suffer for another, the innocent for the guilty. And the answer is, it would not be just if it were *compulsory*. If God had compelled Jesus Christ, or any other being in the universe, to stand in the place of the sinner, it would have been a manifest injustice; but for Jesus to give himself a ransom for many, was perfectly consistent with justice. Let me give a very simple illustration. A gentleman in Concord, New Hampshire, had long been accustomed to teach boys. On one occasion, his boys having made a rule—as, indeed, they made all the rules of the school—that if any one transgressed in a certain particular he should be publicly flogged on the platform, and a pupil was found to have committed this offence; he said, "Boys, what shall I do?" They said with one voice "He will have to be flogged." He was a little fellow, perhaps about fifteen years of age, and, just as he came up on the platform to receive the merited punishment, his older brother came in at the door. He was a full-grown man, a strong, stalwart fellow. He at once caught the situation. He stepped up to the platform, and he said to the teacher, "Will you allow me to take the punishment of my brother upon myself?" The teacher turned to the school and said, "Boys, do you think that the law of this school will be sufficiently honoured if this brother should receive the punishment on his own back?" The boys held up hands in assent. The brother took off his coat and bared his back while the teacher brought down upon that back the heavy blows that would have been administered to the offender. Now, the law of the school was satisfied and sustained, when the elder brother took upon himself the punishment due to the sin of the younger; the law was magnified and made honourable; but the little fellow escaped the punishment, because some one took it voluntarily upon himself. And so God magnified his law and made it honourable, while our blessed Redeemer took our punishment upon himself, and in our stead suffered on the accursed tree. But then, again, some objector says, "Jesus Christ did not bear the exact penalty of sin. The penalty of sin was everlasting destruction from the presence of the

Lord and the glory of his power; and how could Christ's suffering for a few hours, however great, in the agonies of the cross, be bearing the penalty of sin?" Well, I answer, he did not suffer the *exact penalty* due to the sin, but he suffered an *equivalent* for that penalty. You all understand what the word "equivalent" means. I may have here a bag containing ten thousand copper pennies, and on the other side I may have a very small bag containing about forty sovereigns, the equivalent of these ten thousand copper pennies. Now those are by no means *equal;* if you should carry one and then the other, you would very soon see their inequality; yet the one is an equivalent for the other, and that is the reason why it is unnecessary that we should pay a large debt in copper pence, because we can pay it in that which is equivalent to them—sovereigns, or notes upon the Bank of England. Jesus did not suffer the exact penalty due to sin, and which the sinner would have borne, but Jesus suffered an equivalent before the law, something that the law and justice of God could accept as a substitute and equivalent for the sinner's punishment, and as magnifying the law, just as much as though every sinner had come to suffer the due exclusion from the presence of God, and the eternal weight of his holy wrath.

Now, having spoken very briefly about how our Lord Jesus Christ loved us, and what he did for us, I especially desire for a few moments to emphasize the *me;* for all that I have said is but the introduction to what is to each believer a most precious word in this text, that same little word, *me.* "He loved me, and gave himself for me." God shows his greatness in this that even in the mass he never loses sight of the individual. Millions of birds fly in the firmament, and yet there is not a sparrow falls to the ground without

The Individuality of Grace 111

his notice. Millions of blades of grass spring up in the field, and millions of lilies bloom in the valley, yet not one of them escapes the oversight of God; he fashions every one of them in his own perfect way by his own divine handiwork. And we are told that the very hairs of our head are all numbered. On the full scalp there may be counted three hundred thousand hairs; how easy then to lose one of them! Constantly and unconsciously they drop from the scalp, and yet there is not one of them all that perishes without God's knowledge; God notices and counts the very hairs on our heads. The stars are as countless as the sands, yet he calleth the stars by name. There is a very sweet saying in John x. 3: " He calleth his own sheep by name." Some of you have been in Oriental countries and have seen those shepherds with their great flocks of thousands of sheep, and yet there are some shepherds who know every sheep individually by name. A traveller in Syria saw two flocks of sheep numbering some thousands come and drink at one watering trough, and saw each shepherd separate his own sheep and go his own way without losing one, or having one mixed with the flock of the other. He said to one of the shepherds, " How is this possible? Do you know these sheep by name?" " Yes," said he, " I do." " Well," said my friend, " will you call twenty of your sheep by name?" and he called them one after another, and as he mentioned their names, or gave the peculiar call which they recognized, each individual came out from the flock and gathered around the shepherd. Millions of stars —God calls them all by their names. Millions of believers —God calls them all by their names. And, moreover, this traveller said to the shepherd, "How do you distinguish these sheep? I cannot tell any difference between them;

they all look alike to me." "Ah, but," said he, "I will show you how I distinguish them," and he called one sheep: "Do not you see that that sheep's tail is a little crooked?" He called another: "Don't you see that that sheep in jumping over some fence has injured his hind foot?" He called another: "Don't you see that that sheep has got a slit in the ear? Don't you see that other sheep has got a little bend in his nose"? He knew the sheep by their defects. And the Lord knows us by our defects, and he has a great many such marks to recognize. Yes, he knows his sheep by the faults of their temper, and of their will, and of their disposition, and their unguarded speech and their manifold weaknesses and infirmities. He recognises every one of us by name, and he recognises our infirmities, and he has compassion upon them all. He loves each one of us, and cares for each one of us personally. We are told in the eleventh of John, "Now Jesus loved *Mary* and *Martha* and *Lazarus*." How often we thank God for that! It would have been so easy and short to say "Jesus loved the whole family." That would not do; no, "Jesus loved Mary and Martha and Lazarus." So it is with the church in this house, every one of us he can name, and he loves each one separately and individually. And how beautiful is his treatment of Peter! In the twenty-second of Luke, Jesus says, when he warns Peter of the coming temptation, "Behold Satan hath desired to have you"—that is plural, have *you all*—"that he may sift you as wheat; but I have prayed for *thee*,"—singular—"Peter," because Peter was to be in the depths of a great temptation, and was to deny his Lord three times, and with oaths and curses; and so while he said "Satan hath desired to have *you all* that he may sift you as wheat, I have prayed for *thee* that thy faith fail not."

The Individuality of Grace

See how Jesus followed that same Peter. It seems quite incredible that he should think of one poor, weak disciple when he has the interests of the universe on his hands and on his heart; yet so it is. When Peter denied his Lord, denied him again and again, the cock crew; then Jesus turned and looked upon Peter: Peter saw his look, and went out and wept bitterly. And then, when he rose from the dead, the angel conveying the message from Jesus, says to the woman, "Go, tell my disciples *and Peter.*" Why "and Peter"? Because Peter had said that he was not a disciple. He had voluntarily cut himself off from the number of disciples, and if Jesus had sent a general message, " Go, tell my disciples," Peter might have said : " That does not mean me; the Lord does not recognise me, for I have said I am not his disciple, and sworn that I am not, and cursed and blasphemed to confirm my oath and my lie." Jesus therefore knew how Peter would feel, and he sent a special message to Peter. If you will compare the gospel narratives, you may see the reason why Peter, when he heard the message, got up and ran toward the sepulchre. He could not restrain his impatience. The Lord had sent for him, had sent word to him, and the only individual message that was sent was to the very man who had denied him. May this not be the reason that his impetuous nature could no longer be restrained, and so he ran with all his might to the tomb where the Lord Jesus had lain? Oh, yes, he "loved *me,*" " gave himself for *me.*"

Paul says in this same chapter and verse, " Christ liveth in me." Not only did he love me and give himself for me, but he " liveth in me." The thought is that every believer needs a whole Christ for his salvation, and has a whole Christ for his sanctification; his joy and full redemption.

Every little drop of rain or drop of dew gets the benefit of the whole sun. If you look at a drop of rain when the sunlight falls upon it at a peculiar angle, you will get all the colours of the rainbow. Why? Because the *whole sunbeam is in that drop.* In the sunbeam, you know, there is violet, indigo, blue, green, yellow, orange, red, all combined in white light; and when one little drop of rain or dew prismatically separates all these colours and gives the violet, indigo, blue, green, yellow, orange, red, like the rainbow, it shows that the drop that is so small, nevertheless takes in the whole light: all the light, all the heat, all the life-giving power of the sun blesses every drop. And if you are a child of God there is in God the Father no light or life or love that is not for you, just as much as though there was no other person in all the world to be benefited and blessed and saved and sanctified. God gives the whole Christ for your salvation, sanctification, satisfaction, and glorification. This precious feast of fat things and "wines on the lees, well refined," is waiting to give you a visible token of how your Lord gave his precious blood and body for your redemption. But what is the natural and legitimate outcome of this great deed? In the first place, every believer can say of God, "*My God.*" Notice the singular personal pronoun,—not the God of believers only, but "my God." And not only so, but there is a divine sense in which God is to me what he is to no one else; there may be a special revelation and communication of himself to my soul, so that, as though I were brought face to face with God and all other beings in the universe were shut out while I look into his face and he looks into mine, I may appropriate him wholly as my own, and say "my beloved is mine, and I am his."

Of this personal relation let me give an illustration. When God revealed himself to Abraham it was by his name JEHOVAH or JAH; and when Abraham built the altar to the LORD, he inscribed on it, or called upon, the name by which he specially knew God. For instance, when the ram was provided for the offering on Mount Moriah in the place of Isaac, he built an altar, and he called that altar by the name Jehovah-jireh, or Jah-jireh, the Lord will provide. But when God appeared to Jacob he appeared to him specially by the other name of God, EL, the Almighty. And this name of God is traced all through Jacob's experience. For instance, when he took the stone on which he had been reclining for a pillow and set it up to be a sign of God's house, and poured oil on it, he called the name of the place "*Beth-el*," not Beth-jah, not the house of Jehovah, but the house of EL, the house of God, as God made himself known to him in his wisdom. Then, when in the struggle at the ford of Jabbok he received the blessing from above, he called the name of the place "*Peni-el*," the face of EL; and God said "Thy name shall no longer be Jacob, but *Is-ra-el*, prince of EL. Then when he went back to Bethel he called the name of the place " El-beth-el," EL, the house of EL. Meanwhile another altar had been erected, and on it he placed the name "*El-el*ohe-Isra*el*," EL, my EL, of the prince of EL. But what does that mean but that my God is *my* God, and that he is a different God to me from what he is to you, because of the special revelations he makes of himself to me? and because he comes down to me in my infirmity, and in the boundlessness of his compassion takes me up in his arms and calls me by my particular name, he bears to me a particular name that is all my own. He may be JAH to Abraham, but he is EL to

Jacob; he is Jesus to me, and he is my Jesus. He has his own name, his own attributes, his own exhibition of himself to me as a humble believer. Hence, in Revelation we read: "I will give him a white stone, and in the stone a new name written, which no man knoweth saving he that receiveth it."—Rev. ii. 17. May God give us at least a touch of the mystery and majesty of that mercy that can make it possible for him to come down to one insignificant disciple and reveal the whole of himself to him as though there was no one else to whom he needed to reveal himself.

When the blacksmith welds two pieces of iron he puts both into the furnace and sends the blast through it until they are at white heat. Then he places them on the anvil, one upon the other with nothing between, and brings down the huge hammer upon them, and so welds the two into one. Jesus would unite you with him. He says, "Poor sinner, lovest thou me? Follow thou me." As William Arnot said, he puts the "thou" upon the "me" with naught between, and so welds the two into unity. Will you be united with Jesus? Then it is very simple, let him put the "thou" and the "me" together, while you gladly consent to have nothing henceforth come between your Lord and you. If there is a poor sinner that has come in here without Christ, if there is some stray soul, wandering from the Father's house, without peace and rest, open your inmost heart now; and while the Lord Jesus says, "Poor sinner, lovest thou me? Follow thou me," let your heart respond "Jesus, I accept thy love and sacrifice for me, and from this time forth, forgiven, redeemed by blood, I will follow thee whithersoever thou goest."

Sermon Seven

Life by Believing

> But these are written, that ye might believe that Jesus is the Christ, the Son of God; and that believing ye might have life through his name."—JOHN xx. 31
>
> "These things have I written unto you that believe on the name of the Son of God; that ye may know that ye have eternal life."—I JOHN v. 13

THESE two texts belong together. The first of them teaches us the object for which the Gospel according to John was written: "That ye might believe that Jesus is the Christ, the Son of God; and that believing ye might have life through his name." The second text gives us the reason why the first Epistle of John was written: "These things have I written unto you that believe on the name of the Son of God; that ye may know that ye have eternal life." The Gospel was written that we might *have* life; and the first Epistle of John was written that we might *know* that we have life.

We take up the first of these great themes, and leave the other to a subsequent occasion.

Life eternal through believing, is the subject of the Gospel according to John. When God gives a key, it is very sure to unlock all the mysteries to which it pertains;

and when we have such a divine key, it is quite in vain for us to look for any human interpreter. The Gospel according to John has a divine key attached to the lock, and we have only to turn the key, and the door is opened into the mysteries of this gospel.

Here we shall find the expression "life" or "eternal life" about eighty times; and we shall find the expression "believe" about forty times. This is sufficient to show that the gospel fulfils the purpose for which it is declared to have been written. While you will not find in this gospel, in a single instance, the word "repent", you will often find the word "believe," and moreover, notice how explicitly the apostle puts this whole matter. "These are written that ye might believe that Jesus is the Christ, the Son of God." It is not often that those three titles of our Lord are put together, but they are here put together for a specific purpose. Jesus is the human name. "Thou shalt call his name Jesus," was said to Joseph before Christ's birth. "Christ", which means anointed, is the Saviour's Messianic name; it is his name as the Messiah. And "the Son of God" is the Saviour's divine name, and so we have here the three great titles—" Jesus" the human, " Christ" the Messianic, and "the Son of God" the divine title; and these things are written that ye might know that Jesus the human child was Christ, the anointed Messiah, and that both represent the Son of God.

Now, again, the Bible is a kind of encyclopædia and a lexicon combined; that is to say, it gives universal information about the subject of eternal life, and it defines the terms that it uses. My simple object, as the organ of the Spirit and the word of God, is to lead enquiring minds into the study of the subject of eternal life. I should be

Life by Believing

glad, if the time allowed, to consider every instance of the more than forty in this gospel in which the terms "life" or "eternal life" are used. But let me at least call attention to this gospel as a revelation of *the way in which eternal life becomes ours through believing*. Not only does it fully treat this great subject from its first to its closing chapters, but the inspiration of this gospel is partly seen in the fact, that, in every case in which eternal life is referred to, some *new conception* with regard to it is added to what goes before. It is even more remarkable that these additions follow what may be called a *progress of doctrine* in this Gospel according to John. That is to say, the unfolding is gradual, systematic, regular, so that in no instance what we are taught, about eternal life, could change places with what precedes or follows, showing that the apostle John in following the narrative of the life of Christ as recalled to his memory by the Holy Spirit, was also led by the same Spirit, and probably without his own recognition of the fact, to unfold gradually, systematically, logically, and progressively the whole subject of eternal life.

This you will see for yourself if you will gather together the scattered references to eternal life within the bounds of this gospel, and thus make a systematic and orderly presentation of the whole subject.

The first reference to life in this gospel narrative is found in the fourth verse of the first chapter. "In him was life, and the life was the light of men." Now, why should life in Jesus Christ be first presented to us under the figure of light? Because the first approach of Jesus Christ to a human soul as the life of God is in his light-giving power. To show you that you are a sinner and need a Saviour—that you are condemned by the law and need reconciliation and forgiveness—that hell opens beneath your feet, and that you certainly will fall into perdition if you are not renewed by the power of God and lifted to heaven —to show you your disease and your physician, your need and your supply, your destitution and your divine provision —that is the first office of Jesus Christ. He cannot give life until he has given light; and whether you get the life will depend upon whether or not you follow the light, whether you open your heart to the incoming of the light, and rejoice even in the smiting of a righteous God, and turn from your sin to your Saviour.

Jesus is the Sun of righteousness, and from the sun there come three beams in one, the beam of light, and the beam of heat, and the beam of life. And so Jesus Christ, as the Sun of righteousness, throws out a three-fold beam, light and love and life ; but the light is first recognized, and if you receive the light you get the love and the life besides.

The next reference to life in this gospel is found in the third chapter, verses 14-16. " As Moses lifted up the serpent in the wilderness, even so must the Son of man be lifted up : that whosoever believeth in him should not perish, but have eternal life ; for God so loved the world, that he gave his only begotten Son, that whosoever believeth in him should not perish, but have everlasting life." Here first the term " everlasting life " or " eternal life " occurs, and is found twice, and something important is added to what was previously taught us.

Why is this " *eternal* life," not " *immortal* life " ? Why should not God have said that whosoever believeth in Christ should have *immortal* life ? " Eternal life " is more than " immortal life," for eternal life has no beginning nor end. And there is a reason why the Spirit should say that the

Life by Believing

believer in Jesus Christ shall have *eternal*, not immortal life. Suppose you are born of a certain noble sire and mother, and trace your lineage back through all the generations to a remote antiquity, you, as a child in the family, are not only entitled to all that pertains to that family in the future, but you inherit all that pertains to that family in the past. The glory of its past history, of its achievements, of its heroism on the battle-field, of its services in the state or church; the glory of its learning, of its patriotism, of its philanthropy—you, as a child in that family, come into the inheritance of it all. And so there is a spiritual heredity. If I am a child of God by faith in Jesus Christ, all the past of God I inherit as well as all the future of God. Being a child of God, whatever is glorious in the past eternity of God comes to enrich my present and my future. When God has a child born to him in his family by faith in Jesus Christ, the child does not simply start with the present moment of birth to enjoy a future that shall be blessed, but God enriches that new heir of glory by all that there is in the glorious past of his eternal existence. You have God for your Father, and all God's past is in Christ your past also.

The next reference is in the third chapter and the 36th verse. Here is the only instance in the whole word of God in which there is in the original language a perfect stanza with rhyme and rhythm.*

It might be translated, to convey both the rhythm and rhyme—

"Whoso on the Son believeth,
Everlasting life receiveth;"

---

* Ὁ πιστεύων εἰς τὸν υἱὸν
ἔχει ζωὴν αἰώνιον

and there is some reason why, in that place alone, the Holy Ghost has framed the message of salvation so as to form a perfect poetic couplet. The heart of the gospel is there— " He that believeth on the Son hath everlasting life ; " and the Spirit of God has put it into a beautiful rhyming Greek couplet that he may call attention to this gem of the gospel.

What idea is added to our previous conceptions of eternal life, when we strike this marvellous verse? We have had "life" and "eternal life" before, but we have not had that little word "*h-a-t-h*, hath." " He that believeth on the Son *hath* everlasting life " ; not " shall have it." *Hath it.* That is to say eternal life is the *present possession* of the believer.

> "The moment a sinner believes,
> And trusts in his crucified God,
> His pardon at once he receives,
> Redemption in full through his blood."

That is to say, if you came in here to-night, a poor, wretched undone, unsaved sinner, and, while you are here in the presence of God, open your heart to the light and love and life of Jesus, you can pass out of this house saved ! Nay, salvation may come to you in a moment of time if you hear and obey the voice of the living God. We often say in our prayer meeting talks and prayers, that we hope that we *shall* be saved. But if you believe you *are* saved ; and would to God you might have the joy of the present salvation in your soul ! It is a reproach to God that we should so often go to him, years after we have taken Jesus Christ to be our Saviour, and have begun to walk in the narrow way with him, and ask that, after we have completed our course on earth, he would finally save us. We have salvation already. It is only the consummation of that salvation that will come by-and-by. If you trust in Jesus you are saved now. It is a real and a present salvation.

In the fourth chapter we find that beautiful narrative about the woman at the well. "If thou knewest the gift of God, and who it is that saith to thee, Give me to drink; thou wouldest have asked of him, and he would have given thee living water." Christ says, moreover, to this woman at the well, "The water that I shall give him shall be in him a well of water springing up into everlasting life." A most remarkable kind of water that is, indeed! Water from earthly springs has no such property as that. If I am thirsty I drink this water, and shortly my thirst returns, and I must have some more to quench the new thirst; but Jesus says, "Whosoever drinketh of the water that I shall give him shall never thirst; but the water that I shall give him shall be in him a well"—or spring of water—"springing up into everlasting life." Notice the progress of thought : a *drink*, a *spring*, a *stream*. I thirst : I come to Christ, and ask the living water. It is proffered to me in the golden vessels of his grace. I take a drink, and lo, my thirst is quenched! But not only so. That water has the power in me like to that of the seed when put into the earth. The seed begets a plant, and the plant bears other seeds like unto the first. And this water which enters into me, to quench my thirst, becomes in me a spring like unto the source from which that water came, and out from this spring runs a stream like unto the stream that issued forth from that original spring. And so every soul that is enabled to drink into Christ Jesus is made partaker of the Holy Ghost and the nature of God himself; and so life becomes within that soul a springing well, and out from the springing well runs a flowing stream, a stream of living water and living testimony unto the Lord Jesus.

In the fifth chapter and the twenty-fourth verse this life is presented as the secret both of the resurrection of the soul and of the resurrection of the body. " Verily, verily, I say unto you "—" Verily, verily " is used twenty-four times in this gospel, and always prefaces one of the most important statements which Christ ever makes—" Verily, verily, I say unto you, He that heareth my word, and believeth on him that sent me, hath everlasting life." We have had all that before, but he *adds*, " and shall not come into condemnation ; but is passed from death unto life." We have already learned that eternal life is the present possession of the believer; but, in order that we shall not mistake our Lord's meaning, he uses another form of expression which is more explicit, clear, and convincing, if possible, than what preceded. Here is a chasm. I am on one side of it ; as soon as I pass across, I am on the other side. Here is a sinner: he stands on this side of eternal life. He crosses by faith : he stands on the other side. He is on different ground. He has " passed from death unto life "; and, to make that plainer, it is said, " and shall not come into condemnation." The Greek word is " crisis " ; that is, judgment, and it should be so translated : "Shall not come into judgment." I understand by that, that a believing soul shall never come into the judgment of the great white throne. Hundreds of Christian people never seem to have risen to the height where they see their own privileges. It is common among disciples to stand in fear of the judgment. They ask themselves, " How shall I confront God at the great white throne ? " *You are never going to confront him there.* When Jesus Christ died on the cross your sins were judged in him. He undertook to bear your penalty in his own blessed precious person. Now, if Christ has been judged for my sins, how can I be judged for them too? If Christ has endured the penalty of my sins, how can I endure the penalty of them too? If Jesus Christ is my Saviour, can my Saviour condemn me? He is "the end of the law for righteousness"—that is, for justification—"to everyone that believeth." But does not the Bible say that "we shall all appear before the judgment-seat of Christ"? Yes, but that judgment-seat of Christ is not the great white throne. The judgment-seat is the bema. The bema was a platform at the end of the race-course, where the judge stood to deliver the prizes to the successful runners in the race. You and I are to be judged at the judgment-seat of Christ, not as to the question of our salvation, which has already been settled, but as to the question of our service and its reward, which still remains to be settled. So we shall never come into condemnation, for our salvation is assured, though we shall come before the judgment-seat of Christ to receive the proper reward of our service, and to take our places in his kingdom according to the use of the talents or the pounds which he has committed to us. But if this precious gospel teaches anything it is that, if a man believes in Christ, he has passed from death unto life. He can never, therefore, come into death, neither can the question ever be raised as to whether he shall come into life, for he is in life already, and he shall not come into condemnation.

Now, notice, still further. "Verily, verily, I say unto you, The hour is coming, and now is, when the dead shall hear the voice of the Son of God: and they that hear shall live. . . . Marvel not at this: for the hour is coming, in the which all that are in the graves shall hear his voice, and shall come forth; they that have done good, unto the resurrection of life; and they that have done evil, unto the resurrection of damnation."

Let us not confuse these two passages of Scripture. The former tells us that the hour is coming, and *now is*, when the dead shall hear the voice of the Son of God. Nothing is said about their being in their graves. "The dead shall hear the voice of the Son of God, and they that hear shall live, and only "they that *hear* shall live." Manifestly, that has nothing to do with the resurrection of the body. It regards humanity as dead in trespasses and in sins. The voice of the Son of God goes forth proclaiming the tidings of saving grace; and those that, being dead in trespasses and sins, hear that voice, are raised from the death of their sins and their condemnation.

The other passage of Scripture which follows adds, " Marvel not at this: for the hour is coming, in the which all that are *in the graves* shall hear his voice, and shall come forth; they that have done good, unto the resurrection of life; and they that have done evil, unto the resurrection of damnation." The additional thought, put before us, is that, if Jesus Christ becomes life to you from the dead, so that your soul is raised from its death in sin by the hearing of his voice, then your body also, if it sleeps in the grave, shall hear his voice, and come forth to the resurrection of life. That is to say, the Holy Spirit that becomes an inhabitant in you when you believe in Jesus, and grants you an immediate resurrection of soul in the image of God, becomes the secret of the resurrection of your body also out of the corruption of the grave.

In the sixth chapter Christ presents himself as the bread

of life, and tells us that whosoever shall partake of this bread shall live for ever. In the fourth chapter he teaches us that he is the water of life, and here that he is the bread of life. Water may quench thirst, but it cannot sustain life. Water is not properly food; it makes room for food to digest; it supplies the material for secretion; it expands the digestive organs so that solid food has the opportunity to distribute its properties through the human system; but no man could live on water. He must have solid nutriment in order to be kept alive from day to day and year to year. Jesus, in the fourth chapter, tells that woman of Sychar that he is the water of life, because he is able to satisfy all her yearnings of soul. In the sixth chapter he tells us that he is the bread of life, because he is the sustenance and the support, the staff of life, to the believing soul. The water satisfies your desire, but the bread supplies your need. The water quenches your thirst, but the bread appeases your hunger. And Jesus Christ says, " He that believeth on me shall neither hunger nor thirst "; that is, shall neither have unsatisfied or restless yearnings, nor find himself faint or fail because he lacks strength to go on in the right way.

Let us pass to the eighth chapter and twelfth verse, where Jesus says, " He that followeth me shall not walk in darkness, but shall have the light of life." In the first reference, in the first chapter and fourth verse, " In him was life; and the life was the light of men," he is presented as the light of everybody, even of the sinner who does not accept him as Saviour. All he knows about his sins and his salvation comes from the light that shines upon him, even though he may refuse to believe and be saved. But here we are taught that, having had the light shed abroad round us like the sunlight, he that follows that light shall have light *within him.* The reference is undoubtedly to the pillar of cloud and fire. When, in the evening hours of the feast of Tabernacles, they lit up those great candelabra that stood in the court of the women, and flashed their radiance all over the city of Jerusalem; in that ceremony they celebrated and commemorated the pillar and cloud of fire that accompanied Israel through the weary path of their desert journey. When the tents were pitched this pillar came down and stood over the cherubim in the holiest place. So our blessed Lord says to us, " If you follow the light as they followed the pillar of cloud, then shall the same pillar of cloud come down and enter your heart; so that you who follow the light shall have it in your own soul."

In the tenth chapter our Lord is teaching the great truth about his sheep, and he says, " I am come that they might have life, and that they might have it more abundantly." And then, in the 28th and 29th verses he says, "I give unto them eternal life; and they shall never perish, neither shall any man pluck them out of my hand. My Father, which gave them me, is greater than all; and no man is able to pluck them out of my Father's hand." I asked myself for years what force there was in this *repetition,* " I give unto them eternal life; and they shall never perish, neither shall any man pluck them out of my hand, etc." Eternal life is not only a present possession, but is a true and an inalienable possession. You ask me whether I believe in the perseverance of the saints. I tell you, no. I have no confidence in the saints and their perseverance; but I believe in the *perseverance of Jesus Christ.* The reason why the saints persevere is, because Jesus Christ perseveres *in* the saints. If the Lord should withdraw his mighty power from me I should drop into perdition. If he, for a moment, forsook me, what would become of me? Outbreaking sins, outrageous iniquities, a final and fatal apostasy would result. The precious truth is, that it is the keeping power of our Lord and his perseverance which is our hope. Hear what he says, " My sheep hear my voice, and I know them, and they follow me : and I give unto them eternal life ; and they shall never perish, neither shall any man pluck them out of my hand." And now, as if to make it stronger and mightier in convincing power, he says, " My Father, which gave them me, is greater than all, and no man is able to pluck them out of my Father's hand." Why are the two hands of Father and Son represented as ensuring the keeping of the sheep?

Here is a watch : I hold it in my hand. I may have a strong grip and hold it firmly, but if I put the other hand over it, and lock the two together it is going to be very difficult for another to get it out. Here is a wooden rule. When I was a boy, we used to try the power of our grip by taking a rule in our right hand, and defying some fellow to wrench it out. He would take hold with both hands, and it was almost impossible, if a strong fellow got hold, to prevent its being wrested from your grasp. But suppose you yourself take it in both hands. Then he may swing your whole body from side to side without compelling you to let go. " My sheep shall never perish, neither shall any man pluck them out of *my hand.*" There is *one* hand having hold. " My Father, which gave them to me, is greater than all ; and no man is able to pluck them out of *my Father's hand.*" There is the other hand laying hold : who shall pluck the sheep out when held by both those almighty hands?

I pass over the intervening chapters, to call attention

to one more precious thought. In the seventeenth chapter of John and the third verse we read, " And this is life eternal, that they might know thee the only true God, and Jesus Christ, whom thou hast sent." The essence of eternal life is found in a personal, practical knowledge of God in Christ, and that is what these wonderful words mean, which were our starting-point in this study. " These are written that ye might believe that Jesus is the Christ, the Son of God, and that believing ye might have life through his name."

What is his name? A man's name is that which specially represents his own personality. My name means myself. Your name means you. The name of Jesus Christ means him. To have life through his name is to have life through union with him. You can get no life by using the name of Jesus Christ nor even by searching the holy Scriptures, which have no power to give you life, apart from the Holy Spirit of Life. If you would have life it must be by personal union with Jesus Christ. When a boy at school, I was greatly interested in experiments in natural science, as I am to this day. I remember the first time I saw an electrical machine, and being well acquainted with the teacher, he selected me for the first experiment in electricity, which I thought a high honour. I remember the little black-walnut stool with its glass legs, the glass legs being non-conductors to prevent the electricity from passing off into the earth. The teacher stood me right on that stool, and placed the poles of the electric battery in my hand. Then as he turned the cylinder and developed the electricity, I felt it passing from the wires into my body, entering and filling me, until my hairs stood on end, as the electricity sought a point by which to escape. Then as he

Life by Believing 131

touched a hair of my head or brought his knuckle close to my arm, the electric spark passed from me, and I felt a slight shock. But as soon as I got off that stool, the electricity passed from me to the earth. While united to the electrical machine and separated or insulated from all else, I had the electric life in me. The moment I parted from that machine and stood on the earth, I lost the electric fluid.

Jesus Christ represents the life of God. When I take hold of Jesus Christ, and am united to him, I feel the life of God that is in him becoming the life of God in me. Apart from him we are nothing and can do nothing. Joined to him, the very life that is in God is practically ours.

Let me give one illustration from my own pastoral life of how a human soul gets life in union with Jesus. A few years ago, while pastor in the city of Detroit, Michigan, there tarried after sermon a man who, with tears besought a personal interview. He came and sat down by me in my study, and for three hours unfolded to me one of the darkest histories that I ever heard from the lips of a mortal man. I could not in a miscellaneous audience tell that story. It suffices to say that there was scarce one command of the Decalogue, save that concerning murder, which he had not wilfully and systematically violated. He was a profane swearer; an habitual drinker; an adulterer; a liar; and virtually a thief. There was scarcely any sin that had not been his sin; and, when he unfolded to me that dark history, he said, "Now, do you mean to say that it is possible for such a man as I am to be saved?" "Certainly, I answered; certainly." "How long do you think it would take me to be saved?" "Just as long as it would take you to turn your heart to Jesus Christ."

"Do you mean," said he, "that I could be saved while I am here in this room?" "Certainly, if you take Jesus Christ as your Saviour." "But have I not got to get rid of all these sins and evil habits of mine, first?" "You are to cast all your sins on the Sin-Bearer." "But I must get out of these evil relations in which I am living?" "Yes, by the power of God, when first you have taken Christ to be your Saviour." And so I talked with him for another hour. At last God brought him to the point, where he was willing to submit himself at once to the Lord Jesus Christ, and I said, "Let us get down on our knees before God. I will offer a short prayer, and then you pray for yourself." I knelt with him and prayed that Christ Jesus would come into his soul and give him life from above, there and then. And I said, "Now, my friend, pray for yourself." He continued in silence for a few moments, and then began to pray, but he broke down, and said, "I cannot pray." I said, "You must. This is the crisis in your destiny and history. You must call on the mighty God to save your soul." Said he, "I cannot pray." "Well," said I, "try. Let me hear that you cannot pray. If you cannot do anything more, tell God that you cannot pray." And he tried to get up, and said, "Let me up. I know how to curse, but I cannot pray." I drew nearer and put my arm about him, firmly but tenderly holding him down, while I besought him to call on God. Presently with a great effort he began to pray. And then I thought that I had never heard a man pray as he did. It was with a stammering tongue, but he poured out into the ears of God all the story of that vile life, and then and there he opened his heart to Jesus Christ and took him as his Saviour.

We rose from our knees. I say, solemnly, before this audience and before almighty God, with the full consciousness that I may never preach the gospel again, that I have never known, during thirty years of pastoral life, a case of more full and absolute self-surrender to God, or more absolute and full communication of God to a human soul, than in the case of that man on that day. He rose up from his knees a renewed man. He turned from his old sins and habits. His foot was on the head of Satan who had bruised his heel for many a long year; and he told me, not long ago, that from the day when, in my study, he offered himself to Christ to be saved and took Christ as his Saviour, he had *never even had a desire for strong drink*, and that he had never desired tobacco, which he had used in all three forms—smoking, chewing, and snuffing. That man became a minister of Jesus Christ. I had the pleasure of being called to ordain and instal him as pastor of a church; and from that day to this, he has been in no field of labour without a continual revival of religion. A deep experience of what Christ can do for a human soul was his; and men and women have been brought by scores and hundreds to the feet of Jesus through the power of his transformed life.

That simple story shows what Jesus Christ can do for a human soul. If there are any of you here to-night who have not found Christ as your personal Saviour, I pray you turn to him just now, for I call God to witness that with all humility and fidelity I have preached this saving gospel to you and given you an illustration of the power of this gospel, as I have seen it, not in one life only but in many lives. And may the Lord, out of this audience, gather many unsaved souls to himself, through Jesus Christ our Lord!

Sermon Eight

Believing and Knowing

"These things have I written unto you that believe on the name of the Son of God; that ye may know that ye have eternal life."—
1 JOHN, v. 13

IN the twentieth chapter and the thirty-first verse of the Gospel of John, we read : "These things have I written that ye might believe that Jesus is the Christ the Son of God, and that believing *ye might have life* through his name." The corresponding passage to this is in the thirteenth verse of the fifth chapter of the First Epistle of John : "These things have I written unto you that believe on the name of the Son of God that ye may *know that ye have eternal life.*"

The gospel was written that men might believe, and believing might receive life everlasting. And now this first epistle is written that such believers may *know* that they have eternal life. In other words, here is *God's touchstone of character*, by which to test the signs and proofs and fruits of godliness, and so discern whether or not you are a true believer, whether you have the form of godliness without the power, or the power of godliness within the form

The apostle intimates why it is desirable that every child of God should test himself as to these fruits of faith. He says, in the first chapter, "These things write I unto you

Believing and Knowing

that your *joy may be full.*" In order to complete joy there is needed an assurance of a saved state, the knowledge of God's divine operation in the soul, the proof and the fruit of the divine indwelling. No believer who doubts his own saved state, and lacks the evidences of it, can be truly happy. Another reason the apostle hints for writing this epistle. He says, " Be not deceived." There is danger of deception ; in matters of religion deception is fatal. Many who are members of our churches have practically no experience of godliness. During my public ministry hundreds of professed believers have confessed that they have been for many years confessors of Christ, and yet are persuaded that they have never been converted to God. It has been one precious privilege in my ministry to lead out into light aud joy and salvation many such professed disciples who have had previously the form of godliness without the power thereof.

Deception in matters of religion is especially perilous. There is no more subtle snare of the devil than a profession of Christ without the possession of grace. People come into the church of God, but, if their hearts have never been really touched by converting grace, they are very prone to mistake their place in the church for their membership in " the church of the firstborn which are written in heaven," and to cherish a false security through sacraments and ordinances and outward communion with the church of God, and so sometimes go down into the grave still in a state of awful deception. So True..

By their fruits we shall know them. There is great need once in a while to compare our character and life with God's test-fruits of holiness.

There are five chapters in this epistle, and they all treat

the great subject of knowing that we are children of God; and the prominence given to this may be seen in the fact that the word "know," or "knowledge," occurs between forty and sixty times in the course of these chapters. "We know that we are of God." "We know that we have passed from death unto life." "He that loveth knoweth God." The whole epistle is full of the proofs by which we "know" that we are of God—the justification of such knowledge. More than twenty distinct evidences of a child of God are given here. It would be impracticable now to take up each of those tests, but we may do a wiser thing to classify these evidences and consider the classes. When men build a house they quarry the stone, cut, chisel, and fit stones to their places, and then bring them together, and, on the site of the building, erect them into one structure. So we may go down into these chapters as into a quarry, and take out the tests here set before us, and construct them into some simple form that we can keep before our mind and memory.

A careful study of this epistle shows three great words which are very like. They are "*life*," "*light*," and "*love*," and under those three leading words all the evidences of piety, as brought out here, may be arranged. The argument of the epistle is very simple and beautiful. God is *light*, and the fountain whence all light proceeds. God is *life*, the centre and source of life, and all life proceeds from him. God is *love*, the fountain and spring of love, and all love proceeds from him. And the consequence is, that if I am a child of God, I will bear a likeness to my Father, will have in me God's life, God's light, and God's love. Put those simple sentences together, and you have the whole argument. The quarried stones are erected into a building with three parts to it, and all united in one great symmetrical structure. The central part of the whole building is life, and on the one hand light, and on the other hand love, and all point upward to God himself.

I. First, God is life, and if you are His child, you have God's life in you. That proposition needs scarcely more than to be stated to be apprehended and understood. What is life? Life is a great mystery. Nobody can define it, but we know the signs of life, and they are mostly two. First, *vitality;* second, *energy*. How do you know a living babe from a dead corpse? In the first place, there is the spirit of life in it. It breathes, it sees, it hears, it feels; it has senses; it has a measure of intelligence. And then there is energy : action, motion, ability to move the eyes, and the hands, and the feet; and by-and-by ability to walk, and talk, and exercise all the organs of body, and faculties of mind. So are you to know a living child of God. He will have vitality and energy. He will manifest the spirit of life and the power of action. Such is the argument of the apostle. He says, "Hereby know we that He abideth in us, *by His spirit*, which He has given us." The word "spirit," means breath, or wind, which is an expressive symbol of the Spirit. We know the child of God, because he *breathes in God.* The spirit of life is in him ; and as the apostle says again, " God's seed remaineth in him." God has begotten him as a child, and His vital power is in him, and makes him an acting disciple, enables him to do, to confess, to possess Jesus Christ as a Saviour.

You know a dead from a living body, as I have said, because in the latter there is sight, hearing, feeling. How beautifully the apostle refers to this in the child of God. He says in the opening verse, for instance, "That which we have seen with our eyes, which we have looked upon," or as the original reads, "that which we have *glanced at* with our eyes, that which we have *gazed upon.*" If you go along the streets, looking for a certain name on a sign above the shops, you just glance at them all, until you see a sign which has on it the very name you are looking for, and then you stop and *gaze at* that attentively, until you are satisfied that is the very name, with the very initials and spelling which you have sought. "That which we have *glanced at.*" But we were not satisfied with a glance at Jesus. We stopped and *gazed* at Him until our hearts and minds were filled with His image, and we never forgot that image afterwards. There is the spiritual eye, that not only sees, but gazes.

John also says, "He that is of God *heareth* us." That is to say, if we speak in the name of God, the true child of God turns attentive ear, and stops to hear what we have to say. There is the hearing ear. Then he says in the fifth chapter, "He that hath the Son hath life." He that has the possession of the Son of God, has life, his hands have power to lay hold of, and to hold fast to that which they lay hold upon.

The sinner has no eye to see Jesus, no ear to hearken to Jesus, no hand to take hold of and hold fast to Jesus. He may get a glance at him, but he passes by even His cross in indifference. He does not stop to gaze. The words of the preacher may catch his ear, but he does not stop to listen. And the Christ of God may be within his grasp, but he does not even reach out his hand to lay hold upon the salvation, offered to faith. And hence the Bible calls the impenitent sinner "*dead in trespasses and sins,*" because his eye does not respond to the sight of Jesus, or his ear to the hearing of the words of Jesus, or his sensibilities, his reason, his conscience, to the voice of duty, and the offer of salvation. The Lord says, "If you are a living child you will show it by the fact that your eyes are taken up with gazing on Jesus, and your ears with the words that He speaks, and your grasp with the taking hold of the Saviour of sinners."

Life not only shows itself by this vitality, but also by *energy*. What is life but power in action? A living being that has no power to move an eye, a finger, a foot, is paralyzed. If there is life at all, it is life without action; life scarce distinguishable from death. It is life encased in death, and death ensues. Paralysis of feeling and motion is a sign of approaching dissolution. This epistle teaches us that a child of God has power to *do*. He does righteousness. "Every one that doeth righteousness is born of him"; he is an acting disciple, and has power to do, not evil, but good—not unrighteousness, but righteousness. There is the life in action, the power to walk with God, to work for God, to confess Christ and to witness for him, the power to live unto God, to exert oneself in holy works of love and mercy.

God is a God of light. If you are a child of God, you will be a child of light. Light in this epistle means knowledge, and is the opposite of darkness, which here means ignorance, alienation from God, separation from the true light that comes into the world in Jesus.

The peculiarity of light is that it *reveals*. Paul says, "Whatsoever doth make manifest is light." If there were no light in this house, we could see nothing. If there were absolute darkness, you could not see me, nor I you, nor could we see the interior of this building. Nothing would be visible. But the moment you let sunshine into the building, everything becomes manifest.

How do you know that you are a child of light? Some things become manifest to you that were not manifest before. First, you come to *know yourself.* If you are a child of light, the light lights *you.* You see yourself, and somewhat as God sees you.

Some think there is no honest atheism. I believe that there may be perfectly honest atheism; but it does not begin by being honest. Men begin by trying to get God out of the universe because they are uncomfortable in sin. But one may argue to himself and try to persuade himself that there is no God, until by-and-by God gives him over to believe the lie, that he may be damned. Hear Paul: "God shall send them strong delusion that they all might be damned who believed not the truth, but have pleasure in unrighteousness." When you *have pleasure in unrighteousness,* and try to believe such a lie in order to bolster up yourself in sin, God may give you over to believe what you knew at the beginning was false, but which the withdrawal of His spiritual and providential restraints leaves you afterwards to believe.

No man ever saw himself to be a sinner if God did not show him that he was. Hence Jesus Christ is represented as granting repentance unto life, because he helps the sinner to see himself as God sees him. You may have some thought about yourself, that you are not exactly what you ought to be—that, perhaps, you lost your temper with your wife or children before you left home, or you may have a sense that you did not exactly deal honestly with that man who came into the shop to-day to buy something. But I am talking about the sense of deep guilt—the sense of

damning guilt—the sense that I am utterly unclean and
defiled in God's sight, and am not fit to dwell with God at
all. That is a true conviction of sin. That is contrition.
The word "contrition" means ground together and pul-
verized, as though the man's conscience were beneath him
like the nether millstone, and God's law above him like the
upper millstone, and between the law of God and his own
conscience he was being ground to powder.

No man ever comes to such a sense of sin as that if he
is not enlightened by the Holy Ghost. When God sheds
light on him then he sees himself. Job was called a perfect
man, an upright man, one that feared God and eschewed
evil, and he thought himself to be without fault; and when
his friends came to him to talk about his great calamities
and afflictions, and maintained that it was impossible that
God should visit a man with such judgments if he was not a
sinner, Job attempted to justify himself. He said, "I have
not closed my hands against the needs of the poor. I have
not shut my ear to the hearing of the complaints of the distressed. I have not been in the sight of God the kind of
man you make me out to be." But, after all, when God
showed himself to Job and showed Job to himself, then Job
repented himself in dust and ashes and prostrated himself
before God. It is one thing to measure yourself with another
man, or with all other men, and quite another thing to
measure yourself by Almighty God and his standard. In
the first chapter of this epistle we read: "If we say that we
have no sin, we deceive ourselves, and the truth is not in us.
If we say that we have not sinned, we make him a liar, and
his word is not in us. If we confess our sin, he is faithful
and just to forgive us our sins and to cleanse us from all
unrighteousness." Nothing can be plainer than that. If a

man says either that he has not sinned, or that he has been justifiable in sin, he is not a child of God. It is making God a liar, and he shows that God's word does not abide in him. It has been said that nothing shows the character of a man more than his bottom thought about sin, when you get all the rubbish out of the way and get down to the bottom thought. If, for instance, you say, "I love it and I am going to have it," you are not a child of God. That is a sinner wallowing like the washed swine in the mire of his own iniquity. If you say, "I did wrong, but I could not help it; I am not responsible; God is responsible; I am just as he made me," you are not a child of God. You are charging the responsibility of your sin on one who cannot be tempted with evil and never tempts any man to do a wrong thing. And so if you say of sin "It is nothing," and treat it as without moral guilt. But if you come to the point where you say, "Would to God I never had done anything that offended him; God may forgive me for my sin, but I never can forgive myself for sinning against God;" when you come to see sin as a hateful thing, and hate it because it is sin, and not because it brings punishment, not because you have been detected in your sin, not because you are liable to be brought up before a court, but because you see it to be sin, and hate it as sin; when you heartily wish that you never had sinned, and would cut off your right hand if you could deliver yourself from the guilt of having sinned, —then, my friend, God has begun to deal with you, and he sheds his light on your soul, and you are alive, and, instead of being discouraged, then is the time to thank God that you have seen yourself somewhat as God sees you.

If you have light on yourself, you will have light on God. As surely as God sheds his light on you, he will reveal also himself. When the sun shines down on you, it also attracts your glance toward itself. So the light that reveals you reveals its source, and you will read God just as you read yourself, in the light of this new revelation.

Did you ever have a wrong thought of God which afterwards was made right? Did you ever find yourself thinking of God as you had not thought of him before? That prodigal son fretted because he was under the roof of his father, because his father had control and authority over him. The oversight of his father was irksome, and he wanted to get away where he could do as he pleased. So he went off into that far-off land, and wasted his substance in riotous living, and got down to the deepest want. Then he came to himself, and began to see his father and his father's house, and his father's authority, and his father's rule, and his father's love, in a different light. And he took those steps back to his father, out of all degradation and wretchedness, because he thought of his father as he had not thought of him before. That is what brings a sinner to God. God shows the sinner Himself. He is in the foreign land, in an awful famine, in rags and wretchedness and misery, and then God shows to him Himself—what a gracious Father he is!—and makes him sorry to the depths of his being that he has not loved that Father, has not gone in the way of his Father, has not been patient under his Father's rule and even correction; and, coming to himself —that is seeing himself—he comes to his Father because he sees his Father as he never did before.

If you are a child of God, you will see yourself as a sinner, and you will see your Father as your Father, and Jesus Christ as your Saviour; and you will be sorry at the bottom of your heart that you ever gave your Father a distressing or anxious thought about you, or that you ever passed your Saviour by without giving him all the life, power, energy, activity, obedience, and affection of which you are capable.

A word now with regard to love. If you are a child of God, you will be a child of love; you will have the love of God in your heart. What kind of love is that? Three words express this love: it is expansive; it is expulsive; it is explosive.

This love of God is expansive, for when it has once got into the heart it makes the heart bigger. All our human love is selfish. The love a husband bears his wife, and the love a wife bears to her husband, and the love that parents bear their children has, at least, a large mixture of the self element. We love our families because they make us delightful homes, and because we find our happiness in those homes, and the conditions of prosperity and profit. This is not wrong, but it is not the highest kind of love. The highest kind of love is the love that God exercised toward us when we were enemies; the love that Jesus showed when, on the cross, he prayed for those who drove the nails through his hands and feet, and who passed by the cross and wagged their heads and mocked and derided and said, "He saved others; let him save himself and come down from the cross." Then the Saviour prayed, "Father, forgive them; for they know not what they do." This is the kind of love that God had to us; not the love of complacency that is drawn out by those whom we find amiable and beautiful in character and life, but the love that goes out to sinners in their degradation, destitution and misery. We learned this love only by learning the love of God.

Love is not only thus expansive, but it is also expulsive,

for it drives out all that is unlovable ; and it is explosive, for it demands vent in benevolent action. The apostle says, " By this we know that we are the children of God "— not only when we love God, but when we " love the brethren." The argument of the apostle is, " If any man love not his brother whom he hath seen, how can he love God whom he hath not seen?" Look at the argument. When the Bible says that every disciple should love his fellow disciple, it does not mean that we should love without discrimination all those that belong to the same church or body of believers. That is a very wrong conception, though it is often entertained. God never asks you to love that which is unlovely for the sake of its unloveliness. You cannot love, for instance, a hateful disposition. And you cannot love a hateful man because of his hatefulness. It would be very strange for God to demand that we should love that which is not to be loved. That would be contradicting the laws of our being. As well say that we should call white, black, or light, darkness, as that we should regard and treat as lovely that which is unlovely. God would have you love a fellow disciple, but not for the sake of that which is unlovely in him, but for what is Godlike ; and therefore the apostle says, " If any man love not his brother whom he hath seen, how can he love God whom he hath not seen ? " You claim to love God. Well, then, do you love all that is Godlike in God's people ? Here is a disciple, for instance, that may have faults, as all of us have, but nevertheless he is a prayerful man, an upright man, an honest man, a Godly man. He loves souls ; he bears on his heart the interests of Christ's kingdom. Now, if you do not love *what in that man is like God, then you do not love God*, for if you do not love whatever measure of Godlikeness you see exhibited in a fellow creature, how can you love God whom you have never seen? The only way that you know absolutely that you love God is that you respond to the measure of God's image which you see in God's dear people. That is what the apostle means. A brother of Jesus Christ bears Christ's image, though that image may not be perfected, and may even be marred by many faults and failings; but if I cannot look past faults and failings, and recognize the measure of the image of my Master, and respond to the measure of that image, then I do not love God.

That is a severe test of our Godlikeness. We cannot expect perfection in any child of God below, and if we expect it we shall not find it; but we must learn to look past the imperfections, the faults, the follies, and even the lapses from duty, in God's children, and our hearts must be drawn to the image of God as far as that image is manifested in others. That is brotherly love, and that is the sign of our Godlikeness.

There is also a larger love than this—a love to those that are not at all lovely, and have not the image of God in them, and that do not manifest attractive virtues and traits —people down in the slums, profane, blasphemous, intemperate, licentious, everything that is bad. No doubt there is something in them that might be attractive, were we intimately enough acquainted with them to discover where that attractive quality lies. Are we to love such people? Yes, we are. Are we to love them because they are drunkards, and licentious, and profane, and blasphemers? Of course not. What are we to love them for? For the sake of developing Godlikeness in them. We are to look at them, not as to what they are, but as to what they may be by the grace of God. Paul said that he was a pattern or

Believing and Knowing

type of all future believers. A type is something used in printing to make images like to itself. A type reproduces indefinitely like impressions on paper or any yielding substance. Paul says, "I am a pattern so that other people should take comfort and encouragement by me. I was a persecutor, a blasphemer, profane, injurious. I went to drag men and women out of the synagogue and put them into prisons, and I stood by and consented even to the death of Stephen, the first martyr. Now, take encouragement from me. If the grace of God reached me it can reach you. I am a pattern, therefore, to all sinners in future periods of human history that God can reach a man that is repulsive and unattractive, and hateful to disciples, and who is doing all he can to destroy their lives and break up their peace. I was converted partly to encourage you with regard to other sinners."

When the sun looks down on the earth it sees a pond covered with green slime, which breathes malaria and breeds venom. It is a pestilence in the midst of the land. And yet the sun will shine down softly and gently upon that pond, and there comes the white water lily with its delicate fragrance. The sun looks down on the sterile sands where you think nothing would grow, and, lo and behold, up shoots the lupinus, with delicate and many coloured flowers. Or the sun looks down on some mass of filth and slime outside of our great cities. As Ruskin has said, there are brickdust, soot, clay, and sand mingled. But what wonders the sun can do if you let the sun simply shine. That sand may be wrought into new crystalline shapes, and become the opal. By-and-by the clay take on new crystalline conditions, and you will have the sapphire. The soot will be transformed and crystallized, and out of the carbon may be formed the diamond. That filthy water will give up its vapours to the skies, and the frost will send it down again in exquisitely beautiful snowflakes and ice crystals. And somewhat as the sun does with this earth's polluted and barren districts, God's infinite love does with poor sinners. Out of the filth and the slum of their licentiousness and sin he develops the most fragrant and beautiful flowers like unto paradise.

Now, you are to love poor sinners for what God's grace can do for them; and you do not know but that the abandoned man or the outcast woman that you lift up out of the gutter and rescue out of the clutch of vile sins may yet be a saint that shall get nearer to God than nine-tenths of those disciples that pass them by in neglect.

I have spoken of God's life, and of your being a child of God, and having that life in the spirit and power of life. I have spoken of God being light, and of your having the light in the revelation of yourself, and the revelation of the truth and of God. And I have spoken of your having the love of God, of its showing itself in love to God himself, and then in love to your brethren who bear his image, and then in love to a poor dying world, even the most degraded or destitute human beings, in the hope and faith that grace can do for them what it has done for you.

But love always implies hate. A magnetic needle has two poles, and as one pole repels the other pole attracts; nay, at the same pole you find both attraction and repulsion. Our natures, and even God's nature, are so constituted, that where there is love there is hate. You cannot have a God of love without a God of wrath, though some people would construct a God and leave out all holy anger. In a true disciple love and hate are found side by side. By as much as he loves, he hates, and with the same energy he loves and hates. If he loves holiness he hates sin. If he loves goodness he hates unrighteousness. If he loves God he hates the devil. Such a hate is a sign of love, and one of the strongest signs of love. Hence the apostle John in this epistle says, " Love not the world, neither the things which are in the world. For if a man love the world, the love of the Father is not in him ; for all that is in the world, the lust of the flesh, the lust of the eyes, and the pride of life is not of the Father, but is of the world. And the world passeth away and the lust thereof; but he that doeth the will of God abideth for ever." I put this as the closing appeal, because I am persuaded that we, Christian people, are just now under one of the worst temptations that ever beset the church. It is a peril as old as the days of the apostle John. Throughout this epistle, like James and Peter and Paul, he holds up the world as the *irreconcilable foe of godliness*. He says, in fact, that the world and the church are such antagonistic foes as never to be reconciled, and that the greatest danger of the church is to be found not in the world's open hostility, but in the world's proffer of friendship. Now we have come to the time in church history when the world no longer openly opposes, but rather courts the church. The world would like to be esteemed as quite churchly, not losing its worldliness by conformity to religion, but just decently churchly and formally religious. Nay, the world is getting into the church and the church is getting into the world, or has already got there, until it is almost impossible to tell where the world ends and the church begins. The ages of persecution were far safer than these when there is no persecution. Persecution acted as a sieve, that let the grain fall through on God's floor, while it sifted out the chaff for the wind to carry away ; but now there is no such sifting process, and the chaff and the wheat lie together on the garner floors of God, and it is almost impossible to separate them.

Let us judge ourselves lest we be judged. The apostle says, "If you love the world you do not love God." "If any man love the world the love of the Father is not in him." The world hates God. No matter what complexion it wears, how deceitfully it smiles, how it seems even to court the church of God and the things of religion, whatever may be the appearance, the world always did hate, does hate, and always will hate God. The world crucified our Saviour, and loves him no better in the nineteenth century than it did in the first. And if Christ came on earth to-day, the world would persecute him and crucify him, just as it once did, if it had the power.

Let us not deceive ourselves. The objects that satisfy the lust of the eyes, the lust of the flesh, the pride of life, do not belong to God. They are hostile to him, and draw in a different direction, and therefore, if you hold to the world you cannot hold to God. If you are living for this world you cannot be living for the world to come. If you are taken up with this life, you cannot be taken up with the life to come. You may have this world if you want it, but you cannot have the other too. You may have the other if you want it, but you cannot have this too. The world passes away, and the objects of its lust, but he that does the will of God abides for ever. As John Wesley used to say, the child of God ought to be too proud to commit sin. So I say, we ought to be too proud to be satisfied with this world. If I were going to live here a thousand years, why should I care for a little wreath of parsley on my brow, that would not last for twenty-four hours? If I am to have any crown, I want a crown that will last. If I am to live a thousand years, do I want a straw hut, which the fire would burn up in three minutes? No, I want a substantial mansion, and a provision for a thousand years. If you are going to live for ever in heaven with God, why spend your time over perishing things that are enjoyed but for a day?

Let us deal honestly with ourselves. Have we the life of God in us? Are we doing righteousness? Have we the light of God in us? Have we seen ourselves as sinners, and seen God as our Father and Christ, as our Saviour? Have we the love of God in us? Do we love the brethren for the measure of their likeness to God? Do we love sinners, in vice and crime, for Christ's sake? Do we hate this world, that crucified our Lord and that has always drawn Christian disciples away from their allegiance to him? Do we remember that to-day the great danger of disciples is their conformity to the world, locking arms with the world, as though they had nothing else to live for? No more call was there for consecration in martyr days than in these; the martyrs that God wants in the nineteenth century are the disciples *that dare to be separate unto him*. Let men call you a fanatic, sneer at you as a pretender to perfect holiness; an ascetic, that ought to be shut up in a cell. Let them laugh at and scorn you. They hated your Master. Why should they not hate the disciple? God wants a church within the church; within the nominal body of professing Christians, a real body of Christ, joined to him by faith, working with him in love for mankind, dwelling in the light of God as he dwells in the light of God, and parting company with the world as the most dangerous foe the disciple can have.

The Lord help us to live for him!

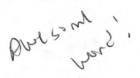

Sermon Nine

The Mountaintop of Prayer

"Now unto him that is able to do exceeding abundantly above all that we ask or think, according to the power that worketh in us unto him be glory in the Church by Christ Jesus throughout all ages, world without end. Amen."—EPHESIANS iii. 20, 21

THIS is the most glorious of all the revelations concerning prayer, to be found in the Epistles of St. Paul.

In order that we may see the connection, let us read the whole of this prayer, beginning at the fourteenth verse : "For this cause I bow my knees unto the Father of our Lord Jesus Christ, of whom the whole family in heaven and earth is named, that he would grant you, according to the riches of his glory, to be strengthened with might by his Spirit in the inner man ; that Christ may dwell in your hearts by faith ; that ye, being rooted and grounded in love, may be able to comprehend with all saints what is the breadth, and length, and depth, and height ; and to know the love of Christ, which passeth knowledge, that ye might be filled with all the fulness of God. Now unto him that is able to do exceeding abundantly above all that we ask or think, according to the power that worketh in us, unto him be glory in the Church by Christ Jesus throughout all ages, world without end. Amen."

The Mountaintop of Prayer

The Epistle to the Ephesians is the Switzerland of the New Testament. It presents a series of Alpine heights, and as we tread over the pathways of this Epistle, we rise from one height to another, and from thence survey the wonders of the grace of God. The subject of the Epistle is the unity of all believers in Christ Jesus, and the subject of this particular prayer of the apostle is, specially, a larger acquaintance with the love and with the power of God, from which he draws his great argument to stimulate saints to fervent and believing supplication. We are standing here on, perhaps the highest of the peaks of this Epistle; it is the Mont Blanc, soaring up into the highest heaven.

We reach the summit of a mountain by ascending first subordinate heights; we climb to the peak itself by going up the mountain side, and from point to point get increasingly large prospects. How does the apostle lead us up to this mountain peak of prayer? In the first place, he conducts us to that sublime height, the love of God, and from that he ascends to the power of God. A moment's reflection will show that to understand each of these is necessary, if we are to apprehehend what prayer is, and what are the encouragements to the praying soul. Our incentives to prayer must be found both in the Love and in the Power of God; for love determines his willingness, and power determines his ability. If God were simply a God of love, but not a God of power, he would be willing but not able; if he were a God of power, but not a God of love, he would be able, but not willing. And in this latter case, his Omnipotence, so far from being turned to our advantage, might become the means of our destruction. But when we have, first of all, a willing God, and then a God of boundless ability, we have the highest assurance possible to a praying soul. And so Paul begins by praying that in accordance with, and by the power of the Holy Spirit, shed abroad in our hearts, we may be able with all saints to comprehend the breadth, and length, and depth, and height; and to know the love of Christ which passeth knowledge.

Paul is introducing us to the science of the divine mensuration, or the measurement of the dimensions of the attributes of God. He treats the love of God as a cube, having breadth and length, depth and height. The reason is that the cube in the Bible is treated as the perfection of form. Every side of a cube is a perfect square, and from every angle it presents the same appearance. Turn it over, and it is still a cube—just as high, deep, and broad as it was before. And so the Holy of Holies—that which represented the dwelling-place of God in the Tabernacle and the Temple—was a perfect cube. By divine direction, it was made ten cubits long, ten cubits broad, and ten cubits high; and if we turn to the Book of the Revelation, and see the Holy Jerusalem of which the Holy of Holies was the type, let down from God out of heaven, we find that the length, and breadth, and height of it were equal: it is still the perfection of symmetry. When Paul leads us to study the love of God, he first of all calls our attention to its breadth. We should be very careful how we misquote Scripture. Believing, as I heartily do, in the inspiration of language, as well as thought, I am very reverent in the commission to memory of the exact words of Holy Scripture. There is a reason why this does not read, as too often it is quoted, " length and breadth ", but first of all " *breadth.*" For what is the first thing that you and I need to know about the love of God? It is whether it reaches to ME—is it broad enough to take me in? And this was the mystery of which Paul speaks in this Epistle to the Ephesians, written especially to a Gentile people—that the Jews did not represent the final election of God, but that that election comprehended all nations and peoples, and tongues and tribes, and those that were sometimes afar-off, worshippers of the great goddess Diana. Yes, the very people of Ephesus itself, far from the living God, and immersed in all manner of iniquities and idolatries, those that were sometimes afar-off were reached by this broad love of God; a breadth that takes in all humanity. The great multitude that stand round about the throne in the consummation of salvation, shall exemplify the breadth of a love that left not the most hardened and desperate sinner outside of its yearnings and its power.

The first thing is, then, how broad is the love of God? and I say, in God's name, it is broad enough to take anybody in, if he will be taken into its holy embrace. You may have gone away, like the Prodigal, from his father's house; you may have wandered as far as you could get from that father's house; you may have wasted yourself and your substance in riotous living; you may have come to such an extremity of spiritual famine, as that no man can minister to you, and you can no longer help yourself; but if, even then, in the depths of your degradation, and your estrangement, you come to yourself, and turn about and come to God, you shall have the robe and the ring, and the shoes and the fatted calf, and the father's kiss of welcome. So broad is the love of God!

When I have discovered that it is broad enough to reach to me, the next question is, the length of this love; how long has God loved me? " I have loved thee with an everlasting love." There never was a time when God did not love you —before you were born, in the ages of eternity, he loved you; he planned your redemption to meet your sin, and planned the gift of the Holy Ghost to supplement the gift of Jesus Christ that you might be regenerated and sanctified and fully equipped for glory. And as that love never had a beginning, it shall never have an end. It reaches from one eternity to another, and so spans the two eternities.

Then the next question is, how deep is that love? So deep that it went down to hell to pluck me out, that it descended to the depths of my sin and guilt and misery and perdition that it might lay hold upon me. You ask how high it is. Not until you can measure the measureless heights to which it lifts you, exalting you side by side with Jesus Christ and making you a partaker of the Divine nature and the Divine glory; not until you can understand those heights, can you understand the height of the love of God. And so Paul prays that they may be able with all saints to comprehend what is the breadth of a love which reaches to the most destitute, degraded, and depraved; the length of a love that reaches back to an eternity without beginning and onward to an eternity without end; a love so deep that it hesitates at no depths when a sinner is there to be rescued; so high that it ascends to the infinite heights of an infinite glory and carries us with it. Such is the love that encourages us to pray, because we know that we have a loving God, and therefore a God whose heart is full of the willingness of grace.

I suppose that this is the real point of the argument in the fourth chapter of the Epistle to the Hebrews when the writer, summing up all that he has to say, concludes: " Let us therefore come boldly unto the throne of grace that we may obtain mercy and find grace to help in time of need." Notice, it is the "throne of *grace*." There are seven thrones spoken of in the Bible appertaining to God—the throne of power, the throne of judgment, the throne of justice, the throne of righteousness, the throne of glory, the throne of majesty, but we are never bidden to come boldly to the throne of power, of holiness, of justice, of judgment. Why? Because such a throne would repel us. But we are told to come boldly to the throne of grace, because grace is favour to the undeserving, and I need not take cognisance of my own demerit when I come to the throne of grace. Power rebukes my weakness, holiness assaults my sin, justice reminds me of my condemnation, judgment threatens me with perdition; but grace assures me of salvation, and so I come boldly to the throne of grace where my loving, sympathetic Saviour is my intercessor and my friend.

Now, having ascended to the height of love, Paul carries us onward to the height of power. And here notice that we are dealing with picked and packed words :—" Now unto him that is able to do exceeding abundantly above all that we ask or think." I challenge any student of the Bible to find, even in the most enthusiastic and glowing descriptions of the power or grace of God, any words that surpass those in emphasis or intensity—" Now unto him that is able to do exceeding abundantly above all that we ask or think." The words that are here, thus picked and packed together, remind us of the old story of the ancients about the Titans. When they sought to scale the heavens we are told that they piled mountain upon mountain, Ossa upon Pelion, Olympus upon Ossa. And so here the apostle Paul is taking words that have in themselves the size and the weight of mountains, and is piling one upon the other in the vain attempt to express omnipotence.

Some illustrations strike the eye as well as the ear, and we are thus enabled to reach the mind through those two channels at once. Suppose, here is a tumbler filled with water, so full that it probably would accommodate scarce another drop. Now, the Greeks would have called that by a word ($\pi\epsilon\rho\iota\sigma\sigma\text{o}\varsigma$) that means "fulness." Suppose I continue to pour into this tumbler and it overflows: that would call for another expression, "over-fulness" ($\H{\epsilon}\kappa\ \pi\epsilon\rho\iota\sigma\sigma\text{ov}$). Suppose that I continue to pour until the overflow exhausts the pitcher and drenches the floor, the Greek would call that "an excess beyond over-fulness," $\H{v}\pi\epsilon\rho\ \H{\epsilon}\kappa\ \pi\epsilon\rho\iota\sigma\sigma\text{ov}$. That is exactly the expression that is used here. The first word means an excess, the prefix means an excess of an excess, and the whole expression means an excess of an excess of an excess. That is what Paul says about prayer—"Now unto him that is able to do excessively and superexcessively and supersuperexcessively"—that is the God you have to deal with. He can not only fill your little measure till it overflows, but he can pour in upon the overflow, and still upon the overflow of the overflow continue to pour in. You perceive that I am labouring to express by the imperfect vehicle of human language what no words can express.

If you examine this passage closely, you will observe that we attain to this height of prayer by a sevenfold ascent. Let me indicate the stages of the ascent. "Able to do"—that is the basis of all, simply a declaration of the general ability of God to answer prayer. "What we *ask*"—that is the first stage. "*All* that we ask"—that is the second. "What we *think*"—that is the third. "*All* that we think"—that is the fourth. "*Above* all that we ask or think"—that is the fifth. "*Abundantly* above all that we ask or think"—that is the sixth. "*Exceeding* abundantly above all that we ask or think"—that is the seventh. It is a marvellous revelation concerning prayer, and the wonder is that any disciple of Jesus Christ can take up such a passage of Scripture as that and ever be prayerless, or lose faith or confidence in prayer, or leave so mighty a power unused in his own personal life.

But notice the *basis* on which all the promises to prayerful souls rest. Let us not pass by that little phrase of so much significance, "according to the power that worketh in us." Notwithstanding the boundless love of God, notwithstanding the boundless power of God, there is absolutely no power in prayer unless there is first, working in the suppliant, that mighty power of God. In the eighth chapter of the Epistle to the Romans we are told "The Spirit helpeth our infirmities: for we know not what we should pray for as we ought: but the Spirit itself maketh intercession for us with groanings that cannot be uttered. And he that searcheth the hearts knoweth what is the mind of the Spirit, because he maketh intercession for the saints according to the will of God." Then we are told in the latter part of the same chapter that Jesus Christ "also maketh intercession for us."

The power that worketh in us is the power of union with the Spirit of God and with the Son of God, and upon that double union with those two Persons of the Trinity depends all our ability to avail ourselves either of the love or of the might of God. This wonderful thought it is essential that we should understand, if we grasp the philosophy of prayer. You have often asked yourselves, "Why do I need two intercessors—one the Holy Ghost, and the other the Son of God? My friend Dr. Gordon, of Boston, has said that it reminds him of a firm of lawyers, where one partner never leaves the office, but collects and classifies and arranges documents and evidence and does the office work. The other goes into the courts to plead, to appear before juries and judges and represent the case. The Holy Ghost corresponds to the lawyer that keeps in his office, and the blessed Son of God corresponds to the lawyer that goes to the court and stands in the presence of the judge to represent the case. Two intercessors: the Holy Spirit in the heart with groanings which cannot be uttered, breathing out to God the desires of the saints. Have you never yourself, in your most prayerful moments, found that there were many things that you could not utter; you could only groan and sigh? But you remembered with thankfulness that—

> " Prayer is the burden of a sigh,
> The falling of a tear,
> The upward glancing of an eye,
> When none but God is near."

Have you never been compelled to say—

> " My God will pity my complaints,
> And heal my broken bones,
> He takes the meaning of his saints,
> The language of their groans "?

When your prayers surpass the power of human language to express, when they are groans and sighs after God that defy utterance, that is the very groaning of the Holy Ghost within you in unutterable longings after God. Such is the office of the Intercessor within. Now as to the office of the Intercessor on high. He takes these prayers that tremble up from the heart, in which the Holy Ghost speaks, but which are corrupted nevertheless with our selfishness and sordidness and carnality, and He purifies them from all these defects and imperfections, and then presents them before the throne of God as perfect prayer. And so we read in this Epistle to the Ephesians, in the second chapter, "through him" (that is Christ) "we have access by one Spirit unto the Father." That is the only verse in the New Testament where we have Father, Son, and Holy Ghost represented in connection with prayer. Through Christ, by the Spirit, unto the Father.

The intercession of Jesus Christ I am satisfied is very much misunderstood. We imagine our Lord as standing before the throne of God and praying for His people. It is true that He does pray for them, but not as we sometimes think. His very *presence* at the throne of God is his everlasting plea. The very fact that He stands there with pierced hands and feet and side, your Representative, is the assurance that you are heard and shall be answered. There is a beautiful story in Greek history: Eschylus, a Greek tragedian, it is said, had committed some offence which made him amenable to a severe punishment—in fact, if I remember rightly, he was charged with treason against the State. He came before his judges as they sat in a semicircular row, and the case was put before them. They were about to say "Condemn!" with one voice, when the door opened, and in came a brother of Eschylus, who on the battle-field for his country had lost an arm. He saw what the position of affairs was, and the danger in which his brother stood, and he stepped before the judges and without a word raised the stump of the arm that he had sacrificed for his country. The judges looked

on Eschylus and then looked at his brother, and with one
voice they cried, " Acquit, acquit ! "

> " Five bleeding wounds He bears,
> Received on Calvary,
> They pour effectual prayers,
> They strongly plead for me.
> ' Forgive him ! Oh, forgive ! ' they cry,
> ' Nor let that ransomed sinner die.' "

What is the assurance that your prayers shall be answered?
It is that the power that works in you by the Holy Ghost
and in your union with Jesus Christ enables you to claim
the love there is in God and the power there is in God for
the fulfilment of His promise to you as a believing and
penitent soul. Have you ever noticed the force of that
expression which occurs in the New Testament,—praying
"in Jesus' name"? Turn to the Gospel according to
John. The most wonderful words that our Lord has ever
spoken on the subject of prayer are in the sixteenth
chapter of the Gospel, beginning with the twenty-third
verse : " Verily, verily, I say unto you, Whatsoever ye
shall ask the Father in my name he will give it you."
Now notice this : "*Hitherto* have ye asked nothing in
my name : ask, and ye shall receive, that your joy may be
full. At that day ye shall ask in my name : and I say not
unto you, that I will pray the Father for you : for the Father
himself loveth you, because you have loved me, and have
believed that I came out from God." Observe that our
Lord three times here bids the disciples pray *in His name*,
and, what is more remarkable, He says, " Hitherto have ye
asked nothing in my name." Not only had no Old Testament saints prayed in the name of Jesus, but not even these
disciples who accompanied Him for three years had yet

prayed in His name, and this was therefore a new revelation on the subject of prayer. If you will compare the Gospel narratives, you will find that the first great lesson He taught was simply to *ask* (Matthew vii. 7). Then in the eleventh chapter of Mark, He says, "Ask *believing*." And now we come to something grander than asking or even asking in faith—asking *in the name of Jesus*. The name of Jesus represents Himself, as my name represents me and your name represents you. To ask in the name of Jesus is not simply to say " For His sake," but it is to ask in the power of my union with Him as my Redeemer; it is to ask in His stead; it is to ask because I belong to Him and He belongs to me; and this union is my authority in the request.

We read in the eighth chapter of the Book of Esther, how on a certain occasion Ahasuerus took his signet-ring from his finger and put it on Esther's, and said to Mordecai and Esther: "Write as it liketh you, in the king's name, and seal it with the king's ring: for the writing which is written in the king's name, and sealed with the king's ring, may no man reverse." To write in the king's name was the same as if he had written it himself: it was to use the authority and power of the Oriental despot to carry out the will of one who might, like Mordecai, be simply a subject. And so our Blessed Lord gives you, as it were, a blank sheet of paper, and says: "Write as it liketh you, in My name; and seal it with My signet-ring, for what you write in My name and seal with My signet-ring no man, no angel, can reverse." When I was in Belfast, in 1890, I desired to visit the celebrated works of Marcus Ward and Son. I could not obtain access to those works in my own name, for strangers are not allowed to go through that extensive establishment, but a friend of mine, who was at the same time my host, said, "If you take my card and *use my name*, I think you will have access to all parts of the works." I simply went down and presented the card of my friend and made my application in his name, and the same courtesies were shown to me as would have been shown to him. Just before the dear pastor, Mr. Spurgeon, left for Mentone, he said: "So much sympathy and kindness have been shown me in this city and in Great Britain that I imagine that if you want to get entrance to any place and will use my name, courtesy will be shown you." Let me put this truth very boldly, but I trust very reverently. When I ask a favour in another's name it is not I that am the suppliant, but the man whose name I use. I simply present the request which he makes through me. And reverently let me say, when, in the name of Jesus, I present my request to the Father, *not I but Jesus Christ is the suppliant*. And therefore I have the assurance that I shall be heard.

Apply this to your condition. In the first place, you see why prayer is not answered. If the fellowship of the Holy Ghost is interrupted by your sins, by your continuance in inconsistencies, and violation of the conditions of your own Christian life, if you live afar from God in a a comparatively indifferent wandering on the border line between duty and inclination, you hinder the work of the Holy Ghost in praying within you. If in any way you impair your fellowship with the Blessed Son of God, you hinder the intercession of the Son of God for you at the throne of grace. And so the power of God must work in you, and work in you mightily, by your cultivation of fellowship with the Spirit within and your cultivation of union with the Son of God at the throne, if your prayers are to be attended with power.

The Mountaintop of Prayer 165

And the second thought is, what a lost motor the Church of God has given up when she lost the apostolic power of supplication! In this Church there has been for months past one of the sublimest spectacles that has ever created joy in heaven, or in the midst of men made both the ears of him that heareth it to tingle. On the second Sabbath of last May your beloved pastor was suddenly attacked with disease. After what appeared to be a partial recovery, he suffered a relapse, went down to the gates of death, was pronounced by competent physicians incurable by human instrumentality, and for twenty-one weeks daily prayer was offered for him in this place at early morning and evening. In those prayer meetings the whole Church of God seemed to be represented. Baptists of all grades of theological opinion, Primitive Methodists, Wesleyan Methodists, Episcopal Methodists, Congregationalists, Independents, Presbyterians, Episcopalians, all united in hearty supplication to the living God to spare a life that they accounted of more value than the precious gold of Ophir, the onyx, or the sapphire. During this time more than 7,000 messages of condolence and sympathy, resolutions from ecclesiastical bodies and all kinds of meetings and assemblies, have poured in upon the devoted head of this your beloved pastor. Fifty telegrams a day came to Westwood enquiring about his health, until it became impossible for telegraphic clerks or private secretaries to open, read, and answer them. And what astonished Mr. Spurgeon beyond measure was that not only from rectors and curates and deans and deacons and archdeacons and canons and bishops and archbishops there came visits of sympathy and enquiries of affection, but that even Jewish Rabbis waited upon him and assured him that all Israel was praying for his recovery. I say with pathos and deep persuasion that since the time the disciples waited ten days before God in continuous prayer for Pentecost, or prayer was made without ceasing of the Church of God for Peter when in prison, there has been no spectacle so sublime presented by the Church of God during all these eighteen centuries ! What a tribute to him who for forty years has been a standing protest against all formalism, all hypocrisy, all scepticism and all secularism, and who has presented the living Christ as an ever-present Saviour ! And now, in the name of God, I challenge this great Church of Jesus Christ to a spectacle more sublime than that which has greeted the eyes of angels and of men. I want to challenge you—and this is the solemn conclusion of this solemn appeal—to as unceasing and united prayer for a new coming of the Holy Ghost on the Church and on the world. If this spectacle was sublime of all disciples of every name uniting for the rescue of one beloved pastor from the jaws of death, how think you the heavenly host would thrill with delight, and even the heart of our Saviour itself, if disciples of Jesus Christ of every name could be found represented in morning and evening meetings for prayer, during six months to come, in this consecrated place in an importunate, believing, and anointed supplication that the greatest manifestation of the Holy Ghost since the days of Pentecost might come upon the Church of God in this apostate age ; and that the world might soon hear the tidings of the gospel, that they might flash like electric lights from pole to pole, till every creature should have learned the message of salvation ; and that gospel having been preached as a witness to all nations, the end might come when the King in His glory shall once more descend to take His throne and wield His sceptre over a regenerate world !

SERMON TEN

The Perfect Peace

"Thou wilt keep him in perfect peace, whose mind is stayed on thee, because he trusteth in thee. Trust ye in the Lord for ever; for in the Lord Jehovah is everlasting strength." The marginal reading is, "for in the Lord Jehovah is the Rock of Ages."—ISAIAH xxvi. 3, 4

"Be careful for nothing; but in everything by prayer and supplication, with thanksgiving, let your requests be made known unto God. And the peace of God, which passeth all understanding, shall keep your hearts and minds through Christ Jesus."—PHILIPPIANS iv. 6, 7

PAUL says, of the love of God, in the Epistle to the Ephesians, that "it passeth knowledge." Here he says of the peace of God, that it "passeth understanding." It may seem very strange that the apostle should bid us undertake to know a love which passes knowledge, and to seek after a peace which passes understanding. And yet there is no contradiction in these terms. When they were laying the Atlantic cable, they came to some places in the ocean which they were unable to sound. They would let down their fathoming line a thousand fathoms, a second thousand, a third, a fourth, a fifth, and even a sixth thousand fathoms, and the lead would still swing clear, and whenever in the ocean such a place is found we call it unfathomable; that is, we express our knowledge of those depths, by saying that we do not know. And so we express our highest knowledge of the love of God, by saying that it passes full comprehension ; and so we express our estimate of the peace of God, by saying that it passeth all understanding.

Who among you, does not need peace? First, look at the word, "peace." It is not joy. It is a greater word than joy. Joy is fitful, transient. Joy sometimes alternates with deep depression, just as the crest of the wave alternates with the trough of the sea. Peace is an eternal and unchangeable calm. The highest expression for the bliss of God is the one here used, "the peace of God." And peace is so characteristic of God, that in the same passage from the Epistle to the Philippians, He is called "the God of peace" as He is elsewhere called "the God of truth." There is what is called "the cushion of the sea." Down beneath the surface that is agitated with storms, and driven about with winds, there is a part of the sea that is never stirred. When we dredge the bottom and bring up the remains of animal and vegetable life, we find that they give evidence of not having been disturbed in the least for hundreds and thousands of years. The peace of God is that eternal calm which, like the cushion of the sea, lies far too deep down to be reached by any external trouble and disturbance, and he who enters into the peace of God, and has the peace of God enter into him, becomes partaker of that undisturbed and undisturbable calm.

There is a difference between peace *with* God and the peace *of* God. In the fifth chapter of the Epistle to the Romans, the apostle says, that "being justified by faith we have peace with God." That is true with regard to any sinner who has just turned from his iniquities and accepted the Saviour. The moment that he finds the Saviour, he finds peace with God, but that is not the peace of God. Sometimes a disciple waits many years before the experience of the peace of God fills his soul, but the moment that a sinner becomes a trusting, penitent believer, that moment he has peace with God, for peace with God is the peace of reconciled relations, but the peace of God is the peace of conscious, divine, indwelling. If a soldier escapes from an enemy by whom he is held in captivity, and seeks to get within the lines of his own army, his own loyal friends and fellow soldiers, he may cross the line that separates the pickets of one army from the pickets of the other, and not be aware of it. He may cross it in the night. And so a man may cross the line that separates between the friends and the enemies of God, and may not know it. He may suppose that there is something more that God demands than that which he has already yielded in penitence and faith, and some error of early education may lead him to expect some sign of God's approval, that the Scriptures do not justify. And so many a sinner has turned to Jesus, and come on the ground of peace with God, through our Lord Jesus Christ, who has not, at the time, known that he was a reconciled son of God, so subtle are the snares that Satan puts round us to rob us of conscious peace.

This perfect peace of God, first of all, surrounds and invests the whole man. The word translated " keep " in Isaiah, and the word translated " keep " in the Epistle to the Philippians, both mean to keep as by a garrison, that is, to surround as with a guard; and this reminds us of what is said in the Psalms, that "the angel of the Lord encampeth round about them that fear him, and delivereth them." The idea is that God sent his angels to walk like sentries, as it were, about a believing soul, and ward off the enemies of his peace and of his holy happinesss and bliss in God. Notice that the whole man is thus kept. The apostle says, "The peace of God shall keep your hearts and minds." That includes the whole man. If the heart represents the loving power, and the mind represents the thinking power, between the two is comprehended all that is meant by heart and mind, and soul and strength.

What is the unrest of the mind? The unrest of the mind is unsettled conviction. If I do not know the truth, or do not believe it, it is impossible for me to have any real rest in my mind. This is an age of doubt, an age when it is fashionable to doubt, an age when men and women are questioning all the great verities and certainties of the Word of God, and the unseen world. You may pride yourself on your scepticism, you may think well of yourself because you doubt what humble-minded believers accept without a question; but I tell you solemnly, here and now, that your life will be a restless and unhappy life, that can never know the peace of God, so long and so far as you do not believe. Paul says to the Ephesian Christians, "That ye henceforth be no more children, tossed to and fro, and carried about with every wind of doctrine, by the sleight of men, and cunning craftiness, whereby they lay in wait to deceive." He uses here two figures to express the condition of a mind that has not anchored itself to any religious certainties. When the wind blows strongly, all little objects that have not much weight in themselves are taken up and tossed to and fro. A feather or a piece of paper will be borne on the wings of the wind, and even if it settles for a moment on a twig or stone, it is borne away again wherever the wind will. So it is with people who have no certain convictions. They come into the presence of believers and, for the moment, the atmosphere of faith in which they find themselves inclines them to believe; but the moment after they may come into the company of unbelievers, and the atmosphere of unbelief inclines them again to deny the truth that they were on the point of accepting, and so they vacillate. They reflect whatever individual sentiments they happen to meet. One day they believe that there is a God, and the next day they doubt it. One day they believe that the Bible is the Word of God, and the next day they deny it. One day they are inclined to think that Christ is God's Son and man's Saviour, and the other they are inclined to think that he is a mere myth, or an impostor, or a misguided man. How can there be any heavenly rest in the soul where there is not heavenly belief in the soul? Paul could say, "For we know that if our earthly house of this tabernacle were dissolved, we have a building of God, an house not made with hands, eternal in the heavens." Paul could say, "I know whom I have believed, and am persuaded that he is able to keep that which I have committed unto him against that day." Paul could say, "I know that all things work together for good to them that love God"; and the power to say "I know" on great religious questions is the power that brings the peace of God to the human mind, and no mind ever knew peace unless there was this rest of conviction in God.

Paul uses another figure to express the unrest of the mind that has no settled conviction. He says, "By the sleight of men and cunning craftiness whereby they lay in wait to deceive." This language refers to the tricks of a magician, legerdemain, skill or sleight of hand. The trickster holds up his silk handkerchief, and makes you believe, for the moment, that behind that handkerchief he accomplishes a certain thing that he does not accomplish. He makes your eyes the fools of your other senses, and you are almost persuaded that a thing is true that is a trick, an imposition. And so, by the sophistries of false argument, men, through sleight of mind, as other men through sleight of hand, make you believe that they prove what they do not prove and cannot prove—that there is no God, that the Bible is a fraud, there was no such person as Jesus Christ, or that his resurrection was a myth and an imposture, and that all belief in Jesus Christ is but, after all, misguided fanaticism. They pretend to prove what cannot be proven, and their forms of logic are the silk handkerchief behind which they perform these tricks of intellectual legerdemain. I bless God that there are some people in the world who can defy any logic to prove to them that there is no God, that there is no inspired book, no divine Saviour, no heavenly life beyond this world. It is as possible to get to certainty on religious things as it is to certainty on other things. Perhaps you say, "How am I going to experiment on the unseen world?" I answer that you can experiment on the unseen world just as truly as you can experiment on the world that now is, and that is material and sensible God says, "Oh, taste and see that the Lord is good." Now the taste is one of our senses. It is the simplest, and the earliest to be brought into exercise; and yet we never think of distrusting our sense of taste, and to that sense God appeals as a figure to express experimenting on him. You may go into the prayer-room and handle God. You may send up your prayers to the throne of grace, and get the answers down. You may look into the Bible and find the testimonies of Jesus Christ within the pages of the very scriptures themselves. You may open your heart to the incoming of the Holy Ghost, and in that have the highest demonstration of the reality of the unseen spirit and the unseen world. If you will have your senses exercised to discern both good and evil, you will, by the power of a holy experiment, demonstrate to yourself the reality and verity of spiritual things.

What is the unrest of the heart? It is the unrest of unsatisfied love and longing. When Noah opened the windows of the ark he sent out first the raven, which wandered to and fro over the face of the earth, and, finding no rest, still continued to wander. But when he sent out the dove, and the dove could find no rest for the sole of her foot, she came back to Noah into the ark. Those two birds, the raven and the dove, represent human souls in all history. Unbelieving souls are restless without God, but they will not fly to his bosom. Believing souls, restless without God, can realize what Augustine's motto means, " Thou, O God, hast made us for thee, and our heart is restless till it rests in thee "; and when they find no place on which to rest, they fly to God, and find in him their refuge and their heaven. You might just as well try to find a resting-place for the human eye outside of the socket provided for it, a resting-place for the joint of your upper arm aside from the socket of the bone made to accommodate it, just as well attempt to find a resting-place for the sole of your foot without a solid substance on which to stand, as to attempt to find a resting place for the heart without God. God never meant that we should find in this world any permanent rest for our hearts, even in the love of human beings. However pure a wife or a husband may be, however beautiful and affectionate a child may be, God never meant that our hearts should rest in marital, paternal, or filial love. Why? Because the objects of our love may be torn from our embrace without a moment's notice. The wife that you hold in your arms to-day and cherish with husbandly affection, who is all to you that any human being could be, you may lay in the earth before another Lord's-day; and the little child whose hand is so omnipotent as it caresses your face and twines about your neck may lie in the coffin cold and dead before another day shall pass. God never meant that you should find the anchorage for your heart on anything that is any less eternal and unchangeable than himself.

The Book of Ecclesiastes records an experiment conducted by a king with royal resources at his hand. God permitted him to have immense wealth and all the facilities for conducting the experiment; and the king tells us that he undertook to find out what was that good for the sons of men, which they should enjoy under heaven all the days of their life. He tried wisdom and folly, he tried mirth and wine, he tried architecture and agriculture, he tried the mechanic arts and the fine arts. He built him great works. He gathered him men singers and women singers and instruments of all sorts. He planted immense gardens and orchards and vineyards, and great pools were constructed by him; and his verdict was "All is vanity and vexation of spirit, and there is no profit under the sun." He turned away from all these things a disappointed man. Not only did he say, "It is all vanity"—that is, all emptiness—but "it is all vexation of spirit"—positive vexation as well as emptiness. But if you pass along from Ecclesiastes to Solomon's Song, you will find that he who, in the Book of Ecclesiastes, tried this experiment and found the world too small to fill man's soul, in the Book of Solomon's Song finds the soul too small to contain God. In Ecclesiastes he finds that man is a half-hinge and that God is the other half, that this world is half a sphere and eternity is the other half, and that as you can never have a complete hinge if you do not put both parts together, or a complete sphere if you do not put both hemispheres together, so you cannot get the whole man, you cannot get the whole bliss, you cannot get the whole satisfaction, if you do not join this world and the other world, if you do not link man to God. And so he gives us his conclusion : " Fear God and keep his commandments, for this is the *whole man*."

What is the unrest of the will? It is the unrest of unsettled resolution. It is to be vacillating in purpose, one day determined to be a meek, holy, upright man, the next day forsaking that determination and plunging anew into sin ; one day resolved to give up all for God, and the next day compromising between God and Mammon ; one day to be strong in my resolution toward the right, and the next day to find, with Samson, that my resolves snap like the green withes and new ropes, in the crisis of a mighty temptation. There can be no such thing as the peace of God when there is not a fixed resolve, when you cannot say with David : " O God, my heart is fixed, my heart is fixed, trusting in Thee." Over in Paris, in the palace of Versailles, they have the " Gallery of Battles." It is lined with pictures that represent great battles in which the French were victorious ; for there is not a single picture in that gallery which represents a French defeat. The " Gallery of Battles " in the word of God is the Book of Daniel, and it is lined with pictures of conflicts conducted by the children of God against the powers of this world, and there is not a single defeat pictured forth in that gallery of battles, for there was not a defeat to be recorded. The ground and secret of those victories was simply a holy, fixed resolve. That third chapter, where we read about the three holy children, is one of the sublimest portions of the Word of God. Nebuchadnezzar set up that great image on the plain of Dura and commanded all the people of his realm to fall down before it and worship. The three holy children, Shadrach, Meshach, and Abed-nego, did not yield homage to his idolatrous image, so he caused the furnace to be heated seven times hot, and he brought them before himself and the image and he said, "Now if ye be ready that at what time ye hear the sound of the cornet, flute, harp, sackbut, psaltery, and dulcimer, and all kinds of musick, ye fall down and worship the image which I have made, well; but if ye worship not, ye shall be cast the same hour into the midst of a burning, fiery furnace; and who is that God that shall deliver you out of my hands?" Hear the sublime answer of those three holy men: "O Nebuchadnezzar, we are not careful to answer thee in this matter. If it be so, our God whom we serve is able to deliver us from the burning, fiery furnace, and he will deliver us out of thy hand, O king." But the sublimest part is what follows: "BUT IF NOT,"—if God does not appear for our deliverance, if there is no divine interposition, if we are flung into the fiery furnace and consumed there,—" be it known unto thee, O king, that we will not serve thy gods, nor worship the golden image which thou hast set up." He could not shake the determination of these holy men by putting them between the image on the one hand and the fiery furnace on the other. And when the decree of Darius went forth that no man should ask any petition of God or man, save of him only, for thirty days,

Daniel was found to be still praying to the Lord his God. The enemies of Daniel came and informed the king, and though Daniel knew that the writing was signed and that the den of lions was the alternative to the abandonment of prayer, he went into his chamber, and still prayed to his God, as aforetime. He might have done as a great many Christians do—knelt down with the windows and the doors shut and prayed in silence. But his testimony for God was at stake. Those mean, contemptible spies were underneath the windows even then listening to see if he dared to violate the king's word, but he opened his window, threw open the casement, and knelt down before the window with his face toward Jerusalem and prayed aloud so that they might hear that he was not afraid of the king's word; and he went into the den of lions because he would not give up praying to his God.

Why do not you have the peace of God which passeth all understanding? Why do not you that are children of God and disciples of Christ, who have been walking as disciples for many years, have the peace of God? Perhaps you are losing all peace of God because you have not a settled resolve for God. There is a border line that lies between the church and the world. Within that border land or line there lie what we call worldly amusements of which you cannot say, perhaps, that there is anything in them inherently wrong and yet you notice that the world loves them, that the world has put its stamp upon them, that they are the favourite employments and enjoyments of men that have no love of God in their hearts; and I am sorry to say that in this border land you will find thousands upon thousands of professed disciples habitually walking. They consort with the world, and follow its amusements.

They are drawn into the world's pleasures, and so find themselves drawn further and further into the world, until they leave the company of Christ's disciples altogether. There never was a child of God that had the peace of God that passeth all understanding until he had made the sublime resolve to let that border land alone that lies between the Church and the world. If you want the peace of God, there must be a separation between you and the world. You must leave chosen employments and enjoyments in which worldly men find their satisfaction, and you must get nearer the heart of true disciples and nearer to the heart of Jesus Christ. President Edwards, on his birthday, made this solemn resolve, "Resolved that hereafter I will never do anything of which I so much doubt the propriety as that I intend, at the same time, afterward to consider whether it be proper or not, except I equally doubt the propriety of not doing it." Whenever you come to make a total surrender of yourself to God; whenever you lay yourself as a burnt sacrifice, a whole offering, on God's altar; whenever, henceforth, you cut off all indulgences that might tend to defile you with worldliness and persuade the world that you hanker after such joys because you have no taste of celestial joys; when you come to the point where you have laid yourself before God entirely to be His, then the fixedness of your resolve makes possible the peace of God, which passeth all understanding.

How shall I get this peace of God? The prophet Isaiah says, "Thou wilt keep him in perfect peace whose mind is stayed on thee because he trusteth in thee." Perfect peace is then inseparably connected with perfect trust. And it is so even in society. Let me appeal to the family. How long would the wife have peace if she did not trust her husband? How long would the husband have peace if he did not trust his wife? How long would partners in business have peace in business relations if they did not trust each other. The whole basis of society is trust, and if trust is destroyed society falls into ruin. Now, much more is it so in our relations with God. There can be no peace in mind and heart and will unless there is trust in God. What is trust? It is simply dependence on truth. Look at the etymology of the word ; true, truer, truest,—trust. Why do I trust God? Because he is the truest being in the universe. Why do I trust you? Because I know you to be a true man or a true woman. The knowledge of your truth leads to trust. How then shall I get more trust in God? By getting more knowledge of God.

The condition of perfect trust is perfect knowledge of God. Many people try to get perfect trust by looking somewhere else but to God himself; but there is one little verse in the Psalms that has a world of wisdom in it on this subject. It is Psalm ix. 10, " They that know thy name will put their trust in thee." Notice about that verse, first, that knowledge and trust are inseparably linked, and secondly, that if we have a true knowledge of God we will trust him that is to say, unconsciously and involuntarily, just as you trust a true man or a true woman. You do not exercise your will about it, but when you come to know another person to be perfectly trustworthy, you cannot help trusting such a trustworthy person. Parents sometimes say to me, " How shall I get my little girl to trust me more? I tell her, 'you do not trust me as you ought to,' and she says, ' I know it mother, but I cannot help it? ' " Poor child, what is the reason that she does not trust her mother? It is because she knows that her mother is not to be trusted. A mother, for instance, wants a child to be quiet while she is gone on an errand, and she says, " My dear child, if you will be quiet, I will bring you some sweets when I come back," but she has not the slightest idea of doing as she says ; and when she returns she makes some shallow apology, such as " Oh, I forgot." The instinct of the child reads through the deceit, and the parent ought to blame herself, if she blames anybody, for the distrust of the child. The fact is that your child knows you too well to trust you. If you want the trust of a child never violate exact truth. Be all that you pretend to be. Do all that you promise to do. Never give your word without strictly fulfilling it, and your child, even though it may be disobedient, will trust you and cannot help it. There will be involuntary trust.

If you look up to God, if you know him, if you get acquainted with him, if you understand how perfectly true and boundlessly faithful he is, you will trust him and you cannot help it. So instead of picking your experience to pieces, and wondering why you do not trust more, just take God's way and resolve that you will know him more. Get better acquainted with your heavenly Father, and see how, without meaning it, without, perhaps, being conscious of it, your trust goes out towards him as naturally as waters flow out from a spring.

So we come to the last question—how shall I get more *knowledge* of God? See how very simple is the train of thought suggested by the text. First, there is the peace of God to keep your heart and your mind and your will, and secondly, that peace is inseparably connected with trust; and thirdly, trust is inseparably connected with more knowledge of God. The vital question is, then, how shall I know God better ? And I have just two answers to that, very simple and very brief. There are two ways in which to know God better. One is to know him through his word, and the second is to know him by prayerful walking with him. The word of God and the walk with God will make you acquainted with God.

Many in these days tell us that we cannot know anything about God through his word, even if there be a God; that nature is a sufficient revelation of God, and that we can learn all that we need to know about God through nature. Suffice it to say in reply, that while nature can give us hints that God is all-powerful and all-wise, and while there are even hints of God's goodness in nature, there are also dark things that make it look as if God might not be a good God; and if we had to interpret God by nature alone, we should be in doubt about his moral character and attributes. You could never infer the forgiveness of God from nature because nature never forgives. If you cut your hand with a sharp instrument it may heal by degrees, but there will be a scar there. If you jump off, or fall off, a precipice, you will be dashed in pieces, no matter how sorry you are for your carelessness or rashness. Nature never forgives, and if we had only nature to judge God by, we should know nothing about God's moral attributes. But God's word is his complete revelation of himself. It was given to supplement and correct the revelation of nature, and the revelation that is in your own mind and heart and conscience of what God is. You are made in his image, and though the image is shattered, yet like a shattered mirror, every fragment of which reflects the light, you still reflect God. But we get no perfect idea of God, except from his word. In that word the precious Christ appears and says, " He that hath seen me hath seen the Father." As you watch the Saviour and trace his life, you get an idea of what God is as you never could otherwise, and, knowing him, you will come to trust him.

There is another way of knowing God, and that is, walking with Him. If you walk through these streets with a friend arm-in-arm, and hear his converse in your ear, you have no doubt of his companionship. Enoch and Noah walked with God, and they had no doubt of God's presence. It was as real, as substantial to them, as the presence of any friend whom they saw, and with whom they conversed. And, blessed be God, there are people who have had no education, who could not construct a sentence grammatically, who can scarcely find their way even through the word of God by their own unaided efforts, but who are wiser than the princes of this world in their knowledge of God. Education tends to make us proud in mind, and to lean to our own understanding, so that we get beyond the simplicity of the faith of little children. You are very wrong in seeking peace anywhere except in God. In Mrs. Fletcher's biography, she tells of a convert who had a strange dream, that he was down in a very deep well in the night, and he looked up and saw a single star shining far above him, and it seemed to let down lines of silver light, that took hold upon him and lifted him up. Then he looked down, and he began to go down. He looked up, and he began to go up; and he looked down, and he began to go down again; and he found, that by simply keeping his eye on that star, he rose out of the well, until his foot stood on the firm ground. A parable is in the dream. If you look down, you go down; if you look up, you go up. You will never find peace from looking downward and within. If you see yourself as you are, it will make you

The Perfect Peace

more unrestful and unhappy, and so the apostle says, "Looking away unto Jesus, the author and finisher of our faith." Get your eyes off yourself and on your Saviour, get them off your disease and on your physician, get them off all your own deficiency and unworthiness, and weakness, and get them fixed on the sufficiency and merit, and almighty strength of the Lord Jesus. Now, and here, turn your eyes to the Lord Jesus. Seek no more to find comfort in doubt. Seek no more to find comfort in the purest object of human love. Seek no more to find peace in a will that is not settled on God. Just as the magnetic needle never rests till it turns to the pole, just as it keeps moving from side to side restlessly until it settles towards the Pole Star, so your heart and mind, and will, must only turn from side to side in restless disquiet, until you come to fix your mind on God, and your love on God, and your will on God, and then you will come to know what is the peace of God, which passeth all understanding.

> "Behold the ark of God,
> Behold the open door;
> Oh haste to gain that dear abode,
> And rove my soul no more."

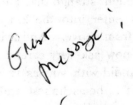

Sermon Eleven

The New Birth, No Marvel

"Marvel not that I said unto thee, ye must be born again."—JOHN xii. 7

To one word in this text it would be well to give special heed—the word "*marvel*." In all that has been said upon the new birth that word has generally been forgotten. If any doctrine of holy scripture is considered one of those mysteries into which it is impossible for us to penetrate—something far above us, and which, if accepted at all, must be simply accepted on the authority of the word of God, it is this doctrine of the new birth or birth from above. And yet it is of that very doctrine that our Lord says, we ought not to marvel; whatever mystery may be connected with it, it is not to be thought strange that He should teach that no man can see or enter into the kingdom of God, without being thus born from above. And it is that precise thought to which I shall now ask very careful attention. I shall be as honest and candid with you as it is possible for me to be, and I pray you to be as honest and candid with God and this truth, as it is possible for you to be.

Why then is it that this doctrine of the new birth, the birth from above, is not one at which men need to stumble or marvel?

1. Consider, first that there is, in every man, that which *is radically wrong*. The word "radical" comes from a Latin word which means the root, and to say that every man is "radically" wrong, is to affirm that there is something, from the root of our manhood upward and outward, through all its developments, that shows sin to be there. When, as a boy, I used in the winter to go out coasting, I found that I could slide down hill very easily, but never could slide up, unless I was drawn up. That led me to infer, that for some reason, it was easier to go down hill than to go up hill. There is a great power in the universe, called "gravitation." No man ever saw gravitation. It is not something that you can see or hear, or touch, or taste, or smell; yet it is a reality. How do you know that there is such a force? Gravitation is the tendency of a body towards a centre. If I drop anything it falls, it does not rise. I may take a weight in my hand, and lift it up, but it is by an effort; but it needs no effort to let it fall or drop. It falls of its own weight. So, although nobody has ever seen gravitation, we know that this force or attraction exists in nature, because we observe that whatever is loosened from its fastening, falls towards the centre of the earth. You never saw anything ascend that had weight to it, unless it was drawn or raised up by some counteracting force.

Now, there is something in man that is like gravitation. There is the tendency to sin, which makes it easier to do wrong than to do right. As soon as we be born, and begin to live intelligently, we begin to go astray. We find that it requires an effort to do right, though it requires little or no effort to do wrong. We slide or fall into the wrong, but we never slide or fall into the right. To do right implies a resolute resistance against this moral gravitation that is in us. Therefore we say that there is something in every man that is radically wrong—something that from the roots of our being reaches upward and outward, until it affects the tiniest twig of our growth, and shows that we are by nature " evil, and only evil continually."

2. It follows, then, in the second place, that there *must be some radical change* if we are to be like God and dwell with God and be happy with him for ever. There must be some radical change; that is, the change must reach, like the evil, down to the roots of our being. It must affect the whole man. If your watch does not keep good time, you may change the hands and set it right, but in half a day, perhaps less, it is wrong again. If the watch stops altogether, you may set the hands exactly with the clock in the Victoria Tower, but in a moment the hands fail to tell the right time. You must reach the evil by applying the remedy from within. The difficulty is in the inside, and the inside must be remodelled and repaired. If a man who raises fruit finds a tree in his garden that yields very poor fruit—that, in fact, never has a perfect apple, or pear, or whatever it may be, on its branches—he cannot remedy it by cutting off a branch here or there. The next harvest time the fruit will be of the same quality as before. The only way to remedy such a difficulty is to put in grafts. He takes a scion from a better class of trees, and inserts it as a graft in the old tree, and by and by there will develop a branch that will bear good fruit—fruit that is eatable. The fruit-grower must put some new life into that tree, or else he will not get good fruit. He must bring somewhat from outside, and introduce into the tree, and depend upon the growth of the new scion or graft to yield an improved harvest.

The New Birth, No Marvel

You don't reap a change in conduct, but character.

3. No man *can radically change himself.* If every man is radically wrong, and needs to be made radically right, he must look to a Higher Power to effect a radical change. The word "disposition" suggests a great truth. It is from the same root as the verb "to dispose." Our disposition is what, in us, *disposes us to this or that course.* We say that such a one has "an amiable disposition," because disposed to be amiable; or that such another has "a hateful disposition," because disposed to say and do malicious things; or that another has "an angry disposition," because disposed to get easily angered, or "a patient disposition," because disposed to bear suffering or sorrow without murmuring.

It will be seen at once that the difficulty in any man's changing himself lies in his disposition. He is not disposed to do right, to be a child of God, to submit himself to the righteousness of Jesus Christ; and this indisposition constitutes the great obstacle. It is the disposition itself that needs the change, and yet it is the disposition itself that is opposed to such change; and such facts in our very being prove without question that no man can radically change himself. Here is a greedy man, an avaricious man; he gets all the money that he can, and keeps all that he can get. He has no disposition to give, to impart. Like the horse-leech's daughter, he cries, "Give! give!" He always wants more than he has, and never inclines to give anything to others. If you try to persuade him to be a benevolent man, what is the difficulty? It is that he is not disposed to be benevolent. You can bring no motive to bear upon such a man that shall make him a different man, because his very heart and soul are poisoned by his greediness. You have no leverage, because the disposition to be different is lacking.

Reformation does not reach the core of our difficulty. Some people have been accustomed to commit certain sins, and give up those sins, and therefore they think they are very much better. It may be so in the eyes of men, and in their own eyes; but so long as a man is not touched by the Holy Spirit of God, he may simply move from one kind of sin which has lost its charm to another that has a fascination for him. Sometimes one who has indulged his appetites and passions finds them wearing out, becoming dull like a weapon that has been ground down, until there is no blade left, and so he forsakes old lusts and passions that once gratified him, but no longer can, for new lusts and passions that retain power to yield him sinful pleasure. Sometimes a young man, when he gets older, leaves the sins of his youth for other sins of his manhood, and when he gets to be an old man he leaves the sins of early youth and maturer manhood for the sins of old age ; for even old age has its peculiar temptations and its peculiar indulgences. You can never safely infer that you are better, in the sight of God, because you have changed the field, or form, or sphere of your sinful indulgences. Again, one might give up a certain sort of sin because it is not respectable in the eyes of men, because it lowers their respect for him and his respect for himself. A man, for instance, gives up intoxicating drink simply because he wants to be a respectable man and succeed in business. Another gives up profane swearing because he cannot be a gentleman and swear, and because he wants to go into polite society. The secret motive that leads one to give up a bad habit has much to do with the virtue of reformation, and, if the motive be not such as God approves, and such as is pleasing in his sight, what does the reformation amount to ? You may take a vessel of metal,

The New Birth, No Marvel

and change its form, but you cannot change the nature of the metal. If it is of brass you may cast it into a new shape, but it will be a brass vessel still. If it is an iron vessel, however recast, it will remain an iron vessel still. And not until you can take an iron vessel and change it into a silver one, or a brazen vessel and change it into a golden one, can you radically change your character. You may change the outward life, and the form and the complexion of the sin, and yet remain at the root the same man or woman still in the sight of God.

4. If, then, there be a radical wrong, and there needs to be a radical change, and the man cannot radically change himself, the only being in the universe that can change him throughout *is the God who made him*. That is why the Bible calls this a re-creation. It is as stupendous a work as the original creation, and to re-create demands the same power that originally created. The same creative hand that made this world must change it, if it is changed essentially; and the same power that made a man must make the man anew, if he is ever made anew. That is the simple doctrine of the new birth, and that is practically all that there is in it. God therefore calls it "new birth," or "birth from above."

Now, what is birth? Birth is the *beginning of life*, the starting point of existence. Birth is the beginning of the forming of character and of habits. Birth is the beginning of the use of the organs of the body, and of the exercise of the powers of mind. What is the new birth, or the birth from above? It is spiritually beginning life again, and in a different fashion; beginning to experience new joys and motives in the soul; starting on a new walk, from a new beginning to a new termination by a new path; having a new life in God. That is the new birth. You may take any other term to express it, but that is the idea. It is beginning anew, not in one respect, but in all respects. It is going back to a new starting point, and taking a new direction, setting your face against sin and toward God and holiness.

Let it then be repeated, on the authority of the holy Scriptures and the Holy Spirit of God, that no man or woman on earth can ever accomplish a change like that, unaided by God himself.

5. If there is something radically wrong in you, and it needs to be radically changed, and you cannot accomplish that radical change yourself, and only God can accomplish it if it is done, then it follows that *either God must do that work for you,* and without you, or *he must do it with your consent;* and certainly God never saves a human soul without the consent and co-operation of that human soul. Man is not a mere machine. If I have a watch that does not keep time, and I take it to the watchmaker for repairs, the watch gives no consent in the case, and has none to give. The watchmaker takes it to pieces, finds where the difficulty lies, and remedies it, and the watch is perfectly passive, has nothing to say or do, for it has no intelligent, voluntary nature with which to consent or co-operate. Any other kind of machinery which is out of order is repaired by the engineer or the mechanic without its own voice or consent. But man was made in the image of God, and that image partly remains to man, even after the fall, in the independent power of thought and choice. I say, with great reverence, that God respects the creatures that he has made, and the consequence is that he does not, and will not, deal with a human being as you would with a machine, which, if it needs repair, you remodel, and which, if you cannot make anything

The New Birth, No Marvel

out of, you do not hesitate to smash in pieces. When God sees a man or a woman conducting in a sinful way, living a sinful life, and cherishing a sinful heart, no doubt the power of God might change such man or woman into a holy being, somewhat as a man changes a damaged machine into a more perfect mechanism; but God never will do it, because he will not treat a human soul as though it were a mere piece of machinery. The Creator respects the mind, capable of thought; and the heart, capable of love; and the conscience, capable of judging; and the will, capable of choosing; and therefore he puts salvation before us as a something to be chosen, accepted, appropriated. You could not earn it, obtain it, work it out; but you can *take* it, and it never will be yours if you do not.

In the sixth chapter of John we are confronted with these mysteries. Jesus Christ says, "No man can come unto me except the Father which hath sent me *draw* him." That is only one side of it. No man is ever saved if God does not draw him to himself. On the other side, Christ says, "All that the Father giveth me shall *come* unto me." That is the other side. *God draws: you come.* Christ says, in the fifth chapter of John, "The scriptures testify of me, and yet ye *will not come* unto me that ye might have life." The perversity of men is a strange thing. They will sometimes take up this precious Bible, and say, "I do not see that I have any responsibility. Christ said to Nicodemus, 'Except a man be born again he cannot see the kingdom of God.' I cannot bring myself into a new existence and start myself in a new history. I do not see that I am responsible for it." Yet on the opposite page of this very same book is another version of the same matter; for, in the first chapter and the twelfth and thirteenth verses, we read: "To as many *as received him,* even to them that believed on his name, he gave *power to become the sons of God.*" What voluntary blindness is that which has an open eye to see the declaration of God's sovereignty, and yet a blind eye for the declaration of man's responsibility? Chemists sometimes take the purest and most fragrant herbs, and obtain from them the most deadly poisons. A perverse reader of scripture is a kind of chemist who, out of the very plants and blooms of God's garden, distils most dangerous and most poisonous juices. Within the compass of the same verse we read: "Work out your own salvation with fear and trembling, for it is God that worketh in you both to will and to do of his good pleasure." "God works in you to will and to do": that is one side of it. But you must work out, to the end, your own salvation: that is to say, you are to co-operate with God. Though you cannot buy or earn salvation, you can take or accept it. God buys it, with the precious blood of Jesus Christ; and he offers it to you freely, but he will not compel you to accept it and be saved. You must accept salvation for yourself. If I understand the scriptures, that is the plain teaching of the Word of God.

Let me illustrate this responsibility of the sinner. Suppose that you are in a house which is on fire. You are in a room on the ground floor, and the key is inside. In such a case you can wait there, until you think it unsafe to wait longer, and then you can unlock the door and go out. Suppose, on the other hand, that the key is not on the inside, but that the door is locked, and the person who has the key has gone away, and there is no way out but through that locked door. In that case you must either be let out, or stay there and perish. But suppose again, that although you are in that room, and the key is on the outside, there is a friendly hand on the key, and if you but call and ask that the door may be unlocked it will be, and you can escape. You see, the three supposed cases are quite different. In the first you have the power of release in your hands, and may go out when you please. In the second case the power of release is in another's hand, and you have no choice but to wait. In the third instance, however, the power of release is, indeed, in another's hand, but the *power to call* is your own, and the call will bring release. You are in the house of doom. You have not the key out of it, and cannot escape when and as you please. Nor is there a despotic being, in whose hands is the key, and who is where you cannot reach him, in which case you might, in helpless fatalism, say, "I can do nothing; it is of no use even to cry, or pray, or ask for deliverance." The fact is, a loving, gracious God has the key to that house of doom, and he says, "You have only to ask of me, and I will give you deliverance."

I am quite aware that I am treading on delicate and difficult ground, for no man on earth can explain the wonderful way in which these two great truths are harmonized. God himself never attempts to harmonize them. He presents the truth in both its aspects, and we are to submit to his teaching, and give up the attempt to explain the mystery. But it is perfectly plain to me that God treats every human being as capable of thought, love, and choice, and the fact that he *puts salvation before us as something to be accepted*—a free gift, but something to be accepted, shows that he does not propose to force it upon an unwilling soul.

6. One step more. If what has been said be true then, *if God withdraws from you, or if you withdraw from God* in such a way that you no longer will or can accept his free

gift, your salvation becomes impossible. This is the most solemn ground that I ever touch in preaching the gospel. And I feel very solemn as I tread here. No one can present such thoughts as these without a sense of shrinking; yet fidelity to God and souls demands that I should tell the whole truth. If salvation is something to be given by God and accepted by man, and if both God's giving and man's accepting are necessary to salvation, answer me this question. If God withdraws the gift, or if you have no longer the will or the capacity to take the gift, how is salvation, for you, possible?

Let us then ask, first, *Does God ever withdraw from a human soul?* Once a member of my church, an aged woman who was dying, sent for me. She was very old, but her husband was still older than she, and at that time little short of ninety years of age. I had been very much troubled in mind about him, and had been to talk with him about his own soul, and had offered prayer with him; and she knew that I was very anxious about him, and sent for me, and from her own dying bed said to me, very solemnly, "Pastor, I am afraid that my husband sold himself to the devil forty years ago." And then she told me one of the saddest stories I ever heard. She said that at that time he was a member of the State legislature, and was very much moved about his own soul; that his pastor and many others came to see him and begged him to give himself up to Christ and accept him as a Saviour; and that she herself pleaded and prayed with him. He said to her, one night, "Wife, I have a scheme to carry through the legislature. It would not do for me to carry that scheme through if I were a Christian man. I am going to see that through, and then I will repent and accept Christ as a Saviour." He carried the scheme through ; but, as she said to me, *from that day he had never apparently had any desire to be a child of God.* That was the end of all penitence and longing for Christ and readiness to accept Christ on his part. He deliberately chose, in the crisis of his history, to carry an iniquitous and dishonest scheme through the legislature, and purposed afterwards to turn from his iniquity and become a Christian. But he grieved the Spirit of God, and hardened himself against God. Does God ever withdraw himself from a human soul ? I pray God I may do no dishonour to his grace when I say that I have no more doubt that God sometimes withdraws himself from a human soul than I have that a human soul hardens himself against God. There is nothing more solemn in the whole word of God than the first chapter of the Epistle to the Romans: Let me read two or three verses : "When they knew God, they glorified him not as God, neither were thankful, but became vain in their imagination, and their foolish heart was darkened. Professing themselves to be wise, they became fools, and changed the glory of the incorruptible God into an image made like to corruptible man and to birds and four-footed beasts and creeping things." Verse 24: "Wherefore *God also gave them up to uncleanness.*" Then in the twenty-sixth verse : "For this cause *God gave them up* to vile affections." Then in the twenty-eighth verse : "And even as they did not like to retain God in their knowledge, *God gave them over* to a reprobate mind." This is the one place in the Bible where this awful truth is taught most fully. Three times over it is here said that "*God gave men up,*" or "gave men over," and each repetition of this truth is stronger than that which went before. First, God gave them up unto *uncleanness*—that is, he suffered them to sin and commit iniquity. The second statement is that God gave them over unto *vile affections*—that is, he left them to habits of sin and to the deliberate choice of their own lusts. But the third statement is that *God gave them over to a reprobate mind*. What is a reprobate mind? It is a mind that justifies the sin that a man has been committing, and that throws the responsibility for sin on God. It is a mind that perverts the conscience and the reason into the upholding and vindication of iniquity. And when God, who has given one up to uncleanness, and then to vile affections, also gives one over to a reprobate mind, that is the last "giving up" that is possible. God then *abandons that soul to destruction;* and let me add with awful solemnity that man thus given over by God is already as truly damned as if he were in hell !

This is very plain language. I feel constrained to deal honestly with souls. If you by perversity get where God gives you over and withdraws his providence and his Spirit from restraining you ; if God no longer touches you by providence or grace, you are a lost man, hopelessly lost.

Why did God give these people over to uncleanness, then to vile affections, then to a reprobate mind ? This passage tells us. In the first place, we read that they "held the truth in unrighteousness"; and the original means that they *held down* the truth in unrighteousness. If a man tries to rob you on the street, and you can get him down and hold him down till help comes, you do with the robber what these people did with the *truth*. God gave them a certain measure of truth and they tried to get the truth down, as it were, and to hold it down and stifle its voice, so that they might not hear its witness against their wrong-doing. We are told also that "they *did not like* to retain God in their knowledge. They sought to get the knowledge of God out of their minds, to shut their eyes to the evidence that there is a God. They tried in every way to blind their own vision to the sight of God, and stop their own ears to the remonstrance of God, and harden their own hearts to the touch of God; and so God found it necessary, however reluctantly, to give them over, and say, "Let them alone."

Do men ever *give themselves over*? What does the apostle Paul mean when he says in the fourth chapter and the nineteenth verse of the Epistle to the Ephesians, "Who, being past feeling, have *given themselves over* unto lasciviousness, to work all uncleanness with greediness." What is it to be "past feeling"? Suppose the eye no longer has sight, or the ear has no longer hearing, or the hand has no longer the sense of touch. It is *past feeling*. Suppose the conscience is "seared with a hot iron." If you took an iron at white heat and applied it to the eye, you would burn the eye into total and fatal blindness and insensibility, and no power, short of God, could give you that eye back sound and healthy. If you habitually apply sin to the injury of your conscience, you burn your conscience into total and final insensibility; and the moral sense will never fully awaken until it awakens in the future state.

This is not preaching any theology, but the theology of common sense. There are some who refuse to hear the testimony of the Bible as to things which are nevertheless going on right before them. Hundreds of people in London are doing to-day just what the heathen did, about whom Paul wrote in the Epistle to the Romans. Here is a man, for instance, trifles with intoxicating drink. He sees himself getting under its control more and more, and finds it more and more difficult to get along without it; he finds also that, whereas he once used it in what he calls "moderation," he now takes too much, as he confesses, and gets tipsy and drunk, because it is going beyond his own control. He tries for a few days, perhaps, to let it alone, but the old appetite has tremendous power over him, and so he goes back to his cups. Up to a certain point he is like a man whose hand is on the helm of a vessel, and who can steer his ship by a determined effort out of danger. But he allows himself to drift on and sweep deliberately farther and farther towards the vortex of the awful maelstrom of destruction, until at last he finds himself where, even if his hand is on the helm, the helm does not guide the vessel, for the vessel no longer obeys its own rudder! Have you not seen those things? And are there not hundreds in this city, to-night, and may there not be some in this house that God has already given up to uncleanness, and even to vile affections ; and perhaps He is now deliberating whether it shall be necessary to give them over finally to reprobate minds and seal them as lost souls?

Preaching the truth is an awful business. It is glorious to tell of a free salvation, but it is terrible to be compelled to tell men and women that, even while you are preaching to them, they are, perhaps, hardening themselves fatally and hopelessly against Almighty God!

7. The concluding point in this argument is now reached. First, we saw that everybody is radically wrong. Secondly, that everybody needs to be made radically right. Thirdly, that nobody can radically change himself. Fourthly, that only God can change him. Fifthly, that God will not save a human soul without the acceptance of salvation. Sixthly, that if God no longer approaches a soul, or the soul is no longer willing or able to accept God's salvation, the lost

state must remain eternal. Let us hear, then, the conclusion of the whole matter. "*Now is the accepted time.*" As you sit here you say to yourself, "I marvel whether I am included among those whom God has given over, or who have so hardened themselves against God as that there can no longer be a response even to the grace of God." How can you find out what your condition is? Is there any response in yonr mind and heart to the truth to-night? Is your conscience giving you disquietude? Have you a sense of restlessness? Do you feel as if God were talking to you? And do you feel as though you would like to turn round and face God, and begin another life? Then you have so far a proof that God has not yet finally given you over, and that you have not yet hardened yourself into fatal insensibility. And I say to you, "*Now* is the accepted time," for not one of you can tell whether you shall to-morrow remain sensible to God's approach. Not one of you can tell whether, if you now harden yourself against the simple entreaty of the truth and the Spirit, which is also the appeal of God, you may not be sacrificing the last hope and chance for your own salvation !

Now, do not turn your ears away, for we are in the presence of God; give yet a moment more careful attention. You go into a blacksmith's shop, when he is about to give a new shape to a piece of iron. He takes the iron and puts it in the furnace, and he sends a blast through the furnace, and then he pulls out the iron at white heat, and puts it on the anvil, and the sledge hammer comes down upon it, and moulds it into the desired form. If he allows the iron to get cold, he must put it back into the furnace, and make it hot again. He cannot mould cold iron without danger of breaking it. He may a dozen times heat the iron, and let it cool, and again put it back and heat it, and although the iron may be somewhat injured by the repeating of this process, it can still be made into the desired form. But *God never repeats His process with a disobedient soul.* I am very desirous that you should grasp this thought. If a truth is impressed upon your mind to-night, and you reject that truth, it can never be impressed upon your minds in the same way again. This is not limiting the power of God except as the power of God is limited by the conditions of the human mind. Man is not a machine. He is not like a piece of iron. He cannot be put through the same process a dozen times, and receive an impression the last time as he would have done the first. Truth depends for its power largely upon its novelty; and an argument when presented as a new argument, with new illustrations and appeals, has a certain power upon us. But, that argument, repeated to-morrow with the same illustrations and the same appeals, will be found to have lost its power, because it has lost its novelty. There is one exception to this law. If you hear an appeal of truth or duty, and *yield* yourself to it by obedience, you keep your mind tender and receptive, so that the same truth presented in the same way again, will still have effect upon you, perhaps even more than on the previous occasion; because your surrender of yourself to the truth will increase your sensibility to impression, and so, what the appeal would have lost by mere repetition, is overbalanced by the gain in your receptiveness. Your obedient nature, your disposition to obey, have opened all the avenues of your being, and the truth has thus more power on you, perhaps, the second time than it had the first, because you are more open to its appeal. If, on the other hand, you hear the word of God and reject it, you shut

The New Birth, No Marvel

your eyes in a measure; you are hardening your heart, and when the truth is put before you again in the same form, it has not half the former power, perhaps no power at all. God may make an impression on you afterwards, but He must take another way to do it ; another truth to do it with, another form of appeal, argument, illustration. Every time you hear the gospel preached, and refuse its appeals, you narrow down the circle of divine influences, within which, for you, salvation lies. Right in this house, before me, are men and women who are making their own salvation more and more impossible, because they hear the word of God without obeying. Evangelists, among the outcast and degraded classes, find that the publicans and the harlots go into the kingdom of God before hundreds of people do who sit in the sanctuary every Sunday. Why? Because these respectable church-goers get *gospel-hardened*, and outsiders are only *sin-hardened*, and it is practically worse to be gospel-hardened than be sin-hardened. Nothing makes one so impervious to the impressions of the gospel as to hear and not obey; and therefore if you could get, into this tabernacle, thousands of people who have very seldom, if at all, heard the gospel before, and are living in the vilest of sin, and will let me preach this same sermon to them, hundreds more of them will be ready to accept Jesus Christ than are likely to do so from among this audience of habitual hearers. This is an awful statement, but awfully true. The very hearers that are paying no attention to God's message, who care nothing about it, and lightly dismiss it, show *by the way in which they treat* the truth, how near they are to a hardened state ! The very fact that one can hear God speak such solemn words, and care little or nothing about it, is the one alarming feature.

It is not in my power to lead one of you to Christ. If I should plead till midnight it would not affect a soul, unless moved by the spirit of God. But I entreat you with tearful tenderness, if there is one of you that feels a drawing towards God, and yet has never accepted salvation, that you will not run the risk of being given over to a reprobate mind, or of hardening your heart against God, by even saying, "Just this once, go thy way, go thy way." Let every unconverted soul say, "I will, by God's help, now take Jesus Christ to be my Saviour. I will not trifle with this matter of salvation. I will not turn away from God. I will not give the word of God an opportunity to harden me any further. I will not give Satan an opportunity to withdraw me from the pale of divine influences. I will not give my own treacherous heart an opportunity, even by the postponement of my own salvation. I will turn about. I will go and say to God, "Father, I have sinned against thee; I have neglected thee; I have hated thy reproof; I have been given over to sinful habits and vile affections. Give me not over to a reprobate mind."

This is a favoured place for souls to turn to God. There are in this congregation more praying souls, probably, than in any other congregation gathered in Christendom to-night, people who daily and hourly pray to God for souls. In some room in this great building prayer is going on almost every hour of the day; while I have been here meditating this sermon, and praying for power to preach to you, I have heard all around, in these various rooms, the sound of prayer and of singing. What does that mean? They have been praying for you, praying that the Word of God might have fruit in human souls, praying that this might be the birth-hour of some into the kingdom of God. And, blessed

The New Birth, No Marvel

be God, salvation is free and full and ready for you. Are you ready for it? I pray you, do not leave this house to-night without a blessing. In the schoolroom below I propose to meet all enquiring people, or those who desire now to make their salvation sure. I want to meet you there. We will have a few words of prayer, and of personal counsel about immediate surrender to the Lord Jesus Christ. Let every one who desires salvation stay, and let us, in the presence of God and with his help, settle to-night this great matter for eternity!

SERMON TWELVE

The Riches of Grace

"The unsearchable riches of Christ."—EPHESIANS iii. 8

THERE is a universal desire on the part of human beings to be rich; the instinctive love of gain seems to be a part of our common humanity. The apostle Paul, in this Epistle to the Ephesians, sets before us the vast riches of God, and tells us how we may be made partakers of this divine wealth. This epistle is especially given to the exhibition of these infinite riches of grace. There are six passages here that I will read, at the beginning, in order that you may understand what is to be said. In the seventh verse of the first chapter we read: "In whom"—that is in Christ—"we have redemption through his blood, the forgiveness of sin, *according to the riches of his grace*, wherein he hath abounded toward us." Then in the eighteenth verse, "The eyes of your understanding being enlightened, that ye may know what is the hope of his calling, and what *the riches of the glory of his inheritance in the saints*, and what is the exceeding greatness of his power to us-ward who believe." Then in the second chapter and the fourth verse, "God, who is *rich in mercy*, for his great love wherewith he loved us." Then in the seventh verse, "That in the ages to come He might show

The Riches of Grace

the *exceeding riches of his grace* in his kindness toward us, through Christ Jesus." Then follows the text, "That I should preach among the gentiles the *unsearchable riches of Christ.*" Again, in the third chapter and the sixteenth verse, "That he would grant you, according to *the riches of his glory,* to be strengthened with might by his spirit in the inner man."

When you remember that this epistle consists of only six chapters, and notice these repeated references to God's riches, and especially the forms of speech used with regard to them, you will feel, with me, that this whole letter of Paul is intended to set forth these boundless riches of God. In that expression in the second chapter, "the exceeding riches of his grace," the word translated "exceeding" is that from which comes the English word, "hyperbole," applied to exaggeration. The word literally means, "to shoot beyond the mark," and expresses therefore the idea of excess. Paul means by it that, though you use the utmost wealth of language, you cannot shoot beyond the mark: the riches of God exceed all power of language to express. In the words of the text, "the unsearchable riches of Christ," "unsearchable" literally means riches that can never be explored. You not only cannot count or measure them, but you can form no estimate of them; and you not only can form no estimate of them, but you never can get to the end of your investigation. There is a boundless continent, a world, a universe of riches, that still lies before you, when you have carried your search to the limits of possibility. I feel as though I had a theme, about which no man ought to speak. An archangel's tongue could do no justice to it. If the intelligence of a cherub were united with the love of a seraph, such intelligence and such love together would vainly seek to set before us the subject that we are now to consider. I would not touch the theme, but for the hope and confidence that, as I labour in my human infirmity to reach the greatness of it, my very failure may show how wonderful it is.

In order that we may consider the subject in such a way as both to remember it and bring out its richest features, I ask your attention to two departments of thought, both suggested by the epistle itself: first, this riches of grace, as seen *in our inheritance in God;* and secondly, this riches of grace, as seen *in God's inheritance in us.* The foundation for the first thought is found in the first chapter and eleventh verse: "In whom also we have obtained an inheritance"; and the foundation for the second is found in the same chapter and the eighteenth verse: "The riches of the glory of *His inheritance in the saints*"—not the saints' inheritance in him, but "His inheritance in the saints." I will say, in advance, that this second thought is perhaps the most overwhelming conception of grace presented from the beginning of Matthew to the close of the Apocalypse—that not only should a saint be permitted to be rich in God, but—oh, marvellous and incomprehensible thought!—that God should estimate himself to be made richer by the love and faith of a believer, so that God should consider that in you and in me He obtains an inheritance!

First, as to *our inheritance in God*, look at what marvels this epistle presents as to that inheritance. First, see what God does to give us this inheritance. The apostle says, in the second chapter and first verse: "And you, who were dead in trespasses and sins, hath he made alive." In the fifth verse he repeats it: "Even when we were dead in sins

hath made us alive together with Christ." We who once
were dead in trespasses and sins are made heirs of God ;
and, in order that we might be heirs, God begins by creating
us anew in Christ Jesus, just as though he had taken dead
elements from the earth, and made a man anew " out of the
dust of the ground." Sin had slain us, and we were dead to
God, and God had first to make us alive in Christ that we
might be able to receive the eternal inheritance. Then,
having made us alive, he took us into his family, and he
gave us what Paul calls, in the fifth verse of the first chapter,
" the adoption of sons ": " Having predestinated us unto
the adoption of children," or sons, " by Jesus Christ."
"Adoption-of-sons" is one word in the Greek, and means
sonship, or the place and the privilege of a son. When we
were dead he made us alive, and then, having made us
alive, he gave us the place of sons, for who could properly
be an heir but a son ? God does not take an alien and will
his property to that alien. <u>When he makes an heir he first
makes him a son</u>. The alien is put into his family of grace,
and, of course, becomes an heir because he is a son. Everything involved in being a son is represented by that word,
" sonship."

A like thought is expressed in other language, when
Paul says : "You who sometime were afar off are made
nigh by the blood of Christ." This probably refers to
the cleansing of the leper. To the Jew the leper was the
walking parable of death and judgment. When he went
anywhere he had to go with bowed head, with distinctive
garments, with a long staff in his hand, and had to cry
" Unclean, unclean," to prevent anyone from coming into
contact with him. He could not enter even into the court
of Israel, much less into the court of the priests ; and, if

God removed his leprosy, he had to be examined by the priest outside of the camp, "afar off," as it were, from the holy place; then when he was pronounced clean, and the sin offering or trespass offering was made in his behalf, he was led by the priest to the tabernacle of the congregation and permitted to enter into the court of Israel. This is another figure to represent our preparation for heirship. We were lepers, outside the camp, having no privileges in the court of God's people, and God took away our leprosy, cleansing us in precious blood, and then brought us into the court of Israel and even into the court of the priests; yes, into the holiest place of all, for the veil had been rent in twain, so that we could come to the very presence of God, and put our hands on the blood-stained mercy seat! You see how the Bible exhausts all figures to express the marvels of this grace. I have preached both the terrors of the law, and the invitations of the gospel, as faithfully as I know how; and I propose now just to hold up the riches of grace in the confident expectation that to display those riches may attract some poor souls to the everlasting inheritance which is the glorious gift of God.

Another wonder about this rich grace is that, having made us sons, as I have suggested, he made us heirs—"In whom we have received an inheritance." Among men a child ordinarily gets the property only when the father or the testator dies. As God never dies, we are come into our inheritance jointly *with* the ever-living God himself! He bestows, not the universe upon us—that is too little for him to give—he gives *himself*. All the wisdom, all the knowledge, all the power, all the love—all the blessedness that is in God becomes ours in Jesus Christ; and, together with God, everything that God owns. This grand thought is too great for our apprehension — that the humblest believer here is going to share the very nature of God, which is the first and most glorious element in the inheritance — going to share the throne, the sceptre, the crown of Jesus Christ, going to share the universe that God owns; that is to say, that there is nothing in God or his possessions that is not to contribute to the everlasting blessedness of the sons and heirs of God.

Another remarkable fact is this—that, having made us alive, and given us the place of sons, and made us heirs, he pays us, in advance of the full redemption of our inheritance, the interest or revenue of the estate. See in the first chapter, in the thirteenth and fourteenth verses, "In whom"—that is, in Christ—"also, after that ye believed ye were sealed with that Holy Spirit of promise which is the earnest"—that is, the foretaste—" of our inheritance until" —that is, this side of—" the redemption of the purchased possession, unto the praise of his glory."

A minor, before his majority, receives, by the appointment of the testator, the revenue from the estate. Stocks are invested, land is rented, buildings are tenanted, and the income from all these investments, gathered in by the executors and administrators, is dealt out to prospective heirs, during their minority, for their support, education, and enjoyment. And so, although we have not come to our majority yet, and have not entered fully upon our inheritance, we get the earnest or foretaste of it; the joys of heaven are in anticipation brought down to earth. The apostle, labouring to express this thought, mixes up two figures in one sentence. He says, " We are sealed with that Holy Spirit of promise which is the earnest of the inheritance." The first figure is taken from the common practice of confirming a document by a seal; and the second figure is taken from the practice of paying over to the minor the revenue of the estate before his majority. God says: "You were dead. I made you alive. You were an alien. I made you a son. You had no possession in me. I made you an heir." Here is the document which is the title clear to mansions in the skies, and the Holy Ghost puts on that document his broad seal, and affixes to it the stamp of God ; and if you ever doubt that you have an inheritance, look at that title and see the seal of the Holy Ghost. You do not suppose that the Holy Ghost seals a lie, putting his attestation to a false and misleading document, do you? If you have in your heart the love of God shed abroad, if you feel the hungering desire after God, if you love his worship, if you sing God's praise because your heart is full of thanksgiving, if you yearn to glorify the Master who died for you, if your passion for souls leads to exertion in their behalf, if your temptations are overcome in a higher strength, if you put forth your efforts to honour your Master who honoured you by making you alive, making you a son, making you an heir—all this is the Holy Spirit putting his seal on the document and saying: "That is a child of God. Bear witness; there is the stamp of God upon him." That seal itself becomes to a believer the most precious advance payment in anticipation of his inheritance. Believers, how many of you have ever had the seal of the Holy Spirit put on your title to heavenly mansions? How many of you have received and enjoyed the earnest of your inheritance? Are not many of you living beneath your privileges, instead of cultivating communion and fellowship with Jesus by the Holy Ghost? Some of you are courting the world and its pleasures, living in the indulgence of some secret sin or the deliberate neglect of some known duty; and, in consequence, you have not the seal of the Spirit of God on your title, and are uncertain whether or not you are saved. Why not come up to the true level of your privileges? Why not claim the sealing of the Holy Ghost and the earnest of your inheritance? Everyone of you may have that foretaste, and it is God's will that you should, and I may reverently say that it disappoints God when his children do not claim the fullness of this blessing.

The apostle expresses kindred ideas in other parts of this epistle. For instance, he says, in the first chapter, "that ye might be filled with all the fullness of God." How can one have such an experience as that, without recognizing in it the sealing of the Holy Ghost? And again he says in the fifth chapter, "Be not drunk with wine wherein is riot, but be filled with the Spirit." It is not a privilege only, but a duty, to "be filled." It is not "you may be filled," not "you ought to be filled," not "it is your privilege to be filled," but an injunction—"Be filled"—as though you dishonour God, as indeed you do, if you are not filled. And then mark that wonderful promise to prayer, in the third chapter, about "Him that is able to do exceeding abundantly above all that we ask or think." All these represent a part of your privileges and of the earnest of your inheritance.

As reference has been made to prayer, let me add that any praying disciple may command evidence that there is a God, and that he is in fellowship with him. You need have no doubts. If you are a doubting disciple you are not really a praying disciple. You do not get the full benefit out of prayer if you have still questionings about God or your own state. If you hold daily communion with him in your chamber, and he touches you and you touch him, you will go through the world like a man who is continually encompassed in impregnable armour, and on your shield of faith Satan's fiery darts of doubt will be quenched. A boy went into the battle and was found without a helmet. Someone said to him, "Your head is unprotected." "No, it is not," he answered, "My mother laid her hands on it before I went to the battlefield, and besought God to be with me." If God's hands are laid on your head, that head is helmeted; if God protects you no arrow from the devil's bow can pierce your coat of mail.

We have now seen how we are made alive, then introduced into sonship, then declared heirs, then paid in advance the earnest of the inheritance. And now a word about the actual inheritance itself. It is said in the second chapter and the seventh verse—and it is one of the most remarkable verses in the New Testament—"That *in the ages to come* he might show the exceeding riches of his grace." It is not said, anywhere in the Bible, that *in the present age* God can show the exceeding riches of his grace. We may get a taste and foretaste of his grace here, but we must wait till the ages to come for the full display of that marvellous riches. There are some paintings that demand a whole gallery for their exhibition; they are too large for a private house. The panorama, on which is emblazoned the riches of God's grace, takes a universe to hold it, and eternity to unroll it. In the ages to come God is going to show the exceeding riches of his grace. Let me use a very simple illustration of what I think God means? Suppose that out of the streets round about this Tabernacle there is taken one of the very worst of men, or—for I think we all feel

The Riches of Grace 213

that if a woman is bad she is worse than a man is—one of the worst of women. And, to make the case more startling, suppose her to have been born deformed—a cripple. She presents in herself the results of generations of crime and lust and strong drink. She is, in body and in soul, a leper, and she carries the leprosy of sin on her body, in the scars of iniquity, and her mind and heart and conscience and will all show the awful fruit of sinful indulgence. Even her companions in sin hate her. She is passed by as a repulsive and loathsome object by everybody, even the members of her own family. She barely keeps a foothold in life, because she is surrounded by those who despise her. Her heart is full of malice. Her mind is a cage of unclean birds. She has almost petrified her conscience into insensibility, and she has no will except for evil doing. Now, suppose that to-night that woman has come into this Tabernacle, and hears the story of the riches of grace, and believes that this rich grace is for her, poor as she is, wretched as she is, foul as she is, despised as she is. We will further suppose that, right here and now, she opens her heart to the Lord Jesus Christ, and takes him as her redeemer. Grace begins at once to work in her soul. Gradually she becomes transformed. Her temptations are resisted, her evil habits are overcome, her evil dispositions are displaced, the love of God is shed abroad in her heart, her imagination and her memory are purified, her conscience quickened and strengthened. The effects are seen even in her body. Her complexion becomes clearer, there is a new light in her eyes, there is a new expression in her face. She goes on, for twenty, thirty, forty years, growing in grace, an astonishment to all who knew her in her sins. But her growth has only begun. You see some little of the riches of grace in her, but, in order to show you the exceeding riches of that grace, God must transport you into the ages to come, and show you that poor degraded, depraved soul after those ages to come have wrought on her their wonderful results. A thousand years hence behold that saint. She has then for a thousand years had a body like unto Christ's glorious body, without the taint of corruption. The scars of sin are all gone, the deformity and the disease and the repulsiveness have been displaced by the charms of everlasting beauty and everlasting youth. Not a thought has crossed her mind for a thousand years that might cause her to blush in the presence of infinite purity; not an affection or an emotion has swayed her heart, but such as rule in the heart of the infinite God. As to knowledge, she has been educated in the university of heaven for a thousand years. All the philosophers of Greece and Rome, all the ancient and modern sages and scholars together could teach her nothing. If you could gather all the knowledge of the ages of the past and the present, it would not be as a drop in the ocean, compared to what she knows by communion with angels and saints and God himself. Yet she is only at the beginning of her true history, though she has been in heaven for a thousand years; for the thousand years are an insignificant fraction to what is before her; and, at any stage of her future existence, there will still be an eternity before her, and at any stage of her future perfection there will still be before her an unattained perfection. Get where she will for height, there are boundless heights beyond; get where she will for progress there are endless paths beyond—growth infinite: eternal advance. Now we begin to see what God means when he says, "That *in the ages to come* he might show the exceeding riches of his grace in his kindness toward us through Christ Jesus?'

You can never understand it here, do what you will. You must wait until this everlasting display of his grace, growing more glorious as the ages go by, unfolds its record to you amid the splendours of his throne.

→II. Perhaps the most glorious part of our theme is yet to be presented, and that is "the riches of the glory of *God's inheritance in the saints.*" This is certainly among the most stupendous thoughts within the pages of the New Testament —that God should regard you and me as worthy to be made an inheritance for himself! See what glimpses the apostle gives us into this subject. In the first place, he teaches us that God *buys* or purchases us for his inheritance, that he redeems his inheritance by precious blood. In the fifth chapter, Paul tells us that Christ "gave himself for us as an offering to God for a sweet smelling savour." When God looked down on us we were slaves of sin, condemned by the law, victims of death and hell; and he first gave his own Son to buy us out of our bondage and captivity and spiritual death that he might introduce us into the privileges of the sons of God, and find in us an inheritance. Then, after this purchase, he proceeds to *make us anew* in Christ Jesus; that is, to make us fit to be his own inheritance. In the second chapter and tenth verse we are told, "We are his workmanship, created in Christ Jesus unto good works." The original word there is ποίημα, a poem, as though the divine Artist were writing a poem full of the rhyme and rhythm of heavenly music, and took us for the theme of the poem. We are his workmanship, his artistic product. God does not make anything imperfect; when he makes you anew in Christ Jesus that means perfection for you in the future life.

So this brings me to the third point. As he bought us

for an inheritance, and reconstructs us in Christ, he carries the work to perfection. One of the sweetest suggestions in the New Testament is wrapped up in this divine truth. A man dies and leaves to his son an estate, with an old house upon it in which the family had lived for many years. In passing by that estate some time after, you notice that the house is apparently being almost pulled down. They have torn off the old boards and shingles, they have taken down the half dilapidated chimneys, they have cut out rotten floor timbers and base timbers; they have built up a new foundation, put in a bow window on the south exposure, and are building a large piazza round the east and north and west sides. The present owner is making it over, improving his inheritance. Is it not in some such way that God perfects his own dear children? He sends to us afflictions, and they seem to tear us to pieces with sorrow and grief. God is only stripping off the rotten boards and shingles, and taking out the dead timbers. He is only remodelling and "improving his own inheritance"; and because he loves us so much he takes such infinite pains with the old building to put in place of its corruption the glorious renovations of the Holy Spirit. That is why God deals with his own disciples oftentimes in a very painful way. He is seeking to make them completely over into the likeness of his dear Son.

Again, he who buys us for an inheritance, and makes us anew, and perfects us by the discipline of his grace, *comes and dwells in us.* He has built his house for a dwelling; and he is going to be the inhabitant himself. " Know ye not that ye are the temple of the Holy Ghost, and that the Spirit of God dwelleth in you?" In the second chapter and twentieth verse: "are built upon the foundation of the apostles and prophets, Jesus Christ himself, being the chief corner stone in whom all the building fitly framed together, groweth unto an holy temple in the Lord, in whom ye also are builded together for a habitation of God through the Spirit." Am I not right in saying that this thought is unsurpassed for grandeur in the New Testament? God buys us from sin, delivers us from captivity and condemnation, then he makes us over in Christ Jesus by the power of his grace, then he disciplines us by sorrow and suffering, and trial and temptation, until he has perfected the building. Then he comes and dwells in it, and makes it a habitation of God.

And so, finally, he glorifies it. He could not dwell in it without glorifying it. But, at last he is going to take this body of ours and make it like unto the body of Christ. He is going to take this soul of ours and wash it clean, not only saving it from the penalty, but from the power and dominion and presence of sin also, and make it a fit place for his glory to shine in, and for his glory to shine through. In the fourth chapter of Zechariah, we read of the wonderful candlestick, with the lamps that are burning in testimony, on its branches. But when in Revelation you get a last glimpse of that golden candlestick, the *lamps* are turned to *stars*. What were lamps on earth, have become stars in heaven, and these stars are held in the right hand of Jesus Christ. We think of Daniel, twelfth chapter and the second verse, " They that be teachers (margin), shall shine as the brightness of the firmament, and they that turn many to righteousness as the stars for ever and ever." If God takes these pains to perfect the building while we are on earth, what do you suppose will be its perfection when it is transplanted to the skies; when the last sign of sin and imperfection disappears, and when the light of a candle, and even sunshine itself is superfluous, because his glory lightens it, and shines through the window with supernal splendour !

Even the great mind of the apostle Paul, with all his learning and culture and philosophy, labours by the Holy Ghost to express this idea. Let me read, in conclusion, the last verses of the first chapter; and let us give good heed, and catch the idea of them if we may: " The eyes of your understanding being enlightened that ye may know what is the hope of his calling and what the riches of the glory of his inheritance in the saints, and what is the exceeding greatness of his power to us-ward who believe, according to the working of His mighty power"— or the energy of his might—" which he wrought in Christ when he raised him from the dead, and set him at his own right hand in the heavenly places, far above all principalities and power and might and dominion and every name that is named not only in this world, but also in that which is to come; and hath put all things under his feet and gave him to be the head over all things to the church, which is his body, the fullness of him that filleth all in all." What does all this mean? That phrase, "According to the working of his mighty power," is the key. If I have a fabric that I want to measure, or a city that I need to take the dimensions of, I must have a measuring reed or rod, like the man in Ezekiel's vision. God puts an infinite prospect before us and gives a measuring rule whereby to estimate it. What is that measuring rule? It is "*what God wrought in Christ, when he raised him from the dead and set him at his own right hand in the heavenly places,* far above all power and dominion and principalities and every name that is named." God says: " If you want to know what I am going to do for you in the exceeding richness of my power

The Riches of Grace

and grace here is the unit of measurement. When you can measure what I have done for my dear Son in raising him from the dead and setting him at my own right hand in the heavenlies, where even angels, principalities, and powers are under his feet, then you have the yard measure by which to estimate the infinite glory to which the saints are to be introduced."

I sink back exhausted, in the vain attempt to set before this congregation the greatest mystery of grace that I ever grappled with. I cannot remember, in thirty years of gospel preaching, ever to have been confronted with a theme that more baffled every outreach of thought, and every possibility of utterance, than the theme that I have now been attempting in the name of God to present.

I have, in Japan, a beloved daughter and son-in law, engaged in the work of missions to the heathen. That son-in-law was almost an idol in his family, and a general favourite, and he deserved to be, for he was amiable, considerate, loving, and unselfish. When he gave himself to the work of foreign missions, and proposed to go to the far East, the question was naturally asked, " How will he ever break away from his father and mother, his brothers and sisters, and especially from his aged grandparents?" We watched to see how God would support him as the time came in 1888, for him to bid a long farewell to all he loved on that side of the sea. But he left on record. as his parting message, the words of the text, " Unto me who am less than the least of all saints is this grace given, that I should preach among the nations the unsearchable riches of Christ." He forgot all about the ties to be sundered, the great ocean to be crossed, the language to be mastered, and the strange people to be confronted; and the one thought that filled his mind, was the inestimable joy and privilege of preaching among the nations the unsearchable riches of Christ. You need not shed any tears over such a man. He has got a glimpse of the infinite riches of God, and like one who knows that he has found exhaustless wealth, and is surrounded by awful destitution and poverty, he yearns to go and scatter the coin of the kingdom among the destitute and degraded peoples of a far-off land. He has never had a mournful moment since he turned his back on his own country. That is the spirit of every true missionary, and I bless God that in some faint measure I know what that joy is. Opportunities have more than once, in my life, apparently opened to me the door to possible wealth, if I would turn aside from the preaching of the gospel, or make a compromise with the world. It cost me nothing to turn my back on the prospect of riches, for I had a grander privilege. The infinite riches of God were at my disposal. I had the wealth of the gospel to scatter among poor souls. You that are yet wandering from Jesus, you do not know what a Saviour we have who believe! You do not understand what riches of grace and glory are in store for you also, if you repent and accept of Christ; and I feel it a great joy to stand here, and carry out and carry on the testimony of that blessed man of God, who preached here for so many years, and like him, to press upon you the gift of God, which is found only in his dear Son.

In Bunyan's great allegory, in the House of the Interpreter, a man was seen, raking among the dust and rubbish, to find coins or gems, while above his head a celestial hand was stretched out with a crown set round with blazing jewels. "*Thou art the man!*" You are seeking amid the pleasures and treasures of this world a satisfaction that you

The Riches of Grace

will never find; and, while you are looking down, you need only look up and see God's hand stretched out, offering an eternal crown, every gem of which represents the riches of God. Will not you come to Christ now? Do not think of your sin. It is not too great for him to save you, and the greater your sin the more he yearns to save you, because the greater is your need. And all that you have to do is to accept him. He is God's free gift. These boundless riches are yours without paying a farthing, taking a step, making an effort, or waiting a moment. It is all yours, if you will hold out your hand and take it. Surely nothing can be added to the glory of this gospel, OF THE UNSEARCHABLE RICHES OF CHRIST!

PART TWO

The Heights of the Gospel

Sermon One

The Three Determining Wills

"But I will come to you shortly, if the Lord will, and will know, not the speech of them which are puffed up, but the power. For the kingdom of God is not in word, but in power. What will ye? shall I come unto you with a rod, or in love, and in the spirit of meekness?"—1 CORINTHIANS iv. 19—21.

IN all the ages there has probably never been another Christian worker that has rivalled the apostle Paul. Whenever we study the character of this remarkable man we are more and more ashamed of ourselves. His great faith, his great courage, his holy yearning after souls, his willingness to be nothing in the eyes of men, his absolute giving of himself to His Master's work, and even his joy in suffering for His Master's sake, put to shame everyone of us, I am sure. And it is well for us to ask what are the secrets of a character and a career so marvellously beautiful as those of the apostle Paul.

I have taken this text this morning because it is one of God's gems that, entirely apart from its beautiful setting in the Word of God, burns with the very fire of the Holy Spirit. It is quite possible that you have never noticed the three great conditions of successful service which are here indicated.

There are three determining wills in every life of power among men : the first is the will of God, the second is the

The Three Determining Wills

will of the man himself, and the third is the will of those among whom he labours; and these are beautifully referred to here. The first, "If the Lord will"; the second, "I will"; the third, "What will ye?"

Now with regard to the first: the Lord's will. The will is the centre of being; it is that on which the whole being revolves as the sun moves upon its own axis. "Thou shalt love the Lord thy God with all thy heart and soul and mind and strength." I suppose that word "strength" means the will, as the strength of the character. Now as the will is centre of being, God's will represents God. What God chooses, what God prefers, what God eternally purposes —that is God's will. And all the relations of men to God are determined by the attitude of man's will toward God's will. If we take the system of the heavenly bodies as an illustration, the sun may represent God moving round on the axis of His own will for evermore, and all obedient souls may represent the planets that move about this central sun in the orbit of obedience, and all unholy and disobedient souls may be represented by wandering stars that will not move in the orbit of obedience to God, and to whom is reserved the blackness of darkness for ever. The great question of the persecutor, Saul, when he met Christ on the road to Damascus was, first, "Who art Thou?" and as soon as he learned that it was the Lord, then the next question was, "What wilt Thou?" And that question he asked for his whole after-life, and may I not say for the whole of the eternal ages yet before him? From that moment he surrendered himself to the Mastership of Jesus Christ, and he knew henceforth no other Master but Jesus Christ; and in the smallest matter the first question he asked was, "What is the will of the Lord?" and as soon as he knew it, immediately he said, "That is my will." So he did in this case.

As to our relation to the will of the Lord, I pray you to notice two or three things. To obey the will of the Lord is the secret first of all, of *safety*—security. "All things work together for good to them that love God." From the moment a planet wheels into its path round the sun, there is nothing that can harm that planet, but just as soon as a star wanders from its orbit, and goes plunging headlong into the depths of space, it is liable to come into clash and crash with the universe of God. I have seen a great piece of machinery that would almost, if not quite, fill this immense building. Now, suppose that in that great piece of machinery, one little wheel, as small, it may be, as a shilling, should drop out of its place and fall into the midst of the machinery, that colossal mechanism moving round and round and round would grind this little wheel among its larger wheels into fragments, if not into powder. The Universe is one great Machine, and God is the Motive Power of it, and when a soul drops out of its place in this great machinery, and falls among the great wheels of God's purpose, it is ground into powder, unless the grace of God puts that wheel back into its place in the vast system. The moment that you find out what the will of God is, and drop into your place, all the universe moves with you, and all the universe moves for you, the whole Godhead is back of you, the wisdom of God, and the power of God, and the love of God, and the grace of God; and you are as absolutely sure and safe as God is. And so Peter says: "Who is he that shall harm you if you be followers of that which is good?"

I suppose you have read the story of William III. of

Orange, and his wars on the Continent. On one occasion he was exposing himself in the thickest of the fight on the battle-field, in order that he might control the forces at his disposal. A lieutenant-governor ventured into the same exposed place on the battle-field, and the sovereign remonstrated. He said, "You have no right here, for this is a place of peculiar peril." "Sire," answered the lieutenant-governor, "I can risk my life wherever my sovereign can risk his life." "Not so," replied the king, "Duty calls me here, and I am safe; Duty does not call you, and you are not safe." And no sooner had the words issued from his mouth than a shell swept by and took off the head of the lieutenant-governor, while the king stood absolutely unharmed.

The supreme question is, Does your duty call you? If it does, you are safe; but if you go where duty does not call you, you are not safe for a single instant. Secure in the cleft of the rock when God's hand is in front of you and hides you in the cleft; never secure in any other place than just where God would have you to be, and where you seek to be in obedience to His divine will. And so it was John Wesley who declared, "I am immortal until my work is done." And so with Paul at Corinth. You remember that, in the eighteenth chapter of the Acts, we are told that after he had that vision of Macedonia—the man saying in the vision of the night—"Come over and help us,"—he gathered that the Lord had called him to preach the gospel in Macedonia and the neighbourhood. And so he left Bithynia, where the Spirit would not suffer him to go, and went over into Macedonia, and down into Greece. And so he came to Corinth, and you know how he was met there. You remember how they persecuted him; how they drew him before the deputy's seat, Gallio being seated on that throne of judgment; but how the Lord had said, "Fear not, Paul, fear not, be not afraid, but speak, and hold not thy peace, for I am with thee, and no man shall set on thee to hurt thee : for I have much people in this city."

And so because one is perfectly safe in following the will of the Lord it is the secret, likewise, of perfect peace or *serenity*. I remember that the President of the United States, Mr. Lincoln, in the midst of the late war, was once approached by a very timid soul who said, "Well, Mr. Lincoln, I am very anxious that the Lord should be on our side." "Sir," said Mr. Lincoln, "that does not give me the least trouble in the world; the only question is whether we are on the Lord's side. If we are on the Lord's side we are perfectly safe."

To be in the cleft of the rock makes the saint serene. It was this that made Stephen smile; and his face was lit up as the face of an angel when the stones were flying through the air that caused his death. And it was this that enabled Luther, when his life was threatened as he went to Worms to meet the Diet. "I would go to Worms," said he, "if there were as many devils there as there are tiles on the roofs of the houses." And it was this that enabled the martyrs, when they lay on beds of coals, to say that they felt as though they were on beds of roses. My friend, are you doing the will of the Lord? Then you are absolutely secure, and you can afford to be absolutely serene. Be not afraid to go right forward, for the Lord is at your back.

So this is the secret of *service*—a higher will controlling my will, not crushing my will. I wish that you might all get hold of this great distinction. When you yield yourself to God, He does not destroy your will. You merge your will into His; you open your whole being to Him, and it becomes the channel through which God shall flow, and pour the stream of His mighty and almighty power. To go as I am led, to go when I am led, to go where I am led, to go as I am led,—it is that which has been for twenty years the one prayer of my life; and I know nothing that is so blessed a help as that in serving God. And we must be willing to have the will of God gradually disclosed. It is not all unfolded to us at once. It is very much like that sheet which Peter saw let down in a vision on the house-top. It came down at the hour of prayer, and it ascended again when the hour of prayer was over, and all that it revealed to Peter was his immediate duty. "There are three men that seek thee; get thee down and go with them, nothing doubting, for I have sent them." That vision did not tell Peter what his duty was the next year, or the next month, but what his duty was just then and there. And it is a blessed thing if you are willing, on the house-top to-day at noon, when you are praying to God, to have Him let down so much of His will to you in the vision as pertains to the immediate duty before you, and leave all the rest to Him.

Do not you see that, as this is the secret of safety and serenity and service, so it delivers you from all worry and anxiety? I have long held, and I repeat it here, that any work which I am doing, which you are doing, which necessitates worry, which compels anxiety of mind, and care, and perplexity, and solicitude, is probably my own selfish work, and not God's work at all. It is something that you or I are doing because of our ambition, or appetite, or avarice, or selfishness, or our desire to get ourselves on in this world. For if it is God's work I am doing, and I am only putting my hand to God's work, why should I worry about it? Is that not a kind of impertinence as though God were not able to take care of his own work? Why, the man that is on the battle-field, and has supreme confidence in the general-in-chief, and follows the general into the thickest of the fight, does not consider himself responsible for the issues of the battle. By no means. He knows that there is a competent hand that is regulating the whole matter, and all he has to do is as a soldier to follow where his leader goes, and strictly to obey his commands. A very beautiful story was told of a gunner at Waterloo, by Dr. Cook, of Belfast. The gunner was describing the supreme moment, just before the new recruits came up under Blucher, that under your great Wellington turned that decisive battle of modern ages, and the dust and smoke cf the battle were so thick and intense, that the gunner, as he stood on the height on which he had been placed by the command of his officer, could not see five yards in front of him. He felt the swaying tides of the battle move this and that way as the troops were repulsed, and then moved forward again to the onset; and he did not know at one time whether he was among Englishmen or among Frenchmen—among friends or foes. Dr. Cook said to him, "Well, my friend, what did you do in that supreme hour of darkness and solicitude?" "I stood by my gun!" said he. That is all you and I have to do. We are not responsible for the swaying tides of battle; we are not responsible for apparent defeat, or apparent failure. The question is, Am I where God puts me, and do I stay where God puts me, and do I do what God would have me do?

And this leads me to say that as this doing of the will of God is the secret of safety, and serenity, and service, it is also the secret of *success*.

Now, I want to have it understood, that in estimating success you can never depend on the world's standards. What the world counts success God may count failure, and what man counts failure God may count as success. Until we get rid of the snares of man's judgment and our own judgment and leave everything to God, we shall never be able to do the will of God with a peaceful soul. When Stephen, early anointed for the work of God and just beginning to make an impression upon the people, fell under the stones of his enemies, I suppose most men would have said,—"What a sad failure is that life, cut off in its very beginning!" But there was a young man that stood and held the clothes of those that stoned Stephen, and looked on the face that was radiant with God's smile, on whom impressions were made at that time that never were effaced. He was Saul of Tarsus; and personally I have very little doubt that the conversion of Saul of Tarsus should be traced back even past the appearance of Christ at Damascus—to the first conviction implanted in his mind when he looked upon the first of the martyrs. So that for aught you know Stephen may have died to give to the Church Saul of Tarsus as Paul the Apostle of the Gentiles. When Paul and Silas went over to Philippi, a city of Macedonia, in accordance with the vision of the night, and when just as they got there they were put into prison, thrust into the inner prison, and their feet made fast in the stocks, I suppose most people would have said, "Well, that certainly is a failure. Paul must have mistaken that vision of the night, and he must have been off his track." But when at midnight Paul and Silas sang praises unto God, and God answered by an earthquake that shook the foundations of the prison and loosened every man's bands, and the gaoler and his family became the first-fruits unto Christ of that midnight hour, I suppose that in heaven it was seen that what man counted failure God counted success. And when Paul went to Rome and was chained by the hand to a soldier of the prætorian guard, and when every morning a new soldier was chained to him, until the whole of the prætorian guard had had Paul under custody, I suppose most people would have said, " It is a pity, is it not, that a man of such power as Paul should have an audience of only one man, and that audience changed every day?" But Paul could say, "I have preached the gospel of Christ throughout the whole prætorian guard." The clanking of the chains of the imprisoned apostle were the voices of the Holy Ghost to tell the story of redemption to those Roman soldiers. And who knows how much the conversion of pagans in Rome may be attributed to Paul's being thus chained by the hand to these soldiers!

Perhaps I am spending undue time upon this part of my theme, but this is where the main stress of the whole subject lies. The one "if" that is the most important in any man's life is this "IF the Lord will." Now, just as soon as you discover what the Lord's will is, then you are to do just as Paul did. Let us hear him. "If the Lord will, I will." Not only so, but, "I will come unto you *shortly* if the Lord will."

I thank God for that word "*shortly*" There are some people who have a sort of a vague intention to do the Lord's will, but the time of doing it is very far in the future. It is a very indefinite and uncertain purpose. There are people who have purposed to repent, twenty years ago, and have never repented yet; there are people who have purposed to believe, twenty years ago, and have never believed yet; there are people who have purposed to be baptised, twenty years ago, and have never been baptised yet; there are people who have long ago purposed to identify themselves with the Church of Christ, and have never done it yet; and they will go along until they drop off into the awful gulf at the close of life, and not one of these half-formed purposes will ever be fulfilled! What did Paul say? "*Immediately*, I was not disobedient unto the heavenly vision."

Now, let us understand that it is perfectly right for you to wait until you clearly understand what God's will is, provided you are searching meanwhile to know that will, earnestly desiring to be acquainted with it, and holding your whole nature open to the communication of it; but the moment that will is made plain to you, then it is impossible for you to be too much in haste to fall into the line of God's purpose and perform His blessed will.

Paul simply waited to know the will of God, and then acted. It is very likely that Paul had some signs of the will of God which are not communicated to you and to me, but I believe there is no child of God, especially in any matter connected with his higher life, who needs be in doubt very long as to what the will of God is; and if you will allow me to stop just here for a moment to indicate some things that must be spoken of more fully hereafter, I will give you what have been to me, for many years, six signs of the will of God. There may be one or more of them at a time; there may be some cases in life when all of these indications must be granted to make you feel sure, but I believe that if you will wait and study these six signs until one or more of them brings clear revelation to you of the will of God, you need never make an essential mistake in the performance of your duty.

In the first place, there is the witness of His Word. If anything is laid down clearly in the Holy Word of God which may be my guide in duty, God will never give me any light outside of that Word. If He says, "Repent," "Believe," "Be baptised," "Do not forsake the assembling of yourselves together," you need no further light. Light is given to you there, and that is to be adequate for you.

In the second place, there is the light of a conscience enlightened by the Word and Spirit of God. If your conscience compels you to a certain course, and you have compared that conscience with the will of God as declared in the Scripture, and it proves to be in accord with the Scripture, then there can be no doubt, so far as your conscience is concerned, what your duty is.

If these two fail to guide, then look for the outward call. Is there a door opened before you for service? Is a path plainly set before you, and does God seem to point providentially to that path? That is another indication.

Then the fourth indication is the inward call. How does your heart respond, in the times when you are considering what the will of God is? How does your better self respond to the voices of the word and of your conscience, and to the outward call of God's providence?

If these four fail, then let us look a little further. What about the rational judgment; that is, the judgment of the reason? Of course, God gave man common sense and the sound mind in order to determine questions of duty. Suppose, for instance, God calls you to a work, apparently, for which you have not the strength. It is impossible that God should call a blind man to do a work that can only be done when a man has his eyes; or a deaf man to do a work that can only be done when a man has the hearing of his ears; or call to a handiwork which can only be done by a man who has the use of his hands, one whose hands are crippled or paralyzed. Here then your reasonable judgment is to come in to weigh questions of a claim of duty with respect to your having ability to do a thing that you are considering.

And then the last of all the indications is this, and I think it is the most important, next to the Word of God: How about your spiritual judgment? That is to say, when you solemnly weigh the question that is before you in the scales of your spiritual life. When you notice how, in prayerful moments, and in seasons of intimate communion with God, a question appears to you, and how in carnal moments when you are most worldly-minded, the question appears to you; if you find that whenever you are nearest to God the claim to this duty comes uppermost and will not go down at your bidding, and whenever you are most immersed in the world, and the flesh and the pleasures of this life, the matter gets lost sight of, and obscured—when you see such lights as those all in a line, you may make up your mind that that is the way to the harbour. And Paul was accustomed to weigh all these considerations—What is the command of Christ outwardly? What is the voice of conscience inwardly? What is the call of God's providence in the outward opening? What is the response of my own nature in the inward impulse? What is the judgment of my reason? And what is the judgment of my spirit when I am nearest to my God? To these may be added the calm judgment of the best and holiest saints.

But when you come to know the will of God by these or any other indications, the quicker you move the better, and the more cheerfully you move the better.

Now, I want you to notice that Paul not only said, "I will come to you shortly," but he said what is more important, "I will know not the speech of them that are puffed up, but the power."

At Corinth and at Athens there were four classes of men that were greatly conceited, and puffed up with pride—those that gave themselves to rhetoric, those that gave themselves to logic, those that gave themselves to wisdom, and those that taught others the snares of sophistry. Paul says, "I determined not to know anything among you save Jesus Christ, I would not come with enticing words, and I would not come with endeavour after excellent speech or worldly wisdom, but the demonstration of the Holy Spirit."

You may be assured that the lost art in speaking to men about gospel truth is the art of commanding the power of the Holy Spirit. There are a few divine artists that have that power, and one of the most conspicuous in modern ages was the man that for thirty years stood in this very pulpit to tell men the story of the gospel. But it is a very rare art in these days to command the Holy Spirit's power in speaking to men. How much do we value the coming of the Holy Spirit? I took up this New Testament the other day, and I noted that fact, that where the Holy Ghost begins to be manifested the bulk of the New Testament began to be written; that is, at the Acts of the Apostles. If the Holy Ghost had never come we might have had the four gospel-narratives, but the Acts and the Epistles and the Book of the Apocalypse we should never have had. And it is just so in a believer's life. There might be a measure of knowledge such as is represented in the four gospels; but, be assured, we should never have the new Acts of the Apostles, we should never have holy service for God, we should never have Christian people engaging in work, and successful work, for the Master, if there were not a personal advent of the Holy Spirit into the heart of the believing child of God. And I would not myself give you a fraction of a penny for an entire ministry if there is nothing of the power of the Holy Ghost in it. There may be poetry and philosophy, and logic and wisdom: all this is good for nothing spiritually; begetting only the inflation of self-conceit and worldly power and confidence. But when the Spirit comes there is not the mere word, but there is the Power of God in which the kingdom consists, and by which it is furthered and forwarded.

Now, let me call attention to one word in the second chapter of this Epistle to the Corinthians—the word "demonstration." I suppose there is not one of you here, even a child, that does not know that the word "demonstrate" means to prove. That word was used by these men who lived in Athens and in Corinth, of those means by which they sought to convince men through the power of logic. Now, Paul said, "I am not going to depend upon the demonstration of logic; but upon the demonstration of the Holy Spirit." How does the Holy Spirit prove a truth? Suppose I tried to prove a truth by logic, how do I do it? I lay down a position which is called the major premiss; then there comes another one on the top of that, which is called the minor premiss, or the second of these propositions. The logician says, if this is true, and that is true, something else must be true, and that he calls the conclusion. That is what is known as the formula of logic. That is what reasoning men have always depended upon throughout the world for power in argument. When the Holy Ghost wants to demonstrate a truth what does He do? Does He say this and another thing is true and so some other thing is true? Not at all. The Holy Ghost has quicker logic than that. You say you are not a sinner, do you? How does the Holy Ghost prove your sin to you? He touches your blind eyes, and breaks up your deception, and shows you your sin like a rotten carcase lying right there before you, and sending up its stench into your nostrils. You say, "I do not believe in a hell." The Holy Spirit just opens the very doors of the infernal regions, and compels you to look down into the bottomless pit. You say you do not believe there is a God. The Holy Ghost rends in twain the veil that hides God, and you feel that you are confronted with God and God is dealing with you. That is the way of the Holy Spirit's demonstration. Logic may fail to carry any proof; but when the Holy Ghost takes a man and shakes him in the hand of His Omnipotence, all the scales fall off from a man's eyes, and suddenly he sees what for twenty years he has been blind to. He knows himself, and he knows God; he knows hell, and he knows heaven. Saul of Tarsus thought he ought to do many things contrary to the name of Jesus of Nazareth, and he went to Damascus, that he might commit men and women to prison; but on the way, in a moment of time, the scales fell from his eyes; he saw Jesus whom he persecuted to be the Son of God; he saw the truth that he hated, to be the truth of God; he saw the Church that he sought to imprison and slay, to be the bride of Jesus Christ; he saw himself a sinner, a rebel and apostate, and at once he said, and it was the question of the rest of his life, "Lord, what wilt Thou have me to do?" Argument might have been spent on the Apostle Paul for forty years, and not have brought him to and strength and support to those that were truly God's. Now remember, that your wants largely and often unconsciously guide the preacher in what he shall say to you, for the natural impulse of a man is to supply the demand that he finds to exist in a congregation; and, especially, your wants will largely determine the message. I suppose that Felix did not enjoy Paul's reasoning of righteousness, temperance and judgment to come; but it was what Felix needed, though it made him tremble. I suppose that Agrippa did not relish being almost persuaded to be a Christian, but it was what he needed—that presentation of the argument from the prophets with which he was very familiar. And so, there may be sinners here that will not relish a plain gospel message, but that is what they need. May God give me grace to give them what they need, even though it is not what they relish. For it is like medicine, that, being bitter in the mouth, may work great changes in the whole body.

And especially remember that your capacity to receive the truth will largely determine the power of the gospel. "If any man will do His will, he shall know of the doctrine." If, as you hear the Word from God, you obey it; if, as you see the will of God, you quickly undertake to perform it, you will find your own capacity to receive the truth, and capacity to obey the truth will grow with every new proclamation of the truth. It seems to me that this church is like a city set on a hill, that cannot be hid. I suppose there has been more of the gospel of Christ preached in its purity here than within any other four walls that stand to-day in the United Kingdom; and I am deeply concerned, that God should come, and, by the power of the Holy Spirit, bless His Word. I am going the conviction and the resolution that forty seconds accomplished on his way to Damascus. That is the demonstration of the Spirit.

I want you to feel with me this morning more deeply than you ever have felt before, that there is going to be no power in my preaching if there is not the power of the Holy Spirit. I would almost better drop dead here this morning than go on preaching to this congregation in any dependence on rhetoric, or logic, or poetry, or philosophy ; and I bless God that I can say, from the depths of my soul as before Him, that my only purpose is, out of love to serve every man and woman, and child in this church, the representative of no part or party, but of the whole church, that with great unanimity invited me in June last to resume this ministry among you. I declare, as I am in the presence of God, my dependence upon just one thing ; I believe God will bestow the greatest gift, the power of the Holy Ghost, and I am going to ask your prayers and co-operation in Christ Jesus, to make this little ministry of mine, that is flung in among you like a stray orb from the other side of the sea, a blessing to many souls.

Just a word in conclusion. I have not left myself any time for it, but you will notice that the apostle not only says, " If the Lord will, I will," but asks " What will ye ? " Suffer me to add just a word of exhortation to a discourse already perhaps too long. A great deal depends upon this beloved people. The same word that is a rod of rebuke to a sinner is a staff of support to a saint. The same message over which a rebel sinner falls and stumbles is a stepping stone to a saint, and the same word that Paul spoke in rebuke to those in Corinth that were apart from God or backslidden from Christ became a word of help to rely on your prayers: I believe I shall have them. Let us meet together often, though we see each other not, in the secret pavilion of God. Let us bring individual cases in our families, Sunday-school classes, among our neighbours and friends, to Him who hears and answers prayer; and let the power of the Holy Ghost be so deeply our confidence that we shall never speak for Him or work for Him without the serene and blessed assurance that we are doing the will of God, and that the whole Godhead is behind us in assuring power!

SERMON TWO

The Secret of Overcoming Satan

"Ye are of God, little children, and have overcome them : because greater is he that is in you, than he that is in the world."—I JOHN iv. 4

THIS General Epistle of John is the battlefield of the ages, and is full of sharp contrasts : life and death, light and darkness, sin and holiness, heaven and hell, love and hate, are put opposite each other all through this epistle. This is the Gallery of Battles which represents the greatest of all the conflicts of history, the everlasting fight between evil and good, between the Son of God as the leader of the good and the devil as the leader of the evil ones.

There is so much in this text to inspire and encourage that I pray God to help us all to enter at once into the heart of it. It is the message of comfort to God's dear children : "Ye are of God, little children, and have overcome them : because greater is He that is in you, than he that is in the world." Now there is no doubt that "He that is in you," refers to God, and there is no doubt that "He that is in the world," refers to the devil; and the first thought that strikes us is that there is no attempt in the Bible to deny or dispute the greatness of Satan. This passage acknowledges his greatness, but it affirms that He that is in the disciples is greater than the god of this world.

First, then, let us consider the greatness of Satan so that we may understand the character of the adversary whom we have to contend with. The Bible represents Satan as the head of a great army of foes. "Satan" is always in the singular number, and although in our English version we frequently find the word "devils," there is but one devil, and the Word translated "devils" should be translated "demons," as it is in the margin of the Revised Version. There is then but one devil, but there are many demons. Satan is the head of this great host, the general-in-chief of the armies of evil. If you will closely examine the Epistle to the Ephesians and the Epistle to the Colossians, you will find that there seem to be seven grades of fallen angels, as there are seven grades of unfallen angels. We read of "Principalities," "Powers," "Dominions," "Authorities," "Rulers," "Thrones," "Wicked Spirits," etc., and above them all, as I believe, there is a rank of archangels, or chief angels. We apparently have the names of three of these archangels given to us in the Bible. One of them is Michael, who seems to have had special care of the dead bodies of God's saints; one of them is Gabriel, who seems to have had special charge of the messages about our Lord's coming in the flesh; and the other of these three, apparently also an archangel, but fallen, is the Devil or Satan. So we are to imagine Satan as the highest over all the ranks of fallen angels.

Suppose that, for instance, one of the provinces or colonies of Great Britain should rebel and cut loose from the parent government; it might carry into its rebellion all its officers, from its governor-general down to the mayors of its cities, and even its police magistrates; and apparently when this great rebellion took place among the angels of God they carried over into their revolt the ranks they had before rebellion came among them, so that Satan is a chief demon, an evil spirit, a fallen angel of tremendous power. He commands armies that may be almost as countless as the sands of the sea. I think the more closely you study the Scriptures, the more you will see this to be the case. For instance, there were seven demons in Mary Magdalene before Christ cast them out; and in the twelfth of Matthew, we read of a man that had an evil spirit, out of whom the evil demon went but came back and brought seven other spirits more wicked than himself. That man in Gadara, who lived among the tombs, we are told, had a legion of demons in him, and when they were cast out they went into a herd of swine numbering thousands, and the whole herd of swine went down into the lake and perished in the waters. This is the first thought, that is suggested by text, that Satan has tremendous power and immense hosts of demons under his control, rendering him obedient service.

Then, in the second place, Satan has marvellous wisdom and knowledge. He has a master intellect, with all the knowledge that you might suppose would dwell in the mind of a fallen archangel. He knows how to reach the human soul; he knows how to deceive you and mislead you. You have seen the magicians when, behind the silk handkerchief that they hold up, they perform their tricks and make you believe that they do a thousand things which they really do not, making your eyes the fools of your other senses. Just so, Satan by his sleight of hand, and cunning craftiness, whereby he " lies in wait to deceive," makes you believe that he proves a thing that cannot be proven, and that what is actually a reality and verity is a sham and an absurdity. When the Duke of Richmond presented his report about " Fortifications,"

The Secret of Overcoming Satan

Sheridan said, "I compliment the noble president on his talents as an *engineer*, which were strongly evinced in planning and constructing that very paper. . . . He has made it a contest of posts, and conducted his reasoning not less on principles of trigonometry than of logic. There are certain assumptions thrown up like advanced works to keep the enemy at a distance from the principal object of debate; strong provisos protect and cover the flanks of his assertions, and his very queries are his casemates." And Satan is a civil engineer. He constructs his fortifications to make the evil strong and repel the good.

And so as he is a demon of marvellous power and wisdom, is he also formidable in his familiarity with evil, and it is this that constitutes the great hold of Satan over the human soul. Remember this awful fact, that Satan has gone over the whole round of possible sin. Remember that he has had age upon age to practise ungodliness, and rebellion, and deception. Remember that he has in himself the very secrets of hell. And so when you come into conflict with Satan you meet one that has not only tremendous power, an immense following, a most acute intellect, and the greatest mastery of knowledge, but you are confronting one that has gone through the whole experience of evil doings, and who by long practice in the art of deceiving and seducing souls has become the master of that art.

Yet notwithstanding this, we are bidden to remember that "He that is in you is greater than he that is in the world." Conceding the greatness of Satan, let us look for a moment at the superior greatness of Jesus Christ.

In the first place, Jesus Christ has all power. Satan has great power, but not omnipotence. Jesus Christ met Satan single-handed and alone. Satan assaulted Christ with legions of demons behind him, but Jesus Christ overcame him without even angels at his back. He said in the crisis of his great passion, "Thinkest thou not that I could pray to my Father and he should presently send me more than twelve legions of angels?" He could have summoned hosts of angels, but he met Satan single-handed like a champion in the fight. He preferred so to meet him that the disaster and the defeat of the Devil might be the more overwhelming and awful.

Christ is not only a God of all power, but he is a God of all wisdom. Satan is very wise, but he is not omniscient, and Christ is. If Satan understood something of the subtleties of a human heart, and the ways to reach that human heart with ten thousand forms of temptation, Jesus Christ is still wiser than Satan, and can discern the movements of the Devil afar off, and warn His servants against the subtlety and secrecy of his approach.

Then Jesus Christ is everywhere present. I speak more emphatically of this because there are some people who seem to think that if there be a devil at all he is omnipresent, everywhere present. For as they argue, "is not Satan represented as moving in your heart, and moving in my heart, and if he moves in the hearts of all men, and at the same time, is he not everywhere present?" That position is founded upon a great mistake, which has long since been exposed by Robert Hall in one of his discourses. There is no one that is everywhere present but Almighty God, and we must not be misled even by the language of Holy Scripture. Let us remember that it is a common thing to speak of a certain person as doing what the agents of that person do. For instance, you attribute to Queen

Victoria, as your sovereign, all that her subordinates do in all parts of the empire and its dependencies. You say that the act of her ministers and her magistrates is the act of your queen, and that is true. A general-in-chief on the battlefield can be in but one place at any one time, and yet if he has ten thousand officers under him, and they are executing his orders, and acting in obedience to his commands, you say these are the acts of the general-in-chief. You say, "He made a sally against the foe over there," or, "He assailed and captured that citadel." You say, "He repulsed and defeated that regiment," although he himself may have been on some commanding height on the battlefield, and all these things were only manœuvres executed in obedience to his orders, by his subordinates. So Satan could personally work only in one human heart at one time, but all that his subordinates accomplish is properly attributed in the Word of God to him, because it is under his mastery or control. But Jesus Christ is an omnipresent God. He is in your heart, and in my heart, and the heart of every disciple, by the Holy Spirit, so that of a true child of God we may still say, "He that is in you is greater than he that is in the world," since He is the all-powerful, the all-wise, and the all-present God.

And, then, remember that Jesus Christ represents perfect holiness. There is a common impression in the minds of people that darkness is as positively powerful as light. That is a great mistake. What is darkness? Darkness is the absence of light. What is light? Light is not the absence of darkness only; light is something real and positive. There was darkness in this house before the sun rose this morning and shone into it. But what is the sunlight? It is something actual and real; while the darkness is only the absence of sunlight, so that the darkness does not drive the light away, but the light drives the darkness away. Let us all remember that. And so Jesus Christ represents infinite holiness, and holiness, like the light of the sun, positively dispels the darkness, that is to say infinite holiness repels evil and drives evil to the wall; and in the great ages to come, when Christ shall be crowned as King, we shall find darkness absolutely dispersed and light pervading the moral universe.

Now I come to the more practical part of this discourse. I have shown you something of the greatness of Satan, and something of the greatness of our dear Lord. The question is, What is the secret of our possession and exercise of this overcoming power? We are told in this wonderful epistle that there are three secrets of overcoming power. It is marvellous how the Bible tells its own story if it is properly read. If you will examine this First Epistle of John throughout, and read it prayerfully and carefully, you will find the whole secret of overcoming power laid down here. In the second chapter and fourteenth verse we read, " I have written unto you, young men, because ye are strong." What is the secret of their strength? " And the Word of God abideth in you, and ye have overcome the wicked one." Now turn to the third chapter. Let us read in the eighth and ninth verses. " For this purpose the Son of God was manifested, that he might destroy the works of the devil. Whosoever is born of God doth not commit sin; for his seed remaineth in him : and he cannot sin, because he is born of God." And then in the twenty-fourth verse of the same chapter, " And he that keepeth his commandments dwelleth in him, and He in him." Here are the three secrets whereby you overcome the devil. ✻The first secret is, *the Word of God* abides in you. ✻The second is *the seed of God* abides in you; and the third is *God himself* abides in you. That is the reason why the apostle says, "Greater is he that is in you than he that is in the world."

Now look successively at these three secrets. The Word of God is represented in the Scriptures as the "sword of the Spirit," "a two-edged sword." A Damascus scimitar has but one sharp edge and a dull back. Hence you can hew with a scimitar, but you cannot thrust with it successfully. But when you have two edges to a sword, and each side is keen, you can cut both ways with such a blade; and the two keen edges unite in one burning point, and you can thrust with such a sword. And so the Word of God is represented as having two keen edges and one burning piercing point. Again, it is represented as a living sword. The Word of God is quick, *i.e.*, alive and powerful, and sharper than any two edged sword. This sword is represented as going out of the mouth of Christ, for he speaks the Word of God. It is represented as being held in the hand of the Christian warrior, because his dependence is on the Word of God. Here, then, is the first secret of strength. You have in this the only offensive weapon that you are recommended to use in the Word of God; all the other pieces of armour are simply defensive; this one piece of armour is added that you may cut both ways among your enemies and thrust them even to the backbone. So that a man who knows the Word of God, and has the Word abiding in him, and is mighty in the power of that Word, is able to make his way among all opposers; and never was that illustrated more grandly than in the career of your own departed pastor whose one weapon for forty years was this Word of God, and who wielded that weapon in such a way that the enemies of God and of the truth were afraid of him, as well they might be. Knowing

the Word, and having it in your heart, you shall find that
Word going forth like a two-edged sword out of your mouth,
a living sword, and a powerful sword, that hews men to
pieces before God, and lays bare their thoughts and intents.

And then, secondly, the seed of God abides in the child
of God. The seed represents the living principle. I suppose
you are all familiar with certain great facts of nature.
You know how, for instance, in the vegetable world the seed
is the most carefully preserved and guarded of all the
products of plant life. Here is a little plant growing up
and putting out its branches and leaves, and by-and-by its
flowers. The flowers may be very beautiful and very fragrant,
and you may value them and consider them the finest
products of the plant, but, if I may use such language, the
plant does not so regard them. The thing the plant cares
most for in the economy of nature is not root nor
stem, is not beauty nor blossom, nor even fruit, but seed.
And you will find that in this great world of plant life, the
most carefully developed, and the most carefully preserved,
and the most carefully scattered, is the seed. Indeed, there
are some plants that, like the dandelion, have the power to
float their seed in the air, supported as by a parachute, so
that it shall be borne on the atmosphere, and then when the
seed lodges it has a little hook to fasten in the soil and root
itself there. And there are other seeds that are variously
supplied with appliances for their distribution and propagation; I think I have counted fifty different methods by
which the seed in nature preserves itself and scatters itself
when it is ripe. Now the seed in the plant and the seed in
animal represent not only the highest products of life, but
the means of producing and propagating life, and therefore
the seed is the most precious thing in nature. And how

significant it is that the principle of life in God which represents the highest perfection of Deity and represents the means by which God's likeness is reproduced in you and in me is called by the sacred name of "seed," and we are told that when the seed of God remains in us we feel that we cannot sin. We have a new *affinity*. I want even these dear boys here to understand what I am saying—I want to use this word intelligently, and so will explain it. Now, my young friends, you have all heard the word "affinity." That is a big word, but it means simply this, a desire or drawing after something that is like myself. We say, "Birds of a feather flock together," "Fishes go in shoals," or "Insects go in swarms." These are all illustrations of the law of affinity in nature, and this law is singularly illustrated in the case of seed. Suppose I take a little germ of sugar-cane and put it in the earth, it will take up sugar. That is what makes sugar-cane sweet, and gives us molasses, as we call it,—or sugar in its refined form. If I set an asparagus germ in the earth that takes up the salt, because the asparagus is a sea-weed and lives on salt. If I set a peach tree, it takes from the ground and the atmosphere what we call prussic acid, and that gives the peachy nutty flavour to the peach as to the almond. Every plant has its affinity. One for sugar, one for starch, one for salt; and these plants take up out of the soil that for which they have affinity. So when the seed of God is planted in us we may be put in the soil of worldly society, but we select out of the soil and atmosphere the things of God not the things of man—that for which we have a divine affinity, and we feel we cannot sin because we are born of God. And so we come to have the sugar of God in us, and the salt of the gospel in us: we do not absorb the poisonous evils of this world, we do not take them up, but we have affinity for the things of God. We are like a tree planted by the rivers of water with its little spongelets at the end of the roots drinking up the blessed water of life, and making sap of it. That is what John means when he says the seed of God is in the disciple, and he feels that he cannot sin because the seed of God leads him to love the things of God and hate the things of the evil one.

But we are told once more that God Himself abides in us. Read John xiv. 23. " If a man love Me, he will keep My words : and My Father will love him, and we will come unto him, and make our abode with him." God would have you to feel this great fact, that if Jesus Christ dwells in you by the Holy Spirit, He makes you strong to overcome Satan, as He himself was strong to overcome Satan in the desert and in the Garden of Gethsemane, and that is the secret of your triumph over evil.

Did you ever ask yourself that question which Friday is said to have asked Robinson Crusoe, " Why God not kill the devil ? " Did you ever ask yourselves how it is that we find sin in the universe of God ? I suppose we shall never be able to answer that question, certainly not on this earth, but it is possible, perhaps, to give you a hint or two about it. Perhaps it is necessary to a free moral agent that he shall have the power to sin as well as to obey. Now I grant you that God could keep sin out of the universe, but it might be by making such beings as we are, little more than machines. If a being is created, free to choose right or wrong, the possibility of sinning may be involved in the fact of such freedom. Certain it is that of all the intelligent beings that God has created, some appear to have turned from their first estate. Satan and his hosts fell from their original

The Secret of Overcoming Satan

innocence by voluntarily sinning against God. Man was created in innocence but in freedom, and like the fallen angels abused his liberty, and fell into ruin.

But there is another thought that I feel more sure of, and I throw out this as a helpful suggestion, that for us who are in a world of sin and sorrow, contact and conflict with sin is one secret of all highest attainment in holiness. I wonder if you have ever thought that the various animals in this world may represent some form of vice or sin that men are guilty of, as though God has put these vices in the form of an animal that we might see how hateful they are. For instance, the peacock represents pride, and the turkey-cock represents vanity. The fox represents cunning, and the serpent represents subtlety. The wolf represents rapacity, the tiger represents ferocity, the panther represents deception and treachery, the lion represents arbitrary use of power and strength, and so the swine represent sensuality, and the sloth represents laziness. When you look at these animals what do you see? You see the vices that curse humanity, embodied in hateful, ugly, repulsive forms. Did it ever occur to you that you have got one of these animals inside of you; that if you are cunning there is a fox there, that if you are treacherous there is a panther there, that if you are revengeful there is a tiger there, that if you are arbitrary and overbearing there is a lion there, that if you are lazy there is a sloth there, that if you are given to lust there are swine there? Did it ever occur to you that you are a menagerie all at once, a cage of unclean birds and beasts; that to-day cunning comes up like a fox, and to-morrow treachery like a panther, and the next day subtlety like a serpent, and the next day some other form of vice that may be represented by one of these animals? I do not intend to awaken a smile, for it is serious business, but as I have lived long, more than fifty years, and have looked into the depth of my own heart from time to time, I have felt that there was a whole menagerie of wild animals right in my own heart needing to be tamed and subdued.

A friend once asked an aged man what caused him so often to complain of pain and weariness in the evening. "Alas!" said he, "I have every day so much to do. I have two falcons to tame, two hares to keep from running away, two hawks to manage, a serpent to confine, a lion to chain, and a sick man to tend and wait upon." "Why, you must be joking," said his friend; "surely no man can have all these things to do at once." "Indeed, I am not joking," said the old man, "but what I have told you is the sad, sober truth; for the two falcons are my two eyes, which I must diligently guard; the two hares are my feet, which I must keep from walking in the ways of sin; the two hawks are my two hands, which I must train to work, that I may be able to provide for myself and for my brethren in need; the serpent is my tongue, which I must always bridle, lest it speak unseemly; the lion is my heart, with which I have a continued fight, lest evil things come out of it; and the sick man is my whole body, which is always needing my watchfulness and care. All this daily wears out my strength."

Now, how are you, as God's saint, to overcome the evil that is in yourself and this world? If, for instance, cunning rises up in your heart like a fox, and you defeat and destroy cunning, there is one animal the less to contend with. If deception comes up, and you subdue your tendency to deception, there is a serpent that is strangled. If some other form of sin, like lust, is slain, there is a whole herd of swine

The Secret of Overcoming Satan

driven out of you. Let us not fear to come into close contact with sin, for every time in the strength of God you vanquish your sin, you vanquish one of those low forms of animal life in you, and you will thus become finally triumphant as a man in God over all these forms of evil.

[These thoughts seem to have no little warrant in the Word of God. The Psalmist says, "I was as a beast before Thee." Jude, verse 10, compares certain ignorant evil speakers to "brute beasts," etc. In different parts of the Word of God, man in his depravity and corruption and sensuality and indifference to holy things is compared unfavourably to twenty different forms of animal life.

To the Ass, in Proverbs xxvi. 3.
To the Bear, in Daniel vii. 5.
To the Boar, in Psalm lxxx. 13.
To the Bullock, in Isaiah xxxi. 18.
To Dogs (wild), in Phil. iii. 2 ; 2 Peter ii. 22 ; Mat. vii. 6.
To Dogs (mad), in Proverbs xxvi. 18, 19.
To the Fox, in Matthew viii. 20 ; Luke xiii. 22.
To Jackals, in Canticles ii. 15.
To the Goat, in Daniel vii. 5.
To the Horse, in Psalm xxxii. 9.
To the Horseleech, in Proverbs xxx. 15.
To the Leopard, in Jeremiah xiii. 23 ; Revelation xiii. 2.
To the Lion, in 2 Timothy iv. 17.
To the Mule, in Psalm xxxii. 9.
To the Ox, Isaiah i. 3.
To the Serpent, in Matthew x. 16.
To the Swine, in 2 Peter ii. 22 ; Matthew vii. 6.
To the Vulture, in Matthew xxiv. 28.
To the Viper, in Matthew xxiii. 33.
To the Wolf, in Acts xx. 29 ; Matthew vii. 15.

Thus the whole round of the animal creation is explored, to find types of stupidity, violence, rage, obstinacy, ferocity, rapacity, bloodthirstiness and cruelty, malice and malignity, cunning and fraud, depredation and destruction, stubbornness and insensibility, wilfulness and waywardness, insatiate greed and selfishness, treachery and stealthiness, wrath and hate, insinuating flattery and subtlety, sensuality and beastliness, slander and venom, and every conceivable form of diabolical passions and warfare against God and man. The theme demands far more careful treatment than the space available now allows.]

Let us also notice that Satan having for ages practised iniquity, represents every possible form of sin in himself; and, therefore, if you come into conflict with him and vanquish him, you practically vanquish all foes in vanquishing him. He is like Goliath, who was the strongest of the Philistines. It would scarcely have been any more a triumph for David to have met every one of those Philistines single-handed one after the other, and to have vanquished them than it was to meet the strength and pride and arrogant defiance of them all in one giant, and bring him to the earth. So God lets you and me come into close conflict with the devil in order that by the strength of Christ in us we may accomplish a conquest over him who is the giant champion of evil, and may in him virtually put all the forces of evil to flight. If you have never thought of this it is worth coming across the sea to give saints the comfort of that thought. If we are in Christ, and He in us, let us not fear even Satan, for " He that is in you is greater than he that is in the world."

I think you have noticed that I never preach a sermon to the children only, and why? There are some of my brethren that have a sort of "prelude"—I do not think that was known in apostolic times, but it is a modern invention—a sort of a preliminary sermon to children, and after they have got through with their ten minutes' talk to them, the children are supposed not to have much interest in what follows. I want these children to understand that I never preach a sermon without thinking of them, and putting something in the sermon that they will understand. And now the rest of you need not listen unless you choose, but I wish to talk to these orphanage boys just for a few moments, and apply this truth to them.

"Ye are of God, little children, and have overcome these foes, because greater is he that is in you, than he that is in the world." Here the Spirit of God speaks to "little children," and I want you to understand that if Jesus lives in you, He is just as mighty in you to overcome the devil as He is in the oldest saint in this house, because it is not the age of the saint, it is not the long life of the saint, or his attainments, that makes him able to overcome the devil. It is only the fact that Jesus is in him; and if Jesus is in a little child he shall overcome Satan just as well as a man eighty years of age. I suppose you have all read about Hercules. Hercules was the ancient god of strength. I suppose that very likely the Romans and Greeks got the idea of Hercules from the story of Samson told by the Israelites. Now we are told that when Hercules was a little baby in his cradle, there were some serpents that came into the room and wound their way into the cradle and tried to sting him, and folding their coils round him to choke the life out of him. But we are told in the fable that with his little hands he just took hold of the necks of these serpents and strangled them to death. God would have you to feel that a little babe in Christ that is rocked in the cradle of the Church, when he comes into contact with the great serpent, the devil, if Jesus is in him, can beat back the serpent, the serpent cannot strangle him.

But then, dear boys, remember this, that you are only strong when you are on the Lord's ground, not on the devil's ground. Now I have read a story about a swan that was walking on the shore of a lake, and a wolf came up and ran after the swan and would have torn him to pieces. But the swan said to himself, " I am not strong on the land, but I am strong on the water." So he plunged into the water, and when the wolf followed him into the water, he with his strong bill just gripped the wolf by the ears, and pulled his head down under the water, and drowned him. There are a great many people, dear boys, who try to fight the devil on the devil's ground, and they always get defeated ; but if you can meet the devil on the Lord's ground you will defeat him. Compel him if he assails you at all, to come to the fountain of water and blood that is opened in the house of David for sin and uncleanness ; and when you are thus on the Lord's ground, and close by the shelter of the Lord's presence and power, you are strong and the devil is weak, and you can easily overcome him, because in Christ you are abiding, and Christ is abiding in you. Yes, little children, greater is He that is in you, than he that is in the world.

Do not let us be afraid even of the devil. Get out of the way of temptation if you can just as well as not, but when you cannot avoid meeting temptation, when you are bound to face it, and when it is cowardice to flee, stand your ground. Meet the devil, and all the foes that the adversary can bring against you, and depend upon it, that He that is in you, by His word, and by His seed, and by His spirit, is infinitely greater than all those that be against you.

Perhaps, that young man is in the house and hears me, who had a conversation with me a few days ago, and told me that he was in the grip of a life of awful sin, that he had long been a sinner, and a flagrant sinner, given to vices of which I could not speak here, and feeling himself to be dragged down to hell by those evil doings. I want that dear young man to feel that God gave me this sermon specially for him. I have thought of him, in that awful fight with the devil that is to issue either in his salvation or in his damnation, and I ask him to think that God means this little message for him. You need not fear the devil if you are abiding in God, and God is abiding in you, and if you are meeting the devil on the Lord's ground, and not on his own ground, you can resist every effort to arrest or hinder your spiritual life. Believe in God, believe in His power, cast yourselves upon Him, and let His Spirit, and word, and seed abide in you and make you mighty to overcome all evil!

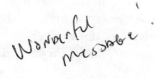

Sermon Three

Sin's Dominion Destroyed

"For sin shall not have dominion over you: for ye are not under the law, but under grace."—ROMANS vi. 14.

THE greatest demand of our day is for a higher type of piety on the part of God's children. John tells us, in his First Epistle, third chapter, eighth verse, "For this purpose the Son of God was manifested, that he might destroy the works of the devil." And if so, the works of the devil in your heart and mine certainly ought to be destroyed. The argument in the sixth and seventh chapters of the Epistle to the Romans covers this subject, the privilege and the duty of the child of God to be freed from the power and dominion of sin; and the key to both of these chapters is supplied in the first verse of the sixth chapter: "What shall ye say then? Shall we continue in sin, that grace may abound? God forbid."

First, then, let us look at the argument of Paul, then at a certain reason or consideration that he urges, for "Ye are not under the law, but under grace"; and then draw some practical inferences.

First, his argument. I am quite aware that this is a very difficult subject to discuss, and I therefore ask your closest attention, for I shall try to make it as plain as I possibly can. This argument is illustrated in three ways. First, judicially; second, maritally; and thirdly, actually. Let me explain these terms. First, it is looked at in the light of a judgment; secondly, in the light of marriage; thirdly, in the light of actual duty and privilege. The word "judicially" refers to that which pertains to a judge; and we are all familiar with the meaning and application of this word in our courts of law. For example, over a dead criminal the law has absolutely no hold. If a man has been executed for a crime like murder, the moment that he is pronounced to be dead by the attending physicians and surgeons, the law has no more control over him; it can execute no more vengeance upon the dead criminal, and his body is often given into the hands of his surviving relatives. to be buried. There are some very remarkable features about this law process. I will give you two examples that will show what is meant. There is a story in law books to this effect, that in one instance a man had been hanged and his body was given over into the custody of his friends, and they succeeded in bringing life back into what appeared to be a dead body; and the decision of the judge was that the law had no more hold over that criminal, he having been executed and declared to be dead, and delivered over into the hands of his friends. They had successfully resuscitated the body, but the law had executed its penalty upon him, and he was no longer amenable to justice. A more remarkable case than this occurred in my own country, of which I was told just before I left home. A judge in one of the Southern States had sentenced a criminal to be executed on a certain day, at a certain hour. Through some misapprehension of the sheriff or a misunderstanding of some sort, the appointed hour and day passed by without such execution. Then the question was, What shall be done with this man? The judge was appealed to, and he said, "This criminal is now unknown to the Court. Such a day and hour were appointed for his execution; he is supposed to have been executed, and the Court knows no such man." Now, whatever you may think of these applications of law they illustrate this: there is such a thing as a man being dead in the eyes of the law, which is the argument of the Apostle first of all in this chapter. He says that by the death of Jesus Christ you, a believer, have become dead to the law, so that you are judicially free. The law condemned you, but Jesus Christ atoned for you, and your faith and your repentance make you one with the atoning Saviour, so that the law says it has no longer any hold on that penitent and believing sinner. You, as a believer, died with Christ, were buried with Him, rose with Him, and, in the eyes of God, ascended with Him, and are now seated in the heavenlies, and the law has no longer any power to condemn you. That is the position of the Word of God. We may find illustrations of this in history. It is said that in the wars of Napoleon there was a man drafted to enter into the French army. There were circumstances which prevented his going, and he hired a substitute to go in his place. That substitute went into the war and died on the battle-field. Another draft was made, and this man was again drafted. He appeared at the recruiting office and said: "I, in the person of my substitute, died on the field of battle, and I can never be drafted again;" which was true, and he was released. Now look at the argument of the first ten verses of this chapter: "What shall we say then? shall we continue in sin, that grace may abound?

God forbid. How shall we, that are dead to sin, live any longer therein? Know ye not, that so many of us as were baptized unto Jesus Christ were baptized into His death? Therefore we are buried with Him by baptism into death: that like as Christ was raised up from the dead by the glory of the Father, even so we also should walk in newness of life. For if we have been planted together in the likeness of his death, we shall also be in the likeness of his resurrection. Knowing this, that our old man is" [not *shall be*] "crucified with Him, that the body of sin might be destroyed, that henceforth we should not serve him. For he that is dead is freed from sin. Now if we be dead with Christ, we believe that we shall also live with Him: Knowing that Christ being raised from the dead dieth no more: death hath no more dominion over him : " so that, just as Christ rose from the dead never again to die, you that are in Him, having died in Him, and risen in Him, have risen to die no more, risen into newness of resurrection life. Magnificent conception !

Now look at the second illustration of the argument, drawn from marriage. Read from the 7th chapter, the first few verses. " Know ye not brethren, (for I speak to them that know the law,) how that the law hath dominion over a man as long as he liveth? For the woman which hath an husband is bound by the law to her husband so long as he liveth; but if the husband be dead, she is loosed from the law of her husband. So then if, while her husband liveth, she be married to another man, she shall be called an adulteress: but if her husband be dead, she is free from that law; so that she is no adulteress, though she be married to another man. Wherefore, my brethren, ye also are become dead to the law by the body of Christ; that ye should be married to another, even to him who is raised from the dead, that we should bring forth fruit unto God."

As the Apostle has illustrated this great argument from the department of judicial life or the law, he now illustrates it from the department of marital life. Let us look at the illustration. There are two ways in which a marriage can be dissolved in the eyes of God. One is by that particular form of abhorrent sin, which, in laying the foundation for another family, saps the foundation of the former family relation; and the other is by death. If the husband dies, the wife is free to marry again; if the wife dies the husband is free to marry again. Now, the Apostle says, you have become dead in the body of Christ to the law; that is, he compares the believer to a wife married, and the law is compared to a husband having a hold over the body of the wife. Paul argues that you are dead to the law, and therefore the law has no hold on you any more; and furthermore, that in Christ the law is dead to you, and therefore you are no longer in bondage to the law. That is the argument framed into a new illustration. Let us look more closely at it. Christ's death slays the law, not as a rule of life, but as a source of condemnation. Faith in Jesus Christ implies the legal death of the believer to the law, dissolving the bond of law and the bondage of sin. We are told that in heaven they neither marry nor are given in marriage, but faith forms a spiritual union with Jesus Christ that is far above the physical union implied in marriage. As, when the wife dies she passes out of the body, and out of the sphere of the body into another where she is no longer under the control of the husband whose marriage covenant had a hold upon her so long as she was in the body; so the believer who dies to the law is free to be married in a spiritual sphere to the Lord Jesus Christ as a husband. That is the illustration. Once you were bound by the law. It was like a husband that had despotic control over you as a wife, but from the moment that you believed in Jesus Christ, His death on the cross had slain the law and destroyed its despotic control over you; and in Jesus Christ you yourself died to the law, and became free in another sphere to be married unto your Redeemer.

There is still another department in which this thought is illustrated, and that is in actual life. The first I referred to was what is called a legal fiction — that is to say, if it is not an actual reality, it is a way that the law has of construing the facts; the second was simply an image or illustration to give us in vivid form the truth presented by the other. But now Paul comes down to the department of actual life: let us see what is here said from verses 11 to 14, " Likewise reckon ye also yourselves to be dead indeed unto sin, but alive unto God through Jesus Christ our Lord. Let not sin, therefore, reign in your mortal body, that ye should obey it in the lusts thereof. Neither yield ye your members as instruments of unrighteousness unto sin; but yield yourselves unto God, as those that are alive from the dead, and your members as instruments of righteousness unto God. For sin shall not have dominion over you."

If you do not understand the argument from the judicial side, or from the marriage side, mark the distinct declaration of God here. This is a series of injunctions. "Reckon yourselves dead," "let not sin reign," "yield not your members," "sin shall not have dominion over you." I wonder that, having read these words a thousand times, I should never have seen the force and power of them as they are now impressed upon me; and I most earnestly pray

God that I may make these commands bear heavily upon your consciences, and at the same time uplift you by their marvellous assurances that God is on your side. What does this mean, "*Reckon* ye yourselves to be dead"? The word "reckon" means to think of ourselves, to count ourselves, as dead unto sin but alive unto God. When you take account of your own condition, look at yourself as a redeemed man or woman and as having been slain so far as the law is concerned. We have an instance of the same teaching in Chapter xiii. 14, and perhaps the best commentary on it is thus in this same Epistle to the Romans: " But put ye on the Lord Jesus Christ" (that is, as a garment) " and *make not provision* for the flesh to fulfil the lusts thereof." Life is a constant providing against the future. You know that your appetite that has been satisfied to-day will return by-and-by. You know that you are liable to be taken ill, and so you make provision against possible illness. You men that are in business know that losses may overtake you, and so you provide a margin of profit, so that what you lose in one transaction may be made up by other bargains. We know that death is before us, and we are constantly making provision against the dying hour, and drawing up a will so that whatever little or much property we may have may be disposed of according to our pleasure, and our sense of right; we are thus arranging things with reference to the dying hour, and many men have insured their lives so that their families shall not be left in destitution. I remember a man who said that he was always accustomed to make such preparation for death, that if it should overtake him at any time his business might be found in order. His rule was, " Think of yourself as about to die to-day; act and live as though you were to live for ever"; that is, go about your duty as though you had eternity in which to do it ; but feel all the time that you are liable at any moment to pass away. And when latterly he did actually pass away his wife said that everything about his business, about his family, and other persons for whom he had been a trustee, was found on the night of his death to be absolutely in order. Now think of yourself as dead to sin : and make no provision for the flesh. If you knew you were never going to be hungry again you would not have made preparations at home for another meal, would you ? If you knew that your shoes would never wear out, you would not order another pair of shoes this week, would you ? If you knew that the clothes you were wearing would never need to be replaced by another suit, you would not trouble yourself to get money saved up for another, would you ? If you knew that there was no possibility of your dwelling falling out of repairs you would not lay aside anything to put in new timbers, or new bricks, or new plaster on the walls. How plain this is ! do you not see that we are constantly making provision against contingencies that are liable to come—want, loss, sickness, death, disaster of every kind? Now the apostle says, " Do not make provision for the flesh as though you expected to fulfil its lusts ; do not reckon yourselves as sinners, but reckon yourselves as saints : and, therefore, do not provide for sin, as though you expected to commit sin, but make no provision for committing it." What an injunction that ! may God help you and me never more to think of ourselves as a stronghold in which sin is entrenched, and where the devil has his habitation ; but to think of ourselves as the sanctuary of God in whom the Holy Spirit dwells. And, just as the care-taker of a temple in charge of the holy courts is not making provision for a theatrical performance where the gospel is going to be preached, is not making provision for all sorts of worldly and secular entertainments, where Jesus Christ is the head and enthroned, so you as the Sacristan that is in charge of God's temple, are not to calculate on its being defiled by sin, but calculate on its being inhabited by God, and sanctified by the power of the Holy Ghost. Would that I could command the trump of Gabriel to declare this truth to this people this morning! I have long as a child of God lived more or less in the expectation of sinning; I am ashamed of it. I have calculated on sin, and calculated on repentance, and calculated on forgiveness, and swung like a pendulum now toward sin, and again toward sorrow for sin, and then back to sin again. I am ashamed of this. I confess it before God and before you this morning. Reckon yourselves to be dead, do not reckon yourselves to be living unto sin; reckon yourselves not to be castles of the devil where he has right and is bound to control, but reckon on yourselves as the temples of God, and say to yourselves to-day, "The Holy Spirit is in me, I must walk softly and keep these courts clean, and free from idols, and see that there is a holy offering on God's altars, and that the holy lamps are kept always burning."

Yes, the Apostle adds, not only reckon yourselves dead and make no provision for your lusts, but let not sin reign in your mortal body. When the devil asserts over you the right to rule, dispute every inch of territory. Say "Thou shalt not?" When Satan advances to assume control of you, stand your ground and reply, "This is God's temple, it is not thy stronghold. Begone; get thee hence"! Go down on your knees; Satan cannot advance over a kneeling Christian, and never did yet. Call on Almighty God, and say, "Lord.

this is Thy temple, drive back the adversary that would take possession and lift the black flag of revolt over the turrets of Thy sanctuary!" Do not let sin reign in your mortal body. Dispute, as I have said, every inch of territory, and every step of advance.

Let us hear Paul once again, "Neither yield ye your members as instruments of unrighteousness unto sin; but yield yourselves unto God, as those that are alive from the dead." Jonathan Edwards said at the Lord's table, "I have this day solemnly covenanted with my Saviour, that as he gave Himself wholly for me I will surrender myself wholly to Him. Henceforth, these eyes shall not look with lust, but they shall look as the eyes of Christ; these ears shall hearken to no impure suggestion, they shall hearken unto the words of my God; these hands shall handle no uncleanness, the name of God shall be written on the palms of my hands, and these feet shall walk not in ungodly ways, but softly and sweetly before my God." I want you to feel, I want to feel, that these members belong to Christ. Shall I take the members of Christ and make them the members of a harlot? Shall I engage in the harlotry of this world while Christ owns me and has purchased my members? Shall I give faculties of mind or body to the service of the devil when Christ owns me wholly? No! let me be obedient to God! And so the apostle who says, "Reckon yourselves dead, let not sin reign in your mortal body, let not your members be instruments of unrighteousness unto sin," teaches us, positively, to "Obey from the heart." Let us look at that suggestive verse, the 17th,—"But God be thanked that ye were the servants of sin—" your service of sin lies in the past,— ye *were* servants of sin, but " ye have obeyed from the heart that form of doctrine which was delivered to you." If you notice the marginal reading it is this—"That form or mould of doctrine into which ye were delivered." Now, I suppose, we have some persons here this morning that are moulders, that are casters, and who know what the foundry business is. You go into a foundry, and there is a cast, or mould, or matrix. The metal is put into the furnace and heated to a white heat, and poured into the moulds, and presently the moulds are knocked to pieces, and you see the various castings. Here is, for instance, the bed-plate of a range. It has only filled out part of the mould; it is imperfect, and it is knocked to pieces, and the pieces are put into the furnace again and melted over. And there is another casting of some sort that has run out in one direction and taken form, but there is a portion of the mould that has not been taken on. That also is knocked to pieces and put into the furnace again. But here is something else that has filled out the whole form, and every impression of the mould is left on the metal, and that is useful for the purposes of manufacture. Now the apostle says, "Once ye were servants of sin"; but you have been broken down by contrition and put into the furnace of God, and you have been melted down into holy surrender and submission, and then you were poured into the gospel mould, and you filled out the gospel form, and took the whole impression of gospel teaching. Ah, dear friends, why should not we take on the whole impression of the gospel mould, and instead of yielding ourselves unto Satan, yield ourselves unto God, get impressed more and more with Godliness, and manifest the spirit and temper of Godliness more and more in our lives?

Now, before I pass to a few closing reflections I would say a word as to what Paul gives as a consideration. He says, "For ye are not under the law, but under grace." That is not exactly a reason, but an argument; and it is very much misunderstood. I suppose nine-tenths of people think when they read, " Ye are not under the law, but under grace," that it refers to two dispensations, one of law, like that of Abraham and Moses, one of grace, like that of Christ and the apostles And they think that the Bible says we are not under the law, but under grace, because we do not belong to a previous dispensation in which men were liable to be justified by works, but belong to the present dispensation in which we are justified by grace. And I must confess, dear friends, that I think this is a very dishonouring interpretation both to the Scriptures and the Lord. I suppose Abraham was saved just exactly as you are saved, by faith in the Atoning Lamb, only he looked forward, and you look backward. That is all the difference. Somewhat dimly he looked forward, more clearly you look backward. Praise God for that. But if you are saved by faith so was he; for he believed, and "it was counted unto him for righteousness."

But now, while in every case in which these words are used they may not mean exactly the same thing, it is perfectly evident what they must mean here. There are motives for your not allowing sin to have dominion over you, because you are not " under the law, but under grace." The idea is that, when a man is under the law, he cannot live a holy life. The moment a man transgresses he comes under the dominion of the law; I do not care whether his transgression is known to other people or not. Suppose that there was a man on the streets here that this day committed murder and nobody knew it but himself. That man goes about with the consciousness that every other man that is looking into his eyes is charging him with murder, every police officer he sees coming towards him he thinks may have a warrant for his arrest; and his conscience proclaims him a murderer, though no man may proclaim him to be such, and from the time he commits that crime he is under the law, although the law may not yet have ferreted him out or put him into gaol. Adam committed sin, and when God came into the garden in the cool of the day to walk with man, Adam and Eve shrank right away from the presence of God, and before God said a word to them, they hid themselves behind the trees of the garden. They were under the law. Do not you see they had broken the law, and the law had its sword hanging over them, and although God had not accused them, and there was no man to accuse them, their conscience accused them, and they knew they were guilty? And when Joseph's brothers stood before him, he did not accuse them. They did not know it was Joseph. God did not accuse them, but they said, "We are verily guilty concerning our brother, in that we saw the anguish of his soul when he besought us, and we would not hear; therefore is this distress come upon us." You see, from the day they sinned against their brother, they were under the law, the penalty of the law, and the sense of the power of the law, and the power of sin was in them. Just so the moment a man transgresses the law of God, he is under the law, and the law has dominion over him.

And then, in the second place, he has become a sinner, and the consequence is that his character is in ruin. If an angel to-day should rebel against God and refuse to do God's bidding, he would not simply become a transgressor of the law, but he would shatter himself as well as break the law of God. The moment you fling the tables of the law down, and break them by your transgressions, you break yourself as well as the law. And as you cannot repair the battered, broken, shattered tables of the law, you cannot repair the battered, broken, shattered character. Once innocent, now guilty, Adam could not recover himself to where he was before. He had sinned. No repentance would do; no reformation would do. Suppose you are going along a level way and you come to a chasm and desire somehow or other to get across that chasm and go on to the level beyond. You must have the chasm bridged. There is no way across the wide gulf unless there is a bridge built there. Now, suppose a man goes along in a moral life and comes to a point where he sins. Sin constitutes an awful chasm, and even if he could begin a moral life again and go on as before, there is that awful chasm to be bridged, and he cannot do it; no good works cannot repair past evil doing. The thought I want you to get hold of is that the moment Adam sinned, the moment any man sins—he is under the law, the penalty of the law overhangs him, and the power of the sin remains in his own shattered constitution and character. The consequence is that no sinner can ever undo his own evil-doing. It is impossible in the nature of the case. Now when Jesus Christ comes and offers salvation, and puts away the penalty of the law because He bore it, He breaks up the power of sin because He gives a new nature, and He will more and more banish the presence of sin if you will allow Him to do it by the entire surrender of yourself to Him, until you come into the heavenly life itself, where nothing enters which defiles, works abomination or makes a lie. Therefore, when the apostle says, "Sin shall not have dominion over you," he adds, "Ye are not under the law, not under its penalty, and have no right to be under its power, and ye ought to be more and more rid of its presence for you are under grace."

Now suffer me to gather these thoughts up as well as I can in a few words of practical suggestion. In the first place, there is a divine call to holiness—mark that, "Be ye holy for I am holy." God does not mock us. The command to be holy implies that there is, in God, power to be holy, and that all we have to do is to lay hold of that power and we shall be holy. I wonder if you have ever noticed these remarkable words in 1 Corinthians vi. 13, "The body is not for fornication but for the Lord, and the Lord for the body." Not only is the body for the Lord. We shall all admit that. That is to say, when I come to Christ and give myself to Him, accept him as my Saviour, my body is for Him, its powers and faculties for Him. But did you ever observe that we are also told that *the Lord is for the body*? That is to say, if you have given your body for the Lord, He has given Himself to you, and as you have consecrated your body to Him—shall I say it?—He has dedicated Almighty power, love, wisdom, and grace, to the sustaining of your body in the overcoming of sinful lust and the carrying out of your purpose to be His! So that you have the whole Godhead on your side in your determination to be holy as He is holy.

Then my second remark is, Do not be afraid that people will say of you, if you are seeking to be entirely the Lord's, that you are a perfectionist. You know I am not a perfectionist. If there is anything perfect in this world I have not yet found it, and I have had a great deal of opportunity to observe; and some of the people that are foremost to claim perfection are foremost to exemplify imperfection. But I am perfectly certain of this, that if there be one danger in seeking perfection, there are a thousand in being content with imperfection. Do not be frightened by the ghost of a word, do not be alarmed because people may possibly say of you in your endeavour to be entirely the Lord's, and to live a sinless life before Him, that you are advocating perfectionism,—let each of you by your life and by your lips witness that you are never going to be satisfied with anything that lacks the image of Jesus, and entire conformity to His pattern. I think there is a good deal of difference between the two forms of expression,— "No longer able to sin," and "able no longer to sin,"— quite two different things. The perfectionist says, "I am no longer able to sin"; the child of God that understands his privileges, and lays his hand on the right hand of his Father, says, "By the grace of God I am able no longer to sin; I put my foot on the old lusts I indulged, and the old appetites that I gratified."

Now, once more. We are saved by hope. What your expectation is about your life will be very largely what your realization is. You remember that when in *Pilgrim's Progress* Christian got into Doubting Castle, and was in despair about himself, he found there was a key that opened its gates, the Key of Hope; and by the Key of Hope he got out of it. Now, your sin is a Doubting Castle. If you expect to sin, you will sin; if by the grace of God you expect not to sin, that very expectation becomes in God the Key of Hope to you, and it opens the doors to let you free. Suppose that this great congregation, to a man and woman, this morning, should go out of this house and lift up holy hands and hearts and say, "O God, Thou hast bidden me to be holy as Thou art holy. Thou hast said my body is for the Lord, and the Lord is for my body; henceforth this shall be Thy temple. I will think of myself as Thy temple; I will not reckon that I am going to sin, but going to serve. I will not yield my members as instruments of unrighteousness to sin; I will not let sin reign over me; I will dispute every inch of territory, and every step of advance on the part of the adversary." And if you have lost the greatest preacher of the age, my brethren, this Tabernacle congregation may remain the greatest preacher of this or all ages in the testimony of what God can do to purify unto Himself a peculiar people zealous of good works.

SERMON FOUR

The Security of the Saint

The text is the first verse of the ninety-first Psalm:

"HE THAT DWELLETH IN THE SECRET PLACE OF THE MOST HIGH SHALL ABIDE UNDER THE SHADOW OF THE ALMIGHTY."

Eleven Psalms in this book of Psalms are, in the Talmud, ascribed to Moses. Over the ninetieth Psalm, we find the inscription: "A prayer of Moses the man of God." Of course the authorship of these two Psalms is ascribed to Moses only by tradition, and we have no certainty about it; yet, if you examine the two Psalms, they bear evidence on their face that this tradition is probably true. And there is a thought which came to my own mind, in the study of these two sacred poems, which serves to illumine them as with a new light, and to explain and interpret their contents.

The ninetieth Psalm is a dirge of death, but the ninety-first is an anthem of life. A very marked contrast is noticeable, as we pass from the ninetieth to the ninety-first, in their entire tone. In the former, the theme is death, destruction, disaster, and the wrath of God; thousands and tens of thousands fall under the judgment of the Almighty, and a whole generation is swept away as in one night. But the ninety-first Psalm is jubilant with the air of exultation and rejoicing. "He that dwelleth in the secret place of the most High shall abide under the shadow of the Almighty"; and from beginning to end there is not a despondent tone or a suggestion of despair; it is hopeful and joyful, and ecstatic in God.

Let us suppose that these two psalms were composed by Moses with reference to the experience of the children of Israel in connection with the Exodus from Egypt. For example, as the midnight hour approached on that fatal night which left one dead in every family of Egypt, and among every herd of cattle, let us suppose that, as the Angel of Death was passing through the land, and the blood had been sprinkled on the lintels and the two side-posts; and as the families were gathered round the Paschal lamb, eating it in haste, the leader of the sacred feast of sorrow, as the Angel might be coming near to the houses which he was to "pass over," in his awful errand, chanted, or offered as a prayer, this ninetieth Psalm. The darkest midnight hour is upon them; the most awful plague ever visited on the children of men is just in the very process of infliction; and these timid and shrinking children of God, that have witnessed all the judgments that God has visited upon Egypt, are now compelled to behold that tremendous visitation which was the last great catastrophe.

We may imagine them with a trembling but trusting spirit surrounding the Paschal lamb and repeating this "Prayer of Moses:"

"Lord, thou hast been our dwelling place in all generations." . . . .

This prayer having been offered, the Angel of Death comes in front of the dwelling; and a voice is heard, outside the blood-stained door, from the Angel himself:

"He that dwelleth in the secret place of the most High shall abide under the shadow of the Almighty."

Again the trembling believer, behind the blood-stained doors, responds:

"I will say of the Lord, He is my refuge and my fortress: my God; in him will I trust."

Again the Angel answers:

"Surely he shall deliver thee from the snare of the fowler, and from the noisome pestilence." . . . . . .

In the concluding verses Jehovah himself, as though confirming all that the Angel had said, in His own person speaks to His trusting people, for this psalm is manifestly a dialogue, in which three parties are speaking.

"Because he hath set his love upon me, therefore will I deliver him." . . . . . .

We are introduced thus, to the child of God, sheltered behind the blood, addressed by the Angel of God:

" He that dwelleth in the secret place of the most High shall abide under the shadow of the Almighty;" and all the rest of this ninety-first Psalm is a sort of commentary on that first verse; and the thoughts it contains fall into two divisions: first, the place of blessed security as found by those thus sheltered in God; and secondly, the conditions by which we get into that place of security.

I. First of all, "Shall abide under the shadow of the Almighty." There is no mistaking this figure. Its natural interpretation is found, not in the wings of the Cherubim in the Holy of Holies, but in words such as our dear Lord used when He said, " How often would I have gathered thy children together, even as a hen gathereth her brood under her wings." As Bunyan says in his *Pilgrim's Progress*, there are four calls by which the hen calls to her brood. The first is the call of *night*, when they need a shelter from the dampness and from the darkness. The second is the call for *food*, when the hen would attract her little ones to pick up some dainty morsel that she has found for them. The third is the call of *danger*, when the hawk descends, or the brood is in peril. And the fourth is the call of *love*, when, with motherly desire and yearning, she would gather her brood where they may feel the softness of her breast-feathers and the warmth of her own body. So, " He shall cover thee with His feathers, and under His wings shalt thou trust." "When the night shadows are falling, when the night-hawk is descending, when food is needed by you in your hunger, or when My love yearns for a closer embrace, you shall find a safe and a delightful shelter under the shadow of My wings."

The one thought of this psalm is *deliverance*. " Surely he shall deliver thee from the snare of the fowler, and from the noisome pestilence ; " and this single verse interprets all that follows ; for all the dangers against which we are warned in the rest of the psalm may fall under one of these two divisions : they are either like the " the snare of the fowler " which may represent the perils that threaten the soul : or "the noisome pestilence" which may represent the dangers that threaten the body; and when the child of God is sheltered within His folded wings, no harm can come either to body or soul.

First, then, as to the security of the believer's *body*. " Surely he shall deliver thee . . . . . from the noisome pestilence. . . . . A thousand shall fall at thy side and ten thousand at thy right hand; but it shall not come nigh thee." "But," you ask, " do not children of God suffer from disease? Are they not prostrated upon beds of sickness, and do they not die like other men?" They do indeed, but notice the limitations suggested in this psalm : "Only with thine eyes shalt thou behold and see *the reward of the wicked.*" There are two aspects in which we may consider disease and bodily sufferings. On the one side it is obvious that these may represent Divine judgments on evil doing, and on the other side it is obvious that they may represent Divine discipline and correction for the children of God. It is not said that you shall escape such suffering as has to do with your discipline, with your education, with your perfection in the divine life ; it is only said that whatever bodily ills represent the reward or the recompense of the wicked, and are, therefore, the judgments of God, abroad in the earth, that the inhabitants of the world may learn righteousness, you, as a child of God, shall escape when you dwell in the secret place of the most High.

How often, when God's scourges sweep over the earth, when awful epidemics of pestilence rage, do the children of God, especially those that are closely abiding with great confidence and fidelity in Him, seem marvellously to escape ! Your departed pastor has often told how, in 1854, when he had been scarcely twelve months in this City, there raged in London a fearful epidemic of Asiatic cholera. With all his youthful vigour he plunged at once into the work of relieving the sick, the suffering, and the dying, and burying the dead, not sparing himself, with his proverbial unselfishness, until weary and worn with much work and much weeping, he came back from a funeral service, feeling as though he, himself, were a ready prey for this awful judgment and scourge of God. He was passing along Dover Street and he observed in the window of a shoemaker's shop a paper, wafered to the pane of glass, on which it was obvious that something was to be found besides an advertisement. He stepped up and looked at it more closely, and he found there inscribed in large characters the ninth and tenth verses of the ninety-first Psalm: " Because thou hast made the Lord, which is my refuge, even the most High, thy habitation; there shall no evil befall thee, neither shall any plague come nigh thy dwelling," and he said, "That was God's message to me. I at once took heart and from that moment I neither felt any fear of cholera myself, nor did I suffer any harm from repeated ministrations to the sick and dying."

When I was a lad in the City of New York, an awful scourge of cholera visited that city; and after the pestilence had departed it was remarked, by the pastor of the church of which I was a member, that, although hundreds and thousands within a short distance of the church had fallen under that terrific scourge, not one solitary church member of all that large communion had sickened or died. God does not assure you that any suffering that is essential to the maturing of your spiritual life and your education for service, you shall be spared, even though you be His child; but He does say to you that, if you are abiding in Him, such scourges and such judgments, as represent the recompense that God administers to wicked and rebellious souls, shall not come nigh you; and though a thousand fall at your side and ten thousand at your right hand, you shall go through such perils with safety. The pestilence that walks in the darkness, and the destruction that wastes at noonday shall not touch you; and you shall, not only be delivered from danger, but be without fear; " thou shalt not be *afraid* of the terror by night, nor the arrow that flieth by day."

We now turn to notice the second and more important part of this divine deliverance. "Surely he shall deliver thee from the *snare of the fowler.*" "Thou shalt tread upon the lion and adder; the young lion and the dragon shalt thou trample under feet." It would seem again that there is no mistaking what this means. There are here four conspicuous names or terms, "fowler," "lion," "adder," "dragon." You recognize at once four names appropriately applied, even in the Scriptures themselves, to the great Adversary of God and man. He is a fowler, on the one hand, that spreads his net to catch the feet of the unwary disciple and especially of the sinning soul.

" Satan the Fowler who betrays,
Unguarded souls a thousand ways."

He is the "roaring Lion who goes about seeking whom he may devour." He is the Adder, the subtle insinuating Serpent, that plants his venomous fangs in man. He is the Dragon out of whose mouth issues the fiery breath of blasphemy and profanity, and all forms of evil speech. And the blessed LORD says, if you will abide in Him, Satan shall neither take your feet in his snares as the deceiver, nor devour you as a roaring lion, nor plant his venomous fangs in you as a serpent, nor breathe his fiery breath on you as a dragon; in other words you will not only be free from all the recompense of the wicked, that comes in the form of judgments of God, that are abroad in the earth : but you shall find in God security against all the subtleties of the devil, all his destroying power, all his venomous poisons, all his blasphemous, and profane, and impure suggestions and accusations against Almighty God. Here is deliverance, deliverance from physical ills and ailments; deliverance from spiritual diseases and disobediences, because in God you have found your abiding place.

II. We turn now to the other side, and ask, what are the conditions of our entrance into such security?

We may still find the answer in this psalm. It will be found to indicate four great secrets of such serenity and security, and we may give them in the language of the psalm. "I will say of the Lord, He is my refuge and my fortress: my God; in him will I trust." That is the first. The second is, "Because thou hast made the Lord, which is my refuge, even the most High, thy habitation." The third, "Because he hath set his love upon me, therefore will I deliver him." And the fourth, "Because he hath known my name." These are the four reasons given in the psalm for such abundant security in God.

First of all, "I will say of the Lord, He is my refuge and my fortress." The power and force of this verse lies in that little word "MY." It is not he who says of the Lord, "He is *a* refuge and *a* fortress," or "He is *the believer's* refuge and fortress," or "He is *the church's* refuge and fortress." It is he who, with the personal power of an appropriating faith, says "The Lord is MY refuge," who enters this safe abiding place. Notice how the eighteenth Psalm begins: "I will love thee, O Lord, my strength: the Lord is my rock, and my fortress, and my deliverer; my God, my strength, in whom I will trust; my buckler, and the horn of my salvation, and my high tower." There are nine "my's" in two verses. The power of the little word "MY" is that it puts me into personal relations with Jehovah: it claims Him as *my God*, just as much as though there were no other sinning, suffering, penitent, believing soul to put trust in the Lord God.

One of the greatest troubles or obstacles that we find in the way of Christian living is the hindrance of a false humility; we think that it savours of pride or self-confidence to take the living God as ours; but the psalmist does not so consider it, and the Angel of God, and God himself, does not so regard it. I am to say of the Lord, boldly, "He is my refuge," just as though there were no other soul that needed to flee to Him for shelter ; and "my fortress" just as though there were no other soul that needed a stronghold: "He is my God, in him will I trust." God says, not only to believers, but to unbelievers, that to look up into the face of Jehovah and say from the heart, "MY GOD," is the beginning and the middle and the end of faith. To write your name in a promise and say, "That promise is mine and I claim it"— that is appropriating faith ; it is that which makes His truth your "shield and buckler," as this psalm indicates. There is the first condition: you get into the secret place of God by claiming God as yours. You leave all other believers out of the question; for the moment you forget all about this dying world in the bonds of sin and perdition; and you just come face to face with God and you look up to Him, and as though you singled out God to be your God, and believed that He singles you out to be His believing child, you say to Him, "Thou art my God and I am Thy disciple"; and He says to you, "I am thy God." That is the first condition of entering into this divine security.

The second is, "Because *thou hast made* the Lord which is my refuge, even the most High, *thy habitation*." You not only say "My God," but you declare this "God to be your habitation." "Habitation" differs from a place of *sojourn* in this : you may stop for a night in a place where you are sojourning, but you *dwell* in the place that you inhabit. In that first verse, the emphasis is on that word "*dwell:*"

"He that dwelleth in the secret place of the most High." This psalm is not a message for every soul, it is not even a message for every believing soul, but only for such believing souls as continually abide in God. It is a most melancholy thing that not every believer does thus abide in God. Jesus says, "If ye abide in me, and my words abide in you, ye shall ask what ye will and it shall be done unto you." This implies that there are some believing children of God that do not thus abide in Christ, and in whom His words do not thus abide, and so their prayers have little power and little prevalence with Almighty God. The psalm tells us that the dear child of God that enjoys such security as this, is the believer that does not run to God for a refuge only in the time of some special temptation or danger; who does not call on God only in the hour of sorrow and suffering, but whose *habitual place of abode is God;* who by night is with God, who by day is with God, who in prosperity finds his very sunshine in his Father's smile, who in adversity finds the light still breaking through the clouds in that Father's smile; the man who daily walks with God, not only on Sunday, to go down in the week into paths where God is forgotten; not the man who reads a verse of Scripture in the morning, and offers a hasty prayer, and leaves the Word of God and prayer behind him to be absorbed through the rest of the day in secular employments and carnal pleasures. The believer who abides in Jehovah is the man who stands before God as Elijah did, waiting for God's command, and walks with God as Enoch did, finding no fellowship so sweet as the companionship of the Lord.

The third condition is, "Because he hath *set his love upon Me.*" It is the deliberate fixing of the love on God that is the next condition of this abiding in God. There is a great deal of misapprehension on the subject of love. Over and over again have I been met both by penitent sinners and believing saints with such a question as this : " I would like to love God more, but really I have little control over my affections, feelings and emotions. I cannot love any object more, simply because I will to do it." That is very largely true. Your feelings are not directly under your control. You cannot awaken more emotion because you think you ought to feel more, and cannot always directly arouse more affection because you think you ought to love more deeply. But did you ever notice that the Word of God does not treat love as an emotion or even as an affection? Love is there regarded as a *law* or *principle of life*. For instance, James says, " If ye fulfil the royal law according to the scripture : thou shalt love thy neighbour as thyself." He does not call this " the royal affection," or " the royal feeling," but the " royal LAW."

Paul, referring to this same thing in Galatians, says, " Bear ye one another's burdens and so fulfil *the law of Christ*," and he is obviously referring to what Jesus said, " A new commandment give I unto you, that ye love one another." Now a commandment is a precept, and we voluntarily obey a commandment; and so love is obedience. It is not simply a feeling, or an emotion, or a movement of sensibility, or even an out-going of affection; love is a law of life. You may not be able to govern your feelings, but cannot you control your choice? When you think of two objects and you determine to which you will devote yourself, do you not make a choice between those two objects? If Mammon is on one side and God is on the other side, cannot you choose Mammon or choose God? Now if you choose Mammon you love Mammon; if you choose God you love God, and so the Apostle John says in his first Epistle, " And *this is the love of God; that we keep his commandments*." And so, when this psalm says, " Because he hath *set his love upon Me*, therefore will I deliver him," it means that you are distinctly and definitely to set the choice of your life on God, that you are to endeavour in everything to obey Him; that this is to be the principle of your life, the governing law of your conversation and conduct. God hath spoken, I will obey; God hath called, I will follow.

" He hath set his love upon Me." You know when you set your love upon God, and you know when you set your love upon something else, because you know which way the obedience of your will and the choice of your whole nature leads. And so the apostle again, in the Epistle to the Colossians, says, " If ye then be risen with Christ *seek those things* which are above, where Christ sitteth on the right hand of God." " *Set your affection* on things above, not on things on the earth." Here we have precisely the same thought. And again the psalmist says, " I have set the Lord always before me."

Let us therefore dismiss from our thoughts henceforth, the mistaken idea that love is treated in the Bible simply as a feeling, or an emotion, and let us settle ourselves upon this conviction that love is a law of life, a principle of conduct, distinctly chosen and followed in obedience to the Master; and thus shall we escape the subtle snare which the Fowler sets for unguarded feet; we shall stop looking inside of ourselves, and worrying over our love and affection because it is not so strong as it ought to be; and we shall, instead, look at our daily life, and mark which way the magnetic needle of our will turns; if it turns God-ward, toward the great Polar-Star of the Universe, we need not give ourselves any concern as to whether or not our life is directed God-ward.

The fourth and last condition is this, "Because he hath *known My name.*" This is, at first glance, the most obscure of all these conditions, and yet, when rightly understood, it perhaps throws more light upon the subject than all the others   In this psalm there are found four names of Deity: the first is "most High"; the second, "the Almighty"; the third is "Lord," or Jehovah; and the last is "God." We may be always confident that, if we want the interpretation of any verse in the Bible, it is most surely found by searching the Bible itself; and so if you would know what is meant in this psalm by "*knowing His name*," you would best compare scripture with scripture. The word "Because" is here conspicuous. "*Because* he hath set his love upon Me." "*Because* he hath known My name." "*Because* thou hast made the Lord thy habitation." This word, "because," assigns a reason: *therefore* it is possible for God to be to you all that He says He will be to a believer.

What is it, then, to *know God's name?* Think of the four names revealed here. The name of God represents His character, as my name represents me and distinguishes me from other men; I am known by my name; my name attaches itself to me, and wherever I go identifies me. So God's name stands for God. You never saw Him, looked in His face, or heard His voice, or felt His touch; and there is no way to know God except as you know Him by His *name*, or become acquainted with His character. In these four names, therefore, we have here a fourfold aspect of the divine character: MOST HIGH, ALMIGHTY, JEHOVAH, GOD.

How do you know Him as the Most High? That which

is "most high" is lifted up above all else. The lower down we are the more perishable everything is. The grass under your foot in the summer is one of the frailest things in nature; it grows and blooms to-day, it withers and decays to-morrow. You ascend a little higher and you find the trees that last not only for one season but many seasons, till you come to great trees like the Sequoia Gigantea in the Californian forests, that have been standing for 3,000 or 3,500 years, but even these decay and fall by-and-by. You rise above the level of the trees, and come to the hills that last for ages, though they are worn away by rains and snows, and are shaken by storms and upheaved by earthquakes until sometimes they disappear altogether as hills and become the beds of lakes. You mount still above the hills, and there are what are called in the Bible " everlasting mountains" that have stood ever since the world began. You soar above the mountains, and you come to the planets that are constantly changing their places in the sky as they move around the sun in their annual journeys; but far beyond the planets stand the "*fixed* stars," that never have changed their place since time began. So you see that, the farther up you go, the nearer you come to that which does not change, and beyond all these is He who is "the same yesterday, and to-day, and for ever." Do you know the name of God as the Most High? He is the unchanging God and the unchanging friend of His people, Who when He says a thing means it and stands by it; when He takes an attitude towards a child of God always preserves that attitude; when He is reconciled is for ever reconciled. Then you have learned what the "Most High" means, the unchanging helper, friend and refuge of a believing soul.

The name "ALMIGHTY" simply means that He who is

The Security of the Saint

"Most High" in His unchanging eternity, is most *Mighty in His power*. So that, if you understand this name of God, you know that there is no time in your life, no place in your history, no need of your soul or body, that God cannot meet. A thousand foes may be around you, all men may array themselves against you, but it makes no difference; the All-powerful God is your friend, and beneath His Almightiness you take shelter. Do you know that name of God? If so, then you understand God's power and know that almightiness is on your side, and if He is for you none can be against you and succeed. A man might as well lift up his arm and try to stop the planets in their courses round the sun, or hurl the sun out of the heavens, as to interfere with the plans of God. If, therefore, you are sheltered under God, the arrow from the enemy's bow must pierce His wings before it reaches you!

Do you understand the name of Lord, or Jehovah? Jehovah is the name of the God of Covenant. The only thing that gives you a right to claim the Most High as yours, or the Almighty as yours, is that you have first claimed Jehovah as yours by the blood of the Covenant which Christ sealed with His own life. You must first be able to say, "I come in Christ, I come to enter into covenant relations by the blood-stained door; I come taking God to be my God, through the sacrifice made for me by His dearly beloved Son, my brother in the flesh, but the Son of God, by the power of the Holy Spirit and the participation of Divine nature." Do you understand what it is to say "Jehovah, my Jehovah"? Then you have come to know it, only by covenant relations with God in Christ.

Finally, do you know what it is to say "MY GOD"? I have been searching in this psalm to see what new thought it is that would be added when we came to consider this fourth name of "God." The key seems to me to be given in the verse where we read that name, "my God, *in Him will I trust.*" Now, what is trust? Trust is confidence in truth. You see it in the word, "trust." Did you ever ask yourself where the word "trust" came from? Look at it closely, *true, truer, truest*—trust. Leave out the "e" in "truest," and you have "trust." What is "trust" but *confidence in truth.* What is the highest trust but confidence in the *truest Being* in the universe? He who, as "Most High," never changes; Who, as Almighty, possesses power which none can resist; Who, as the Jehovah of the Covenant, becomes mine in Christ, He is the Truest of all beings, the God of Truth. Truth is the foundation of His character, truth is the secret of His Word, truth is the bed-rock of His promises. If therefore, you who believe in Him as the eternal unchangeable God, and the all-powerful God, and the God of the Covenant, believe in Him as the infinitely True,—that whatever He saith to you He means, that you can take every word of His promise to build upon it as a sure rock of foundation; if therefore, you have fastened and girded His truth around you as a "buckler," and held it up before you as a "shield," then you know the four names by which He reveals Himself: the "MOST HIGH," the "ALMIGHTY," the "JEHOVAH," the "GOD" of all truth.

I feel ashamed of my own incompetency to deal with one of the greatest themes that has ever come to me through a ministry of thirty years. In the study of this subject I have felt my mind overpowered and overwhelmed, and have asked for special grace to bring to you this message from the Lord your God.

In conclusion, I ask your reverent and thoughtful

The Security of the Saint

attention, first to the fact that such privileges as these are the portion of every man and woman that fulfils the conditions laid down in the psalm. If you are willing to set your love on God as the one object of your obedience, to appropriate all there is in God as your own by faith; if you are willing to trust on every word of His promise, and study to know Him in all the aspects of His wonderful character, as "the same yesterday, to-day and for ever," the All-powerful, the God of the Covenant, and the Truest of all beings; if you are ready to call on Him in the secret place and give Him the chance to show you that He is there, and that He is your friend; and if, with all this, you do not simply run to God in times of danger and special need, but constantly abide under the shadow of His wings, you shall find Him your security against physical judgments and against all the powers of the Adversary of your soul.

I am seeking to bring out of this great congregation at least a few believers who will dare to appropriate all there is in God, and consecrate themselves entirely, spirit, soul and body, property and family and influence, to His service and glory. Malachi hints that God is "weary" of professing disciples that are so mixed up with the world that you cannot tell the difference between them and the children of Mammon; and what God yearns for in these days of a secularized church, split up into factions, and pervaded with the venomous influence of scepticism and infidelity, is, at least, a few souls, if only few there be, who believe the Bible and the whole Bible, who take Christ and the whole Christ, who believe in the Holy Spirit as a Person, resident in the Church and in the believer, who know the secret of prayer in the secret place, who understand the names of God because they have had experience of His own abiding in them, and who defy all the powers of man and all the enmity and malignity of the devil in their persistent, wholesome, unswerving fidelity to Him that bought them with His own blood. It is to such heights of holy living that, if need be, as with dying breath, I would call my fellow-disciples, beckoning them up to these lofty summits to which few attain, but upon which, even while on earth, we find the days of heaven brought down in advance and foretaste.

One word to the unbelieving portion of this audience— one solemn word. There is no possibility of getting into that secret place with God, except you pass through the blood-stained doors. It is not by a mere worldly morality or nominal piety, that leaves out Christ, that this Refuge and Stronghold in God is entered, but like the Holy of Holies, only through the "rent veil," the Saviour's flesh. And if there be one of you that is willing to take the bunch of hyssop and dip it in the blood of the basin, and sprinkle the blood on the lintel and on the door-posts, and then humbly hide behind the blood, the Angel of Death and Judgment that passes through in retribution, will pass over you and you shall be absolutely safe. But apart from the blood there is no safety, and apart from the blood-stained doorway there is no entrance into this secure place, where, under the shadow of the wings of God, warmed by His heart and protected by His love, you shall for evermore abide!

SERMON FIVE

The Present Rest of Believers

"For we which have believed do enter into rest."—HEBREWS iv. 3.

IN the ninth and tenth verses of the same chapter we further read: "There remaineth therefore a rest to the people of God. For he that is entered into his rest, he also hath ceased from his own works, as God did from His." The emphasis of this whole passage is therefore on the present rest of God's saints, another of the high privileges to which God invites believers.

The greatest work of John Bunyan, and perhaps the greatest religious book except the Bible, that was ever given to men, we call *The Pilgrim's Progress*. But there is in the Bible itself a " Pilgrim's Progress " that was written long before John Bunyan was in Bedford Gaol. It is the account, begun in the Book of Exodus and concluded in the book of Joshua, of the pilgrimage of God's people from the borders of Egypt into the Holy Land of Canaan. We cannot read this history of the wanderings of the Israelites without saying, with Paul, " which things are an allegory."

It is quite plain to the attentive student of the Word of God that there is back of the simple historical narrative a meaning that can be explained only by spiritual things. And this is one of the most remarkable allegories that has ever been written for man's learning: it is a parable throughout. The history we are very far from questioning as actual history; we simply intimate that beneath the history there lies the allegory. There is Egypt with its bondage, with its darkness, with its plagues, with its sins, with its judgments; there is the blood-sprinkled doorway with the Israelite hiding behind its shelter; there is the deliberate leaving of Egypt, and the crossing of the Red Sea; there is the wilderness journey with the law given at Sinai, and the pillar of cloud going before God's people; there is the Kadesh Barnea on the borders of the Holy Land with the steps that were taken backward toward Egypt, and the long forty years of journeying; there is the crossing of Jordan, and the occupation and conquest of Canaan. And who cannot see in all this a higher spiritual meaning? Egypt is the world with its bondage to sin and to Satan; the blood-sprinkled doorway is the atonement of Jesus Christ, with the security from the judgments of God accorded to the believer; the crossing of the Red Sea may represent justification, passing away from Egypt and beginning the new life under the leadership of God; the wilderness journey may represent the uncertain and the unsettled course of those that are disciples, but have not learned the fulness of their privileges; and the crossing of Jordan may represent the disciple coming into the possession of his present privileges, realizing the rest that is given to him in Christ and by the Spirit even in this world. There is a mischievous notion that has found its way into the Church of God, and sometimes even into our hymns, that Canaan represents heaven, and Jordan represents death; and so we read such verses as this :—

> "On Jordan's stormy banks I stand,
> And cast a wishful eye,
> To Canaan's fair and happy land,
> Where my possessions lie."

Well, I thank God our heavenly possessions do *not* lie in such a Canaan. Palestine was a very poor type of heaven, was it not? Canaan was a land of enemies, and wars, and conquests, and conflicts, and by-and-by of fatal and awful apostasy of the people of God from His worship; a very poor type of heaven, where there are no conflicts because all conquests are past; where there are no possible sins and no possible snares; where the people of God shall never depart from the knowledge of His ways or cease from a perfect worship and service. Jordan is never treated in the Bible as the emblem of death, and Canaan is never treated as the symbol of heaven. Jordan should be crossed in this life, and Canaan is the type of privileges into which the disciple may enter here, and which are a foretaste and foreshadowing of privileges that lie in the ideal land of promise far beyond. We shall consider then, the present rest into which believers may enter in this world, the foretaste of heaven anticipated upon earth, imperfect but still far more complete than most of the experiences that Christian disciples actually enjoy.

We shall ask two questions, and seek, by God's grace, to answer them from His Word: First, What is this rest? and secondly, How shall it be entered?

First, What is this rest? A present rest. Suppose we take this wilderness experience as the illustration of the theme. We have already seen in the reading of the Holy

Scripture that "My rest," to which here Jehovah refers, was the rest of Canaan, the land of promise, that the Jesus referred to here is the Joshua that led the children of Israel after the death of Moses, and, as Moses had led them over the Red Sea, led them over the Jordan. So that we shall find, in the passage of the children of Israel over the Jordan into the land of Canaan, a very complete illustration of the Christian disciple's entrance into the rest that God gives him in this life.

For instance, this rest which God offers the disciple is a rest from *wandering*. When these Israelites crossed the Jordan into the land of Canaan they ceased to wander, and entered upon a settled and permanent habitation. They had been moving about in tents; pitching their tents to-day and striking them to-morrow; staying a few months, it may be a few years, in one locality, and then, as the Pillar of Cloud might go forward or backward, advancing towards the Holy Land or going back again towards Egypt. That life in the wilderness was unsettled, and uncertain, and unsatisfying. They hungered and they thirsted, they were weary and worn, they went over hot desert-sands under dry skies that withheld moisture, they fought enemies, they suffered defeats, they passed through plagues and pestilences, and all manner of evils; but just as soon as they crossed the Jordan and came into the land that God had given them for a possession, the tents were laid aside, and settled habitations were built; the tabernacle of God ceased to be, and the temple was erected in its place. God says to you, who believe in Jesus Christ, that it is your privilege to stop a life of wandering to get out of your unsettled, and uncertain, and unsatisfying experiences into a settled, a certain, a satisfying life. You are harassed with doubts, it is God's will that you should have assurance; you are burdened with discontent, it is God's will that you should be content; you hunger and thirst, it is His will that should be filled; <u>you are tired of a tent life</u>, it is His will that you should have a house, and that you should have, near by His temple, the place of your abode. That is the first element of rest: that wandering should cease, that you should come into something certain, and satisfying, and settled, and comparatively permanent.

Then, again, when these children of Israel crossed the Jordan they got *out of the wilderness* into a favoured land. They had been across the desert sands which yielded no crops, and where it was not worth while to sow. They may, here and there, in some comparative oasis, have raised some harvests for a time, but for the most part they had been over sterile desert tracts; had wandered in a wilderness way where no man was, where there were no springs of water, and no green and fair and fragrant meadows. But when they went across the Jordan they went into the garden of the Lord. Palestine, in those days, was one of the most fertile, one of the most beautiful, and one of the most attractive sections on the surface of the earth. Its hills teemed with harvests and had oliveyards, vineyards, and orchards; the early and the latter rains were God's benediction upon their crops, and those crops did not fail. And when they went up to worship God in the temple and left their homes comparatively without protection, God, according to promise, watched over their harvest fields, and their homes, and no enemy was ever permitted successfully to invade Palestine, to destroy the fruits of their ground at such seasons, until after they crucified the Lord of Glory. So God says to you,—" You have been in the wilderness, you have been journeying through desert-sands, you have been where there were no crops and harvests, where you had not abundance, but a sterile land, an unfertile soil. Come out of the desert and go into the garden; get out of the barren sands and come to the fertile hills; your past life has brought forth no fruit to God: come where you shall have abundance to repay you for your sowing, and where the Lord's benediction of early and latter rain shall cause your seed to spring up and bear abundant fruit in the salvation of souls, and the glory of His dear name. So there is a second element in this rest,—it is the rest of service; it is the rest of a fertile, and beautiful, and useful life, over against a life that has comparatively wasted its powers and resources, and energies, in a half-and-half obedience, and unfruitful, half-hearted attempts at serving.

Then, again, when the children of Israel passed over the Jordan, into the Holy Land, they got rid of what may be called a certain *weariness* of their desert experiences. Perhaps you think it strange that we should speak of people as being weary of doing nothing. Yet, no doubt, a human soul becomes more weary of doing nothing than of most diligent working for God. There is nothing so absolutely wearying as an idle life, an aimless life, a life without a purpose, without any definite end before it, any definite object toward which to press. The young man who is the heir to property, and with it the heir to laziness, the spendthrift who has nothing to do in this world but to enjoy himself, to waste in pleasure what his father has accumulated, who goes about aimless and purposeless, must be a very weary man. I like to see a human soul get thrilled with a purpose! a life that has been like a trumpet hanging up on the walls of society—silent, getting rusty, losing lustre and even musical power, and that some warrior comes forth and seizes, and puts to his lips, and blows a blast through it. Blessed be God when He takes some idle and aimless and purposeless life, and, by the breath of His Spirit, turns the old rusty trumpet into a clarion that sounds the peal for advance. Here was a people that, all through this wilderness journey, had been aimless. They had had no definite object before them; they had been consulting their own pleasure, the gratification of their appetites, feeding themselves to satiety with quails, trying to be contented with the manna that fell, having nothing before them but each day's endurance of privation, of labour, of the weariness of their march. But, when they came into the land of Canaan, they had a definite object. The land was full of enemies, of Canaanites to be driven out, of Anakim, the giant sons of Anak, that had to be dispossessed and driven back with their chariots of iron; and the Lord set Canaan before them, with its fair hills and verdant valleys and limpid streams and charming woodlands, and all its attractions and resources, and said, " Go, and take possession, build your houses, build My temple; I will dwell in the midst of you, and you shall be My people; and I will be your God." That is what He says to you to-day, that have been living an aimless and purposeless life, and are weary of the very life you have been leading, because it has had nothing of the blast of the breath of God through its old rusty trumpet!

Then, once more, these children of Israel, when they went over Jordan, forsook a life of *backward movement* for a life of forward movement. There is a little phrase in the previous chapter which very few people have ever thought about: " As in the *day of provocation*." What is that? If you turn to the fourteenth chapter of Numbers, second to fourth verses, you will find out what the provocation was. When the people murmured against Moses and Aaron, and said, "Why hast thou brought us out of Egypt to die in this land?" When they threatened, as they often did, to go back into Egypt, and even to make another captain that should lead them back into the bondage of slavery and the misery of their Egyptian life, they cared more for the leeks, and onions, and garlics, and cucumbers, of Egypt, than they did for the presence of God, in the wilderness journey with His tabernacle and pillar of fire. When they entered the land of promise they began to make an onward advance and stop their retrograde movements. May it not be said, on the basis of the Word of God, with entire reverence, that there is nothing that is such a *provocation* to the Lord of grace and glory as that, when disciples have tasted of His Spirit, of the powers of the world to come, and of the good Word of God, they should turn back again to a worldly life, and desire the leeks, and garlics, and onions, and cucumbers, of Egypt? caring more for a worldly bill of fare than for the dainties that God sets on the banquet table beneath the banner of His love. How many of us, since we crossed the Red Sea and became children of God by faith in Christ Jesus, have been continually tempting, grieving, and provoking God, by our worldly appetites asserting themselves, and by a willingness at times to go back again into the bondage of sin, and slavery, and misery, in the world we have forsaken! Sinners no doubt provoke Him, tempt Him, grieve Him; but scarcely more than backsliding children of God provoke Him, tempt Him, grieve Him. When you have found out Christ, to go back from Christ; when you have tasted the glory of grace, to go back to law and, worse still, to condemnation under sin ; when you have looked into the riches of the Word of God, to absorb yourselves in man's poor productions, as though the Word of God were of no value : what a provocation that must be to Almighty God! God says to you, " Come out, come out of this wandering of yours into a settled, certain, and satisfying life ; leave the desert for the garden ; leave the sterile life you have been leading, for a fertile life of usefulness and service ; stop your weary aimlessness, and idleness, and shiftlessness, and laziness, and come into work, and war, and conquest, for God ; and leave your waywardness, your backward movements, your longings for past and forsaken things, and move straight on and forward into a higher and holier, and more beautiful, and more consistent, Christian demeanour and character." That, it seems to me, is the rest that remains now for the disciple, and which the passage of the Israelites over the Jordan represents in type—the present privilege of a believer.

The second question is, How do we enter into this rest? Though that question has been already partially answered, let us give it a candid and careful answer now. I think it will be found that this passage of Scripture indicates to us what the method is by which we enter into this most blessed rest.

First of all, we enter it by BELIEVING : " For we which have believed do enter into rest." Faith is the beginning, middle and end of all holy living. Every successive step in the upward and onward progress of the disciple, is a step in newness of faith, in more cordial and complete belief, in more absolute confidence in the Word of the living God. " We which have believed do enter into rest." I have already referred to the " provocation" to which we have subjected God. And how is it that we have provoked Him? By unbelief; and the whole passage, of which the text is part, emphasizes the hardening power of unbelief. " To-day if ye will hear his voice, harden not your hearts, as in the provocation. For some, when they had heard, did provoke." There is nothing that hardens a human heart like unbelief. The rejection of the testimony of God, turning away from Christ as a Saviour, turning away from the Holy Ghost as a Sanctifier, turning away from the Word of God as a guide, that is unbelief. Notice the difference between unbelief and disbelief. Disbelief is denial, disbelief is dispute, disbelief is rejection of a thing as truth. But unbelief may entirely consist with a state of mind in which there is no real disbelief or disposition to deny the truth of the Gospel or the reality of Christ's work. If I shut out that gospel and that work from possessing and controlling my life—that is unbelief, which is thus very different from disbelief.

There are a great many who think they will be saved because they do not dispute the truths of the Gospel or the reality of the life and death, the resurrection and ascension of Christ. But one may be a believer in one sense, and an unbeliever in another sense. The devil believes and trembles. The devil is an unbeliever of the worst sort; but the devil is not a disbeliever. He believes, for he dares not deny; but he has no faith; he has no reception of Christ; he knows no taking in of the great truths of salvation, for his own personal uplifting. Yes, there is nothing that petrifies the heart like unbelief. Even disbelief hardens the heart less rapidly, for a man may have been brought up in certain circumstances, in which he is surrounded by an atmosphere of scepticism; his father was a disbeliever and an infidel, and he has always breathed the air of infidelity. Such a man is not as much hardened by disbelief as another is hardened by unbelief, who dares not deny the truth of the Word of God, and yet shuts out that Word in its power, and hinders its transforming influence in his own heart.

As unbelief hardens, so faith softens. Just as soon as you believe Jesus, your heart at once turns from a heart of stone to a heart of flesh. The heart upon which no impression could be made before, becomes a heart keenly sensitive to touch, now. The heart that before had no throb, pulses now with life; the heart that before had no feeling, is full of feeling that responds to God's appeal; and every time you take a step in advance in believing, in more fully believing, in more cordial, in more absolute belief, the more tender and soft and responsive your heart becomes; until, like an ear that was once half deaf, but is now keenly sensitive to every sound, or like an eye that was before half blind and only saw men as trees walking, but now sees everything clearly; every new step in faith makes the heart softer, makes it more responsive, makes it more receptive to the influences of God.

A second thing which helps us to enter this rest is, *ceasing from our own works*. Notice the tenth verse of this fourth chapter, "He that is entered" (that is, has already entered) "into his rest, he also hath ceased from his own works, as God did from His." Now what was the first rest of which we read in the Bible? It was the rest of the original Sabbath. When God had completed the works from the foundation of the world then He set apart the seventh day for rest, and He ceased from His own works. And so we find that rest has always in the Bible been linked with, and never more can be separated from, Sabbath keeping. Sabbath keeping, what is it with us? It is ceasing from our own works. You were busy at your trade yesterday, or profession, or whatever be your calling. You laid it aside and you came up to the House of the Lord this morning, not to handle the tools or implements of your trade or calling during the Lord's-day; you have excluded worldly pursuits, you have banished business affairs from your mind; you have left sealed your secular letters as you have shut up your secular warehouse, and you took the Word of God and read it, and besought God in prayer to give you His personal presence and blessing, and came up for worship here where only God is acknowledged, His Word magnified, and His Spirit besought. You have ceased from your own works in order that you should keep the Sabbath. If, while you are here, you are meditating business schemes, studying about what you shall say in answer to letters that you have received—if you are opening your mind to things outside of the limits which God has set to guard His day of rest, and doing it voluntarily, you are not keeping the Sabbath ; you have not ceased from your own works. So the rest that is in store for God's people, and which He invites them to enter, is a rest in which, in three senses, they cease from their own works.

First, _sinful_ works. If there is anything you have been doing that you know to be a sin, or any duty that you have been neglecting that you understand to be a duty, you never can enter into this rest of God till that sin is abandoned and that duty is taken up. There can be no rest in a soul where voluntary sin still exists, or where there is voluntary non-performance of duty. How important this is! To enter into God's rest, that is just before you to be possessed by you, put away your sinful works. If there has been a lie that you have been telling, acknowledge that lie, confess it, forsake it. If there has been a slander that you have circulated about one of your brethren, acknowledge it before God, and go and acknowledge it to your brother. If there has been a disposition that you have been cherishing that has been malignant, malicious, uncharitable, unkind, forsake it, and ask that the spirit of love may possess you. If there has been any neglect of the Word of God, of prayer, of Christian fellowship, of the ordinances of the sanctuary—if there is any act you ought to have performed that you have not performed, or if you have performed any act that you ought not to have performed, you must cease from your sinful works; that is the only way to enter into rest. Any other rest than the rest of voluntary abandonment of sin is deceptive, delusive and utterly false.

Then you must cease from your own *legal* works, that is cease relying on the law; you must rely on grace. Remember that while Moses led the children of Israel across the Red Sea, he could not lead them into the promised land; it was Joshua that led them into the land of promise. Moses represented Law, Joshua represented Jesus, or Grace. If you turn back to the works of the law you can never have the rest that is in God. Ah! many of us—I trust very many of us—know what it is to stop resting upon our own works for justification, and know what it is to fall back on what Jesus has done for us, and say, " Dear Lord, henceforth this is the rock on which I build; my strength, my righteousness, is found only in Jesus."

Then you must cease from your own *selfish* works. If you are doing something for self-gratification, for self-advancement; if you are living in this world to gather riches, to get pleasure to yourself, to get fame for yourself, to gratify your ambition, to mount to some elevated point of influence and power among men; as long as you are seeking your self-interest you never will have rest. There is nothing so restless as a selfish man, and the very gratifications that he gathers to himself only make him more restless.

Then, again, we must not only cease from our own works, but we must take a *definite step of consecration*. That is a much-abused word, and has become very offensive in the ears of some devout and earnest disciples, because it has been used so much in the interests of cant and rant and offensive forms of pietism. But there is a true consecration that we never ought to lose sight of, because of false types of consecration that we hear of and see round about us. What is consecration? It is made up of two words, and it means to set apart wholly unto the Lord our God; as when the Tabernacle was completed, Aaron took the gold, the silver and the brazen vessels, the tongs, the snuffers and all that pertained to the slightest matters connected with the Tabernacle; he gathered them all together and poured the holy oil upon them; he consecrated them to God. And God will never give a disciple the rest unto which the child of God is invited if he does not cross the Jordan of a new consecration. Half a life for God brings no rest to anybody; it is a tiresome life, it is an unsatisfying life. You cannot mix oil with water; you cannot mingle light and darkness; you cannot wed Christ and Belial. There must be a whole heart for God, or there can be nothing known of the rest into which God invites you.

The Jordan, in my judgment, stands for that consecration fully to God as the Red Sea stands for conversion, passing from Egypt into a life of dependence upon Jesus. There is a great deal of difference between acceptance of Christ as my Saviour, and acceptance of Christ as my Master; a great deal of difference between taking Christ as my

Redeemer to save me from hell and lift me to heaven, and taking Christ as my Sovereign to rule over me, to reign in me, to direct my conduct, to govern my thoughts, to give an end to my purposes, and to control my life. May God's grace help each one of us to comprehend what blessings come to a child of God who simply takes his Redeemer and his Saviour to be also his Ruler and his Sovereign. You should ask Jesus what His will is concerning your life and what work He would have you to do, what of your present activities He would have you forsake or diminish because they are worldly and selfish, and what new forms of service for Him He would have you assume in His dear name; how, when you have sought to sanctify your family altar, you may sanctify the counter in your business shop; how, when you have sought to sanctify yourself at the Lord's table, you may sanctify yourself at your own family table; how, when you have sought to give one day in seven wholly unto the Lord, you may keep every day holy unto the Lord, so that, in a sense, every day should be a Sabbath of rest; so that you should go to your place of business to-morrow morning as truly to transact business for God as when you come to the Lord's supper to-day to take the bread and the cup in His dear name; so that, as you sanctify the Sabbath day wholly unto His service, you should seek to pervade all your daily life with the conscious presence of your Master; so that He shall be a partner in your daily business, a sharer of its profits, and the constant companion of your daily walk.

If you would see what a difference there is between a man before he crosses that Jordan and after, look at Peter as a single example. There he was, a child of God—no one dares to doubt it—but he was in the wilderness; he was moving up towards to the land of rest, and then going downward and backsliding from his Master; and when he met the maid and she said, "Thou wert also with Him," he said, "I know Him not," and, when afterwards, again and again, he was accused of being one of the company of which Jesus was the head, he denied with curses and with oaths. That was when he was in the wilderness, a wanderer, a wayward man, without his impulses and his purposes being yet firmly fixed on Jesus. But he crossed the Jordan in that baptism of tears and prayers after Jesus looked upon him, and especially when the Holy Ghost came down in a mighty flood, and he trod, as it were, through the very midst of that flood and reached the other side. Peter was now a new man, and we hear him on the day of Pentecost preaching a sermon for Christ, the immediate result of which was three thousand converts. And we find this same man that shrank from the sight of the maid in the garden and the courts of the High Priest, actually confronting the great Sanhedrim, the supreme council of the Jewish nation, and when they threatened him with scourging, and intimated even death as the possible result of his fidelity to Christ, he calmly said, "We ought to obey God rather than men." And he went forth rejoicing to be counted worthy to suffer shame for his Master's sake. Ah, there is a world of difference between Peter in the desert, and in the Lord's garden; in the wilderness, and in the Land of Canaan; between Peter sighing and longing for the leeks and onions of Egypt, and Peter sighing and longing to be a sharer in the sufferings and the glory of his Lord Jesus.

When Paul went to Ephesus he found twelve disciples there, who had not received the Holy Ghost since they believed; they had gone over the Red Sea, but they had not gone over the Jordan; and he asked them carefully about their experience, and found that they knew only the baptism of John, a baptism unto repentance; then he taught them the fuller things of Jesus, and they were baptized again in His name, and down upon them came the same Spirit as at Pentecost in Jerusalem, and they began to prophesy and speak with tongues. Have you known the Spirit of God since you believed? Have you got any further than the baptism of John, which was unto repentance? Have you known what the fulness of the Holy Ghost is? If you have not, I beseech you come to God, and ask that your share in Pentecostal blessings may be bestowed upon you this day, that your tongue may be anointed for His service, and your whole soul animated and stimulated and cheered by His presence.

Let me add two very brief applications of these truths. First, a word to disciples. Just before they crossed the river, Joshua said, "Prepare you victuals, for within three days ye shall pass over Jordan." The Lord comes to you and says, "Prepare to cross this Jordan, for within three days you may enter this rest of God." Nay, more, within three minutes you might enter this rest if the obstacles were removed out of God's way, and your feet dared to cross the river Jordan. Think how these children of Israel came out of Egypt, and moved on to Kadesh Barnea, within, probably, less than three days of Canaan; and, from that point on the very borders of the Holy Land they went back, to and fro, through the wilderness for forty years; because of unbelief, because of disobedience, because of the provocation of their hard hearts, God sent them to wander to and fro, almost, in sight of the hills of Palestine. You have been wandering, some of you, forty years in the wilderness. When you first accepted Jesus Christ, and moved, under the impulses of your new life, onward toward the rest of God, you came to your Kadesh Barnea, and, perhaps, you got a few bunches of grapes from Eshcol to indicate to you what was the glory of the rest that God set before you. But your wayward and disobedient hearts backslid from God, and you have been wandering all these long years in the wilderness. But the Lord says to you to-day, within three days ye may pass over Jordan." And how many of you are ready to pass over? If God should see to-day, not a show of hands but a show of hearts—if in this great congregation some people that have been wandering from God in an unsettled and uncertain life of doubt and difficulty and almost despair, backsliding from God, loving the leeks and onions, looking back towards their life of slavery and misery, dismayed by their adversaries, having no courage for God, no aim for God, the old rusty trumpet still on the wall, and the Holy Ghost never having pulsed His breath through it—what if God should see in this great congregation to-day many hearts opening their doors to Him, and saying, " Come, blessed Lord, lead me over this Jordan, I will undertake a consecrated life for the service of my Master," what tremendous issues might hang on such consecration.

There are some of you, that are not even yet out of Egypt. You are in the land of plagues and darkness, you are in danger from the angel of judgment, and have not even taken refuge behind the blood-stained door-way; the Red Sea of justification is yet to be crossed, as well as the wilderness and the Jordan. What shall I say to you? I can only entreat you this very moment to begin your departure from the land of slavery, and poverty, and misery; come to the Red Sea, the blood of Jesus Christ, and pass over and begin your pilgrimage with God. The year 1892 is almost at its close ; a few Sabbaths more and it will be numbered with the everlasting past, and it is quite possible that some of you that have heard the Gospel preached here for some years, and have hardened your hearts, like Pharaoh, in disobedience to God, may, before the close of this year, be given up by God, as Pharaoh was, to the visitation of final judgment. I beseech you, believe in Jesus Christ to-day, no longer harden your hearts, and enter, by fulness of faith, into fulness of blessing for Jesus' sake.

Sermon Six

The Christian's Crown Jewels

"Unto you therefore which believe he is precious."—1 PETER ii. 7.

WE shall now have a glimpse of the crown jewels of the Christian. Peter uses one adjective frequently and conspicuously, viz., the word "*precious*." Seven times this word is found in these two epistles, and once we meet the same thought in other words—" of great price."

Let us first get these seven texts before us :—

Chapter i. 7.—" The trial of your faith, being much more precious than of gold that perisheth," etc.

Chapter i. 19.—" But with the precious blood of Christ"

Chapter ii. 4.—'A living stone . . chosen of God, and precious."

Chapter ii. 6.—" A chief corner-stone, elect, precious."

Chapter ii. 7.—" Unto you therefore which believe He is precious."

Chapter iii. 4.—" The ornament of a meek and quiet spirit, which is in the sight of God of great price," that is, very precious.

Second epistle, chapter i. 1.—" Like-precious faith with us."

And, last of all—

Chapter i. 4.—" Exceeding great and precious promises."

The text, "Unto you therefore which believe He is precious," differs from the rest, for, in the original, we find not an adjective but a *noun*—" Unto you therefore which believe he is THE PRECIOUS ONE," or, "THE PRECIOUSNESS," *i.e.*, the one object of inestimable value. Among all this cluster of precious thing *one stands central*, that is, *Jesus*; and if these are crown-jewels in the diadem of the disciple, there is one jewel whose brilliance outshines all the rest—The Pearl of Great Price.

The text furthermore suggests, that all the precious things that belong to the child of God cluster about Him. They only serve to show us the different characters, or the relations, which Christ sustains to the disciple, the various sides and angles of this one priceless Crown-Jewel !

I. In the experience of disciples, first of all we come to the "*precious Blood*" which is the price of our redemption. Jesus Christ finds us slaves to the law and its penalty, to sin, guilt, and condemnation ; and the first thing He does is, to deliver the slave and captive. There was only one ransom sufficient for the slave, whose life was forfeited by sin, and that was to give another life for that forfeited life ; and, because "the Blood is the Life," Christ's Blood was shed ; for the giving of His Blood was the giving of His life. " He gave His life for us." No other ransom would redeem the slave ; no other price would satisfy the demands of a broken law, would expiate the guilt of sin, would answer to the penalty of evil-doing ; and so this precious Paschal Lamb of God was slain for us, and his blood was sprinkled on the side-posts, and the upper door-posts of the house, that we might hide behind the blood-stained doorway. A wonderful

Ransom that was! It not only delivered us from the bondage of the law and penalty, but from the power and dominion of sin; it freed the slave, and made him a son; it redeemed the victim and criminal, and set him in the high places of the family of God, reconciled and restored. So Jesus Christ is precious, first, because of the precious Blood He shed; the first aspect of his "preciousness" is that which He presents as the Redeemer of sinful souls, who restores and reconciles us to God, and sets the slave in the household as a son and heir.

II. The second aspect of this preciousness of Christ is that He becomes the *chief corner-stone*. For, it is not enough for the slave to be redeemed, for the penalty of sin to be put away—beyond pardon, forgiveness, reconciliation, there must be the building up of holy character into the image of God. And so every redeemed slave that becomes a son of God is built up into the likeness of the Father. Every builder needs first a foundation and a corner-stone. "Other foundation can no man lay than that which is laid, which is Jesus Christ." There is no necessity for another corner-stone, for here is Christ, scoffed at and scorned by unbelievers, but the chosen, chief and only corner-stone, the *living* corner-stone. Deliverance from sin is not complete until you are made pure, for it is only "the pure in heart that shall see God." You must, as a new-born babe, feed on the sincere milk of the Word until you grow thereby and become a man, able to feed on the strong meat which alone befits a strong man, and develops him into his full stature and strength.

There is a peculiar expression found in connection with this corner-stone; sometimes it is called, as by the old prophets, the head-stone of the corner, (Ps. 118: 22, etc.) *i.e.* the chief corner-stone, or the stone of the angle. The head-stone is manifestly not the corner-stone; it is the stone laid on the top and not at the bottom of an edifice ; and the chief stone of the corner may refer as well to the chief stone of the *upper* corner as of the *lower* corner of the structure. If the figure be that of a pyramid, there is a corner-stone whose angles determine all the lines of the pyramid, and there is another head-stone of the corner which is laid on the apex of the pyramid to complete it. Possibly these mysterious expressions of Scripture refer to both. Jesus Christ is the corner-stone, laid beneath our character and life, but He is also the head-stone, laid at the apex of our life to complete and finish it. He is " the author and finisher of our faith, that is, He begins it and He completes it.

In the ancient Olympic games, the *stadium* was an ellipse or circle, and the starting point was also the goal ; instead of running from one end of the race-course to another, in a straight line, the racer passed round the curve and came back to the same point whence he started. Jesus Christ is the author and the finisher of our faith, because we start from Him, and we come back to Him. The same thought is suggested here. He is the corner-stone, because we begin to build on Him ; He is the head-stone because we finish building in Him ; and from the time that the first stone is laid at the corner till the last stone is laid, with shouts of rejoicing, it is Jesus Christ all the way from bottom to top, from beginning to end. So he is the preciousness to the builder of character, and life, and destiny, for he inspires and completes our effort. He lies beneath us as an everlasting rock, and when we have finished and done all we can do and the best we can do, he crowns and consummates and completes the scructure as the very stone that lies at the top of all. What a beautiful thought this is! Christ is not content to redeem a slave or even to make him a son; He will never leave him till He has made him perfect in the likeness of God.

III. The third aspect of the preciousness of Christ is His "*precious promises.*" He is the Promiser of all good. As His precious blood redeems; as the precious stone of foundation and of completion regulates the building of character and life, so Christ is the source of our access to, and appropriation of, the precious promises of God.

Upon this head it is well to expand somewhat. The Word of God is here brought to our attention in the light of its exceeding great, glorious and precious promises. The promises present only one aspect of that Word, for there are in it precepts or commandments, warnings and invitations, instructions and admonitions; but Peter takes this one particular feature of the Word of God and separates it for our special thought—"The exceeding great and precious promises." His mind was probably on the Land of Promise that was the type of the promises of the Word of God, and which God would have his people survey, enter into, and take possession of, as the present Rest of the people of God.

How are you to make these promises your own? Keep before you the thought of a *land*. Suppose some poor man in this congregation should learn that there had been left to him a large and valuable estate. He had never seen it, or thought of its possession, but suddenly, by some legacy, this great tract of territory, with its buildings and its woodland and all its resources, becomes his own. How would he make that property practically his possession? As soon as his title was established he would go and examine it for himself; see what there was in the estate, where the woodland was, and what kind of wood grew there, and to what uses it could be put; he would see where the garden spots lay for the culture of all sorts of fruits and of flowers. He would want to know what water there was to irrigate the soil and make it fruitful, and whether there were any mines of coal or metal, especially of gold and silver, to be worked; in other words, there would be first an investigation of the land, and then there would be an attempt to utilize or make serviceable what the land contained.

In some such way we are to take possession of the Promises found in the Word of God. We are, first, to "search the Scriptures," to find out what is in them; even to dig down into their depths for the precious hidden truths that they contain; we are to turn over their soil that the sweetest fruits and flowers possible may be developed by the cultivation of our knowledge of the Word. We are to find out what there is in the Bible that is meant for us, and then make it useful in our lives, our character, our service.

Suppose an apothecary shop in which are gathered all the various remedies from the vegetable, the mineral, and the animal world, that can be applied to the treatment of disease; suppose also a community cursed with all forms of sickness and bodily infirmity; and that there is a remedy on these shelves and in these vials for every ill to which flesh is heir. He who is to use that apothecary shop to a purpose must first know what is there, and then how it ought to be applied to human disease, infirmity, and weakness. God's precious Word is the great apothecary shop of the universe, with the Divine medicine for every spiritual ill, need, and infirmity. Or it may be considered as God's great banqueting hall, with food and drink for every hungry and every thirsty soul; or as God's great armoury with the full armour of

God—offensive and defensive weapons for the warrior in the fight ; or as God's great workshop with an implement for every child of God that would do effective work in the Master's service. The Bible is the great resource of the Christian. We need to know what is in it, and then lay hold on what it contains, and appropriate it.

In this way this Book of God becomes to a disciple the most precious book in the world. It is well to have *one Bible* for constant use, so well made and bound, that it will not easily come to pieces. Every believer needs one Bible as his constant companion, which may be filled with his own private, personal, marginal notes made by his own pen. Most precious will such a particular Bible become, because, in every circumstance of trial, temptation, sorrow, conscious guilt, conscious need, he will go to this one book, and find something in it that is exactly adapted to himself, and will note on the margin the date, the day, the month, and the year, when each particular promise has been sanctified to his good ; and if he gets into circumstances of peculiar trial and trouble, he will again search this dear Book of God and look at the entries on the sacred leaves, which indicate where God has enabled him to dig down and find mines of gold for his conscious poverty, or to appropriate some precious Word of God in times when his need was especially great. I would rather lose everything else I have in the world, than the one Bible which has been the companion of many years, and which is thus full of my own sacred memoranda. And the blessed thing about this is that there is not a man, woman, or child that cannot have one Bible that is just as precious, and for which all the wealth in England would not be a sufficient price.

In one's own Bible it may also be well to indicate the

texts that have been specially blessed to other souls. For
instance, when George Müller was working to build up his
orphanages in Bristol,—when he had the beginnings of his
buildings, but very few orphans themselves—and afterwards
when he needed yet larger buildings for the great work that he
felt must be done, he was one day on his knees in prayer to
God, and he opened at the eighty-first Psalm, and tenth verse,
which may be marked as " Müller's text "—"*Open thy mouth
wide and I will fill it.*" And he says that from that time he
has been asking great things from God, and expecting great
things from God, and has not been disappointed.

When Mr. Moody began his work in America, timid,
uneducated, opposed, maligned, and sometimes persecuted,
he needed peculiar strength from God to help him meet his
difficulties; and one day he was reading in the fiftieth
chapter of Isaiah, at the seventh verse, and these words he
took as the motto of his life from that time forth, "*For the
Lord God will help me; therefore shall I not be confounded:
therefore have I set my face like a flint, and I know that I
shall not be ashamed.*" That text is "Moody's text."
When he started his great institutions in Northfield and in
Chicago for the training of young men and women in
Christian life and service, the whole undertaking was one of
faith and prayer. He had no money back of him to sustain
these great institutions, which cost in Northfield alone
£100,000, and in Chicago about as much more; and he
found in Isaiah xxvii. 3, another motto for those institutions,
"*I the Lord do keep it; I will water it every moment: lest
any hurt it, I will keep it night and day.*"

When Luther was in the midst of the Great Reformation,
and the Word of God was assailed on every side, he found
in the hundred and nineteenth Psalm at the eighty-ninth

verse, the words which have since been known as "Luther's text," "*For ever, O Lord, thy word is settled in heaven*"; *i.e.* far beyond the reach of all disturbing causes.

Paul found, in Habakkuk ii. 4, the text which he repeats more frequently than any other in his writings, "The just shall live by his faith." That is " Paul's Text."

" Carey's text " was, Isaiah liv. 2, 3, "*Enlarge the place of thy tent, and let them stretch forth the curtains of thine habitations: spare not, lengthen thy cords, and strengthen thy stakes; for thou shalt break forth on the right hand and on the left,*" etc. And so I might give you a thousand texts, that have been known as the texts of individuals, because they have supplied special the inspiration and the strength for their Christian effort.

Suppose you are in need of food and raiment, and you want comfort. You turn to Matthew vi 33, "*Seek ye first the kingdom of God, and his righteousness; and all these things shall supply all your need* according to his riches in glory by shall be added unto you." Or to Philippians iv. 19, "*My God* Christ Jesus." You are in circumstances of temptation, and you turn to 1 Corinthians x. 13, "There hath no temptation taken you but such as is common to man : but God is faithful, who will not suffer you to be tempted above that ye are able; but will with the temptation also *make a way to escape*, that ye may be able to bear it." You are in circumstances of peculiar trial through sorrow, and you turn to 1 Peter iv. 12, "Beloved, think it not strange concerning the fiery trial which is to try you, as though some strange thing happened unto you : but *rejoice, inasmuch as ye are partakers of Christ's sufferings;* that, when his glory shall be revealed, ye may be glad also with exceeding joy."

You are undertaking to preach the gospel in the midst of the destitute and degraded of the earth, and you need help. You turn to Matthew xxviii. 19, " Go ye therefore, and teach all nations," and, *" Lo I am with you alway even unto the end of the world."* Perhaps you are discouraged and disappointed about your work—it seems to you to be vain —and you turn to 1 Corinthians xv. 58, " Therefore, my beloved brethren, be ye stedfast, unmoveable, always abounding in the work of the Lord, forasmuch as ye know that *your labour is not in vain in the Lord."* Or you are approaching the dying hour, and your heart gives way to anguish, and again you turn to Psalm xxiii. 4, " Yea, *though I walk through the valley of the shadow of death, I will fear no evil: for thou art with me;* thy rod and thy staff they comfort me." And these examples could be multiplied by the hundred thousand.

Nothing is more astonishing than that, with such a land of promise which we are bidden to enter and take possession of, we do not even know *what is there,* much less appropriate it to ourselves. No doubt there are professing disciples even in this great congregation that spend more time over the daily newspapers than over the Word of God, and who know more of the current news than of the exceeding great and precious promises in this Book. May God help His believing children to understand that every word of promise here is for them, because the precious blood of Christ has been applied to their redemption, and they have chosen Him as the foundation stone and the capstone for the building of character and life. Find out what is in this land ; dig down into its depths ; explore its forests and timberlands ; seek out its garden spots, well watered as the garden of the Lord ; grow fruits and flowers for your table and your dwelling, and build the timber into your homes, and decorate yourselves with the gold and the silver and the precious gems. Let us know what is in the Word of God, and compel other people to see that we do know what precious promises are in it. Think of having such a celestial treasure, and then going about, with heads bowed down as a bulrush, as though there were no riches of glory in the inheritance of the saints!

IV. Let us cast a rapid glance at the other "precious" things to which little reference has been made. "The *trial of your faith*," &c. In the Bible even trial fires are treated as precious; and yet, if there is anything from which a man shrinks, it is from contact with the flame. To be burnt represents as terrible agony as any to which a human being can be subjected, though happily it is often brief. One anguish may possibly surpass it, *crucifixion*, to which the Lord of Glory gave himself that he might show his love, in that He endured the most terrible suffering.

And yet trial fire is precious. Metals, that are not purified, are worth little for manufacture. The ore out of the great mines is worthless for ordinary purposes, until ground to powder, and until the metal has been separated from its alloy. God thinks so much of His children that He must get the dross out of their character, the pure metal separated and purified from all its surroundings and foreign admixtures, and so He kindles a fire and puts the disciple in the crucible and melts him down by those fires, which are sometimes very hot, until the dross is released and rises to the surface and is skimmed away. When he looks down into the crucible and sees in the metal His own face reflected, He knows that the dross is all removed; and he removes it from the fire, and moulds the metal for honourable purposes and makes it into chosen vessels. Malachi says of Jesus Christ, that, "He shall *sit* as a refiner and purifier of silver." Why not *stand?* Because in the purification of metals by fire, the refiner sat by to watch for the precise moment when the metal is purified. In the great iron foundries, in making Bessemer steel, the process is watched through a spectroscope, in which the changing colours of the flames show exactly when the metal is completely ready for its uses.

When the flame reaches a certain shade of colour then the great crucible is turned upside down, released from the fires, and the metal is poured into its moulds. "*He shall sit as a refiner and purifier of silver.*" The Divine Refiner sits down by the crucible, watching intently to see just when the fire has done its full work and when the metal should be removed from the flames.

God puts you in the crucible because you are *so precious* in His sight. He sits down by His crucible, and watches the progress of your purification, and when He sees that you are made like unto Himself, He releases you from the fire. There will not be a pang, or a pain, not be an instant of sorrow or anguish after the perfect work has been accomplished.

V. "The ornament of a *meek and quiet spirit*, which is in the sight of God of great price." The inmost obstacle to holy character is the disposition, or temper, where envy, and jealousy, and malice, and uncharitableness hide. The great impulse which controls our tongues, our conduct, comes from our disposition. The word means that *to which we are disposed*, as fire toward the sun, or water toward its level.

To that inmost place no stranger penetrates; it is known only to ourselves and to Almighty God. Would you be precious in God's sight, and wear the only ornament that God cares for? It is not plaited hair, nor silks and satins, nor broadcloth and doe-skin, nor gold and gems. For these He cares nothing. One gem alone is bright to God, and like His own Pearl, "of great price;" it is a spirit " *meek*," *i.e.*, unselfish, and "*quiet*," *i.e.*, peace-loving and peace-making! the soul that has conquered all wrong dispositions, out of which has been rooted up whatever interferes with the peace, and the purity, of other souls! The disposition is the stronghold of evil. It is comparatively easy to shape the speech, to avoid falsehood, and malice ; but the last thing to be changed is the disposition, or temper—the tendency to be easily provoked, to misconstrue the motives of others, to speak quickly and impatiently, to be despotic, and arbitrary, and overbearing, to be fault-finding and petulant—all the thousand forms of evil temper, that unhappily are often nourished and cherished, even in Christian bosoms !

VI. "The *like-precious faith*." That forms a proper conclusion to this series. We have seen the precious blood that redeems, the precious corner-stone and capstone of the character, the precious land of promise, and the precious trial of faith, the preciousness of the meek and the quiet spirit. What is the "*like-precious faith*," but the faith that in all disciples is alike? How precious is that *bond of union* between all God's dear people, the world over. Jesus Christ is the hub of the wheel, and all the spokes, although separated at the circumference, meet in the hub. Christ is the Sun of righteousness, and all the rays, however dispersed, meet in the Sun. There are millions of believers on the face of the earth, that we never saw, but who hold the same precious faith with us, and if we met them to-day we should love them and they would love us, and we should feel that we were all bound to one Christ. Brought up in other lands, their hearts would at once be knit to yours as though you and they had been reared in the same land, in the same house, and under the same father's care. There are Episcopalians, Congregationalists, Methodists, Presbyterians—disciples that differ from you in some things, but those things in which they and you agree are far more numerous and infinitely more precious than those in which you and they differ. When we all meet in the presence of God, alike redeemed, our differences will all have passed away, and our agreements will be seen to have constituted "*the like-precious faith*" of all true children of God. Believers sometimes, upon platforms, discuss matters that are very trifling, split theological hairs, and draw nice distinctions and discriminations; but when those very controversalists *get down on their knees together they pray exactly the same theology!* When true believers pray and praise their dialect is the same always, so that, if you should take the prayers and the hymns of true disciples from the Cross of Christ till now, you would find no essential difference as to the truths to which have been held and which have practically ruled the life.

Whatever may be the distractions that divide God's people, blessed be His name! we have "*one like-precious faith*," for we hold to one redeeming Blood, one corner-stone and capstone, one inheritance of promise, one final Purification from sin, one Divine "ornament of the meek and quiet spirit," one Saviour who is the infinitely precious One. We shall come, by-and-by, where we shall see all truth in the same light, and the errors and the mistakes of this life will have passed away,

But, remember, He is the Precious One, only to those that *believe*. It is by faith that we are redeemed by that precious Blood, built on that corner-stone, finished with that capstone, tried as by fire and made pure, made partakers of these promises, decorated with that meek and quiet spirit, and bound to all others who hold like-precious faith. How much hangs on believing! Who of you all will by faith accept this Precious One, and to-day begin to find out how all other precious Crown-Jewels become your own only by first possessing this Pearl of Great Price?

Sermon Seven

The Transformed Temper

"And be renewed in the spirit of your mind."—EPHESIANS iv. 23.

THE most subtle element in character is what is called the "*disposition.*" There is that about a fruit that we call its flavour or savour; there is that about a flower that we call its odour or perfume: and the savour of a fruit, and the perfume of a flower, no natural science has been able to explain. You may have the fruit or the flower without the savour or the odour, but not the savour or the odour without the fruit or flower. This subtle element in character, the "disposition," is as difficult to describe and define as are savour and odour; but, though we can never have the sweet savour and odour without the character, we too often find character lacking this indescribable, undefinable charm.

The language of this text is very peculiar, nowhere else found in the Word of God. We find similar words, "renewed in your mind," "renewed in heart," &c.; but here only do we find that peculiar expression, "Be renewed *in the spirit of your mind,*" as though the mind itself had some mysterious quality about it that might be called "spirit," and this spirit of the mind needs renewal.

There is in nature that which reminds us of this strange

something, called "disposition," and it may be illustrated by plant-life. For instance, there is a disposition in a plant to seek the sunshine. Down in the cellars beneath our houses sometimes there will be a bulb or a germ of plant-life which begins to grow, and sends up a long, pale, unhealthy stem, not like the green stalk which is to be found in the open fields; and when this stem has grown, it may be to, many feet in length, it finds a window or crevice through which it winds itself and creeps out into sunshine, and then it begins to look green and healthy and put forth leaves. Because the plant has this disposition towards the light, it seeks and finds the light, even through the darkness. The apostle says, "Be renewed in the spirit of your mind," *i.e.*, made anew in the temper or disposition of your inward being and nature. Get the savour that belongs to God's fruit, the odour that belongs to God's flower, so that when others get a taste or scent of your spirit it will be not as when a bitter morsel or a foul stench offends us, but as when one plucks a fruit or smells a sweet odour from heavenly gardens. Not so much to duty as to delight, not so much to obligation as to privilege, does this Word of God invite us when it bids us be renewed in the spirit of our mind.

Before we go further, let us notice how this invitation, "Be renewed in the spirit of your mind," lies between two other injunctions: "That ye *put off*, concerning the former conversation" (or course of life) "the old man, which is corrupt according to the deceitful lusts: and be renewed in the spirit of your mind: and that ye *put on* the new man, which, after God, is created in righteousness and true holiness." Here the figure is suggested of a man laying aside a filthy robe,—"the old man,"—and deliberately putting on a white robe,—" the new man." The garment stands for the outside life, and the mind or disposition for the inside life; and when the apostle bids us to put off this corrupt outward life, and put on this pure outward life in its place, between the two he imparts the real secret of this complete transformation in the external conduct. We must aim at a thoroughly renewed character; not content simply to change what is outward, we must be renewed in the spirit of our mind, for the inward disposition and inmost temper will determine, control, and give tone to the outward conduct.

Disposition, then, the spirit of the mind, is the theme to which our thought is now turned; and, out of God's own Word, we may get the clue to what is here meant. A most instructive passage is found in Luke ix. 46-56, which alone may suffice for the amplest illustration of the whole matter.

There are here accounts of three different occasions when our Lord was constrained to rebuke his disciples for indulging a wrong disposition, for manifesting a wrong spirit of mind. It is also very significant, that these three instances cover all vicious dispositions or bad tempers. The first evil disposition here rebuked is *ambition;* the second is *intolerance,* or *bigotry;* and the third is *vindictiveness,* or *revenge.* When our Lord dealt with these three wrong tendencies he embraced in them, as representative forms of unholy dispositions, all other evil tempers, for all others are wrapped up in those three. To consider these in order, and see how vicious, how depraved, how destructive they are, will help us also to see the contrast between them and a thoroughly renewed spirit of mind.

I. First, *ambition.* "Then there arose a reasoning among them, which of them should be greatest. And Jesus, perceiving the thought of their heart, took a child, and set him by him; and said unto them, Whosoever shall receive this child in my name receiveth me: and whosoever shall receive me receiveth him that sent me : for he that is least among you all, the same shall be great." Comparing Matthew xx. we get a fuller account of the occurrence here recorded. "Then came to him the mother of Zebedee's children with her sons, worshipping him, and desiring a certain thing of him. And he said unto her, What wilt thou ? She saith unto him, Grant that these my two sons may sit, the one on thy right hand, the other on the left, in thy kingdom. But Jesus answered and said, Ye know not what ye ask." The vital matter about this interview lies in the ambition for the chief seats of honour and trust. The two brethren, James and John, had joined with their mother in the request for these seats on the right hand and the left in the kingdom. But Jesus taught them that he who would be chief of all must, as Mark says, be "servant of all," "even as the Son of man came not to be served but to serve others, and to give his life a ransom for many." The wrong disposition was ambition, whose motto is self-will, self-interest, getting up, and getting on, and getting ahead of others. James and John, with their mother, petitioned for the chief seats of honour beside His throne or His banquet-table. This was perfectly natural to an ambitious soul. But our Lord here taught them how evil the ambitious spirit is, and what evils are its offspring This determination to get on, to get up, to get ahead of other rival claimants, begets jealousy and envy, which are counterparts of each other. Jealousy is envy, directed toward another's prospect of success; envy is jealousy, directed towards his actual success. We are jealous of others *lest they should* do or should get; and we are envious of them *after they have* done or got. Ambition makes me jealous of my neighbour who bids fair to attain, accomplish, achieve, succeed; and makes me envious when he has accomplished and succeeded. Ambition also leads to covetousness, which is desiring what belongs to another, whether property, fame, intellectual gifts and attainments, or worldly success. The soul and secret of, perhaps, a third of all the evils that curse humanity, may be found in this one vice, ambition. It is found in the church of God :—in "Diotrephes," who still "loveth to have the pre-eminence." If there could be cast out of the church all that evil spirit that is ambitious of office, of power, of influence; that is jealous lest other people should attain the pre-eminence, or envious of those who have attained it, what a true brotherhood the church would become ! Some there are who want prominence, and even pre-eminence, and are ready to rend the church of God in twain because they cannot have their way ! Destructive influences are thus sadly at work in the assemblies of believers, as in worldly society. When a minister would be lord over God's heritage, when a deacon or elder would hold a sceptre for the sake of power and the glory of self-advancement, what a mischief-maker he becomes ! What incalculable evils come to the whole Body of Christ when any member seeks to be supreme ! What a monster of selfishness one may grow to be simply through feeding ambition ! In political life, a man aims to get some lofty position, to hold some honourable office, to secure his own advancement and emolument ; and so he plots to get ahead, and even plans the ruin of other people, that, on the wreck of their fortunes, their disappointed plans, their blasted reputation, he may mount up to the throne of his own exaltation ! That was the spirit of Napoleon, willing to demolish all the thrones of Europe, that he might build up his own; that was the spirit of Xerxes and Alexander, willing to put a world in waste for the sake of the sceptre of a world-wide Empire.

What does Jesus teach us? He sets a little child in the midst of his disciples: he points them to the humility of the child-like spirit, and he says, "Whosoever would be great among you, let him be your servant; and whoever would be the chiefest of all, let him be the servant of all;" and when, in John xiii., we read, how Jesus, in the midst of the Passover feast, rose from supper, laid aside his outer garment, girded about him the long slave-apron or towel, and then took a basin and a ewer of water, and poured the water over the disciples' feet, and with the end of the towel-apron wiped their feet,—which the Jews thought was as menial an office as could possibly be performed, save one, the loosing of the latchet of another's shoe,—our Lord, in that visible posture of condescension and humility, illustrated how the greatest among them could be the "chief servant of all." When the Master thus stooped to the most menial act, He showed us that no deed can be drudgery when it is done in His name. We may dignify and glorify the most menial service by doing it for the love of God, and so redeem it from association with what is low or vile, or mean or servile.

II. The second of these malignant tempers, and unholy dispositions, is the "*intolerant.*" "And John answered and said, Master, we saw one casting out devils in thy name; and we forbad him, because he followeth not with us. And Jesus said unto him, Forbid him not: for he that is not against us is for us," and, as Mark adds, "No man can lightly speak evil of me who shall do a miracle in my name."

What is the essence of intolerance? As ambition says, "Myself;" intolerance says, "My way;" "No other way is right but that which I walk in; therefore if you want to be right, you must go in the same path where I tread. No other doctrine is right but that which I hold; so that if you would be a true believer, you must believe as I do. No other practice is proper but that which I pursue; so that if you want to be a proper man, you must follow my practices." That is the real way in which the intolerant spirit dictates to others. See how our Lord treats it. He says, "Forbid him not." They were going to forbid a man *to cast out demons* in the name of Jesus, because he did not follow in their train, did not belong to the twelve apostles, did not attach himself closely to their company. Here was one who was actually casting out demons, and honouring the all-powerful Name in so doing, and yet they would have said to him, "Have done with your casting out demons! You do not belong to our company! You do not walk in the same way with us! What right have you to be exorcising evil spirits!" Jesus *forbids them who would forbid him!* "He that is not against us is on our part." "There is no man that can cast out demons in my name that can lightly speak evil of me, or work against my interests." Our Lord has here given his disciples a lesson for all time to come. What is intolerance after all but the disposition to *compel uniformity in minor matters?* We often talk about the persecuting spirit of the Roman Catholics because they set up the Inquisition in Spain, and put people to the rack and various tortures, and even burned them at the stake because they did not bow to the Pope and worship the Virgin; but it is to be feared that there is not a denomination of Christians in the world that could be safely trusted with supreme power; human nature is too frail to hold an absolute sceptre. There are probably those in the Anglican church, who, if they had the authority, would shut up every Noncomformist chapel; but are there none in Nonconformist bodies, who, if they had their way, would shut up every Episcopal church? Have any of us an ecclesiastical garment in which if He should closely examine, the Lord would not find at least a *scarlet lining of intolerance!* Human nature has never yet been entrusted with absolute power without abusing it, and this is as true in the Church as in the State, that the possession of a sceptre needs to be guarded by constitutional limits to prevent its despotic abuse. There remains much unsanctified territory, even in the hearts of professed disciples, and so it is that intolerance and bigotry are so common even in the Church of Christ.

And as ambition is fruitful of envy, and jealousy, and covetousness, and similar evils, so intolerance or bigotry begets a whole progeny of vipers. Has not this evil despotism been at bottom of the pulpit exclusion which shuts out faithful preachers because they have not been ordained in a certain fashion? And has it not been at the bottom of the exclusion of unquestionable believers from the Lord's table because they have not been able, in the matter of baptism, to see quite as others do? Whence came persecutions but from intolerance! There is no question, as Dr. Schaff says, that heresy is an error, but let us remember that intolerance is a vice and a sin, and persecution is a crime; so that not even in order to rebuke heresy must we cultivate a vice, encourage a sin, and commit a crime. The disposition to say to another, *" You must be like us,"* implies an immoral tone of mind!

Now, what is our duty? Four things are plain:—First,

hold your own views. There is no reason why, because we are bidden to be charitable, we should be without convictions. I honour a man who has an honest, earnest, intelligent conviction, and lives up to it. Hold your own views, tenaciously if you will, intelligently as you can, persistently as it is possible. Let every man be fully persuaded in his own mind, but at the same time, concede to others the right to be as fully persuaded in their minds and to hold their views as earnestly, intelligently and pertinaciously as you hold yours.

In the second place, whenever an error that is held by another is fundamental, striking at the foundations of the Christian system, come out from among those who hold and teach such error, and be separate from them; have no fellowship with the unfruitful works of darkness, but rather reprove them. If there is a man that denies the Lord Jesus Christ, the centre of your faith; who denies the Bible, which is the revealed Word of God, or takes out from its inspiration the supernatural element, you are under no bonds even of charity to recognize and hold fellowship with such a one. You are bound to be separate from such, otherwise how can you sustain the fabric of the Christian church, and the truth as it is in Jesus Christ?

In the third place, magnify the essentials, but comparatively forget those things that are indifferent. Remember what Augustine said: "In essential things, unity; in non-essential things, liberty; in all things, charity." The whole enemy of God is massed against the church of Christ, and stands in solid phalanx over against the truth; so much the more reason why we, who do love Jesus Christ, and stand for His truth, and for the majesty and glory of His Deity, should stand shoulder to shoulder in this great war. If the regiments of the devil can possibly get parted, let us part them ; but let the regiments of God's army stand close by each other, and whatever may be the denominational flags that are raised, let them all be lowered when the blood-stained banner of the cross appears, for that is the standard of our common Master. After one of the most disastrous battles in the American War, Gettysburgh, a man went into the hospital bearing with him aid and comfort which Massachusetts had sent, and he went round from cot to cot, and inquired, "Any Massachusetts soldiers here?" Nobody answered. He continued going round, "Any Massachusetts soldiers here?" Not a word. By-and-by, one voice answered, "No! *Only United States soldiers here.*" What a blessed thing if, instead of talking about our denominationalism, we would forget that, in view of the great war of the ages, and say, "However proud I am that I am a Baptist, or a Methodist, or an Episcopalian, I am, after all, only one of *Christ's soldiers*, carrying on Christ's war."

And fourthly, "By their fruits ye shall know them." It has been well said that it does not make a donkey a horse, because he is brought up in a horse's stall, and fed on oats ; and it does not make a man a true child of God, that he has been brought up in a Christian family or a Christian church. What makes him a child of God is, that he has received of the Spirit of his Master. That is the only test. Now the Lord teaches us if we see a man casting out demons in His name, we are to remember that no man can cast out demons except by the Spirit of God, and we are to recognize the Spirit of God in that man, though he may not follow in our train. A man may differ from us in some minor points of doctrine or polity : the great test is this, Does he cast out demons ? Has the demon been cast out of his heart ? Has the Spirit of God taken possession of his soul ? Is he doing God's work ? Are men brought to trueness and newness of life through him ? Does he magnify the essentials of the gospel, and does the Lord crown his gospel labours with abundant success ? Do not forbid any man who is obviously doing God's work. It is at the peril of your acceptance with God that you put a hindrance in the way of the man that is moved by the Holy Spirit, and is used by the Holy Spirit for service to God and souls.

III. The third of these evil dispositions is the *vindictive* or *revengeful*. He " sent messengers before his face : and they went, and entered into a village of the Samaritans, to make ready for him. And they did not receive him, because his face was as though he would go to Jerusalem." That is, the appearance was that He was going by them, and they took offence at the apparent slight, so that they would not extend their hospitality to Him. " And when his disciples James and John saw this, they said, Lord, wilt thou that we command fire to come down from heaven, and consume them, even as Elias did ? " You remember how Elijah called down fire on two companies of fifty soldiers that were sent to arrest and apprehend him, and they said, " These people will not receive you, shall we revenge ourselves on them by calling down celestial fire to consume them ? " And our Lord somewhat severely, though sadly, replied : " Ye know not *what manner of spirit* ye are of,"—you know not how malignant is the disposition you are indulging. " For the Son of man is not come to destroy men's lives, but to save them."

You never, perhaps, wanted to call down fire from heaven to consume anybody else, but have you never indulged that subtle, vindictive, revengeful disposition in other forms? What is the vindictive temper but the disposition *to return evil for evil*? A pastor asks one of his members to call on another who lives round the corner, and the sharp answer is, "I am not going to call on that party." "Why not?" "Because he passed me by in the street and did not speak to me, and I always pay people back in their own coin." Did you ever hear anything like that from fellow disciples? A man treats you with some indignity, and you wait the opportunity to pay him back with like indignity. He says a word against you, and when you have an opportunity you say a word against him. He has neglected you, you neglect him. He did not come to your house when he was invited, you do not go to his house when you are invited. What is that but a vindictive spirit, returning evil for evil; and there is not one of us, before God, who is not answerable to the charge, that over and over again we have indulged the vindictive spirit, even within the circle of the church of Jesus Christ. The most terrible disorders and divisions come to pass among disciples, from the spirit that returns evil for evil; and, as ambition leads to envy and jealousy and covetousness; and as intolerance leads to bigotry and persecution and malice; so vindictiveness leads to the violation of every command of the Decalogue; so that there is not a form of crime from lying up to murder, that revenge has not prompted, all through human history. There is a golden rule, "Whatsoever ye would that others should do to you, do ye even so to them." But there is a silver rule that men take instead of the golden rule, "Whatever *other people do to you*, do you even so to them." What is the Divine remedy for the revengeful temper? Paul says in the twelfth of Romans, "Dearly beloved, avenge not yourselves, but rather give place unto wrath; for it is written, Vengeance is mine; I will repay, saith the Lord. Therefore if thine enemy hunger, feed him; if he thirst, give him drink: for in so doing thou shalt heap coals of fire on his head." "Do not avenge yourselves." God is the God of vengeance. "Give place unto His wrath," stand back and let the Lord God of holy vengeance repay the insults and the indignities of man. Do not burn your hand by putting it on the sword of vengeance, held in the flaming hand of Jehovah. "If thine enemy hunger, feed him; if he thirst, give him drink." It is devil-like to return evil for good; it is man-like to return good for good and evil for evil; but it is God-like to return good for evil, and so, if you would be God-like you know how.

"For in so doing thou shalt heap coals of fire on his head." When the silversmith refined precious metals, in old times, he put the crucible on the coals, and when the metal was being reduced to a liquid form, he took some of the coals from beneath the crucible and put them on the top of the metal. In this way he put the metal *between two fires*. Now, when you do kindness to your enemy, you subject him to a *top-fire;* his own conscience is already accusing him of wrong, and your kindly act intensifies the accusation. While conscience reproves him, your love adds its gentler reproof, and between the fire of his own moral sense and the fire of your charity, his heart is melted down. How often, when a man is wrong, we rather freeze him into greater hostility by our retaliation of his wrong-doing, by our reciprocal insults or slights.

The history of Jamaica furnishes a most wonderful illustration of holy vengeance on evil-doers. When the evils of slavery in the West Indies were exposed to the view of Britishers they said, " This evil shall be wiped off of the escutcheon of our nation." On August 1st, 1834, the children of the slaves in Jamaica were set free. The whole Act of emancipation did not take effect till the first day of August, 1838, when all the adult slaves were also liberated. The night before that Act took effect there was not a coloured man or woman or child of any age in the island that went to sleep. The day of liberation was at hand, and so they kept that night as a night of prayer and praise. Fourteen thousand adults and five thousand little children met together in prayer, with William Knibb, the missionary and evangelist, leading them on. They meditated a terrible "vengeance" against their former masters. They constructed a large mahogany coffin, which was polished and trimmed after the best style by their best cabinet makers, and into this coffin they crowded all remaining relics of their former condition of slavery : they filled it with whips, with torture irons and branding irons, with handcuffs and fetters, with thumbscrews, the coarse rock, and all that pertained to their former slavery—they put all these in the coffin, and then screwed the lid down tight. Midnight came on, and when the great bells sounded out the hour of twelve, as the first stroke was heard thrilling through the air, William Knibb said, "The monster is dying!" another stroke, " Dying!" another stroke, "Dying!" until when the last stroke of twelve pealed out, he said, " The monster is dead! Let us bury him!" And they lowered the mahogany coffin into the grave. That was their Christ-like vengeance on their former masters, not insurrection, not massacre, not insult for insult, not injury for injury, not blow for blow, but burying out of sight all relics and remnants of their former bondage that they should be no more brought to their minds or the minds of their oppressors.

Nothing can bring about a change of heart like this except we be born from above. No amount of self-reform can purify us of ambition, intolerance, and vindictiveness. We must be flooded with the love of God. The holy Dove must take his abode in our souls, and we must learn love from Him who is love. You cannot do that yourself. Come unto the Lord Christ, and unto the Holy Spirit, to be renewed in the spirit of your mind, and learn the beauty and the power of a disposition which is so transformed by God, that you are no longer ambitious to get ahead, except in serving; nor anxious to have your way, except so far as it is first of all God's way; nor disposed to avenge yourself, save with the holy vengeance that returns deeds of love for acts of malice! Nothing makes more manifest our need of the new birth, than the impossibility of re-making that most subtle heart and core of character, the disposition. But what is impossible with man, is possible with God. Let Him try His grace on your hard heart, and it shall be as soft as the clay on the potter's wheel. Let Him shine into your inmost soul, till His light becomes life to the spirit, and abide in His love till He imparts to you the secret of exercising celestial love yourself.

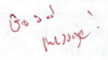

SERMON EIGHT

The Height of Transfiguration

"Verily I say unto you, that there be some of them that stand here, which shall not taste of death, till they have seen the kingdom of God come with power."—MARK ix. 1.

IN the famous Yosemite Valley, in California, there is a place, called "Inspiration Point," because from it you command the entire valley. The bold rock, El Capitan, stands on your left; the Bridal Veil, the Cathedral Rock, the Three Brothers, Glacier Point, Eagle's Nest, on your right; the Washington Arches, the North and South Domes in the distance. From no other point is the entire scene so completely spread before you.

It has been customary on Christmas day to study our Lord's life from the point of His incarnation, or coming in the flesh. This is not the "Inspiration Point" from which to command the best view of the valley of His humiliation. There is another, far more exalted and inspiring, from which to study the true character and career of our Lord Jesus Christ, namely, His Transfiguration.

The Transfiguration occupies the central point in our Lord's public life. If we follow Matthew, especially, we observe that Christ more and more manifests His glory in His words and in His works, until He reaches the Mount of Transfiguration. From that time miracles comparatively disappear; He utters no more great discourses to the multitude; there is a gradual descent from that mountain height until He touches the lowest point in His humiliation, namely, His crucifixion between the thieves. Here then is the central point in His human history. From His birth, everything leads up to that; from that, everything leads down to His death; and there is, subsequently, but one real glimpse of His glory, and that is in His resurrection and ascension, which really lie beyond His mortal career, for He had then passed through the sorrows of death.

It is quite surprising that the Transfiguration is not more studied as the "Inspiration Point," from which everything about the life, and the character, and the career of Christ receives a new glory and a new illumination. Let us get this point of view, and so look at Christ; not from His cradle at Bethlehem, not from His cross at Calvary, but from the summit of the mountain where He revealed His essential glory.

The significance of this event can be seen only by combining the accounts of the different Evangelists. In Mark ix. 1, we read: "There be some of them that stand here, which shall not taste of death, until they have seen *the kingdom of God come with power.*" But in Matthew xvi. 28, we read: "There be some standing here, which shall not taste of death, till they see *the Son of man coming in his kingdom.*"

Uniting the two, the narrative would read: "Verily I say unto you, there be some of them that stand here, which shall not taste of death, until they have seen the kingdom of God come with power, and the Son of man coming in his kingdom." In these two statements we have the key to the Transfiguration; it represents *the kingdom in its power*, and the *King coming in His power*. From this point, then, we get both the glory of the King and the glory of the kingdom.

The value of this event lies in this, that it is the only glimpse of this double glory that has ever been given to the sons of men; and therefore it is the most exalted point of prospect found within the pages of the Word of God. There is only one that can compare with it, and that is in the visions of the seer of Patmos in the Apocalypse, where we have what John saw on the Mount of Transfiguration unfolded in part among the "things to come."

Now, what is a kingdom? It is a territory ruled over by a king. There is a great distinction, however, between the kingdom in an individual, and the kingdom in relation to the whole community over which it extends. Every vessel on the high seas that bears the British flag is a part of the British kingdom, but a very small part, and very inadequate to represent the glory of that kingdom. Every soldier that wears the uniform of the British soldiery represents that kingdom, and yet again how insufficient to display the real grandeur of that empire on which the sun never sets! Again, there is a great difference between the outskirts of an empire and the centre, between a kingdom at its capital and at its furthest borders where civilization ends and barbarism begins, just as there is a great difference between the rays of the sun, scattered at the limits of the solar system, and concentrated in the glory of the shining orb itself. Again, there is a great difference between the subjects of the king and the king himself. They may, perhaps, be robed in plainest, coarsest and rudest attire, and living in the plainest huts or hovels; but the king is invested with kingly raiment, and dwells in a palace such as befits royalty. There is also a great difference between the kingdom in its obscurity and in its glory. The kingdom of Christ however real, is just now unseen. A veil stretches between us and the glory, so that we catch only as through a veil now and then a faint glimpse of its splendour, or seem to hear a voice speaking to us faintly, and scarcely audible in the distance. But when the veil is removed, as it was on this occasion, and the full blaze of the kingdom bursts upon us, we shall learn what Paul means in the Epistle to the Colossians :—" Ye are dead and your life is hid with Christ in God ; but when Christ, who is our life, shall appear "—when the veil shall be rent asunder—" then shall ye also appear with him in glory." We shall see Him then, and we shall see ourselves and the kingdom then as we never have before.

"Till they have seen *the kingdom come with power.*" Taking this Transfiguration scene as an exhibition of the kingdom, how wonderfully complete it is !

First, remember, that the two who met with Jesus Christ on the mountain of Transfiguration, Moses and Elijah, were two of the greatest characters that ever appeared in history— Moses, the leader, the lawgiver, the historian, the poet, the organiser of a great nation, one of the greatest generals of all history ; Elijah, perhaps the foremost of the prophets, a man who suddenly springs into existence, of whose early life we know nothing, who comes before us as a grown man, remonstrating against the iniquities of Ahab and his court ; and passing away as suddenly, with horses and chariots of fire, borne up to heaven without knowing the mystery of death. What do these two men represent? Moses stands for a resurrection life, for Moses died, and was buried by God Himself, in the land of Moab : " The place of his sepulchre no one knows unto this day." Moses stands for saints who have passed through the ordinary experience of death, who have been buried in the grave, but who, nevertheless, live, and live in glory with Christ, and shall hereafter be united with their own bodies in His presence, at His coming. Elijah represents those who have, like Enoch, passed through from one world to another without the experience of dying at all.

These two men belong to a period of history before Rome or Athens were founded—before authentic history began, twenty-five hundred years ago—for Moses lived fifteen hundred years before Christ; and Elijah lived at least nine hundred years before Christ. One of them died, and the other passed to glory without death.

You have in both these glorified saints the testimony to a continuous and endless life. We are told in the Epistle to the Hebrews that Jesus Christ is " made not after the law of a carnal commandment, or ordinance, but after the power of an endless life," and the word translated, "endless," means undecaying, undying, a life that knows no such thing as death. Elijah and Enoch were " translated that they should not see death," in order to impress upon humanity that there is such a thing as life that knows no dying. The body itself dies and decays, but life itself cannot decay, and the child of God has the secret of life that is absolutely undying, undecaying, undiminished as the ages go forward. If you have lost a saint from your sight, whose body you have buried, Moses stands as the pledge of the present glory and existence of your sainted dead, as much so as Elijah is the pledge of a life that knows no death at all, into which those that remain at the coming of our Lord shall, like Elijah and Enoch, be translated without the experience of dissolution.

These saints appeared then with Christ in glory; they shared His glory: Their raiment was white like His, and their faces shone like His, and they talked with Him about "His decease, which He should presently accomplish at Jerusalem."

If you ever ask yourself what is the condition of the saints in glory, these two men indicate the answer.

First : *saints retain their individual character*. Moses was not confused with Elijah, nor Elijah with Moses, nor either of them with anybody else. Moses remained Moses, Elijah remained Elijah, and they were recognised instantly and instinctively by the disciples. There was apparently no introduction of them as strangers, nor any mention of their names in conversation. Probably the disciples, by a kind of spiritual instinct, knew Moses and Elijah, as we shall recognise each other in the future life.

And yet saints in glory *have an associated life*. We shall remain individuals in the future life, but we are to form a society of saints and hold communion and converse with one another in the "general assembly and church of the first-born whose names are written in heaven."

Further, we learn that besides this individuality, this association, there is a *familiarity of converse* with regard to things which are going to happen. Knowledge on the part of immortal souls partakes somewhat of the character of God's knowledge. The future is probably unveiled and revealed before them, so that many of the present limits that surround our knowledge will there be removed. This coming crucifixion of Jesus Christ at Jerusalem was something that was on their tongues in glory, and they understood the purpose and the purport of it, and talked freely with each other and with Christ with regard to it.

What a complete picture of the future glory of the saints! each one retaining individual character, all being gathered together in holy association, instantly recognising each other in glory and conversing familiarly, their minds being open to a knowledge, even of the events that lie in the future and are to make more glorious to the universe the character of our God.

There was still another department of the kingdom illustrated on the mount. Here were three disciples looking up at this glory, dazed, dazzled, affrighted, by its splendour. Who were they? They represent another department of Christ's kingdom: Moses and Elijah and Christ represented the kingdom *triumphant*; Peter and James and John, the kingdom *militant*. Those are the saints in glory; these are the saints in suffering. Those are the saints crowned with exaltation; these are the saints going through the Valley of Humiliation for Christ's sake. But remember that John and Peter and James were just as much a part of that kingdom as Moses and Elijah were : here for a time, bound to be there by-and-bye; here, encompassed round about with ordinary bodies, in ordinary raiment, but destined to share the same lustre and glory as that which they beheld. Yes, this is a wonderful exhibition of the kingdom of God. It has not here come with power, but it has there come with power, and those poor saints that had to go through struggle and trial yet for a while, two of whom were for Christ's sake to be slain, and another to endure persecution and exile in Patmos—they were heirs of that kingdom, only waiting for the day when the glory of it should be revealed in them as it was then revealed to them.

II. This Transfiguration scene revealed the *Son of man coming in His kingdom*. All this glory would be incomplete without the person of Jesus Himself. That is an imperfect conception of Heaven, which does not make the King the centre of its attractions: what would any kingdom be without its king?—his palace, court, throne are the glory of its capital. It was not Moses and Elijah that those disciples saw mainly, it was Christ; and when they came down from the mountain they forgot all about Moses and Elijah, and "saw no man save Jesus only."

It is a very curious and suggestive fact, that, when the kingdom was represented in power, the smallest number of saints appeared which can constitute a company. Christ says, "where two or three are gathered together in my name, there am I in the midst of them." The smallest number that can gather in His name is two, and that is all that were gathered in glory there, because He would show to us that the kingdom of God comes with power whenever two glorified saints meet to hold glorified communion with each other and their Lord.

As to the King, as He prayed He was transfigured. It was not simply that His raiment became white and glistering, or that His face or countenance shone, but that the whole person became radiant. It was as though the prayers that were moving in His soul and breathing through his lips were a sacred fire within Him that the body ordinarily would conceal, but which, on this occasion, the body, becoming transparent, revealed, so that the glory of the holy affections and emotions that were burning in His mind and heart, shining through its body, made it radiant, so that it became lustrous like the sun. And then the raiment—coarse and common as it might have been—was likewise lit up with the inward glory, and shone itself like a garment of golden sheen or sunlight. When Jesus was transfigured, His whole person was glorified; and so they saw, for the first time, the King in His glory.

→ It will now appear why the incarnation does not furnish the true "Inspiration Point," from which to study the person of Christ. The babe in the manger cannot represent our King; nor the swaddling clothes in which He was wrapped, the royal raiment, the purple and ermine of the King and Judge. That stable was not a fit palace for the King of Glory, nor a woman's arms His fit resting-place.

The babe was the King in disguise. His infancy, and even His humanity, constituted that disguise; and, therefore, so long as we look at Christ in the stable at Bethlehem, or on the Cross between thieves, we see Him *veiled;* we cannot behold His glory. Neither at the cradle nor the cross, but on the Mount of Transfiguration the King is seen in His essential glory.

When we come to think of His "*essential glory*," we look down into unfathomable depths, or up into immeasurable heights. We are wont to think of Jesus Christ as leaving His throne in heaven and coming down to earth, and becoming a babe in Bethlehem; as passing through life on earth, poor, forsaken, despised, rejected; as suffering on the Cross as a malefactor between thieves; as buried in the tomb; and, then, as rising from the dead and returning to glory; in other words, His human life becomes to us a sort of a gap or gulf, or interval of thirty-three years, in His divine and eternal existence.

But is that altogether a true conception? If Christ, during His earthly life, wholly gave up His heavenly life, what becomes of His Omnipresence and essential Deity? We may readily concede that, during His humiliation, His essential glory was veiled to human eyes. But are we justified in supposing that His human existence was like the sheet Peter saw, let down from heaven and suspended for a time, and then drawn up again into heaven? He said of Himself, "No man hath ascended up to heaven, but He that came down from heaven, even the Son of Man WHICH IS IN HEAVEN." Observe the present tense: "IS in heaven." While on the earth, as to His human manifestation, was He not, in another sense, also in heaven as to His essential divine nature?

His own words suggest an unfathomable mystery. What is omnipresence? Not simply an influence pervading the universe as the rays of the sun pervade all space; but a real presence of God, alike in all places at all times. If Christ were the Omnipresent God, then there is a mysterious sense in which, while, as to His humanity, He was in the cradle and on the cross, He was, in His essential Deity, still in heaven and on the throne.

I fear that there is a tendency so to emphasize His human manifestation and incarnation, as to lose sight of His essential glory as a person of the Godhead. Great as is the mystery, *essential* glory is something which may be *veiled*, but cannot be *surrendered* or left behind like a garment that may be laid aside and re-assumed. Let us ask ourselves whether, even in the days of His humiliation, He ever ceased to be "God over all, blessed for ever." We may not fathom the mystery. But it may help us to think of His incarnation as rather the veiling of this essential glory, so that men could not see what they could not have borne had they seen it; and that His Resurrection and Ascension was a partial unveiling of His true self, as the Transfiguration was a complete revelation of the hidden glory, so that for once it smote with its full lustre the eyes of His wondering disciples.

Possibly, in the Garden of Gethsemane, there was a

sudden flashing out of this glory for an instant when the soldiers, who moved forward to apprehend Him, suddenly "went backward and fell to the ground." There is no explanation given, but it seems as though, for a moment, the "glory of the only begotten of the Father, full of grace and truth," shone out and dazzled and smote them, so that they scarcely knew what it was that, for the moment, overwhelmed them with awe.

If what has been said appears not only mysterious but contradictory, be it remembered that the Godhead will always be, to our feeble human comprehension, beset with apparent contradictions. Certain it is that for once the veil was removed. The earthly disguise was lifted, and the radiant star of world-wide empire was seen flashing from the breast of the King of kings. The glory that He had from the beginning and will have to the end, and which, being essential and not circumstantial, He must always have retained, was for once beheld by mortal eyes.

Do not His own words teach us, that, while on earth, He was also "in heaven?" and that, if at any moment of His humiliation, He could have been seen as He was, eternally and essentially, the glory would have shone out and dazzled those that saw it. Was not the Transfiguration meant to teach us that the King essentially glorious is always glorious? Is it altogether correct to speak of the coronation of Christ as a coming event? Is Christ, as the essential King of glory, not already crowned and reigning? If so, all that remains is for that coronation to be recognized. Is He still to ascend His throne, or is He already and eternally on that throne, so that it only remains for men to see that He is, and fall at His feet in homage?

Many events which, "because of the infirmity of our

flesh," are represented to us as yet awaiting accomplishment, are *real present facts to God*, for whatever has taken place in God's purpose is to Him a reality. The everlasting future is for ever present to Him and everything that to us is yet to be, is to Him as that which now is. He already sees Christ swaying the sceptre of the universe with undisputed authority.

This vision showed "the Son of man *coming* in His kingdom." That word " coming " is so linked with His Final Advent at the end of the age, that to many it has no other meaning. Possibly this is an error. " The coming of the Son of man in His kingdom " certainly in this case must refer to the Transfiguration, not to His final coming. It was not true that there were "some standing there that should not taste of death " till they saw the *Second Advent* of the Son of man. Even if by His " coming " the destruction of Jerusalem was meant, the only one of the three who could have witnessed that event was John. Perhaps we have too limited notions of the phrase "the *coming of Christ*." "Coming " means a personal presence (παρουσια), and wherever Christ manifests His personal presence He may appropriately be said to "*come.*" Dr. F. W. Upham suggests that the coming of our Lord is a progressive event, having its steps or stages. One was the Incarnation, when He became a babe at Bethlehem : one was the Transfiguration when He disclosed His glory to His disciples : one was His Resurrection and Ascension, when He went up to the glory that He had with the Father before the world was: one was His coming in judgment on the City of Jerusalem and on the Jewish nation, for their rejection and crucifixion of Him : one coming of our Lord may have been at the destruction of the Roman empire, which was responsible for His crucifixion—when the Goths and Vandals and Huns swept down from the north. Every time Christ exhibits His personal presence to a praying saint in answer to prayer, is there not a "coming of the Son of man?" And so, in the 18th of Luke, after a parable on prayer, he says, "Nevertheless—although God does surely hear and answer prayer—when the Son of man cometh shall he find faith on the earth." It is most natural to refer this, not to His final Advent, but to His speedily avenging his saints in answer to their entreaties. When He does come to them to give them their hearts' desires, will He find them *expecting His coming?*

The Lord's coming has then its steps and stages, and this may be illustrated familiarly. Suppose that there was in some very remote part of the earth a great universal king, who was proposing to come to these shores and here set up his visible throne. There would be many different stages in his coming or approach. Suppose him to set sail from the ports of Japan. When he touched at any port on the way, it might be said "He is coming!" If he landed at Calcutta, or one point after another in the homeward journey, at Port Said, Brindisi, Calais, Dover, till he came into the River Thames and landed on the quay at London, at every point it might be said "He is coming," and it would be so. But when he came to take possession of the Imperial Palace prepared for him and his, and actually to sit on the throne erected for his reception, that would be the *final coming*, and would be the end of the successive and progressive comings. Now, is not it so with our Lord Jesus Christ? He always has been coming since the foundation of the world, and every single step and stage of His coming is only an advance towards the last great advent when He shall sit upon the throne, and the whole world shall be brought beneath his benignant sceptre. To Him universal dominion belongs. He has long been on the way to take possession of His rightful throne, moving towards its ultimate and perfect possession; and every time He has displayed Himself to the sons of men, as the babe in the manger, in the synagogue at Nazareth, on the cross, by the rent tomb, but especially in this transfiguration, it has been a new stage in His coming. The ages are the pathway of the Son of God, and the centuries are His strides forward : and when He comes at the end of the age that will be the complete manifestation of His glory, when to our eyes He is seen to ascend the throne that in God's eyes He has occupied ever since the foundation of the world.

We see the nature of the kingdom of Christ. It is as yet an unseen kingdom. The carnal eye cannot behold it; it must be seen by the eye of faith. Its capital city is not in this world, it belongs to another. Its throne is not of marble, its pillars are not of silver, or of ivory, like the famous throne of Solomon, in Jerusalem. It is the "great white throne," with pillars of light; and the robe that He wears is the very glory of God.

The kingdom is unseen, but it is *real!* How little those disciples thought, when they went up to the Mount of Transfiguration, that the kingdom of God in its glory was so near. Their Master felt weariness and faintness, and hunger and thirst, like the rest of them, but in a moment they saw the being that had been clambering up the mountain side with them, wearing the glory that no man can approach unto or behold with unveiled eye. If the veil were torn from our eyes we should find the King in the midst of us, and the saints in glory holding converse with Him. There is a

Presence here grander than any presence of man, and all that is necessary is for our vision to be perfect, and we might see what they saw on the Mount of Transfiguration.

"Lord, open his eyes, that he may see," said Elisha, and immediately his servant saw the mountain full of horses and chariots of fire round about the prophet. Our eyes are holden that we should not know Him, but He is in the midst of us, and that is the only warrant for our being here. We have come to meet the unseen Lord, and though we cannot behold Him now, we can hold converse with Him by the way, and rest in the sweetness of His presence.

It is a sad thought that even here, in this place of worship, there are some that have no share in the kingdom. Christ the King is waiting for new accessions to His kingdom. Every time a rebel against God lays down the weapons of warfare, puts his hand to the solemn covenant with God, and signs and seals it with his own name, the Lord's kingdom extends over a new soul; there is an added province of that kingdom represented in that penitent believer. The only way you can enter into that kingdom is that that kingdom shall first enter into you. If Jesus Christ becomes to you to-day your King, you become a part of His kingdom, and when the glory of the Lord the King is revealed you shall be revealed with Him sharing His glory. And that is the reason why the gospel is preached: it is a humble effort on the part of one who undertakes an embassy for God to tell men how they may become subjects of His kingdom, and sharers of His glory. To-day the King comes in humiliation, as a babe in Bethlehem's manger, a crucified Saviour on Calvary's tree: He comes and says, "Will you let me reign over your hearts? will you open the little territory within you that has been in rebellion and raised the black flag of revolt against Me? will you let into that territory the King of kings?" And if you will open your heart to Him to-day and say, " Lord Jesus Christ I am Thy servant and subject, take the throne in my heart, reign in me, rule over me, be my King, let me be Thy subject and Thy servant, Lord," to-day Christ may take His throne in you; and by-and-bye you shall see Him seated upon His throne over the universe, gathering you round about Him in His court and presence, making you the sharers of the glory that He had with the Father before the world was.

Sermon Nine

Awaking, Arming, Acting

" And that, knowing the time, that now it is high time to awake out of sleep: for now is our salvation nearer than when we believed. The night is far spent, the day is at hand: let us therefore cast off the works of darkness, and let us put on the armour of light. Let us walk honestly, as in the day; not in rioting and drunkenness, not in chambering and wantonness, not in strife and envying. But put ye on the Lord Jesus Christ, and make not provision for the flesh, to fulfil the lusts thereof."—ROMANS xiii. 11, 12, 13, 14.

IF there be, in all the Word of God, a message appropriate for the Sabbath which ushers in the New Year, certainly it is this.

To study it intelligently, we must first inquire as to the figure here employed and its meaning. Paul was familiar with the customs and manners of the Roman soldiers, for, when he was himself a prisoner in the City of Rome, he was chained to a new soldier every morning, and it is probable that this Epistle was written subsequent to his first imprisonment. The Roman soldier appears to have been permitted to lay aside his armour when the night came, and spend the night as he would, but in the morning he was required to assume his armour again, and, with the dawning of the day, appear at the barracks or at any post to which he was detailed. It would frequently happen that a soldier, after laying aside his armour, and spending the night in riotous carousing and drunken revelling, would fall asleep as the day came on, and sleep very heavily after his sensual excesses; then, as day began to dawn, he would awaken or be aroused, hurriedly put on his armour, remove from it the mud or filth that might have accumulated upon it during the previous day, and then march off to the post where he was expected to appear, or to the barracks where the soldiers assembled to receive their rations and enter upon their duties for the day. Familiar with these customs and habits of the Roman soldiery, Paul adapts his language to these well known facts: "Knowing the time, that it is now high time to awake out of sleep: for now is our salvation nearer than when we believed. The night is far spent, the day is at hand"—is even now upon us. " Let us therefore put off the works of darkness and put on the armour of light: let us walk honestly, as in the day; not in rioting and drunkenness, not in chambering and wantonness, not in strife and envying. But put ye on the Lord Jesus Christ, and make not provision for the flesh, to fulfil the lusts thereof." We shall see how beautifully and how closely the figure fits the life of a disciple, for this is not a message to the ungodly but to God's own people, and its pertinency will appear as we come to consider it more carefully.

Paul uses the words "day" and "night," "darkness" and "light," in three marked senses. Sometimes the word "night" expresses the period of past sinful experience and indulgence, and the "day" would then mean the time of our acceptance of Christ, and our conversion unto Him. Again, he uses the word "night" in the sense of the past of our entire life, and, in that case, the "day" would mean the time of our entrance into glory, our passage from this life into the scenes of the life beyond. He also uses the word "night" in the sense of the period of the withdrawal of Jesus Christ from among His disciples, and the "day" would then mean the reappearing of Christ in His second coming, without a sin-offering unto the full salvation of His people. It is possible that he uses these words in all these senses in this passage. There is a sense in which the "night" of our sin is spent, and the "day" of our conversion has dawned. There is a sense in which the "night" of our past life is far spent, and the "day" of our ushering into the presence of God is fast approaching. There is a sense in which the "night" of our Lord's withdrawal is very far spent, and the time of His return and glorious appearing is drawing nigh. Perhaps we shall most honour the truth of God if we are not particular to discover which of these three senses Paul especially adopts in this passage, but rather look at its general trend and import as pertaining to the child of God. We shall observe two things here: first, a command or injunction; and, second, a reason or consideration. Paul first puts a duty before us, and then assigns a ground for the performance of that duty.

The duty is expressed in several forms—"Awake," "Put on the armour of light," "Walk honestly, as in the day," "Make not provision for the flesh, to fulfil the lusts thereof."

The reason is mainly this—"The day is at hand: and our salvation is nearer than when we first believed."

There is an important double injunction which claims special consideration: first, the duty of awaking, and, secondly, the duty of clothing ourselves with the full armour of God. As to the duty of awaking, disciples are supposed to have passed the time of their carousing, their fleshly indulgences, their riots and revelries; but how often it comes to pass that, even after we have given up the open sins of our evil life, we fall into lethargy, and apathy, and indifference, into carelessness, and sluggishness, and sloth. In the Church of

Awaking, Arming, Acting

God to-day, professed disciples are rarely drun tioners, adulterers, blasphemers, revilers, and id be thanked, the time when it was common for professing Christians to commit such awful, flagrant, and criminal iniquities is past; only now and then do we find even a nominal child of God guilty of transgressions of the ten commandments, and standing before men as an open violator of the law of God. But the great evil, especially of this age of ours, is that so many who have put off these "works of darkness" are yet asleep as to all responsibility, activity, duty. What is sleep? A period of unconsciousness, when the whole mental as well as bodily powers are sluggish; a period of sloth, of idleness, of inactivity; a period when we are unclothed, and defenceless, so that our foes have us at an advantage. During sleep time is passing without the recognition of the fact that it is passing—slipping through our hands as the water passes through the hands of statues in our public squares, where the stone or the iron is unconscious of the outflow. How many disciples of Christ there are who are not flagrantly wicked, not open violators and transgressors of God's commandments; but who have never been roused as yet to the full sense of their responsibility and duty to God or man. "The day is at hand," the night is gone by, the sun has risen above the horizon, the world is waiting to have the message of salvation carried to it, the Church of God is waiting to have its young converts strengthened and trained into noble-hearted disciples and effective workers for God; waiting for the contributions of Christian people to be poured into the Lord's treasury; waiting for the self-giving of disciples, who offer themselves willingly unto the Lord, as the messengers of salvation to the ends of the earth. And yet in the opening of this year, 1893, the great proportion of professed disciples of Jesus Christ are asleep, some of them dead asleep, some of them just awaking, half asleep and rubbing their eyes, and recognizing the fact that the day is upon them, but turning over like the sluggard and saying, " A little more sleep, a little more folding of the hands in slumber, a little more indulgence of the spirit of sloth and of sluggishness."

We have just been celebrating the centenary of that wonderful era of modern missions, that was inaugurated by William Carey's offering of himself in 1793 as the first English missionary to India. The greatest obstacle that Carey met with, during the ten years that he was seeking to awaken interest in foreign missions, was found not in the open and flagrant iniquities of his brethren of the Baptist denomination, but in the dead sleep in which whole Churches were abiding, rocked in the cradle of their indulgence, swung in the hammock of ease, one end of which was fastened to the cross of Christ and the other to Mammon, fanned into a delicious slumber amid the intoxicating odours of this world. He found it almost impossible to arouse even his brethren in the ministry, to the fact that a thousand millions of human beings had never heard the gospel of Christ, that the missionary of the Cross had never gone forth into the major part of the regions beyond to carry the gospel to the dying; and was he not told even by one of his Baptist brethren, to "sit down," and that "if God wanted to convert the nations he could do it without him"? It almost seems as if that famous rebuke of John Ryland belongs to the myths of past ages, so impossible does it seem to us in these days ever to have been an historical fact. But let us not suppose that the periods of sleep in

Awaking, Arming, Acting

the Church lie away back in the past centuries. This very day, in January, 1893, the vast proportion of the nominal Church of God lies in the slumber of apathy and the sloth of indifference. There is no design to be offensive to Christ's disciples in this great congregation, when I say that, after preaching here the major part of an entire year, it is quite plain to me that even here the large proportion of members give little evidence of doing any actual systematic work for the Lord Jesus Christ. That a considerable number of people here are engaged in holy activities for God there can be no doubt; but that many others are simply sanctified sponges that imbibe all that they can possibly receive, having no proper conception of their duty to distribute the benefits and blessings of this gospel to a dying world, is a fact of which a careful observer is likely to be sadly convinced. And what is the case here, is true in all Christian congregations the world over. The major part of those who confess Christ as Saviour, have never yet awakened to the fact that He is their Lord also,—Master of their lives, that He owns their purse, their properties and their possessions, that He owns their hands, their feet, their ears, their eyes; that they are His, that their children are His, that their homes are His, that their business is His, that their treasures are His, that all that they have they hold as His stewards and trustees; that they owe a debt to the dying world that can never be paid, however diligent they may be, but that they are also trustees, put in trust with the gospel as the only riches by which that debt can even in part be discharged.

To this beloved people, this morning, the Spirit of God is saying, " Knowing the time, it is now high time to awake out of sleep; the night is far spent, and the day is at hand."

Still a thousand millions of people have not Christ, still more than one half of the population of this earth have never even seen a missionary or a Bible, or heard the first proclamation of the gospel; and as every pendulum stroke of the clock beats a second, a soul passes into the other world, and the greater proportion of those dying people have never yet been told that there is a Saviour for them. Let everyone of us, in the secrecy of the heart, solemnly look back over the year 1892, and ask, how many souls have I spoken to with regard to salvation; how many homes have I visited in which are sickness, sorrow, and suffering; how large a proportion of my income have I given to the Lord Jesus Christ for the service of dying people the world over, and the distribution and dissemination of the Holy Scriptures; how many days have passed in which I have offered no intelligent and devout prayer to God for a soul that is lost without Christ; how many days have passed in which I have prayed and worked for my Master, or have actually asked myself what work He had for me to do? On the other hand, how often I have been absorbed in the treasures and the pleasures of this world, given myself to that mad pursuit of riches or almost equally insane pursuit of what I shall eat and drink, and wear, as if the things of this world were all that had any interest for me, or any importance for me! How many days are there that I have passed almost without a whispered prayer to God, or perhaps, behind the formality of prayer, disguising a heart that had little interest in spiritual things; into how many shallow joys of this world have I plunged, as though they could satisfy me; after how many fleeting baubles have I run, as though if I grasped them they would not burst in my hand, leaving me only the agony of disappointment!

I saw a picture once, "La Chasse de Bonheur"—the chase of fortune—which represented a man as moving, as it were, through the air, after a fleeting vision, a woman, with a golden ball representing boundless wealth and treasure. On he is plunging, with his eye on the golden bait and the seductive female form. He is passing just over a bridge that is broken in the middle, and the chasm opens and yawns just before him. Down beneath his feet there lie the wife and the children, dear to him by natural ties, whom he is rudely trampling down in the mad pursuit of that which he is bent on reaching. That allegorical picture represents human life—a parable in action. In every street in London there is that Chase of Fortune, that insane pursuit of a bauble or a bubble, that subservience to the seductive forms of pleasure, that trampling under foot of all that is dear to God and man, in the vain ambition after personal gratification and selfish advancement. God says to us, "The day is far spent, the night is at hand. We know the *season*, that it is now the high *hour* to awake out of sleep." The very sun itself smites our eyeballs with its brilliance while we turn over in bed for another morning nap, another indulgence of sloth and sluggishness. And if the trumpet voice of God might call some nominal child of God, some sleeping disciple, out from sloth and inactivity, out of unconsciousness and indifference, out from the idleness and waste of time of a life that pretends and professes to be God's, but is as yet half-wedded to the world; if these words of the Spirit could rouse some of you to take up the work of Christ, to have a new zeal for God according to knowledge, and to expand unto new activities of service for men, what a blessed year this would be! If everyone in the membership of this Church of over five thousand souls, should resolve in the strength of God to be the means in 1893 of adding at least one new member to the body of Christ, would three hundred and sixty-five days of prayer and labour pass without at least one soul being so gathered to Christ ? And that would mean more than five thousand sinners converted in this congregation alone during the year to come, instead of two or three hundred, which is the average of the forty years that have preceded. Nothing more needs to be said to prove that the major part even of a great Christian congregation like this have never been fully aroused yet to the idea, "I am God's, my labour is God's, my witness is God's, my money is God's, my time is God's, my strength is God's," all to be poured without measure into the open treasury of the Lord for service and sacrifice in the cause of Jesus Christ.

Permit a word of personal confession and testimony. Two years ago to-day, in solemn meditation and prayer, I was led to see that I had been, in a sense, embarrassing the plans of God all my life long, by scheming for myself, by laying out work that I had called work for Him, but which was really largely work for myself and my own interest. These personal schemes reached sometimes a year and more into the future, so that, if God opened to me a new work to do with wider promise of usefulness and service, I found myself bound hand and foot, so that I could not enter into the open door. It was made clear that it was unwise, henceforth, to have any plan that reached far into the future, and that a servant of God should hold himself open to the leadership of God, day by day, to follow as He might guide. It is a privilege reverently and thankfully to bear witness that the last two years of my life, left thus without any human plan, have been blest in the abundance of service and in the abundance of joy in God, beyond any ten years that preceded. Some of you may be led to make a solemn new year's resolve, that this shall be the best year of service, of entire consecration, of devout praying, of intimate communion with God, of absolute self-surrender for His service; and surely this is one way to awake from sleep, and arouse ourselves on the morning of this new year; one way to consider how the day is far advanced and the night is far spent, and to obey the challenge found in the very dawn of day, calling us to new holiness of life!

The other part of this injunction is, "Put ye on the Lord Jesus Christ," or, as it is elsewhere expressed in the same passage, "put on the armour of light." When the Roman soldier awoke in the morning, before he put on his armour he first cleansed it from everything that had defiled it, or obscured its brightness, on the day before. It so became an "armour of light" or a shining armour. So the Apostle says, "Let us cast off the works of darkness, and let us put on the armour of light." The figure is plain. What is expressed in one verse as putting on the armour of light is expressed in another verse as putting on the Lord Jesus Christ; but there is no contradiction between the two. When the Roman soldier put on his armour, in a sense he put on Rome; for you might have seen on the various parts of that armour the signs of the empire and Cæsar, whose soldier he was. On the helmet were the silver eagles spreading their wings as if for a flight, the signal and symbol that floated from the standard that was unfurled over Rome's battalions; on the breast-plate you might have seen the coat of arms of the Roman Empire with the mark of the Cæsars, and, just as in the cordage of the British Navy if you cut it at any part you see the scarlet thread running through which marks that cordage as the property of the Crown, so you might on any part of the armour of the Roman soldier have seen some mark or stamp of the Roman authority and ownership.

In every part of the Christian armour there is something that reminds us of Christ. The breast-plate reminds us of faith in Christ and love towards God, and the helmet, of the hope of salvation; and every part of the armour is impressed with Heaven's " coat of arms." God's golden eagles are on the helmet to indicate the soaring of the soul after God; the Cross is stamped on the breast-plate to show that our faith is in Jesus; there is a burning heart on the armour to indicate the yearning of the soul after God, so that when you put on the armour of light you put on Jesus Christ. In every part of that armour He is remembered, signified and signalized.

What does the Apostle mean by "Casting off the works of darkness"? He tells us what the works of darkness are—"rioting and drunkenness, chambering and wantonness, strife and envying. Here six forms of sin are arranged in three couplets or pairs: rioting and drunkenness belong together because they have to do with the indulgence of bodily appetite; chambering and wantonness belong together because they have to do with the indulgence of carnal lusts; strife and envy belong together because they have to do with the indulgence of evil tempers and malignant dispositions; and so these "works of darkness" cover the whole range of iniquity, for all the sins to which men are given may be reduced to one of these three classes. They are either sins of bodily appetite, such as intemperance and gluttony, or sins of carnal lusts such as lead to sensual indulgence, or they are sins of disposition, that exhibit themselves in strife and envy, covetousness and jealousy, anger and malice, contention and disorder, breaking up peace, and bringing war on a small scale or a large scale. All these belong to the past life of a child of God. He has nothing to do with them henceforth, and is but half a disciple until he has learned to put these things for ever behind him. He should be ashamed when he sees in himself any remaining tendency to gluttony or to sensuality or the indulgence of evil tempers. What if every Christian man and woman would let strong drink alone, let carnal lusts alone, let alone all strife and envy! What if we had the body in such subjection that no appetite could ensnare us: the lusts in such holy control that no carnality or sensuality could ever betray us: the disposition under such rule that nothing but love should reign in our hearts and govern in our lives, what days of heaven on earth would be brought down to earth! Paul could say—"I keep my body under and bring it into subjection." The body is the residence of the soul. Reason and conscience were meant to occupy their double throne and sway their benign sceptre over the body, and the Holy Spirit was given to occupy His imperial throne over even the reason and the conscience; so that there should be restored the true and normal order of a human soul—God's Spirit ruling the human spirit, and the human spirit ruling the body, so that the whole body is brought into subjection to the divine law. That alone is "casting off the works of darkness"; that alone is putting away revelry and rioting and drunkenness and gluttony, chambering and wantonness, sensuality and indulgence; that alone is truly putting away covetousness, envy, jealousy, malice, and all uncharitableness; that alone is being a whole man in God because

God occupies the whole man; that is being a saint indeed among saints, a promoter of godliness and of God's glory among men.

One must never attempt to put on the Lord Jesus Christ without first putting off the works of darkness. I met Rev. William Haslam at Melchet Court, the residence of Lady Ashburton, and, speaking to him about this text, which then occupied my mind, he said, "Yes, dear brother Pierson, tell the people they must not put on the new man without putting off the old man." There are too many who are trying to put Christ on without putting off the old Adam. It may do in conversion to sing, "*Just as I am* without one plea, but that Thy blood was shed for me," putting the garment of an imputed righteousness over our old self, but we are not to *let the filthy rags remain there.* In *sanctification* the rags are to be put away, and the Lord Jesus Christ is to be the true garment that robes the soul. We should not be satisfied only to be justified by faith, and still permit any filthy thing to remain under the garments of our imputed righteousness. God says to us, "Be ye holy, for I am holy!" and we should not be satisfied to have a wrong lust, an ungodly passion, an unholy temper, or any other form or remnant of evil, to defile the body and the spirit, and so dishonour our blessed Lord. Not until we find out that the fulness of our salvation demands this entire transformation of soul and spirit and body into the image of Jesus Christ, and that sanctification implies a growing and daily progress in divine things so that we are not only invested with Christ but come to represent Christ in the reality of our personal character, will the Church of God be what it ought to be, harmless, blameless, undefiled, separated from sinners.

When the newly-fallen snow has covered the face of the earth, there are pools of filth and accumulations of all kinds of refuse underneath the snow, but its white mantle covers over and for the time obscures all else. That snow white robe of nature may represent to us what Christ does for us in conversion when His pure mantle comes down over our filthiness and hides it, so that for Christ's sake God sees only the pure whiteness of His Son's infinite vicarious merit. But when the snow disappears the filth remains, and so even this imperfectly represents Christ's work. On the other hand when the sun is left free to shine he purifies the filth, dries up the marshes and the stagnant pools, and changes the very nature of the soil on which he beams; so that, as Ruskin says, the clay and sand and soot that may be found everywhere on the outskirts of our manufacturing towns, the sun, if he has only time enough, will so transform, as that the clay becomes the sapphire, and the sand becomes the opal, and the soot becomes the diamond. Even this feebly represents what Christ, as the light of the world, does for a soul that he first covers over as with the white mantle of His snowy purity. Christ is not satisfied to cover your sins; He must purge them away; and if you found in Him the covering of your sins in conversion, in sanctification you may find Him now purging your sins by His refining and purifying power, by the Light, the Love, and the Life of the Sun of Righteousness.

II. The reason or ground of all this exhortation is, "The night is far spent, the day is at hand: now is our salvation nearer than when we believed." We shall best interpret these words if we remember how often in the Bible the "day" is used to represent the *progress of our salvation.* The night is the period of our past life when we groped in the ignorance and darkness of sin; the day-dawn is the acceptance of Christ, when the Light of the world first shines upon us for our salvation; and then, as the sun mounts towards the zenith till it stands at the height of the heavens at the noon-tide, so there is to be progress in our salvation, from one degree of glory and grace to another, until the sun reaches its zenith, when the coming of our Lord Jesus Christ completes our salvation, and He receives unto Himself those who first received Him into themselves.

Here, then, are two great suggestions :

First, *the day is come, and therefore we ought to put on the armour that belongs to the day.* How beautiful is the association of the Lord of Glory with the child of God. We are told as, in the first Epistle of John, that God is light; so we are the children of the light; our armour is the "armour of light," and the day in which we work, is the day of light. All must be consistent and harmonious. When the Roman soldier polished his armour and put it on and went out into the sun, every part of that burnished armour became a reflector of sunlight and shone with the sun. So the Apostle would have us burnish our armour and clothe ourselves completely with it, so that when we go out into the world, that is still in darkness, they who have never seen the Sun of righteousness shall see the shining of His beams in the reflection of our armour; so that, wherever we go into the midst of the deep night-shade men's eyes shall be dazzled with the brightness of our godlike character. In other words, put on Christ's image and likeness ; for the day is already come, and it is no time now to carouse or to sleep. Now the high hour is come to put on your armour, and in it march forward to the barracks, to the post of duty wherever it is, accept as your rations the provision that God gives you for your spiritual life, and for ever cease to make provision for the flesh, to fulfil the lusts thereof.

Secondly, the day of our life is passing, the day of our opportunity is passing, we are drawing very near to *the coming of our Lord.*

"Now is your salvation nearer than when you believed." There is no doubt what is meant. When Christ went away He said, "Yet a little while, and ye shall not see me: and again, a little while, and ye shall see me;" and because he had never communicated to them the day nor the hour wherein he should come, the early Christian Church stood continually as on tip-toe, watching for the appearing of the morning star which heralds the day, when, after the night of Christ's absence, the Sun shall arise with healing in His wings. Two thousand years have nearly swept by, since Christ ascended. The time of His coming is drawing nigh, for it must be at least nineteen centuries nearer than when He first went back to the Father. There would seem to be wanting *not one of all the conspicuous signs* foretold in the twenty-fourth chapter of Matthew, and in the Epistles to Timothy, the second Epistle of Peter, the Epistle of Jude, and the book of the Revelation, as those that indicate the coming of the Lord as drawing nigh. For though Christ did not tell the day nor the hour wherein He is coming, He gave certain indications that should serve to show when the day-dawn was nigh, as the signs in the eastern sky indicate the rising of the sun, although we may not know the exact moment of his mounting above the horizon. Look round the historic horizon to-day, with eyes cleared of carnal prejudice, and see if there be no signals that the coming of the Lord draws nigh. One of those signs, indicated in the Word, is that there should be a *widespread apostasy in the Church*, especially with regard to the doctrine of the divinity of Christ, the inspiration of the Scriptures, and the coming of the Lord. May not that apostasy be now a fact ? There are many desiring to be teachers that know not whereof they say nor what they affirm, blind leaders of the blind, going into the ditch themselves and dragging their pupils with them. Certainly there is a widespread and alarming defection from the faith. Another sign that was given of Christ's coming was the deceptive "peace and safety" which men should feel from the *uniform order of nature;* sneering at the idea of any great revolution or change in the world's condition, and the condition of human society, because, as they say, "all things continue as they were from the foundation of the world." What is the conspicuous doctrine of science in these days, but the "uniformity of nature"? We are told that, so uniform are nature's laws and operations that they have continued ever since the foundation of the world the same, and shall continue to the end of time the same; that there is no use of any Creator because this " clock-work " of the universe carries everything on without the need of a regulating hand. Another great sign of our Lord's coming was given, namely, evangelistic activity such as was never known in the earth before, the *world-wide witness of the gospel;* casting, into the sea of the world, the drag-net, the universal net-work of missionary endeavour reaching into every part of the world, and gathering of every kind. What do we see now? Never was such missionary activity known from the beginning of Christian history, never such widespread missionary organization, the drag-net borne into all parts of the world-sea, with seven thousand labourers to draw it towards the shore, and so many fish gathered within it.

And what is that "full salvation"? Six great words, all of them beginning with the same letter, are, in the Bible, used to indicate what this full salvation of Christ's people is. These words are Refreshing, Regeneration, Revelation, Restitution, Redemption, and Resurrection. These words will prove of unspeakable help to any believer in the study of the Scriptures.

The first is the word "*Refreshing*." "Times of refreshing" are to come "from the presence of the Lord and the glory of His power." These are to be the Days of the "Regeneration," or making of all things new. This Day is to be one of "Revelation," or the perfect unveiling of the glory of our Lord Jesus Christ. These are to be "Times of Restitution," that is the full accomplishment of all the prophecies spoken since the world began; also the Times of our full "Redemption," or the entire release of the soul from the bondage of sin and of death; and of "Resurrection," or the final release of the body from the bonds of corruption, and its introduction into the glorious liberty of a resurrection life. All these are necessary to our full salvation. By "Times of Refreshing," we understand that the Spirit of God shall be outpoured on "all flesh," as it was before poured out on the Christian Church at its beginning. In the "Times of Restitution" not one unfulfilled prophecy shall remain in Scripture; the predictions, so long delayed, as to the literal regathering of the Jews into their own land, or at least a portion of them, representative of the Jewish nation, shall be accomplished. There will be "Regeneration,"—even this world is to be renewed—a new heaven and a new earth wherein righteousness is to take the place of the present order of things—and it may be God's purpose that, in the very world in which we now live, glorified, purified by fire, redeemed saints may tread over the very scenes of previous service and sacrifice, and recall their labours for Christ in the very spots which have been dignified by association with the Saviour in His work. Then shall come the "Resurrection," when this body is to be made like unto His glorious body with all its powers, with eyes that see things that no carnal eye can see, ears that can hear things that no carnal ear can hear, with organs and faculties, glorified and sanctified, enlarged and strengthened, and made susceptible of pleasures and service to which we cannot even in imagination now attain or aspire. The word "Revelation" suggests that Christ came in disguise when He first came, but there will be a glorious unfolding of His perfect character when He comes with the glory of the Father and of the holy angels. The word "Redemption" indicates absolute and final release from all bonds of corruption, and introduction of soul and body into the wondrous participation of the divine nature and presence.

This text has a peculiar connection with the conversion of St. Augustine, who had been through the round of human philosophies as well as of human pleasures, trying to find something, like Solomon, that would satisfy the unsatisfied cravings of an immortal soul. And one day, while sitting down in a little arbour in the garden and meditating upon his dissatisfied state, he had a scroll of the Epistle to the Romans on his lap, and had been looking in it to see if he could find there what he had never found in any heathen philosophy, something to content his long unresting soul. He fell asleep, and it seemed to him in a vision, that an angel came near and touched him, and said, "Tolle, Lege!" "Awake, and read in the thirteenth chapter of Romans, eleventh verse." He sprung up from his sleep, so vivid was the vision, and opened the scroll and read. "And that, knowing the time, that now it is high time to awake out of sleep: for now is our salvation nearer than when we believed. The night is far spent, the day is at hand: let us therefore cast off the works of darkness, and let us put on the armour of light." By the seat in his arbour, Augustine knelt and poured out his soul to God, that he might then awake to the full conception of his need and the greatness of the redemption that was in Christ Jesus, and there began that day the marvellous career of that man who, with Chrysostom at Antioch and Constantinople, and Origen in Africa, and with Athanasius, head of the great council of Nice, with John Calvin in Switzerland, John Knox in Scotland, John De Wycliffe in England, Savonarola in Italy, and Luther in Germany, became the great advocate and apostle of the new faith in Jesus Christ, the faith of the New Testament, and the reformed Church of God.

Sermon Ten

Appointed and Anointed for Service

"But the manifestation of the Spirit is given to every man to profit withal."—1 CORINTHIANS xii. 7.

When Paul began this first Epistle to the Corinthians, he wrote, in the second chapter, "I determined not to know any thing among you, save Jesus Christ and him crucified." These words have been pressed into a narrow mould of meaning, which it is plain the writer never intended should confine and limit them. For instance, there are those who infer from them that every sermon should be a distinct and literal setting forth of Jesus Christ on the cross as the only hope of sinners, and that it is incomplete if it does not deal directly with His atoning work. Whatever prominence is to be given to the great central doctrine of Christ's vicarious sacrifice, it would seem that Paul never could have meant that he would confine himself to this one theme. The same Epistles in which this sentence is found, present the greatest possible variety in the discussion of all topics pertaining to Christian faith and life, conduct and service; and among them many themes that do not bring to the front the atoning work of Jesus Christ as the hope of sinners, as in the eighth and ninth chapters of the second Epistle, where he discusses the great question of Christian giving. In the passage also which is now before us, in this twelfth chapter of the first Epistle, we have a full treatment of the subject of service as rendered to Christ by disciples.

This most important theme is opened with a sentence that reveals Paul's sense of its value : " Now, concerning spiritual gifts, brethren, I wish you not to be in ignorance." If Paul regarded it as of the utmost importance that a sinner should understand that there is no salvation without Jesus Christ, it was equally necessary for a saint to understand that every saved man is a servant of Jesus Christ, and has positive work to do for his Master.

We are apt to think that the spiritual gifts here referred to, were peculiar to apostolic days. Many who profess to believe in Christ have no conception that they also, like Paul, Peter, John and James, have spiritual gifts. Spiritual gifts are here treated as the fruits of the Spirit in every believer, as also in the twelfth chapter of Romans. Paul says these Corinthians had been the servants of Satan, led by him into the worship of idols; they once said of Jesus Christ, " Let him be anathema," or "accursed of God." But when they turned to Christ as a Saviour, the Holy Spirit taught them to serve God, and led them to call Jesus Christ, Lord or Sovereign—Master of their lives.

This *Mastership of Jesus Christ*,—not simply *Saviourship*, but *Mastership*,—lies at the basis of all service. He was crucified to bring to men atonement sufficient to save, but He was glorified to send to men equipment sufficient to serve. And no gospel is complete that shows Christ's atonement as sufficient for salvation, that does not show the Spirit's equipment as sufficient for service. And to this latter half of this double truth I call attention because it is the neglected half, namely, the Mastership of Jesus Christ. Have you accepted Him as your Saviour? Accept Him as your Lord. Have you looked to Him for salvation by faith? Look to Him now for service by the power of the Holy Ghost. Spiritual gifts are distributed to every believer—special spheres for service are appointed to every believer, and certain operations or definite workings are manifested in and through every believer. That is the truth taught in this chapter.

There are many obscure references to the Trinity, which the careless reader will not notice, and these three verses (fourth, fifth, and sixth), contain one of those references. " Now there are diversities of gifts, but the same *Spirit*," that is the Holy Spirit. "And there are diversities of administrations," or forms of service, "but the same Lord," that is *Jesus Christ*. "And there are diversities of operations, but it is the same God which worketh all in all," that is *God the Father*. So that the different gifts bestowed upon disciples, are here traced to the Spirit as their bestower, to the Lord Jesus Christ as Him to whom the service is offered, and to God the Father as Him through whom all power works in believing souls.

Let us fix in mind, then, this great fact, that the Holy Spirit never calls a sinner into the kingdom of God without giving to him his share of the gifts by which he is made serviceable; that the Lord Jesus Christ never saves a man without appointing to that man a sphere of special service; and that God never works by His grace in any believer without working in him fitness for service. The Mastership of Jesus Christ implies spiritual endowment and enduement, or the gifts of the Spirit's bestowment, and the equipment of power for the service to be rendered.

To refer all this back to the apostolic age, as though it has no reference to us, is to commit a great wrong both to our Saviour and to ourselves. We must learn the Divine principle of distributing spheres, and energy to work in those spheres, and call our Saviour our Sovereign Master; and begin at once, if we have not already begun, to render service to this Master as a grateful recognition of salvation freely given to us. Turning from all the idols that we have served, we must recognize the Holy Spirit as residing in our hearts and presiding over all our activities.

As already said, spiritual gifts were not confined to apostolic days. Nine of these *charismata* are here mentioned. "For to one is given by the Spirit the word of wisdom ; to another, the word of knowledge ; to another, faith ; to another, healing; to another, miracles; to another, prophecy; to another, discerning of spirits; to another, divers kinds of tongues ; to another, interpretation of tongues"—nine different spiritual gifts or endowments. It is not necessary, however, that spiritual gifts should in all ages be bestowed precisely in the same *form*, or to the same *degree*, as then. There may have been reason, then, for very marked gifts of the Spirit, because the Christian religion was being introduced among mankind, and needed the seal and sanction of God upon it ; but, when once God's seal was broadly and plainly put upon this gospel message, as upon a document, it was not necessary that the seal should be repeated. There is not, however, one of all these spiritual gifts, bestowed upon apostles and disciples in the first age, that has not some closely corresponding gift, in the age in which we live, differing not so much in kind as in degree.

Can we see, for instance, any signs in our own age to the bestowment of the word of wisdom upon disciples ? What is wisdom ? Spiritual wisdom is insight into truth with power to apply that truth to the wants and needs of others. Wisdom differs from learning, for a wise man is one that knows how to use knowledge, but many a man may have knowledge who has no wisdom. Spiritual wisdom implies this power both to see into a truth and into the wants and needs of souls, and the sagacity and skill to apply to them that truth. We may take as a single example of spiritual wisdom, John Wesley, one of the most remarkable men that ever lived. There was not one among the apostolic twelve that had more spiritual wisdom than he—insight into God's truth and insight into the needs of human souls and the methods by which spiritual life might be cherished and nurtured. The influence of John Wesley lasts to-day, and is growing every day, not only in the denomination of which he was the founder, but in every other body of disciples.

Have we nothing that corresponds to spiritual knowledge —knowledge especially of the Bible and of Christian truth ? Take John Bunyan as an example. Let anyone read Bunyan's "Pilgrim's Progress," and note how, from the beginning to end, this man shows himself a master of the Word of God. See with what deftness and skilfulness he brings in the dialect of Scripture to describe his characters, their doubts and difficulties and trials and triumphs ! See also with what marvellous power he uses the key of Holy Scripture to unlock all the conditions, perplexities, mysteries, and experiences of the human soul.

Have we nothing in these days that corresponds to the faith that wrought miracles ? Study the work of George Müller, in Bristol; see those five orphan houses with their two thousand seven hundred windows looking out on Ashley Downs ! Think of the millions of pounds sterling that have been gathered and expended there without ever an appeal being made to a human soul directly for any aid whatsoever,—all in answer to prayer!

Is there in these days that which corresponds to the gift of healing? Follow Florence Nightingale in the Crimea and see her system of ministry to wounded and suffering soldiers, the like of which for efficiency and serviceableness has perhaps never been known in the ages of the Christian era; under her supervision a revolution took place in the condition of those soldiers which can be appreciated only by those who witnessed it.

The gift of miracles has its counterpart still, especially in that department of supernatural power that is exhibited in the preaching of the Word of God when the preacher is invested with that strange nameless charm which is called "unction." None of you ever heard George Whitefield, but when that mighty evangelist gathered 20,000 souls on Boston Common, in the United States of America, and that vast audience was bowed before him as reeds are bowed by heaven's winds, or as waves are swayed by a storm at sea, the American people felt, as the English people had felt long before, that such a man represented as much spiritual power or unction as any man who had lived since the days of the Apostle Paul.

In apostolic days there was the gift of prophecy. What was prophecy but insight and foresight and the faculty of teaching divine truth? Take a single illustration from many in modern times. Francis Wayland, an American, and one of the most remarkable men whom that country ever reared, a man, who not only saw into the state of things in the Church of his own day, but with mysterious forecast of the perils before it, uttered prophecies which are even now being fulfilled in the Churches of this generation.

Is there nothing in our age that corresponds to the gift of tongues? Think of William Carey, the humble cobbler of Hackleton, going forth one hundred years ago, this very year, as the first missionary from England to India; and who was the means of translating the Bible into forty languages and dialects, and making it accessible to 200,000,000 of the human race.

Is there anything in these days that corresponds to the interpretation of tongues? Think of the great work of such a man as Matthew Henry, whose volumes are on the shelf of every theological student. Look at that man's power of interpreting the Word of God, and bringing out its hidden meaning to thousands upon thousands of God's dear saints!

How nearly correspondent to the discerning of spirits is that power of discerning or discovering the motives of people, of reading their inner disposition and temper, and of detecting in the suggestions, made even by nominal disciples, the marks of the Holy Spirit or of the spirit of evil. When you find a man, for example, like Charles H. Spurgeon himself, who never met an enquirer after the new life in Christ, or a disciple who was searching himself for spiritual growth, for whom he had not instinctively the very word of Scripture or revelation of Christian experience which met the case,—what have you but a marvellous instance of the modern gift of discerning of spirits?

These few examples might be multiplied almost indefinitely, to illustrate the corresponding spiritual gifts of Christ's disciples in the very day and generation in which we live. But let us remember also that all the *graces* of the Spirit, when truly enjoyed by us, become also gifts of the Spirit; and it is quite remarkable that, as there are nine spiritual gifts here, there are just nine graces spoken of in the Epistle to the Galatians, in the fifth chapter,—" The fruit of the Spirit is love, joy, peace, longsuffering, gentleness, goodness, faith, meekness, temperance. These are the nine graces corresponding to the nine gifts.

Examples abound in modern history of these graces. For an instance of *love* take Coleridge Patterson, the missionary Bishop to Polynesia, the man who won the very savages themselves, through the intensity of his devotion to Christ and his devotion to the souls of men. *Joy* is exemplified in Count Zinzendorf, giving up everything for Christ,—fame, position, social rank, and wealth, and willing to go anywhere for his Master; and yet so jubilant in God that he said, "I feel as if I were walking on air," even when treading through the most difficult and dangerous paths of self-sacrifice.

Peace was marvellously illustrated in Pastor Schmolke. With his parish burnt up, his wife and children in their graves, his own body afflicted with palsy and blindness, yet such was his peace that he dictated on his bed :—

" My Jesus, as Thou wilt,
Oh, let Thy will be mine,
Into Thy hands of love,
My all I would resign."

We read of Captain Allen Gardiner, at Tierra del Fuego, dying of starvation, with a piece of chalk writing on the rock, over the place where he fell and died, " Wait, O my soul, upon God, for all my expectation is from Him." Even death by starvation could not break up the joy of that wonderful saint !

Longsuffering is illustrated in all the martyrs. Think of John Huss, of Bohemia ; Jerome, of Prague ; Savonarola, in Italy ; David Livingstone, thirty-nine times scorched in the furnace of African fever, going on with his work of exploring, and making a pioneer path for missionaries, dying on his knees in the little grass hut at Ilala. *Gentleness* is a special grace of the Spirit, and reminds us of Fenelon, the Archbishop of Cambray, whose gentle spirit was so winning that even unbelievers could scarcely abide in communion with him without yielding themselves to Jesus Christ, and one infidel actually fled from his presence because he could not endure the light of his kind, mild, beautiful eyes. *Goodness* finds modern example in John Howard, going on that "circumnavigation of charity," as Burke called it, visiting the prisons and the lazzarettos of the world, and dying himself from the infection of a fatal fever, and refusing to have a monument put up to his memory. Such goodness has had rare illustration in human history. *Faith*, as a grace, found in Martin Luther a unique illustration, bringing to resurrection the doctrine, which had long been buried,—justification by faith—and standing before the whole world as the apostle of faith in his own generation. Hudson Taylor is as remarkable an example of faith as Martin Luther was, and perhaps there was none in apostolic days that exhibited more of the charms of this grace than this modern apostle of missions. *Meekness* makes us think of Archbishop Usher, a man who had no superior in the history of the Irish Church, and yet whose whole soul was absorbed with a sense of unworthiness, and who died with this exclamation upon his lips, "Oh, my God, forgive me my sins of omission." *Temperance* is simply the bringing of the body under control, holding its appetites and its passions in absolute surrender to Jesus Christ. General Gordon, in the Soudan, has given us one of the grandest and most illustrious examples in history, of such complete keeping of the body under, and bringing it into subjection to God.

Thus we have spiritual gifts, corresponding to those of apostolic days, differing not in kind but only in degree ; and spiritual graces, corresponding to those mentioned in Galatians, exemplified before our eyes by men and women of our own generation.

But, what shall be said about *natural* gifts, qualities, faculties, acquisitions and attainments; natural endowments and studious attainments? If the Bible teaches anything, it is that any gift which God has bestowed, or anything acquired and attained by study and effort and industry, may be made *the equivalent of a spiritual gift*, provided it is baptized with the Holy Spirit and consecrated by personal holy self-offering to God.

We might perhaps mention nine natural gifts which may thus all be turned to the uses of spiritual gifts. First, the gift of *speech*. What a marvellous thing is the human tongue and the human voice as the vehicle for the conveyance of ideas! How grand, when a man like Robert Hall consecrates to God the powers of utterance, and uses the years of his human life in testimony to the gospel of his Master! Is not such consecrated speech a spiritual gift?

Take *song*. Many can sing who cannot make a speech. Philip Paul Bliss, the famous singing Evangelist, was the finest singer of gospel songs I ever heard. He fell in the great catastrophe at Ashtabula in Ohio, but he had for years given his entire self to the singing of the gospel, and reminds us of Frances Ridley Havergal, who said, " I will henceforth never sing but for my Master," and the echo of her song is yet in our ears.

Musical composition is another gift. Whenever you hear Handel's oratorios of the "Messiah" and "Creation," remember that those oratorios were consecrated on the same principle as a true preacher prepares a sermon; and the glory of the "Hallelujah Chorus" was the especial outburst of a devout soul when meditating on the final triumph of Christ and His gospel.

Even *handiwork* can be made of service to God. Christian women sometimes think that they can do little or nothing for Jesus Christ; but one of the most remarkable of all miracles in the New Testament was performed on Dorcas or Tabitha, that saint of Lydda. Peter was called to raise her from the dead, and all we know about her is this, that she had *used her needle* to make garments for the poor. She may have been a bed-ridden cripple, unable to lift her feet or her head, but she could use her hands. God has left upon the needle of Dorcas the stamp of divine approbation through all the ages. If you cannot do anything else, wield a needle for the Master—your needle work may be used by Him as a spiritual gift.

As to *invention*, God gives to some men power to find out new truths, invent new arts, organize new sciences, as He gave to Sir Isaac Newton, Sir Humphrey Davy, and Michael Faraday, three great Christian discoverers and inventors, to do their important work both for the Church and the world.

Then as to *learning*. When a man studies books, and digs into the roots of ancient tongues, that he may be the means of helping the missionaries of the Cross to master foreign tongues, and to prepare grammars and lexicons and translations of the Word of God for the use of various native peoples, is that no spiritual gift? Dr. Riggs, of

Constantinople, as he stood on the bridge at that city of the Golden Horn, heard some twenty different languages spoken by the men that crossed that bridge, and he understood all those tongues. Such learning as that, consecrated by a beloved missionary of the Cross, becomes a spiritual gift, used by the disciple for the glory of Christ and His kingdom?

Some men have the faculty of *teaching*, like Thomas Arnold of Rugby, who, on English soil, set up a school the fame of which has reached round the world, so that Arnold's school at Rugby became the model school. Was not that a service rendered to God, and was not the power of such teaching thus used by the Spirit, a spiritual gift?

Suppose a man has *leadership*, like Gladstone, the greatest statesman, and perhaps the greatest genius of the century—is not such power of leadership something that may be so hallowed as to be turned to the purposes of God's kingdom? Dr. F. E. Clark, the originator of the Society of Christian Endeavour, out of whose little organization in his own rural church in America have grown thousands upon thousands of societies of the like character, the object of which is to lead young Christians into a holy service for the Master, has made his faculty of leadership and organization a spiritual gift blessed to the whole church of God.

If you have not learning, the gift of speech or the gift of song, could not invent or discover, and have no acquisitions of any large character, and are not fitted for leadership, still remember that you may at least be a *helper* to those who can organize and can lead. Blessed be God, there is no service so small, no tribute to Christ so insignificant, that it has not a record on the book of God's remembrance. The humblest child who, by seeking simply to help in the least ministries to saints, or promote the kingdom of God, turns such faculty of helping into a spiritual gift.

In the seventh chapter of this same Epistle a like doctrine is taught. The seventeenth verse reads thus :—" But as God hath distributed to every man, as the Lord hath called every one, so let him walk." The twentieth verse reads :—" Let every man abide in the same calling wherein he was called " ; and the twenty-fourth verse reads :— " Brethren, let every man, wherein he is called therein abide with God." Combine these verses, and what have you ? " As God hath distributed to every man, as the Lord hath called every one, so let him walk. Let every man in the same calling wherein he is called therein abide with God." This shows us that anybody, anywhere, in any honourable business, calling, trade, or profession, if he will bring God to his help and make Jesus Christ the partner of his toil and the Holy Spirit the inspirer of his effort, may *in that calling abide with God* and fulfil the work of God. Here are hundreds of working men and women who could not aspire to what in human eyes is a large and important and influential sphere of service, but who from this teaching of God may gather this great lesson : "*All I have to do is to stay where I am, to bring God into my work, and glorify Him in my service.*"

May God write these five principles on our hearts and minds !

I. *Every lawful employment may represent a calling of God.* Observe the vast variety of human needs, and of the corresponding gifts, adaptations, and spheres. All this exhibits a divine arrangement, as in the body there are no two members exactly the same, even the two hands and the two eyes and ears being different; and yet there is not a member, faculty, or organ of the body that is not contributing to the full strength and health and usefulness of the body. There are little capillaries, as they are called, or blood vessels, so small that it takes a microscope to see them, but if one of them does not do its service the health of the body is impaired. When I put my thumb over the palm of my hand I am covering thousands of little vessels which have to do with perspiration. Each one of these little vessels is like a drain, with its entrance and its exit, and the drain has to be flushed at times to get rid of impurities. So minute are these that one square inch will cover thousands of them, and yet if one of them does not do its service the health of the body is hindered. The body of Christ also consists of many members, organs, and faculties, and all that God asks you to do is to stay where He puts you and do the very best you can for Him and for the whole body.

II. *Every human faculty and acquisition may be construed as a gift of Almighty God distributed to us by the Holy Ghost.* In Exodus xxxv., from the thirtieth to the thirty-fifth verses, we are told, "The Lord hath called by name Bezaleel, the son of Uri, and Aholiab, the son of Ahismach, and hath filled them with the Spirit of God, to work all manner of workmanship in gold and silver, and brass and wood-carving, and embroidery." Think of that, that the Lord called a man to work in metals and in woods by His Spirit, endowed him by His Spirit to apply carving instruments to wood, to beat metal into shape, and embroider and weave. Think of that! a man may be just as much called to work in metals and in woods, as Aaron was called to officiate at the altar.

III. *Every sphere of honest and honourable work is a*

possible sphere of service to Almighty God. God *may call you out of one sphere into another,* but, in the absence of such a distinct call, the presumption is, that you are to abide just where you are, and instead of changing your sphere, bring into your sphere the Spirit of the living God. In the Baptist Churches of Great Britain are men, engaged in business, who undertake the charge of a mission hall, and, without leaving their business, preach there, administer the communion, and look after souls. They go to their place of work and spend a portion of their time in gathering that which is needful to supply temporal wants, and then go to minister to God's poor and sick and suffering ones. Why might not many more of the Churches at home be administered to by converted business men, who would preach the gospel as God gives them grace; while the trained men from the colleges and universities, might go to other countries, where we cannot depend as yet on the native labourers to do the work of God, but must have scholars, and teachers, and organizers, to translate the Bible and plan and conduct the missionary campaign. Conversion implies no necessary change of sphere, but only of the spirit with which the work is done—a new principle: all for God and all with God.

IV. *Every tool of trade is a possible weapon or implement with which to serve God.* When God saw Moses in the wilderness he had a crooked stick in his hand, for he was a shepherd, and had his crook; and God said, " *What is that in thine hand?* " He said, " A rod." God answered, " With that rod thou shalt do signs." God comes to you, a carpenter, to-day, and says, " What is that in thine hand?" "It is a plane, a saw, a chisel." " With that thou shalt do signs." " What is that in thine hand?"

You are a mason. "It is a trowel." "With that thou shalt do signs." "What is that in thine hand?" "It is a shoemakers' last, or awl and thread." "With that thou shalt do signs." "What is that in thine hand?" "It is a clerks' pen." "With that thou shalt do signs." "What is that in thine hand?" "It is a scrubbing-brush, or a broom." "With that thou shalt do signs." There is nothing that you have in your hand which is a proper implement or tool of your trade or calling, that God is not ready to sanctify by the Holy Ghost, and make it a means of service in His kingdom. And happy is the Church or the individual believer, that learns that great truth of the New Testament.

V. *Every gift and sphere must be consecrated, and then every lack will be supplied.* God never makes a mistake. When He called Moses to go to Pharaoh's court, with his stammering tongue, He knew what He was doing; He who could make Moses' stiff rod flexible as a serpent, could have made Moses' stiff tongue as flexible and fluent as that of Aaron. And if God calls you to any service all you have to do is to obey Him to the very best of your ability, just as you are and where you are. If you have not even accepted Jesus Christ as Saviour, much less as Lord, see what you are losing. You are not only forfeiting salvation, but you are forfeiting service. Begin to live, and to live for God. Accept Christ, to be saved by Him, first of all; and then ask the Holy Ghost to anoint you for your work for God. So shall the whole of your life hereafter be consecrated to His service; your workshop shall be your pulpit; the very tools of your trade shall preach His gospel; and however humble and commonplace the sphere in which the Lord has placed you, it will be blessed to abide therein with God!

SERMON ELEVEN

Renunciations and Compensations

"Rejoice in the Lord alway: and again I say, Rejoice."
PHILIPPIANS iv. 4.

THIS verse sounds the key-note of this entire epistle: "Rejoice in the Lord alway: and again I say, Rejoice." Three words may be written over this letter to the Philippians, and they will explain everything in it: *"Satisfied in Christ."* This is the disciple's profit and loss account, and the key-word of the epistle is the word, "GAIN." "But what things were gain to me, those I counted loss for Christ" (iii. 7). "I press toward the mark for the prize of the high calling of God in Christ Jesus" (iii. 14). The prize of the high calling is the highest form of gain, the ultimate reward of the disciple. Add to these the text, already quoted, "Rejoice in the Lord alway: and again I say, Rejoice;" and we have the scope of the apostle's thought: all renunciations for Christ have abundant compensations.

You will see that on one side, as is customary in an estimate of losses and gains, Paul puts all that had been gain to him, and which he counted loss, and refuse, to be trodden under foot for Christ; and, on the other side, he puts down all that he has gained or won by the surrender of himself to Christ, and all that he will yet know and attain when the final sum of his gain shall reach its completion. After having thus put on opposite sides of the account the two classes of items, he strikes his balance, and the result is a showing of infinite enrichment; he is, beyond expression, the gainer by the excess of what he receives over all that he surrenders, so that he forgets everything that has been forsaken as of no value in comparison, and presses on toward the mark for the prize of the high calling. The motto of Paul is also found in this epistle : " For to me to live is Christ, and to die is gain " (i. 21).

This is a letter to the Church at Philippi, founded by Paul, as we learn from the sixteenth chapter of the Acts. That Church was linked inseparably with the conversion of Lydia, a woman of Thyatira, and of the cruel jailor, whose hard heart was softened " that same hour of the night," so that he began at once to exhibit all the graces of a Christian disciple.

When God presents before us in the Holy Scriptures, a locked door which He intends we shall open and enter, so as to explore the riches of His glory and His grace, He always hangs the key very close to the lock of the door; and he who will only search a little will find the key, and opening the door, enter into God's palace of Truth, and be free to roam through all its glorious apartments and fill himself with its contents. It is the more pity that so many should read this Epistle to the Philippians, and not have seen that in the sixteenth chapter of the Acts of the Apostles, God has hung the great key that unlocks all its doors. Paul wrote this epistle while a prisoner at Rome. He could not think of Philippi without thinking of Lydia, and the women at the riverside; without thinking of the mob and the riot, and the apprehension, and scourging by the magistrates; without thinking of the jailor, of the stocks, of the prison, of the praises and the prayers of the midnight hour; of the earthquake, of the conversion and baptism of the jailor and his household; of his own assertion of the rights of a Roman citizen, and the servile manner in which they that had beaten him came and besought him to leave their city without making a disturbance, alarmed because they had inflicted on a Roman citizen an unlawful scourging. If the reader will bear in mind these experiences of Paul in Philippi, as he reads this epistle, upwards of fifty references to those experiences may be traced in the course of this letter; and it will have a new charm and a new beauty for every reader who will take this key, and with it open and enter these chambers of truth, where so much instruction, promise, comfort, and consolation are stored for disciples.

Before we go further, it may be well to note a few of the references in this epistle to that experience at Philippi. Take, for instance, the twelfth and thirteenth verses of the first chapter: " But I would ye should understand, brethren, that the things which happened unto me have fallen out rather unto the furtherance of the gospel." He came to the city to preach the gospel, yet he meets a riot, is thrown into prison, and his feet put into stocks; and it seemed as though the whole purpose of his coming to Philippi were frustrated by the power of the devil; as though Satan, the hinderer, had gone before the apostle to make it impossible that he should accomplish the end for which he had been called into Macedonia. And yet, the very things that happened unto him were rather, in the end, unto the furtherance of the gospel, for the jailor that thrust him into prison was, next to Lydia, the first convert in the City of Philippi, and he and his household were baptized that same hour of the night, believing and rejoicing in God. When Paul was a bondman, a prisoner at Rome, chained by the hand to a soldier of the Prætorian Guard every morning, to have another soldier take his place as guard the next day, he recalled this experience in the Philippian gaol, so that he says: "My bonds in Christ are manifest *throughout the whole Prætorian guard*, and in all other places; and many of the brethren in the Lord, waxing confident by my bonds, are much more bold to speak the word without fear." How plain it is that this prisoner at Rome wrote these words, thinking of the imprisonment at Philippi, and how God there made his bonds in Christ to turn unto His glory. Then, again, in the twentieth verse: "So now also Christ shall be magnified in my body, whether it be by life, or by death." In this epistle, over and over again, reference is made to the condition of things when he was in that city. In the third chapter, twentieth verse: "For our conversation is in heaven." The Greek word means: "Our *citizenship* is in heaven." It was at Philippi that he asserted the rights of a Roman citizen, and he could not write to Philippian Christians without remembering that fact, and reminding them that it was not in his *Roman* citizenship that he took most joy and pride, but in his citizenship of that city, the heavenly Jerusalem, the capital of the Kingdom of God; and that his final appeal and allegiance was not to Cæsar as his lord and master, but to Jesus Christ Himself.

So when, in the fourth chapter and fourth verse, he says: "Rejoice in the Lord alway: and again I say, Rejoice," he must have thought of those praises and prayers offered when he and Silas were held fast in the stocks in that inner prison; and, when he adds, in the eleventh verse: "For I have learned, in whatsoever state I am, therewith to be content," was he not thinking of the pain of his scourged back and fettered feet, and how the peace of God still filled his heart, in the midst of this most trying experience? In the words of the twenty-third verse of the first chapter, he may refer to the confinement in the stocks: "For I am *in a strait betwixt two,* having a desire to depart, and to be with Christ; which is far better: nevertheless, to abide in the flesh is more needful for you." A man with his feet in the stocks yearns to get them out of their wooden fetters and be a free man, and yet he is bound fast. May not Paul have had those stocks in mind when he wrote of the strait in which he was, fastened to this world by the decree of God, while yearning to get up yonder, where the "lame man shall leap as a hart, and the tongue of the dumb sing." But let these brief examples suffice to call attention to the way in which that experience, narrated in the sixteenth chapter of the Acts, opens the door to the understanding of this epistle.

Let us now catch more clearly the key-note of this whole anthem of joy, as found in the words of the text: "*Rejoice in the Lord alway.*" You cannot always rejoice in man, nor in yourself, or your external surroundings; but you can always rejoice *in the Lord.* In this epistle, twenty times at least Paul uses such words as "rejoice," "joy," "peace," "contentment," or some other of similar import. Even his heavy cross was forgotten in the crown, and the crown was anticipated even in the earthly experience of suffering and sorrow. And so the supreme idea of this epistle is seen to be the idea of GAIN. Paul's zealous love for the Philippian Christians brings him gain, for it makes him magnanimously forget even his bonds in Christ Jesus for their sakes. The supremacy of Jesus Christ in his heart brings untold gain, for it lifts him into the regions of boundless joy if only Christ be preached, if only Christ be magnified, if only Christ be glorified. His very self-denials are turned into joyful triumphs, his crown of thorns blossoms into roses, and the cross on which He is crucified becomes the tree of Life and Glory, like that which John saw on the banks of the river of life; privation ceases to be privation and becomes privilege; death is not death but the doorway of life, and therefore of infinite gain.

No less than twelve of the fruits of this self-surrender are referred to in this epistle, and they seem to present to us in one view the sources of his confidence and the grounds of his rejoicing.

1. First, as we have already seen, Paul *rejoiced in his bonds* in Christ Jesus, because, being chained to a soldier, he was enabled to speak the gospel message to that soldier; and, having a new guard chained to him every day, he was enabled in the course of due time to speak in turn to the whole of the Prætorian Guard. What a blessed triumph it is, when a man rejoices in fetters, thanks God for his bonds! The very clanking of the chains of the apostle Paul had a voice for his Master! When Dober, the Moravian missionary, first went down to St. Thomas to labour for the blacks, and was told that he could never get a chance to reach and teach the slaves there because he was not a slave himself, he said, "We will sell ourselves into slavery and work by their side." Dober rejoiced in bonds for Christ Jesus if those fetters could be the means of telling the gospel story. Paul and Silas rejoiced in the

stocks if the stocks could be the means of a wider preaching of the gospel; and Paul writes that his own imprisonment, and his own boldness in preaching Christ notwithstanding his imprisonment, became the means of inspiring courage and confidence in more timid souls, so that many other brethren were waxing bold and confident to speak the Word of God in the face of opposition. Here, then, are the first fruits of the joy in God that filled his soul. Bonds could not bind such joy, fetters could not restrain the exuberance of such rejoicing in God; he thanked God for chains that preached the gospel, for a prison that echoed with his testimony, and for permission to set an example of suffering, that made other timid souls bold to bear the cross.

2. Observe, secondly, how he rejoiced *in the fact that Christ was preached.* Here we meet one of the strangest paragraphs in the whole of the New Testament. He says, in the first chapter and fifteenth verse, "Some indeed preach Christ even of envy and strife ; and some also of good will. Some indeed preach Christ of contention—in a contentious spirit—not sincerely, supposing to add affliction to my bonds: but the other of love, knowing that I am set for the defence of the gospel. What then? notwithstanding, every way, whether in pretence, or in truth, Christ is preached; and I therein do rejoice, yea, and will rejoice." We can understand how a true disciple will rejoice when Jesus Christ is preached by some who do not believe exactly as he does ; as a Baptist may rejoice in the testimony of a Methodist, or a Presbyterian, or a Congregationalist, or an Episcopalian. Any charitable, godly man, would be glad to have the gospel preached by a brother of another denomination; but Paul's charity goes farther. There were those who were not preaching Christ sincerely, but in

a jealous spirit, an envious spirit, an ungodly spirit; yet this devoted man was so glad to have Christ proclaimed that he could still rejoice even when Christ was preached by his own enemies, by those who were insincere, or even hypocritical. Of course he did not rejoice in their insincerity or hypocrisy, but he was glad to have the gospel message go forth even from unanointed lips. No doubt God has used some men who have never been themselves converted, to bring home the gospel message to other souls. We would by no means encourage an unconverted ministry, but we thank God that He has sometimes used men that have not been themselves regenerated to tell the story of the gospel to others that needed that gospel; and we ought to rejoice when, in any way, or by any means, Christ is preached, even though God may please, for the time, to use those that have a contentious and an insincere spirit. Did not Leigh Richmond preach the gospel, when yet an unconverted man, and awake people to a sense of sin when, as yet, he himself had not been awakened? No doubt, in some cases, the spiritual progress of the hearers has greatly exceeded that of the preacher, and God has used His own Word to lead them to the Saviour, and then to a sanctified life, when the preacher himself had not as yet found salvation and sanctification. Chalmers used to say that, before his great sickness at Kilmany, he had preached the gospel without being a converted man; he had at least grave doubts about his own saved state up to that time. It is certainly a marvellous triumph of grace in any man that he can rejoice in any method by which the grace of Christ is made known and sinners brought to the acceptance of salvation.

3. Again, Paul rejoiced in *Christ's being magnified* through his own suffering. "According to my earnest expectation

and my hope, that in nothing I shall be ashamed, but that with all boldness, as always, so now also Christ shall be magnified in my body, whether it be by life, or by death. For to me to live is Christ, and to die is gain" (i. 20, 21). Whether by life or death, he resolved that Jesus Christ should be glorified. His words here are often carelessly misquoted:—"For me to live is Christ, and to die is gain." He does not say, for me to live is to advance the cause of Christ, or Christ's glory is the object of my life and of my death; but he says, "*for me to live is Christ*," as though his life were a sort of continuation of Christ's incarnation; as though Christ were to be so embodied and represented in the life of the true disciple as that there should be a practical perpetuation of the life and ministry of Jesus among men. In a sense that is true, for the Church is called "Christ's body," and the body is the incarnation of the spirit. So far as you represent Christ in your temper, your disposition, your spirit, your affection, your conduct, so far is Christ incarnated in you and you become a manifestation of God to the world, somewhat as Christ was God manifest in the flesh. If the disciples of the Lord lived in God and lived for God as they should, there is a sense in which Christ would still be manifest in this world, and manifested to the ungodly, for He would be seen in the disciples somewhat as God was seen in Him. Paul was so thoroughly united with the Lord Jesus Christ that for him to live was a practical perpetuation of Christ's presence among men, and he rejoiced in anything that happened to his body—imprisonment, fasting, scourging, death—it was all one to him if it thus magnified and glorified his dear Master.

4. Paul rejoiced also in *the mind of Christ.* "Let this mind be in you, which was also in Christ Jesus" (ii. 5). What

was this "mind"? It was the mind of self-renunciation, which was most of all exhibited in Christ Jesus in His self-surrender for the salvation of men. He exchanged His throne for the manger, the crown of glory for the crown of thorns, the royal raiment for the swaddling clothes, the worship of angels for the mockery of persecutors and revilers. The Lord of Life came down to die, and He who held the keys of death went through the grave for our sakes. That was "the mind of Christ." It is called in this same epistle, Christ's *emptying Himself*, for such is the force of the expression, "made Himself of no reputation." The same word could be used of a vessel that, having been filled with some precious substance, was turned upside down and so emptied. "He emptied Himself, and became obedient unto death, even the death of the cross." Paul rejoiced to partake of that mind. From the hour that he became a disciple he was entirely given up to God; he ceased to love himself and live for himself and seek his own ends. On the way to Damascus he lost his life for Jesus' sake, and found his life anew in serving Christ and saving souls. That mind which was in Christ was the innermost secret of Paul's joy. As long as we seek anything for ourselves we forfeit real bliss, but as soon as we stop all self-seeking and seek everything for our Master, we attain unto that felicity which is the forecast and foretaste of heaven.

5. Paul rejoiced in *being offered for the sake of men*. "Yea, and if I be offered upon the sacrifice and service of your faith, I joy, and rejoice with you all" (ii. 17). What is the difference between "sacrifice" and "service"? The ceremonies of worship in the tabernacle or temple consisted of two things; there were bloody offerings or sacrifices, and there were unbloody sacrifices; the former signified the

expiation of sin by blood, and the latter, like certain peace offerings and thank offerings, were an expression of gratitude to God. In the ancient ritual of the Levitical dispensation, the priest, after slaying the bullock or kid, and pouring out the blood beside the altar, carried the blood and sprinkled it on the table of shew bread, the golden candlestick, the altar of incense, and the mercy seat; and this activity of the priest, who thus passed from altar to altar, and from one to another of the sacred furnishings of the Holy place, was known as *service*, as the offering of the victims was known as *sacrifice*. Paul therefore says, "Yea, and if I be offered upon the *sacrifice and service* of your faith, I joy, and rejoice with you all." He could rejoice to be a slain victim on the altar for the sake of developing faith in unbelievers; or to spend his whole life in service for the sake of other souls; to be both priest and victim, both officiating minister and sacrificed offering. Can there be any higher joy in God than that? The ancient Moravian seal which seems to have been originally taken from pagan Rome, had upon it, an ox standing between the altar on one side, and the plough on the other; and the motto underneath was, "Ready for either." The true disciple is ready to toil at the plough in service, or ready to bleed on the altar in sacrifice. Paul lived out the whole meaning of that motto, which he may have seen on old Roman seals, and could say, I rejoice with you all if I am permitted to be offered as a sacrifice, like a bullock on the altar, or to toil, in the service of your faith, like an ox at the plough.

6. Another element of his joy was his *knowledge of Christ*. "Yea doubtless, and I count all things but loss for the excellency of the knowledge of Christ Jesus my Lord: for whom I have suffered the loss of all things, and do count

them but dung, that I may win Christ, and be found in Him, not having mine own righteousness, which is of the law, but that which is through the faith of Christ, the righteousness which is of God by faith : that I may know Him, and the power of His resurrection, and the fellowship of His sufferings, being made conformable unto His death ; if by any means I might attain unto the resurrection of the dead " (iii. 8, 9, 10). The knowledge of Christ here is a very large term, and includes four things : justification by faith in His blood; the fellowship of Christ's suffering ; the power of his resurrection life ; and the literal resurrection from among the dead.

Let us tarry a moment to consider these four things. First, if I am in Christ Jesus I stand before God justified and accepted; nearer to God and dearer to God I cannot be, because in Christ I am as near and as dear as He is, since God for Christ's sake loves me as He loves Him ; and, as a member of the body of Christ, I am loved, for the whole body, head and members, stand before God as one. Again, Paul was a "partaker of Christ's suffering." Christ gave up the crown of glory for the crown of thorns, and the throne for the cross. Paul's fellowship with Christ was found in doing as Christ did, emptying himself of all that he counted gain—worldly glory, fame, riches, power, influence—for the sake of his Saviour and Lord. So he writes to the Colossians, first chapter and twenty-fourth verse: " Who now rejoice in my sufferings for you, and fill up that which is behind of the afflictions of Christ in my flesh for His body's sake, which is the Church." If those words are a mystery, let us ask ourselves, " How are souls saved ? " Of course you will reply, by the blood of Christ, by His atoning death. But how does the *knowledge* of that death and of the blood shed by Him reach the sinning soul? Some human teacher proclaims the Word, the tract distributor goes with his tracts, the Bible distributor with the Bible, and the worker for Christ with his witness, into the midst of misery and poverty and sin; and so disciples tell others of the Lord Jesus Christ. The believer in Christ Jesus is the ordinary, if not the indispensable link, between Christ on the cross and the soul in bonds; between Christ on the throne and the sinner in the poverty and misery of sin. The believer, who carries the tidings of salvation to the unsaved, is "filling up that which is behind of the afflictions of Christ in his own flesh for His Body's sake, which is the Church." Just as a hand, stretched out and grasping another hand, may become the link between some fallen one and a new life, the believer stands between the Saviour and the sinner and becomes the link of connection between the two. And so Christ permits us to partake of His self-sacrifice and join Him in uplifting souls into a saved state. That is "the fellowship of Christ's suffering." What is "the power of His resurrection?" In His resurrection Christ left the elements of corruption in the grave and rose never more to know death. In resurrection life you leave the old man of sin in the grave, and put on the new man of holiness, renewed in the whole nature as that life is created anew in Christ Jesus. The term here used, *resurrection from the dead*, is the translation of a Greek word, used nowhere else in the Bible, which is a compound word. To the word which means resurrection is prefixed another word which makes it mean an *elect resurrection, from among the dead*. We are taught that there is to be a first resurrection, referred to in the fourth chapter of first Thessalonians, and fifteenth verse, and which in many other parts, both of the Old and New Testament, is more or less clearly indicated or anticipated. What is a resurrection *from among* the dead? When Christ rose, the dead did not all rise, but some saints rose, after His resurrection, and went into the holy city and appeared unto many. In the twentieth chapter of Revelation we are taught that there is coming a day when the *dead in Christ* shall rise, while the rest of the dead shall remain sleeping until the general resurrection; and that those who rise in that first resurrection are to be associated with Christ in the manifestation of His glory, and the exercise of His power. Paul knew he should have a resurrection, for all the dead are to be raised; but he wanted a part in the *first* resurrection from among the dead, that elect resurrection, when the bodies of saints, which sleep in Jesus, waiting for His appearing, shall rise to meet Him, and be for ever with Him. And so Paul says, " If by any means I might attain unto the resurrection from among the dead," the elect, first resurrection. This, then, is the knowledge of Christ: to know Him as my righteousness by justification, to know Him as my sanctification in the power of a new life, to know Him as my companion in fellow-suffering, to know Him in the fellowship of His resurrection from among the sleeping dead.

Paul hints six other grounds of rejoicing, all of which are in this fourth chapter : such as the peace that passeth all understanding, the thoughts of God, contentment with God's dispensations, the strength which Christ supplies to all His servants, and the fulfilment of the assurance that we shall be with Him at last. " Be careful for nothing ; but in everything by prayer and supplication with thanksgiving let your requests be made known unto God. And the peace of God, which passeth all understanding, shall keep your hearts and minds through Christ Jesus." Four things express the sentiment of those verses: careful for nothing, thankful for anything, prayerful for everything, peaceful at all times; carefulness is gone, and prayerfulness, thankfulness, and peacefulness, take its place. We seem to see the imprisoned apostle, his feet fast in the stocks, smarting with recent scourgings, in the darkness of midnight, in the foul air, fasting, yet praising and praying; careful for nothing, thankful even for the prison, the stocks, and the scourging, prayerful in everything, and filled with the "peace of God, which passeth all understanding."

Paul hints that he found joy in thoughts of God. "If there be any virtue, and if there be any praise, *think on these things*." The highest object of reading books is not to gather a little information, or store a few facts and truths in the memory, or even to have communion with authors, or to acquire through literature culture and refinement of taste. The highest object of reading books, or of communing with men, is *to leave in the mind a precious deposit*, as a stream flowing over its bed leaves its residuum on the very sands and pebbles over which it flows, the red of iron, the green of sulphur, and the glitter of gold. The object of holy thoughts is to grow like God. Chalmers once asked a little boy who was absorbed in thought, "What are you thinking of?" "I was thinking of how God can be eternal," said the boy. "Go on thinking, my boy," said the great Scotchman, "many a man has grown great by thinking of God." Blessed are they, who, banishing from their minds the frivolities and pleasures of this world, the intoxicating vanities of time, open their minds and hearts so that God pours into them the stream of everlasting life that leaves in its very channel the precious deposits of Heaven.

Paul enjoyed perfect contentment. "For I have learned, in whatsoever state I am, therewith to be content." How few know anything of such satisfaction! Paul's content came from his confidence that God was *his God*. I thank God for one sweet lesson that He has taught me in the last few years, for which I would not take all the fabled riches of the Indies. When I came to see that I had been doing work *for myself*, He taught me how much sweeter and better it is to work *for Him* than to work for myself; but there was another lesson still sweeter yet to be learned: *to think of Him as doing the work, and of myself as only the instrument that He uses.* It is quite enough to be a rod that He shakes, a saw that He moves to and fro, an axe with which He fells a foe, a sword with which He pierces a conscience, a vessel of earth which He fills. If it is God who does all the work, and you are nothing but an instrument, you are rid of all care and worry and anxiety; surely the Lord can take care of His own work; and if He chooses to lay down the instrument He once took up, you may glorify Him just as much when you are silent as when you are speaking; if He who chose to fill the vessel, chooses to empty it again for another filling, let Him choose His own way in which to use you, and in any way seek to glorify Him. If He sets you aside, and you seem to be imprisoned and in the stocks, still praise Him, and learn, in whatsoever state you are, therewith to be content.

How stands your profit and loss sheet? Is there anything you count gain? Then count it loss! Is there anything you count as of particular value? Bring that to the Lord! What costs you most to surrender and renounce will give you most satisfaction and compensation. Have you been working for self? Cease all selfish work at once, and come to Christ as your Master, and take His yoke upon you. What things you counted gain count as loss, and tread under foot as the refuse of the dung-hill, that Christ may come and fill your soul; so shall you know what it is not only to be justified in Him, but to be sanctified in Him, and satisfied in Him; and so at last you shall know also what it is to be glorified with Him!

SERMON TWELVE

Duty, a Delight

"I delight to do thy will, O my God: yea, thy law is within my heart."—PSALM xl. 4.

THE sign given to Hezekiah was that the shadow went backward on the dial Ahaz. The Psalms show that they are inspired because on their dial the shadow goes forward: that is, they foreshadow or forecast conceptions of divine things and attainments in divine life far beyond the age in which they were written. The most advanced saints find in these breathings of holy men of old, marvellous spiritual maturity. Their standard or index was set up in faint light of dawn, yet the shadow on their dial marks the full glory of noon. The religious development of centuries discovers no blemish in their beauty, no flaw in their spirituality; we are amazed at the aspirations they breathe, the aims they inspire, and the truths they unfold.

Upon a closer study of the Psalm, whence these words are taken, the first thing which arrests our attention is the true and clear view here found as to the Jewish sacrifices. The whole course of Hebrew history shows us that the drift of the Mosaic ritual was toward formalism. Through the perversion of a sinful nature, men laid stress on the sacrifice but passed over its real significance. Now and then, an Abel's altar with its expression of faith in the lamb that should be slain; but over against it, many a Cain's offering which corresponded to no inward flame of pious love. While men burned their victims, their sacrifice could not be accepted because sin lay at the door. With eyes strangely blinded by depravity they saw not the spirit beneath the letter, but vainly thought that the blood of bulls or of goats, or the ashes of an heifer sprinkling the unclean, could in some way suffice to cleanse moral guilt; and so when to God's altars they led the firstling of their flock, with a narrow literalism they persuaded themselves that duty was done, independent of their state of heart.

But the writer of the Psalm before us reveals a deeper insight into the true spiritual significance of these rites. "Sacrifice and offering thou didst not desire: mine ears hast thou opened: burnt offering and sin offering hast thou not required." He, who thus writes, saw and recognized the real import of smoking altars. His ears had been opened to hear, beneath the letter of the command, the whisper of its spirit. He saw that it was not the outward sacrifice which God desired, but a sincere sorrow for sin: not the offering of a victim which He required, but a holy self-dedication: "The sacrifices of God are a broken spirit." "Then said I, Lo I come!" The pious soul, whose holy emotions find language here, feels that in themselves all mere oblations and libations and ceremonial rites are useless when divorced from habitual obedience. Instead of contenting himself with presenting a victim, with a sublime spirituality, he says: "Lo *I come*"! He becomes himself the victim, offers himself a living sacrifice, to drag at the plough, to bleed at the altar; and, lest it should seem that even this were but an unwilling, constrained service, he adds: "I delight to do thy will, O my God." In other words, God's pleasure is his pleasure. "Yea, thy law is within my heart," the object of choice and love.

I. We instinctively recognize here an expression of the *highest type of piety*. This marks the Psalm as Messianic, since it was fulfilled only in Christ. He, above all who in heaven or on earth ever sought to do God's will, manifested a *habit* of obedience, a *choice* toward obedience, and a *delight* in obedience; and when we remember the peculiar relation he sustained to those rites and sacrifices as himself the sacrifice of which those rites were figures, we cannot but apply especially to Him the language of this Psalm.

We must not, however, limit its application to the Messiah; for, though this ideal became perfectly real only in Him, the piety here breathed is not to be thought of as beyond the imitation of every disciple. Jesus stands as the divine model and pattern of a believer's life. He may well take the first rank and place in the van while holy hearts march onward: yet he goes before us as Leader: we are to come after as followers.

Let us then endeavour to grasp and bring home to ourselves the thought of the text. The days of the old ritual have passed away; but the days of heartless sacrifices have not passed with them. How often do we bring to God's altars the offerings of our service, goaded on simply by a sense of obligation? How often do we give our money to benevolent ends without any benevolent impulse, seeking to silence conscience rather than to satisfy a craving to do good! How often do we outwardly discharge some duty under no nobler impulse than a cold, hard necessity! How many have no heart in their sacrifices:

feel no interest in their offerings ; find no joy in doing right; and are glad when right is done only because they have got out of the way of a claim ! Dr. Watts, in his hymn, wrote that

"God abhors the sacrifice
Where not the heart is found."

Yet what is a constrained and unwilling obedience but a heartless sacrifice ? Is an outward, or even a conscientious, compliance with God's commands all that He asks and has a right to expect of us ? When the Jew brought his bullock to the altar, if it was merely to meet the letter of God's requirement, the flame of his sacrifice bore no incense to God ! And how can we expect our offering to yield the savour of a sweet smell unto Him if He looks down upon us only to see that, behind all our outward compliance, there lies a real reluctance !

The text suggests a sublime contrast to all this : it represents a phase of obedience so far in advance of this that the two cannot be placed upon a level, even for a comparison. These few words reveal a profound sympathy between a human soul and God. Why does *He* do right? Not from any constraint of duty. There is no law, back of himself, to which He conforms : He is a law unto Himself. In being good and doing good, he cancels no debt save that which he owes to His own character. He is holy in his sympathies and in His administration for the same reason that the sun shines, because *it is His nature!* When a holy soul can therefore say, "I delight to do thy will, O my God," it reveals a holy affinity, a profound sympathy with God.

Noah and Enoch walked with God. "Can two walk together except they be agreed ?" It is not passing over the

Duty, a Delight

same path which makes us true companions in travel; there must be an inner agreement, a sympathy of soul, a fellowship of feeling. To walk with God, then, is not merely to follow a right course, to live a life of moral rectitude; many a moral man is blameless in his outward conduct: there must be secret harmony of thought, and love, and life, a oneness of desire and purpose between man and God, before one can ever become worthy of so grand a record as that which is written of those holy men of old. He only has true fellowship with God to whom duty is delight. The text expresses therefore the highest conception of life, and lifts us to the loftiest level. No child in piety ever uttered this rapt exclamation. The maturest manhood in Christ gets no higher than where duty is delight; and Heaven itself promises no nobler maturity—no riper godliness, than to bring such fruit to perfection in a complete union of obedience and happiness; and, therefore, the nearer we come to finding a true, sure, positive and permanent joy in doing right, the closer we approach in spirit to those gates of pearl, within which no desire is known, save the will of God.

The highest type of obedience is never assumed by a soul till its purest happiness is found in a full surrender of itself to God, to serve or to suffer. When we bring *ourselves* to the altar, then there floats up to God, an odour of sweet incense.

When we look at the believer's experience we find in it three stages. First, a sense of *danger*, when fear rouses him to flee from the wrath to come; then a sense of *duty*, when conscience urges him to do that which he feels to be right; and last, a sense of *delight*, when choice impels him to do and bear God's will. Then it is that perfect love casts out tormenting fear as a motive to obedience, and we obey God's law, not because we are in terror of its penalty, but rather because we love and choose to do it. Duty has become delight. This last stage of experience is the highest, and heaven only is higher. We assume this without argument; it is beyond argument. Like an axiom it proves itself; our instinct tells us it is true. We can see in our own children the contrast between these three motives: fear of punishment, constraint of filial duty, and that love towards us that, by a secret sympathetic union of heart, makes our wish their will. And we know this last to be the noblest impulse to obedience, for it implies no constraint. It is not submission but sympathy; it is scarcely obedience, so much as a simple harmony of wills : and to just such a Christian life as this Our Father would have all His children aspire. He tells us, He "loveth a cheerful giver," and what does He mean? Think with yourselves how we commonly give, " grudgingly and of necessity," not because we yearn to bestow but because we dare not withhold. Conscience acts like a force-pump within us, and our benevolent offerings, so-called, come drop by drop into the cup of God's thirsty poor; whereas love, rather than duty, should, like springs of water in a dry place, pour forth our charities, naturally and spontaneously, in obedience to a law of our inner life, plentiful and constant, yet leaving fulness of joy and love, behind.

Indeed, what we call spontaneity is, everywhere, a law of the highest life. What principally distinguishes God's work from man's work is this : Man never makes anything which sustains or supplies itself; what God has wrought He seems to have endowed with a life of its own. Man makes a lamp : however brilliant its light, he must feed its flame every instant, or it goes out in darkness. God lights a million lamps in the sky and they shine on for ages. Every product of human skill has a forced mechanical life, while what God creates has a life to all appearance spontaneous, natural. Facts correspondent to these exist in the spiritual sphere. The man who tries to make himself better reaches no higher than a life of outward morality. His conduct may be blamelessly correct, but it is a forced development. His education, ambition, selfishness, self-righteousness, and a hundred other motives, are called in to prompt and prop up propriety of deportment. When God makes a man better, He begins *within*: He changes his moral sympathies: plants the germ of a new principle whose growth is to develop hatred to sin which he once loved, and love to holiness which he once hated. All this is the preparation for a spontaneous life of obedience which is the fruit of a new nature. He means that the germ shall root itself in us; that we shall choose to do right, so that, were there no law, we should be a law unto ourselves. Then, if every outward condition changes: if society grows so corrupt that religion is no longer popular or respectable; if education is so perverted that vice is crowned instead of virtue—if every outside motive to a correct deportment is gone; then, while the worldly man, whose moral life is the result of expediency, shapes his conduct and his creed to suit the change of outward conditions, the Christian still chooses what his new nature recognizes as the will of God, delighting to do what may bring upon him hatred, persecution, martyrdom.

With the Psalmist he exclaims: " Blessed is the man that feareth the Lord, that delighteth greatly in His commandments." Or, with Jeremiah: "Thy word was unto me the joy and rejoicing of my heart," or, with St. Paul, who from the holy company of the apostles responds to the goodly fellowship of the prophets: " I delight in the law of God after the inward man." Or, with Job, he can say, even amid deep darkness, "I have esteemed the words of His mouth more than my necessary food." How elevated such a life! Jesus could say no more than this: "My meat is to do the will of Him that sent Me." Thus the spirit of the old and the new dispensations is one. Holy men of all ages affirm the same law as regulating the highest life of piety. Prophets and apostles, saints of old time and disciples of latter days, sympathize with each other, and with Him whose delight it was to do God's will.

II. To delight in God's will supplies the *noblest motive*. It is quite common to hear the idea advanced, that he who acts from a sense of duty is controlled by the noblest of motives. Is this so? Where duty and delight seem opposed, a commendable self-denial will give up the delight and take up the duty. But he who thinks duty and delight are opposed, lives a comparatively low life. If he gets high enough up for a true view, he will see that all opposition between happiness and holiness is only apparent. The roads of duty and delight never cross each other. "Her ways are ways of pleasantness and all her paths are peace."

Does he command a true prospect of life, who does his duty only as he pays any other debt? If God had given His only Son to die, so as to pay a debt He owed to the race, the sacrifice had lost nearly, if not quite, all of its moral sublimity. It was because it cancelled no obligation, but sprang from the impulses of pure pity, that it transfigures His character with perfect glory, and vindicates His claim to that highest of titles, Love!

The *godlike* life is swayed by the same golden sceptre. It acknowledges no constraint but that of love, and knows no unwillingness whatever. You and I cannot deny that to do

Duty, a Delight

God's will because it is our delight is nobler than to do it because it is our duty. Duty is often the dictate of a moral or religious education and may be accepted as a yoke. Thousands read the Bible, pray to God, go to church, keep the Sabbath, simply yielding to the pressure of early training: a mother's lessons or a father's prayers have built up barriers which fence them in, leaving open no other road but that which from the force of habit they follow. Does it index no higher life to find such happiness in God's word, and day, and house, as that we should seek our delight amid such surroundings, even were there no command to compel, no duty to urge, no conscience to constrain? If we act simply as a beast of burden obeys the goad, because we would silence the voice of duty, is there not something selfish in such action? Can we claim anything noble or magnanimous, in an obedience whose main object is to give us ease of mind? Is there not an element of meanness in doing right only because conscience will lash us if we do wrong? Is it not possible to do some things, "consulting only a sense of *duty*, which a magnanimous *love* to God and man forbids"?

Piety is not so much any conformity of outward life, as it is a disposition toward the divine, which in a growing Christian will become more and more habitual as a law of life, and in a sense unconscious. It will become less a struggle and more an impulse of the new nature to love divine things, and duty will thus change to delight, till it will be almost involuntary to do right, so little hesitation will there be in choosing the path of duty. A young disciple is thus like the musical pupil, who, in playing his exercises, keeps thinking how he is sitting, holding his hands, and managing his fingers. The mature disciple is more like the master in whom practice and habit have made it possible to lose sight of what is merely mechanical in what is spiritual about music, till he forgets the instrument in the inspiration of musical enthusiasm, and becomes no longer merely a practicer of scales or an imitator of others, but a creator and composer of musical harmonies. It may be that this spontaneous life of obedience is an elevation to which but few ever attain, this side of heaven, yet it is not because it is beyond practical reach. He who makes it his habit to aim after true holiness will find more and more that it ceases to be an effort to be good and to do good, as he rises to real and almost unconscious sympathy with goodness. And this unconsciousness therefore is another mark of the highest life.

III. The text expresses also the *highest spiritual liberty*. In civil government, the nearer we get to a true idea or ideal of liberty the less does government seem to exist at all, for the highest freedom involves unconsciousness of restraint or constraint. The law sits upon us like a perfectly fitting robe; so unfettered are all our motions that so long as we are loyal subjects we forget we are subjects : in a sense we are not restrained. St. Paul wrote, as a philosophic statesman, "The law is not made for a righteous man, but for the lawless and disobedient." Perfect law in a perfect government never makes itself felt until it is transgressed. Under God's administration both legislative and executive powers are exercised with such perfect wisdom and goodness that a holy subject in His kingdom should be wholly unconscious of any pressure of external control, free from every rein of government, a law unto himself. How is it? Gabriel never asks himself whether he is acting in conformity with the law of God. He is in complete subjection, yet unconscious of restraint or constraint. Obedience is natural because delightful. But one path is open to his choice, and he knows no other. The orbit of duty is the perpetual circle of delight. I do not believe the unfallen angels ever knew such a thing as law with regard to themselves. Inperfect sympathy with God, they choose the right independently of its being His will. They are drawn into the same line of direction with His life without feeling controlled by Him!

That this is the highest estate of liberty no one will deny. On earth we may not reach a perfect obedience, but our freedom will be directly in proportion to the completeness of our subjection. The divine government will be a burden or restraint only so far as we violate the rule of right. The 119th Psalm, a splendid monument to the law of God, abounds in such raptures as these: " Thy testimonies are my *delight*," &c. Is it strange that he who could so enthusiastically and repeatedly say this should also exclaim, " I will walk at *liberty*, for I seek Thy precepts!"

It seems strange to us that so many unconverted people, when they speak frankly, confess that they " have not the slightest interest in religious things." Yet, aside from the general effect of a sinful nature, there is a special reason: they have never learned the consistency between law and liberty. They think of religion as bringing an irksome round of tasks, as hedging them in with stern restraints, as offering a life not of self-advancement, but of severe self-denial. They think if they become disciples of Christ they can no more do what they *wish*, but only what they *ought;* they have never imagined that a human soul can rise to a stage of experience where one shall wish to do only what he ought; or if they dream of such a harmony of choice and duty it is as of something far beyond their own reach.

And do not some disciples give the world too much reason to think that living unto God is at best but voluntary acceptance of irksome servitude, instead of delightful service? We betray dislike toward duty, and talk of what we *ought* to do as though we yearned to shirk it. But what if we should delight to do God's will—what if when we impress others with an idea of the new life, we should lead them to feel the truth that it is in every sense the only real good, the highest spiritual liberty—would others then feel so little interest in religious things?

"If the Son therefore shall make you free ye shall be free indeed." The Christian is the Lord's freeman : it is the sinner who is wearing a yoke of bondage; and he who has escaped the obedience of fear and learned the subjection of love enjoys the highest liberty of the sons of God. And we misrepresent and belie Christianity before others whenever we lead them to suppose that it rules by the iron sceptre of duty. We may not have known its golden sceptre of love, but it is the fault of our narrow, selfish worldliness. He who will surrender himself completely to its sway, shall find the Christian experience such a blending of God's life with man's life, as maketh His will our will, and His service perfect freedom!

IV. The text expresses the truest preparation for a *life of service* to Christ. When duty becomes delight we are fitted for our highest usefulness, for that is inseparable from the highest piety, the noblest motive, and the truest liberty.

It takes us needlessly long to discover or realize that to serve God successfully we must serve him spontaneously. Those who most win souls are those who delight to do God's will. If others see that it makes us happy to be disciples of Christ, that we are under no constraint, galled by no fetters of conscience, confined by no severe restrictions; that we are simply walking at liberty because we love to do God's will, we become to them living epistles. They learn to think of our religion as lovely and winning. So, in direct effort to be of service, he who acts under pressure of a sense of duty to another soul becomes formal and mechanical in attempting to do good. His approaches are coldly intellectual, not emotionally fervent. They chill others.

Let it once be seen that duty is delight; that, like Jeremiah, one feels the word of the Lord like a burning fire shut up in his bones, and that he cannot hold his peace because he is aflame with love to Christ and souls, and how will all he says thrill with new life, and power, and inspiration! It becomes a two-edged sword, keen at the edge, burning at the point. Men may feel little interest in hearing another say what he is forced to utter because he feels that he ought; but no man will lack attentive audience who speaks from a full heart, which would burst if denied expression.

Here, perhaps, lies one point of difference between the "righteous man" and the "good man," of which St. Paul speaks. The righteous man acts from a sense of duty. His outward life is blameless, yet it is coldly mechanical in its compliance with God's commands. His rigid adherence to the maxims of virtue and religion challenge respect without winning love. And "scarcely for a righteous man will one die."

The good man acts from love to God and man; while his outward life is no more exemplary, its impulse is nobler and grander. He delights in doing good. Always in the way of duty, there is a naturalness, a spontaneity in his obedience, which makes his life a centre of attraction. He tests his sense of duty by the law of love, lest under a mistaken abstract idea of right he should be gratifying some really ungenerous feeling. His conduct is shaped, not only upon the principle of building up a fine character, which is kindred to selfishness, but upon that nobler principle of exercising the best influence. The righteous man goes about doing *right*; the good man goes about doing *good*; and "peradventure for a good man some will even dare to die." For he wields the noblest influence, and wins the strongest love of others, who delights to do God's will.

The text finds its ideal fulfilment only in Jesus. Yet mark how natural were his efforts to do good. In fact, he made no effort ; not a word was forced from him ; nothing was by constraint ; everything was of choice. Holy influences flowed out from his soul into others. So natural were all his approaches that they took others captive as by surprise. Without knowing how or thinking why, they found themselves won alike to hear his words and lay bare their own hearts. His conversation at the well of Samaria is perhaps the most remarkable instance on record of a purely religious talk with an entire stranger. Yet nothing can be more easy, natural, graceful, than His approaches to her inmost soul. And his words to her tell us the secret of his own success, and how we may secure a similar influence. "Whosoever drinketh of the water that I shall give him . . . it shall be in him a well of water springing up unto everlasting life." There is the secret : a heart gushing up and running over with its own full life, knowing no force but from within.

Ordinarily a sculptor does not himself work the marble : he fashions the clay model, leaving to the mechanical workman to work out in stone what he has not the imagination to invent, or think out in mind. What a wide difference between them! The workman, for a certain sum, undertakes the task of giving to the creation of the artist's genius simply a more enduring form. He feels, perhaps, but little interest in his wearisome work. His aim at most is to be rigidly accurate and correct in copying the model. Everything is done by rule. How different the experience of the sculptor! He finds in his work a rest, a relief. An image is stamped upon his mind, his brain burns, his heart throbs! Yearning to realize his idea, and give it a tangible shape, a rapture thrills him. The consciousness of a power to create fires his soul and stimulates his energies. The Greeks called such a state of mind "*enthusiasm*"—an inspiration from God.

We are too often only the mechanical workmen when we ought to be sculptors of life. We aim to shape our lives after the pattern showed us in the word of God, without aspiring to intense sympathy with Him who wrought out the only model of a perfect life! He did not design that we should simply imitate His life: that makes a righteous man; but rather that we should resemble Himself: that makes a good man. In one case we are the mechanical workmen aiming after an outward conformity to a divine pattern: in the other case we imbibe the spirit of Christ, catch the inspiration of His purpose, become His disciples, pupils in the art of holy living, and He the great Master; we are learners not of the letter, but of the Spirit. Then we are prepared to work out a result which is in a sense, our own, original. The principles which underlie all true life appear in our own, but in new combinations. It is the likeness of similarity rather than of sameness—of inward sympathy as well as outward conformity. The disciple, like the Master, delights in duty, and that delight is his inspiration.

Ask yourself, then, whether you would do right from choice, even in the absence of a law of right. Had God not said, "Thou shalt reverence my house," could you say, "A day in Thy courts is better than a thousand?" Then do you in so far delight to do God's will. By such tests try every act of obedience, and if you find that any act done from a sense of duty is essentially an unwilling act, rest not content until you can say, "Thy word have I hid in my heart: I delight to do Thy will." Then will you be conformed more and more to the image of His Son.

But, perhaps, you ask, how may duty become delight? And all that has been said finds its practical value in the answer. What then are the secrets of such divine attainment?

There are at least four great helps to attaining delight in duty.

1. First, we must habituate ourselves to *think of God's law in its true light*. We do great injustice to Him when we construe the rule of duty as an arbitrary regulation. God has, in Himself, infinite will-power; yet His perfect goodness forbids the framing of a code, without consulting the best good of His creatures. His perfect *law* is the expression of His infinite *love*, and is designed to promote the highest happiness of His subjects. If we accustom ourselves always to think of His law in the light of His love, we shall see more and more clearly the perfect consistency between obedience and happiness. The more we learn to interpret His commands by His benevolence the more shall we delight to do His will.

2. Secondly, there must be *holy fellowship with God*. No unregenerate man can know such experience of delight in duty, for it is born only of the Spirit. It is not a fleshly

product, and to it the carnal mind is a stranger. Except a man be born from above he cannot enter into, or even see, this truth. Only so far and so fast as the Holy Spirit of God possesses, controls, and transforms our spirit, can we delight in doing God's will. There must be a new creation, new appetites, and tastes, and longings. Nor will it do to be merely a child of God, unless there is actual and growing sympathy with God. This must, therefore, be distinctly sought *in prayer*.

3. Thirdly, there must be a *full surrender to God*. No half-hearted disciple can ever know this bliss, which is at once the fruit and crown of self-oblivion. God can reveal His supreme joy only to those whose whole being is open to His incoming and indwelling. One unbarred shutter may keep a room dark, and one unsurrendered idol may keep out the light of God's presence. To lay at God's feet one's whole self, like an unmutilated victim laid on the altar, is to know the descent of that fire from above, which is the sign of an accepted offering, and the foretaste of heavenly glory. No man delights to do God's will whose whole will is not given up to God.

4. But, most important of all, duty will become delight in proportion to our *faithful discharge of duty itself*. If any man will do His will, he shall know of the doctrine we have now taught. Experimental proof transcends all argument: it is the irresistible logic of life! The more perfectly His will is done, the more delightful will it be to do it. The more complete your obedience, the more positive your happiness. Heaven alone has perfect bliss, for heaven only has perfect obedience. And if you will never let the voice of duty speak in vain, if you will obey every holy impulse, if you will cheerfully take up

every cross, it will become a second nature to you to do right. The ways of heavenly wisdom will seem more and more the paths of pleasure and of peace. You will desire no other, and a growing attachment to the right will be the certain fruit of increasing adherence to the right, till at last you will be able with truth to say, I delight to do Thy will, O my God !

We are reminded once more of the beautiful myth about the "wingless birds," who first took up their wings as burdens to be borne, but found them changing to pinions, which, in the end, bore them. We are the birds without wings. God puts our duties before us to be patiently assumed for His sake. But, though at first they are loads, we shall be able afterward to say, with dear Rutherford, "The cross is the sweetest burden that ever I bore : such a burden as wings are to the bird," that help it to soar ; " or, as sails are to the ship," that help it to catch the breeze that wafts it to the desired haven.

PART THREE

The Hopes of the Gospel

Sermon One

The Perfection of the Law; or, No Hope in Legal Obedience

"The law of the LORD is perfect, converting the soul :
The testimony of the LORD is sure, making wise the simple.
The statutes of the LORD are right, rejoicing the heart :
The commandment of the LORD is pure, enlightening the eyes.
The fear of the LORD is clean, enduring for ever :
The judgments of the LORD are true, and righteous altogether.
More to be desired are they than gold, yea, than much fine gold :
Sweeter also than honey and the honeycomb.
Moreover by them is thy servant warned :
And in keeping of them there is great reward."

PSALM xix. 7—11

THE first of the Psalms strikes the key-note of the whole collection. There we learn that the hidden beauty of the Holy Scriptures can be discovered only by meditation; meditation, so constant and so close that it becomes microscopic, as when we look through magnifying glasses at some minute but beautiful object. This psalm, also, so frequently read, is perhaps as little understood as almost any passage in the Word of God. It is a parable, to which are appended both an interpretation and an application. Careful examination reveals *three parts*, that evidently have a close relation to one another. There is, first, a description of the heavens, the firmament, with its peculiar glories. There is, secondly, the description of the law of God, or the Scriptures of the Old Testament; and there is, third, a personal meditation upon the subject, accompanied with a personal application of it to the writer's experience and need.

It will most honour God, if we follow the train of thought which the Spirit has thus indicated, for power always flows in the channels which the Spirit Himself has prepared in the Word of God.

That there is evidently an intimate connection between the first and the second parts, appears from their peculiar and similar structure. In English versification, we recognize the correspondence of related poetical passages, by the similarity of their verbal structure; not only does one thought run through one verse, and its companion through another; but one set of words, in one line, bears close correspondence with a similar set in another line. There is a rhyme and a rhythm of words which make up our poetical stanzas, or the sections of our great epic poems. When the Hebrew seer constructed a poem, he depended not on a rhyme or rhythm of *words*, but of *thoughts;* he constructed the parts in parallels which corresponded with each other. The companion phrases, or sentences, corresponded, each for each, and were called parallels, because, like parallel lines, which run in the same direction, they bore a peculiar and uniform relation to each other. If this Psalm be examined, it will be found that there are ten things which are said about the heavens. Then there are ten things said about the law of God; and the rule of poetic parallels demands that there should be a relation between these two sections, and their minor members. Let us examine into this mutual relationship.

First, what is said of the heavens? Five things : (1) They declare God's glory; (2) they show God's handiwork; (3) day and day speak together; (4) night and night hold converse ; (5) there is a universal witness, a world-wide testimony. Then five more things are said as to the sun, the principal glory of the heavens. (1) He has his tabernacle in the heavens ; (2) he is like a bridegroom that emerges from a bridal chamber; (3) he is like a giant that runs a great race with rapidity; (4) he makes a world-wide circuit; and (5) he reaches with his light and heat and life-giving beams all things on the surface of the earth.

In order to discover the beautiful correspondence between this tribute to the sunlit skies, and what is said of the law of God, we should examine still more minutely into this surpassing description of the heavens and the heavenly bodies. "The heavens declare the glory of God:" their brightness and their brilliance are the expressions of Him who is light and glory, supreme and eternal. They show His handiwork; as the dome of St. Peter's or St. Paul's shows the handiwork of Michael Angelo or Sir Christopher Wren, they show God's handiwork. The golden balls that He rolls along the floor of heaven—what a testimony they furnish to God's power and wisdom and greatness. And then the days are represented as speaking together, holding converse one with another; one day discourses with another with regard to the wonders of God. And the nights are represented as holding similar converse for purposes of mutual instruction, one night becoming the instructor of another, and different nights holding a divine dialogue together upon the mysteries which their darkness and their glory alike represent. And then, when we come to the sun, what a magnificent description! In these heavens, God has set for the sun a tabernacle, a tent, a dwelling-place. The pavilion of the sun is represented by the clouds and the darkness; and his rising is the emerging of a bridegroom, who lifts the curtain of his bridal chamber, and emerges thence in the glory and beauty of his bridal attire. He goes forth like a giant to run a race. Once in every twenty-four hours, as the earth moves on its axis, the sun accomplishes its apparent circuit, moving with tremendous rapidity through the heavens, and coming back to the point of starting; and so he completes the world-wide circuit. He rose in the east this morning; he is setting in the west to-night; but he will as surely rise in the east to-morrow morning, coming forth again, and throwing aside the curtains of his pavilion of darkness and cloud, like another giant, to begin another giant's race round the whole world. And, as in such a giant career as this the whole human race might be represented as standing and looking on his marvellous majesty, the splendour of his chariot, and the speed of his celestial steeds, so, as the sun goes round the earth, every part of the earth is illumined by his beams, and nothing is hid from the light and the heat thereof. If that can be surpassed, or even equalled, in any uninspired poem, where shall such competitor or parallel be found? There is nothing like it, outside of the Word of God, for splendid imagery, for poetic conception, for minute and exquisite elaboration.

But now, when we come to read what is said here of the law, or Word of God, we trace the most accurate and beautiful suggestion of correspondence; so that we recognize

No Hope in Legal Obedience 437

this poetic description of the heavens as a parable, the interpretation of which is the law of the Lord, the Holy Scriptures inspired by Almighty God. The Holy Scriptures declare the moral glory of God, as the heavens declare His natural glory, and with brighter beams they testify to the light and splendour of His character and of His dealings. They show God's handiwork, in the structure of this marvellous Bible. The foundations of it are laid in the first five books which we call the Pentateuch. Then over them are arranged the pillars of history and the arches of prophecy; and all of these overspread as by a dome, with the glory of the revelation of the coming future. What is this but a building erected by God, and manifesting the handiwork of a divine architect?

And then, as the days talk with the days, so the truths of the Word of God mutually speak one to another, and discourse together upon the divine attributes. One book answers to another through the ages, and is interpreted by another. The prophets all agree, though they saw not each other's faces, and could have had no possible meeting or mutual conference; and, as the nights hold converse together and mutually instruct each other, so the very mysteries of God, the darker and deeper truths of the Holy Scripture, illuminated here and there as by some marvellous out-gleaming of a star of prophecy or of God's declared purpose—what are these mysteries but the counterparts of the nights which, glorified by stars, are speaking one to another the language of sympathy and mutual instruction?

And then, as the sun goes round the earth, and has its everlasting witness to give to all parts of the earth, the Scriptures witness to man as man, the earth over. They do not shine on America, or on England, or on Protestant

Prussia, alone: they shine on Pagan and Papal lands, on heathen lands and Mahometan peoples; and, wherever you will find a man, black or white, or of whatever hue or colour, whatever his condition, low or high, or whatever his grade, cultivated or ignorant, or whatever the measure of his intelligence, be he high up in morality or deep down in depravity, this precious Word of God has a message for him wherever he is, and an uplifting power, a power to make him a man in Christ, and a fruitful tree of righteousness planted by the rivers of water, bringing forth fruit in his season. Glory of God!!

And now, as the sun is the main object in the firmament, before whose presence the moon grows pale and the stars entirely disappear, this firmament of the Word of God has in it a Sun, whose glory is so intense, that everything else, even the lights of prophecy, grow dim and pale when this Sun of righteousness appears. His abiding place is in the Word of God, and, wherever you touch the Word of God with discriminating eye, you shall see that Jesus Christ is there. As the sun in the morning throws aside the curtain of his pavilion of darkness, and comes forth like a bridegroom, so the Heavenly Bridegroom emerges in the Scripture from the deep darkness of a world's midnight. The first glimpse we get of His face is in the dawning of prophecy, in the opening up of prediction, as in the 3rd of Genesis: "The seed of the woman shall bruise the serpent's head." And then as you go on through the various periods of prophecy, and the curtains are thrown wider and wider, the person of the Messiah comes forth more and more prominently, more and more unmistakably, until His whole figure is revealed in the 53rd chapter of Isaiah, when the man of sorrows stands before us, His hands and His feet and His side pierced for us, His back bearing the scourging of His enemies for our sake, smitten, afflicted, grieved, oppressed, down-trodden, yet, although the man of sorrows, still being God's Messiah, "glorious in His apparel, travelling in the greatness of His strength, mighty to save." He starts on the race of the ages like a giant, and you may follow him through that race, from Genesis to Revelation. His footsteps, bloody as they are with the sorrows of the cross, have left their scarlet mark on every page of Holy Scripture. You shall find Him in the histories, in the prophecies, in the poems, in the Gospels, in the Acts of the Apostles, in the Epistles of the New Testament, until you get your last glimpse of Him, when He says, "I come quickly," and the Church, in its love and longing, responds, " Even so, come, Lord Jesus." And so He has a world-wide testimony in the Holy Scripture, and a world-wide office to fulfil as the Messiah of men ; and wherever the fall has gone, and wherever sin has left its curse, and wherever the trail of the serpent has passed over human joys and pleasures, Jesus Christ comes to redeem man, to redeem even the earth itself from the curse of the thorns and the thistles, and to bring redemption to the whole creation of God. He is the light and the love, and the life of the world, as the sun is the light and the heat and the life of all nature. More than this, we may follow the glorious analogy still further ; for as we turn from the sun-setting back toward the sun-rising, so we turn from the ascending Christ, and look toward the new daydawn for His re-appearing ! Thus the 19th Psalm contains first a description of the sun and sky, a parable, of which the second part is the divine interpretation. Awesome.

Now, having these introductory thoughts to aid our

closer study of this Psalm, let us notice the ten things here said about the word of God.

"The law of the Lord is perfect;
The testimony of the Lord is sure;
The statutes of the Lord are right;
The commandment of the Lord is pure;
The fear of the Lord "—what produces such holy fear,—
"is clean;
The judgments of the Lord are true and righteous;
More to be desired than gold;
Sweeter also than honey and the honeycomb.
Moreover by them is thy servant warned;
In keeping of them there is great reward."

Ten particulars. The six names here given to the word of God are the same six names that are spread through that 119th Psalm, which is, like the 19th, a splendid tribute or monument to the glory of the Holy Scripture, but surpasses even this companion Psalm. These six names are law, testimony, statutes, commandment, fear (what produces fear), and judgments. Studied more closely, it suggests that law and testimony have a close relation, as also have statutes and commandments, and fear and judgments. There is here even a deeper and profounder suggestion than possibly has ever struck many a reader—namely, that as law has three main features or departments, first, *common law,*—principles or precepts upon which all specific statutes are based,—then *statute law*, or the commandments and precepts themselves, built up on the basis of common law,—and then *legal sanctions*, of reward and penalty, which sustain both common and statute law, giving the law authority, certainty of execution, and glory in the eyes of men, so these three things are distinctly referred to in this inspired poem. Law and testimony concern the *common* law. Law is the one word of the six, most general and covering the largest meaning. Testimony is another name very wide in its application, for it is God's witness to men concerning His will and His character. *Statutes,* however, represent specific precepts ; and so do commandments. But, when we come to consider that which in the law produces *fear* in the subject, and overawes by its judgments or irreversible decisions, we at once think of the sanctions which sustain the whole fabric of law and rule, as we have already been reminded of common law and statute law.

These distinctions are too important to be grasped in a moment. Let us understand what common law and what statute law are. Beneath every commandment or statute issued by any civilized or enlightened nation, there is a basis of so-called common law ; that is the common basal principle on which all laws are predicated and established. In the Word of God the common law has two great principles which characterize and regulate it : first, what is *right in itself,* and secondly, what is *good for man*. Those are the two great principles of common law. They are recognized, both of them, in the Holy Scripture. For instance, when Moses spoke to the people and gave them God's statutes and commandments, what did he say when he bade them obey ? What was the great motive which he put before them ? He said, "For it is *your life:*" that is to say, "This body of commandments is based upon a deeper principle. It is not simply an expression of God's will, but back of God's will is God's love, God's benevolence, God's kindness to man. He wants to promote man's true life ; to make every man like a tree planted by the rivers of water, rooting itself down where the sources of moisture lie, reaching up and spreading itself out towards the heavens, the sunshine, the atmosphere, the dew, and the rain, and bearing abundant fruit. And so He gave this law, not to satisfy the arbitrary will of a great tyrannical governor, but to satisfy the loving and the longing heart of a Father toward His children. 'It is for your life.' It is the best thing for you to keep the commandments of Almighty God." And then Paul says, in the 6th chapter of Ephesians, "Children obey your parents in the Lord, for *this is right*." There you have the other principle of common law—what is *right* in itself, as well as what is *best* for the subject. Those are the principles on which all common law is based; and if there be any statute law in any truly great nation which can be shown to interfere with common law, any statute law that can be proven to be not right in itself, or not best for the interests of the people, the intelligence and virtue of the nation would be prompt to abolish that statute, for no precept not in accordance with common law can long be promulgated and enforced.

Now, what about the *sanctions* of law? We need these sanctions, as appears so soon as we understand their purpose and object. What are sanctions? They are what sustain law. They are two-fold: the reward of righteousness, and the punishment of disobedience. Both are equally necessary to support law and government; and they are equally beautiful and lovely and desirable in themselves, and both of them reflect equal glory upon God as governor.

This should be said with emphasis, because most people do not see matters in this light. They turn toward the *love* of God, but turn away from His *wrath*. Men justify His

No Hope in Legal Obedience

rewards, but feel an aversion as to His penalties. They seem to think that rewards make God attractive, but that punishments make Him repulsive! We like to talk about His mercy, but we do not like to talk about His judgments. But mercy and judgment are equally beautiful in God, equally necessary to God, equally essential to His law. Suppose you build an arch. You put beneath it two massive pillars. Each pillar is equally necessary to support the arch. If you take away the right-hand pillar, the arch comes down, as surely as when you take away the left-hand pillar. Now, reward for righteousness and punishment for sin are the two colossal pillars which the arch of God's law spans, and upon which His government rests; and both are necessary to support that arch, upon which is built the whole structure of the government of God throughout His moral universe; and, if you take away the retribution of evil, you as surely break down that government, and overthrow the arch, as though you took away the rewards of righteousness. Christian disciples ought therefore to learn to magnify the sanctions of Almighty God. It is sometimes said that the Old Testament is vindictive, but the New Testament is merciful. I utterly deny the distinction. The Old Testament is full of mercy and full of wrath, and the New Testament is full of mercy and full of wrath; and when God said to His ancient people that, if they would obey, they should be prosperous even in temporal things, He simply meant to make temporal prosperity the type or the prophecy of spiritual prosperity, as much as to say, "It is impossible to serve God without getting the smile and the favour of God; and it is impossible to sin against Him without receiving punishment and retribution for sin." What would be thought of a judge who, having the power of life and death, should show himself favourable, lenient, indulgent, to offenders who resisted the whole power and authority of the law? No such judge would be allowed to disgrace, on the bench, any enlightened, law-abiding community. We all know perfectly well that it is the man who, in the execution of law, will show absolutely no favour, who will acquit the innocent and condemn the guilty, who helps to preserve the whole fabric of society from overthrow and ruin. And it is the glory of God that He is not insipidly and irresolutely amiable. His love is not at the expense of His justice. His mercy is not in conflict with His judgments. The sanctions of reward and penalty unite to hold up His throne, and those sanctions are equally sacred in His eyes, and equally to be maintained. As surely as you obey He will smile upon you; as surely as you disobey, He will frown upon you. If you conform to the law of God, prosperity will attend you; and if you disobey the law of God, adversity will be your portion. A great truth it is that is revealed in this Psalm; not only the law and the testimony, accordant with right and with goodness, but the precepts and the statutes all based on and conformed to the principles of the common law; and then above, beneath, around all the rest, the preserving, sustaining sanctions of a sure retribution of evil, and a sure reward of righteousness. God's abhorrence of wrongdoing is as certain as His complacence toward goodness.

Thus the lofty morality and righteousness of this Word of God leaves nothing whatever to be desired in it as a code of law. It regulates the whole character and life of any obedient subject. There are three relations which need to be adjusted in this world. One is the relation between man and God; one is the relation between man and man;

and one is the relation between man and himself; and every one of these, this precious Holy Scripture adjusts, regulates, and perfects.

Take, for instance, the relation of man *to God*. Man has sinned. Man has come short of the glory of God. God in justice and in truth must visit punishment upon the unrepenting rebel. This Word of God interposes, and declares to us that, if there be repentance toward God, faith toward our Lord Jesus Christ, and an obedient will in place of a rebellious one, there is a provision made by which the punishment of sin shall be visited— has, in fact, been visited, so that the sanction of penalty is maintained, and that the fearful stroke of God's outraged government shall not fall on your head as a destroying power. There is an adjustment of the relations between God and man, in this, that God can be just and can yet justify the ungodly. He does not smile on sin. He frowns on sin, only the frown falls on your Substitute and mine, Jesus Christ the righteous; and the smile that Christ alone deserves is reflected on you and me in Christ. God looks at us, not as we are, but as we are in Him. And then God does not leave us simply justified: He creates in us what is called an affinity for Himself. Affinity is attraction founded on likeness. "Birds of a feather flock together" by animal affinity. Filings of steel or iron are attracted to the magnet by metallic affinity. Certain substances combine chemically because they have chemical affinity. God creates in the forgiven soul an affinity toward Himself, which answers to His love, answers to His drawing of the soul; and so we are not simply justified by repentance and faith, but we are sanctified. We have a new nature, a new heart, a new longing, and so we come to know what never could have been known by us otherwise. And the highest liberty is found in obedience to God. We once looked upon His law as a means of restraint and restriction, as putting fetters on our hands and feet, as encircling us by a prison wall, so that we could go only a certain distance without coming up against the stone barrier of prohibition. But the true disciple finds in this affinity toward God, this holy sympathy with the God-like, a delight in doing God's will, so that if he were left entirely free,—if the law were abolished so far as he is concerned, he would do exactly what God commands, because the new life runs in the same direction with God's life, and there is an inward sympathy with the Redeemer and Lord.

And then these Holy Scriptures adjust man's relation *to man*. Suppose your sin has involved your fellow man. You have injured him, robbed him, wronged him, slandered him, traduced him; you have done something iniquitous toward him. This Word of God comes in, and tells you not only to repent and confess your sin as one toward God, but to repent of your sin as one toward man. Not only so; but that you can never have peace with God, never have peace with yourself, unless you repair the injury that you have done. You have made a breach; you must heal that breach. You have struck a blow; you must atone for the blow. You have robbed; you must restore. You have wronged; you must undo the wrong. Reparation or restitution is the indispensable companion of repentance and obedience. God's law teaches you that there is to be no retaliation of injury inflicted on you; that, while it is manlike to return good for good, and evil for evil, and devil-like to return evil for good, it is God-like to return good for evil. And so you are to pray for your persecutors and oppressors, and traducers and slanderers, and to have pity on those who malign you and misrepresent you, and impute to you motives of which you have never been guilty, and which have never prompted your conduct.

What a wonderful morality this is which is taught us in the law of God, and how soon would wars and strifes, and contentions and dissensions cease, if, when men were wronged, they returned the wrong with generous and gracious treatment, and if every man who has injured his brother should hasten to make reparation and restitution for such wrong. The Bible teaches us even more than this. This holy morality holds up before us a *new law of love*. Love is benevolence. Benevolence is giving one's self; self-sacrifice for others ; losing my life that others may find life ; giving up my liberty that other men's liberty may be increased ; denying myself extravagant and useless expenditure that the nakedness of the naked may be clothed, and the hunger and thirst of the needy be filled ; mutual self-sacrifice for each other's sake.

And then, this law of God finally adjusts man's relation *to himself*. Man is a kind of double being. He can sit in judgment on himself. He can turn the mirror of reflection around, and look at his own image, and consider what manner of man he is, and improve and reform himself. He can see the wrong, and turn himself from the wrong by the aid of the grace of God.

Sin has broken up this little empire. It has put a usurper on the throne. Where conscience and reason should have taken their place, on their twin seat of empire, passion and lust have held the throne. Appetite, and ambition, and avarice, that should have been slaves, have become rulers. Now, what does God do when, by the lofty and holy morality of the Holy Scriptures, He restores this empire to its right condition? He casts down from this throne the usurper, sin, and He lifts conscience and reason—on whose necks the unholy lusts have placed their feet, from their prostration in the dust, puts the crown of empire on their brow, and sets them on the double seat of the little kingdom in man's heart; and then, over and above them all—for they are nothing, after all, but regents ruling in God's name— over them all is God Himself, controlling these twin sovereigns of our nature; while they hold in check the lower carnal propensities and evil desires, making all the faculties of mind and body subservient to their mission, which is to glorify and honour Jesus Christ as the Lord and Sovereign.

Such is the divine mission of the Law of God to every obedient soul.

We are now prepared to look at the concluding meditation and application of this psalm.

"Who can understand his errors? Cleanse thou me from secret faults. Keep back thy servant also from presumptuous" (or outbreaking) "sins; let them not have dominion over me: then shall I be upright, and I shall be innocent from the great transgression. Let the words of my mouth, and the meditation of my heart, be acceptable in thy sight, O Lord, my strength" (or, as the original has, "O Lord, my rock"), "and my redeemer."

Let us, with a spirit of awe, draw near and examine this divine meditation and application of these great truths. This law of God is His mirror, held up before us, to show us not only our outbreaking and presumptuous sins, but our secret sins; reflecting not only our faces and our forms, but our inward life, motive, desire; not only the adultery but the lust, not only the murderous blow but the hatred; the pride of spirit, as well as the boastful, ostentatious behaviour. This mirror takes out the heart of a man, shows him the inside of his own being, and compels him to confront himself, his past sins, and his present life of iniquity and coming short of the glory of God. I have seen in connection with medical study an instrument that is a combined lance and speculum or mirror; that is to say, while the mirror shows the disease, the lancet cuts out the tumour or the cancer. The law of God is a combined speculum or mirror, and lancet, or sharp two-edged blade. It shows me the cancer and it cuts the cancer out. It shows me, as in the placid water of the laver, whether there is filth on my person, and, like the waters of that laver, washes the filth away. It shows me myself, and it shows me my Saviour. What a wonderful Word of God this is that searches your open act and spoken word, and your silent thought, and that, like the sacrificial knife of the priest when he slew the bullock for the altar, cleaves at one blow to the dividing asunder of soul and spirit, joints and marrow, and discerns the thoughts and intents of the heart!

It is perfectly plain from our study of this psalm that there is *no hope of salvation in the law of God;* not the least; no hope of salvation in the law. There is hope in the *Word* of God, for the Word of God contains more than law; it presents Christ to us; but in the law of God as such there is no hope, for we are all transgressors, and its very perfection assures our condemnation. And when the psalmist has been thinking about the law, noticing how it searched him, how it opened up his innermost being, how it drove him into despondency and despair of self-help, what does he say? "O Lord, my rock and my redeemer." He does not say, "O *law* of God, my rock and my redeemer";

for he knew that the law of God furnished no rock for a standing-place for his feet, and no redeemer for the salvation of his soul. But, having looked at the law, seen its lofty morality, seen how he never could come up to the grandeur of its standard, seen how his very sins challenged that law to punish his guilt, and how the very rewards of the law mocked him because he could never hope to deserve them—he turns to Jehovah, and he calls Him " my rock and my redeemer." What is the law of God? Nothing but sinking sand underneath the sinner's feet. No transgressor can ever take a position on the law of God for his justification. It may be a rock, but it is a rock from which he could only plunge down into everlasting despair, and whose very exaltation would make his fall the more terrible and destructive. No, the law never can be a rock of refuge to you; but Jesus Christ can. "*Having access by faith into this grace wherein we stand.*" Notice that phrase, "*grace wherein we stand.*" There is no standing-place before God, no standing-place for a sinner in judgment, until he finds it in Christ. He is the Rock of Ages, riven and cleft for me, to provide both a hiding-place and a standing-place; and, though every earthly thing should be dissolved; the stars lose their light, the moon her lustre, the sun cease to shine, the heavens be rolled together as a scroll, and the earth be consumed with fervent heat, so that the rocks melt, and the everlasting mountains bow before destruction—that Rock of Ages shall stand, like a petrified shaft of eternity, never to be dissolved, never to be wrecked even by the earthquakes that may wreck the world, never to be melted by the fires that consume the universe. And God is beckoning you up from the depths of your condemnation to the heights of this rock, that you may stand firm amid the chaos that is again to involve this cosmos, in order to make place for the new heavens and earth wherein dwelleth righteousness.

Yes, the law can never bring you redemption. Paul in the Epistle to the Galatians, says, "The law is *our schoolmaster* to bring us to Christ." The Greek word is "pedagogue." The pedagogue was a slave who conducted the children from their father's house to the house of their teacher. He would come in the morning, and knock at the door, and receive them from parental care, and lead them to him who was to instruct their ignorance. And so Paul says, "The law is our pedagogue, to lead us to Christ." The law comes and knocks at the door of the house of our bondage and rebellion, and says, "Are there any poor, penitent, believing sinners here who, despairing of any self-help, or any self-justification, want a free redemption in Christ Jesus?" Those who are willing to be led, the law conducts out of bondage and captivity and hopeless despair, to the house where the Great Teacher lives, knocks at the door of mercy, and introduces the poor, penitent sinner to Him who can satisfy all the needs and demands of a broken law, vindicate, justify, sanctify, save.

Dear friends, abandon for ever all hope of being justified, except in Christ. Such hope is a quicksand beneath your feet; this broken law can only be a destructive sword of God to consummate your perdition. Pray, "Lead me to the Rock that is higher than I!" Stand on the high place that God has given for such poor sinners as you and me; and may the law to-night be your schoolmaster to lead you to Him whose precious blood was freely given to atone for a broken law, and purchase for you salvation! Amen.

SERMON TWO

The Five Revelations; or, The Hope of Justification

"I am not ashamed of the Gospel of Christ ; . . . for therein is the righteousness of God revealed."
"Therefore we conclude that a man is justified by faith without the deeds of the law."—ROMANS i. 16, 17, and iii. 28

ALL human history is one great interrogation point. Some questions are of such profound importance, and concern interests so vital, that they force themselves upon the attention of men : Is there a God ? Is there a law of right and wrong ? Am I a sinner ? Is there a judgment to come ? Is there a way of salvation from sin ? The true answer to such questions vitally touches and involves every human being. We may affect indifference, or assume to treat such matters lightly, and toss them aside as mere trifles, but they are, in themselves, so weighty and massive, that they sometimes sink the soul, in its more thoughtful and serious moments, to the very gates of hell !

The words, chosen as the text, belong respectively to the beginning and end of Paul's great argument on justification, the whole of which must be mastered, if any part of it is to be thoroughly understood. There are some ten words, so similar in meaning as to be very close of kin, which form the keys to the whole passage, such as "revealed," "manifested," "shewed," "witnessed," "declared," "made known," "clearly seen," "understood," "set forth," &c. If we trace these words as they occur, they will conduct us step by step up the ascent of this grand argument, till we reach the climax found in chapter second, verses 19 to 28.

The careful study of this whole passage shows that Paul refers to *five great Revelations* of truth, each having its own peculiar form or method of demonstration—namely, the existence of God, the law of right and wrong, the fact of sin and guilt, the certainty of a judgment, and the one way of justification. Let us examine them in order.

I. *The Revelation of God.* This, it is noticeable, is not traced to the Word of God, but to *the natural universe.* "That which may be known of God, is manifest to them (margin); for God hath shewed it to them. For the invisible things of Him, since the creation of the world, are clearly seen, being understood by the things that are made, even His eternal power and Godhead; so that they are without excuse." (i., 19, 20.)

This question, *Is there a God?* is the fundamental question of all. When a great religious meeting was held at Belfast, some years ago, and brethren were engaged in a somewhat heated, and even acrimonious discussion, as to whether it was proper to use, in public worship, hymns that were not inspired, a French delegate rose and said : "Brethren, while you are engaged in a warm controversy as to whether hymns or psalms only should be used in praising God, over in France the people are asking whether there is any God to praise." That is the bottom question of all—whether there is a God.

As we have said, Paul does not adduce any proof of this from the Word of God. The Bible takes for granted that there is a God, and never once attempts to demonstrate His existence by argument. That first verse in Genesis,—one of the grandest in the whole Scriptures,—says, " In the beginning God created the heavens and the earth." There is no more attempt to prove that there is a God than to prove that there is an earth and a heaven. Here before us lies the creation. A created thing implies a creator; that which is made, implies a maker; and so the Bible grandly assumes that there is a God, otherwise there could not be a creation; and, moreover, it tells us that " *The fool* hath said in his heart, there is no God;" and even the fool says so, only *in his heart*, because even a fool would be too wise to say so in his *head*. Yes, the fool's creed is, " There is no God;" but the wise man instinctively says :

" Every house is builded by someone."

" But He that built all things is God."

There is a certain grandeur and sublimity in the way in which this book of God thus takes for granted the existence of God in the very first verse, and all the way through, assuming any man to be lacking in common sense, who disputes or denies that there is a God. There is nothing new under the sun; and the way in which, in modern as well as ancient times, men have tried to get rid of a personal God, is an exhibition of consummate folly.

For instance, some tell us that this universe is all the work of *chance*. Isaac Newton made a small globe to represent this earth, with its continents and seas, river systems, and mountain ranges, and an atheist came in and, admiring it, asked, " Who made it?" " *Chance !* " said Sir Isaac, with stinging sarcasm. Rufus Choate, a great American lawyer,

The Hope of Justification

said, "Talk of this world coming into existence, with its symmetry, order and beauty, by accident? You might as well talk of dropping the Greek alphabet, and picking up the 'Iliad'"! Francis Bacon said, "I would rather believe all the fanciful fables of the Koran and the Talmud, than to believe that this universal frame is without a creative mind." No chance coming together of atoms could ever have made this world; this universal " House " was " builded by God."

Others would account for it on the "*clockwork*" *theory*: that it is nothing but a wonderful piece of mechanism, that goes of itself, moving uniformly like a clock ; but they do not tell us how there came to be such a clock, or who wound it up, or why it never runs down, or gets out of order. A universal clockwork demands a clock-maker.

Others would get rid of God, accounting for the universe by natural law, as though natural law or any kind of law ever made itself or could administer itself. What is law, but the voice of the law-giver, or his mode of operation? What we call " laws of Nature " are nothing but God's *modus operandi*—His ways of working in the sphere of nature. It is to be hoped that I address no one who denies a God,—yet, let me add, that law must be uniform in its working : it can never make exceptions to its own operation. If the universe were a mere clockwork, it could never reverse or vary its own motion. When a clock runs too fast, it cannot turn the hands on its dial, backward ; they move always in one direction, so long as they move at all ; but the interposition of an intelligent hand is necessary to reverse the movement of the hands, so that they show the correct time. So all " natural law " must work in a uniform way, never making an exception, or moving backward, even to adjust what is wrong. It might be well for any who would get rid of God, by substituting for Him "natural law," to tell us how it comes to pass that one remarkable exception exists to the great uniform law, that *heat expands* and *cold contracts*,—namely, in the case of *water*. If you heat water, it continues to expand up to the boiling point, and then becomes a very expansive vapour; but if you reduce the heat, the water contracts in bulk as you lower the temperature, until it reaches the freezing point, when it suddenly begins to *expand;* and the result is that ice, being lighter than the water, floats upon it and sheets it, and thus protects the vegetable and the animal life beneath, which otherwise would be held fast in eternal bands of ice that no summer sun could melt. Now, if uniform law were regulating this universe, and there were no God back of it, how could this uniform law make this strange exception, just at the very point where the exception must be made, in order to serve a benevolent purpose? That question has never been answered; and it never can be answered without admitting a personal God into the universe.

Other sceptics account for the marks of design in Nature by what they call "*adaptation to environment.*" But how about an adaptation to *unforeseen* surroundings? Let us grant that some winged and creeping things adapt their colour to objects about them, to escape detection and destruction. What shall we say of a fitness for new conditions which the insect or animal could not have foreseen? For example, a caterpillar that is wont to crawl on the earth, living on leaves and refuse material, passes into a chrysalis state, and emerges a winged creature, henceforth to soar on wings, and live on honey. It could not have foreseen this new mode of life, of which it had had no previous experience; yet, if you cut carefully through the enclosure of the chrysalis, you will find all the organs of the future butterfly folded up within this case, ready for use when the hour comes.

No theory will therefore account for creation, that leaves out a personal God; and, therefore, the Word of God sublimely assumes that the creation implies a creator; thought, a thinker; design, a designer; and that this universal house had an architect and builder. The revelation of the existence of God depends not on the Book of God at all, but on the Book of Nature.

II. Secondly, the *Revelation of Law*. And here, again, Paul does not trace this revelation primarily to the Bible. In the second chapter of this epistle, 14th and 15th verses, we read, "For when the Gentiles, which have not the law," (the written law of the Old Testament,) "do by nature" (in a condition of nature), "the things contained in the law, these, having not the law, are a law unto themselves : which shew the work of *the law written in their hearts*."

As the Bible never once attempts to prove that there is a God, neither does it undertake to prove that there is a law of right and wrong, but takes the law for granted; it opens with law, and it closes with law, and law is recognised all through it. And, here, Paul says that even those who were without any written law of God, were still not altogether without law, because "they showed the work of the law written in their hearts," and were thus "a law unto themselves," and that, in a state of nature, untaught by God's Word, they had ample proof of an existing code of moral law.

What does he mean ? We know that there is an external universe, by our bodily senses. We know there is a law, by other senses of the soul, which detect its operation—namely, reason, conscience, moral sensibility. A tribe of savages, who never heard of God or His written law, have rules of conduct, standards of right and wrong, which regulate their social life. This law within is the reflection of God's law without. Law is a rule of right and wrong. It says, "Thou shalt" or "Thou shalt not"; and so there are, in the human heart, tables of law which are a counterpart of the two tables that God wrote with His own finger. I do not need that God should reveal the law to teach me my duty: that written law, without, simply answers to the unwritten law within; that, in the mouth of two witnesses, every word of command may be established.

See how reason, also, tells me of a law of duty. If I become the slave of my appetite, I become the victim of gluttony and intemperance; if I transgress certain fixed principles of bodily health, weakness, illness, acute disease, and then chronic disease, follow; if I continue in such a course, death ensues. Reason thus shows me that certain effects follow certain causes, and that no right course of living produces evil effects on my body. And thus reason shows me a law written on my body—a law of bodily health, temperance, self-restraint, for the promotion of long life, and health and vigour. Again, I see that if husband or wife are false to each other, the foundations of the family life are wrecked; that, if parents do not exercise authority over their children, and children are not brought up to obey, all harmony and well-being in the household become impossible. And so, apart from the written law of God, reason reveals a law of right and wrong in household life. So of society at large. Where men are allowed to take each other's property, or to commit acts of violence and wrong, Society becomes disintegrated, and anarchy takes the place of government. Surely no written l needful to assure us that what works disaster soul, to the family and Society, must be wrong, ar promotes individual and collective well-being, mu... be right. To know that, is to know law.

III. *The Revelation of Sin.* Paul says, in this same epistle, that "by the law is the knowledge,"—the full knowledge—"of sin" (iii. 20). Man would not have known sin but for the law ; but, having the law, he cannot escape the knowledge of sin. Here are the tables of law before or within me : Do I not know whether I am a sinner ? Whoever hears a voice saying, "Thou shalt," or "Thou shalt not," knows whether he has done, or has not done, accordingly. And so, by the law, whether written or unwritten, comes the knowledge of sin. To know the standard of duty, is to know whether or not we have conformed to it. Every man who hears the voice of the law also hears another voice, testifying that he has not conformed to that law ; and so every man is not only a law unto himself, but the witness against himself, for he has also the consciousness that he has not kept that law, and that he is, therefore, a transgressor.

IV. *The Revelation of Judgment.* So we come to the next question : Is there a judgment to come ? Paul asked Agrippa, " Why should it be thought a thing incredible with you, that God should raise the dead ? " And we may ask him who doubts : Why should it be thought a thing incredible with you, that there is a court of judgment—a great white throne, where the books shall be opened, and where souls shall be judged out of the things written in the books ? Here again, the Holy Scriptures do not announce, as some new and strange truth, a judgment to come. They do announce it, but they do not attempt to prove it, because there is another announcement made in advance of the written word of God, and independent of it, in a man's own self. Look again at the second chapter of this epistle, at the fifteenth verse: "Which shew the work of the law written in their hearts, their *conscience also bearing witness*, and their thoughts the meanwhile accusing or else excusing. one another;—in the day when God shall judge the secrets of men by Jesus Christ according to my gospel." Paul reminds us of that court in the human soul, before which every man is daily tried, and from this he infers that it is no incredible thing that there should be another and supreme Court beyond this world, before which every man is to appear.

Let us enter this Court of Conscience in the human soul. There is a bench; on it sits the Reason. The ethics of etymology are very suggestive. When we talk of a man's *judgment*, what is that but the concession that there are assizes in the human soul? Grander assizes than in the highest Courts of this realm, for there never was any human tribunal so awful and solemn as that which is for ever sitting within you! There is the Reason, seated on the Bench of Judgment, ready to weigh, and decide upon the evidence, as it comes before the Court. You may, perhaps, bribe some earthly judges, but you cannot *bribe that judge*, who will impartially render his decision according to the testimony. Memory presides at the witness stand, and one by one marshals her witnessess, and you have to hear their testimony. These witnesses come up from the past, one by one,—your evil thoughts and plans, your dishonesty, perjury, lust, drunkenness, your ill-treatment of wife or children, your deception of your fellow-beings, your slanders, your selfishnesses, your ingratitude to a mother, your disobedience to a father—these, and other witnesses like them, come trooping up from the by-gone years, and take their place, sometimes a score of them together, in the witness box, and you cannot drown their testimony, or deny its truth. The imagination aids the memory, and spreads before you, as in an awful panorama, the whole of your past life, and, like a solemn procession of ghosts, the evil doings of the past haunt your recollection, and will not lie down at your bidding.

We sometimes talk of things forgotten; it is doubtful whether anything is ever really forgotten. I know of a man who keeps, in a little case, an old penny, which has a history. When sixty-five years old, he thought he would like to visit his birthplace, which he left when a boy, six years of age. He went along the streets, and recognized the cottage where he used to live. Immediately opposite was a little shop which, in his boyhood's days, was used as a grocery, now used for hardware, but looking as it did sixty years before. He borrowed a hatchet for a moment, and going across the way, loosened the bottom board of the wood-shed, and putting in his hand, drew out a penny. When a little boy, sent by his mother to the grocery, on some errand, he had lost that penny behind the crack of the board, and he had never thought of it for sixty years; but the sight of that old wood-shed and the little shop opposite, awakened the remembrance of this incident of sixty years before. You think you have forgotten the past, but the day will come when you will begin at the beginning of memory's book, and turn over leaf after leaf and read the dark records of your past life—presumptuous and secret sins, unchaste acts and impure lusts, hateful thoughts and violent blows, blasphemous thoughts and profane words, neglect, disobedience, transgression, contempt of laws, human and divine, and there is not a particular circumstance of your life, O sinner! that will not come up before you in dreadful and awful review, in the Court within, when Memory calls her witnesses to the stand. And there, is the incorruptible jury of the conscience, which, when the evidence has been heard and sifted, will bring in their unanimous verdict, "*Guilty.*" Your own thoughts or convictions are the jurors that will condemn you as guilty, or will vindicate you as innocent, and you cannot escape their verdict. And, when the witnesses have been heard, and the jury has given its verdict, "Thou art verily guilty," the judge from the bench will remand you to the sheriff, for the punishment due to your sin.

What is that sheriff in this inner Court? An American statesman, who led a very bad life, was on his dying bed observed to toss restlessly to and fro. He was asked if he were suffering pain. He only reached out his hand and took from the table a card and a pencil, and with his trembling, dying hand, wrote one word, "REMORSE." The sheriff of that Court of Conscience is remorse, and it is armed with a whip whose lash stings like a scorpion, and burns like fire!

A woman, down in the East End of London, was asked if she would accept a tract. "No!" "Can't you read?" "Yes." "Then why don't you take this tract and read it?" "Because, if I read it, I shall think, and, *if I think, I shall die or go mad!*" It has been found necessary to stop confining criminals in solitary cells, for they cannot live thus; either they become insane, or by violent suicidal acts, destroy themselves. They are put at work, so that they

have less chance to think, and for the time being, the voices from this awful Court of Conscience are not so loudly heard.
If I have thus a court of judgment within me, why should I need a court of judgment without me? Simply because the court of judgment within you cannot completely administer the awards due to sin. During man's lifetime, much sorrow, restlessness, anguish, and remorse, follow evildoing; but many offenders and offences cannot, in the nature of the case, ever meet, in this world, the full and just penalty of sin. There was a man who, for the sake of a little money in the hands of the gate-keeper, went at midnight, murdered the man, his wife, and their little children, leaving behind him one pool of blood. As he fled, the neighbours were roused up, and pursued him. When he was nearly overtaken, he blew out his own brains. Where is that man's retribution if all punishment is meted out in this life? For that man, at least, there must be a judgment to come, a penalty beyond this world. When we see the wicked flourishing like a green bay tree, we have to go into the sanctuary of God, and learn of a Court beyond this world. God's balances only then appear equal.

We have now glanced rapidly at four of these revelations. The fact that the universe exists, and that you *are*, proves a God; the fact that you have a voice of witness to duty within your heart, proves that there is a law; the consciousness that you have not kept that law, proves that you are a sinner; and the fact that you have a Court in your conscience with judge and jury, witnesses and sheriff, proves that you are accountable, and foreshadows the day when God shall judge the secrets of the heart, according to the gospel.

V. And now we are prepared for Paul's conclusion. There is a fifth revelation, and that is *of Justification;* and that revelation wholly depends on the gospel of Christ. We have seen that the Book of God was not given to reveal that there is a God, a law of right and wrong, or sin and penalty, a judgment here and beyond—all these are assumed—taken as not to be disputed. What is it, then, for which the Word of God is given to us; and what *does it reveal*, which cannot thus be taken for granted? " Therein is *the righteousness of God revealed.*" "A man is justified by faith, without the deeds of the law." " The righteousness of God," in the sense that Paul uses it, in this epistle, is *not* the inherent righteousness or rectitude of God's character or decrees; because, if that were all that were revealed, we should only be driven to despair. If we had to look only at the awful anger of a just God, at the awful holiness of an incorruptible God, we should have no hope; but Paul tells us in this epistle what he means by the righteousness of God. Let him define his own terms, in the third chapter, and 26th verse: "To declare, I say, at this time *his righteousness: that he might be just, and the justifier of him which believeth in Jesus.*" This is what God's righteousness means. The problem before God was, how to maintain Himself as a righteous God, and yet forgive the unrighteousness; how to be a just God, and yet justify me, the sinner,—that was the problem which love solved in the eternal ages, and whose solution is given in the gospel. The supreme reason why this gospel is given to us, is that, although you might, without the Bible, know there was a God, and a law, condemnation for sin, and a judgment to come, you could never have known, without the Bible, how God could be just and yet forgive sin. And so the whole Bible, from Genesis to

Revelation, is given to exhibit this righteousness of God, this plan of salvation.

Could I learn about forgiveness without God's gospel? Does nature or my own conscience hint pardon? Where did you ever find any trace of forgiveness or of mercy in the natural universe? Nature knows no such thing as pardon, or even discrimination between offenders. If in any way I wound myself, I must wait for the wound to heal, and even then there will be a scar, and that scar is a proof that, in the natural universe, there is no hint of forgiveness, or even restoration. Suppose I throw myself from a precipice, or fall accidentally, or am maliciously hurled over, I am, in either case, dashed to pieces; for the law of gravity makes no discrimination in visiting penalty, as to whether such a fall is accidental, intentional, or malicious. Surely it is plain that there is no hint of forgiveness in nature?

Do we find, within ourselves, any hint of pardon? A sensitive conscience never forgives your wrong act. Another may forgive you, but you never forgive yourself, or wipe out the record of your offence. It is for ever there to accuse you, and rises up, again and again, to remind you, to reproach you, to rebuke you, to lash you, and so there is no possibility of finding, within, any hint of forgiveness.

We turn now from the natural universe, and from the Court of the Conscience, and ask : Is there forgiveness *with God?* Blessed be His name, "there *is* forgiveness with Thee." You cannot wipe out those records of your memory and conscience, but the blood of Christ can cleanse them all away from God's book of remembrance. They may recur to your remembrance, but only to awaken new thanks to God for such a great salvation and such a great

Saviour. If, in eternity, we cannot forget the guilt that compelled Him to die for us, neither can we forget the grace that led Him to atone for such guilt!

And so, how wicked soever you are—though you be the chief of sinners—though you are loaded down with the burden of such guilt as would sink you to the lowermost hell—if you will reach out your hands and receive Jesus; if you will cry, like the publican, "God, be merciful to me a sinner," there is One who is ready to cover up your sins with the mantle of a divine righteousness.

Blessed be God for this gospel! I need not send you away with that terrible message about God and His law, and your sin and your conscience and judgment to come. I can dismiss you with a sweeter word: God is just, and yet He justifies him that believeth in Jesus. I know it, because He has forgiven me. I used to be afraid of my sin; I have lost that fear. I used to be afraid of the judgment to come; I have lost that fear. I used to be afraid of death; I have lost that fear. I used to be afraid of eternity; I have lost that fear. And because God can do this for me, He can do it for you. Will you have Him do it? He can do it NOW!

Sermon Three

The Vision of the Candelabra; or, Hope in Divine Power

"Not by might, nor by power, but by my Spirit, saith the Lord of hosts."—ZECHARIAH IV. 6

THAT is, "Not by might"—the might of a host, or of numbers, "not by power," or mere carnal strength,—"but by my Spirit, saith the Lord of hosts."

Three times in Holy Scripture the golden candelabra comes into prominence: first, in the twenty-fifth chapter of the Book of Exodus, among the directions there given for its fashioning and its setting up in the holy place; then, in this fourth chapter of Zechariah, the vision which we are now to consider; and finally, in the last part of the first chapter of the Revelation, and the beginning of the second, where the Lord Jesus in glory appears, walking amid the seven golden candlesticks, which are declared to be the seven churches, and holding in His right hand the stars that represent the angels, messengers, or pastors, of those seven churches.

There is, undoubtedly, a reason why these three references to the candlesticks should thus be found in these three parts of Scripture,—one in the law, one in the prophets, and one in the close of the New Testament, which is pre-eminently the Revelation of the Gospel. In the Book of Exodus, the candlestick seems mainly to stand for Jehovah as the source of light to His people. In the Book of the Revelation, the seven candlesticks represent the seven-fold Church of Christ as the light of the world; and here, in the Book of Zechariah, which lies midway between these two, we see the dependence of the Church of God, for its being a light to the world, upon Him who is the original and only Source of light; so that the three, taken together and combined, afford a complete representation of the whole truth, necessary to be taught in this connection—namely, God, the One, original Source of light; the Church of God as a light-bearer in the world; and then the great condition of all true light-giving power. The church is a light only when, and so far as, it is kept in *close and constant contact* with the Source of all light, illumination, and glory.

From this threefold representation, the vision of Zechariah has been selected for our present study, from the deep persuasion that from cover to cover the Word of God contains no message more appropriate to this bereaved and stricken congregation.* "Not by might,"—our dependence must not be on numbers; "nor by power,"—our reliance must not be upon worldly patronage,—"but by my Spirit, saith the Lord of hosts;" and therefore, in proportion as the Holy Spirit abides in the midst of us, will every work which was begun by the departed Pastor, be carried forward; and every new work which ought to be begun, be initiated and established.

---

* Pastor Charles H. Spurgeon had died only Jan. 31 previous, and the impression was that of an event of yesterday.—A. T. P.

I. In the first place, notice the *characteristic features of the vision*. It would be a great help to have an accurate representation of that vision, depicted before our eyes, that at once the impression might lay hold of us in a *pictorial* manner; but we may, at least, try so to picture forth this vision, as that the main features of the representation may be borne in mind. First, there is in the centre a golden candlestick or candelabra, having seven branches—or more properly, six branches proceeding from a central stem, somewhat more exalted than the rest. These six branches, three on each side, rise to a common level, but a little below the level of the central bowl which crowns the main stem of the candlestick; and in each of these branches there is set, at its upper extremity, a lamp. The branches are hollow, and contain pipes or conductors for the oil; and the oil is conveyed from the central bowl through these pipes to the little bowls that feed each particular wick. On the right hand and the left hand of this candelabra, there stand, in the vision, olive trees, which, of course, are the sources of the precious oil of the sanctuary. These are living trees, and they represent therefore unfailing sources of supply, rather than simply reservoirs of oil like the bowl; they are living fountains whose supply cannot be exhausted. And these are curiously connected, by golden pipes, with the bowl in the centre of the candelabra, and they pour through these golden pipes, as the Hebrew beautifully expresses it, *liquid gold* out of themselves. Then this liquid gold is conveyed down through the channels of the candelabra to the lamps at its extremities, and so the lamps are enabled perpetually to burn.

We have thus a poetically and pictorially perfect representation, and one whose lesson seems transparently plain. These olive trees, we are told in the vision, represent two anointed ones. The common interpretation of these anointed ones is, that one represents the anointed high-priest Joshua; and the other, the anointed governor, or king, Zerubbabel. They stood as the visible heads of the Jewish state, in this time of great trouble and trial; and, whatever strength came to the Jewish nation would come naturally from the divine source through this high-priest, Joshua, and through this governor, Zerubbabel. But it needs but very little reflection to find, in all this, a very obvious, suggestive and indisputable type of *our blessed Lord Jesus Christ*. He is, on the one hand, the " High-Priest of our profession," and, on the other hand, our " Lord and King ": two great titles that in the Word of God cover the main part of His official work. Every tongue that confesses that Jesus Christ is Saviour and Lord, speaks by the Holy Ghost. If, on the one hand, the believer acknowledges his indebtedness to Christ's atoning work, as High-Priest, for the forgiveness of sin and for reconciliation with God; and if, on the other hand, the disciple reverently and humbly bows at His feet, accepting all orders from Him, as the Captain of his salvation, and his laws from Him, as the King over his whole nature, then is the believer giving sure proof that he is redeemed; for no man or woman can recognize Christ in His high-priestly function as the atoning Saviour, and His kingly function as the ruling Soverign, without having been born of God.

II. Now, having the vision before us in its general teaching, we may look a little closer into the details. Here is a central bowl, and from that bowl oil is distributed to all the lamps. As to what the candlestick represents, we can have very little doubt when we turn to the first chapter of the Book of Revelation, and there find that, whatever else it may represent in type, it certainly does stand for the Church of the living God. And a surpassingly fine type it is. The candlestick was a divine invention, a divine institution, set in a divine place. The Church of God is not a human invention, but a divine institution; and it is set up in this world, not by the authority of Pope, or Archbishop, or Bishop or Priest, but by the authority of Almighty God. It has the primary warrant for its existence, not in the wisdom of man, not in the approbation of human rulers, not in any blessings it has brought to man; but, first of all, and above all else, n the fact that it is by the decree of God that the Church exists in the world, and that only so long as Christ is practically the head of the Church, has the Church any right to be at all; and therefore if His headship is denied, or divided with any other, the Church forfeits her right to be known as the Church of Jesus Christ. Note the significance of this name: Church *of Christ.* When any *man* is accepted as the head of the Church it is a displacement of her true Head, and a forfeiture of her privileges. Through all her creeds, past all her ministers and officers, we must look up to Him who ordained that the Church should be, and gave it a place in His earthly tabernacle.

We have seen how the central bowl communicates by pipes with the individual lamps. How well does that represent the Church, as a receiving reservoir of the grace of God, distributing her blessings through appointed means or channels of grace to every individual believer! And then the two olive trees, those perennial sources of supply! The capacity of all the bowls on the candlestick is limited, but the capacity of the olive trees to furnish the oil is unlimited. The capacity of the Church to receive blessing is limited, but the capacity of the Lord Jesus Christ to bestow blessing is unlimited; and, as the central bowl cannot accumulate a stock of oil to last for all future time, but must take the supply as it is communicated; and as the burning and shining of the lamp consumes the oil and makes more necessary, so neither the Church nor the individual believer can accumulate any stock of grace against the time to come, but must receive daily renewed supplies from the everlasting fountains in Jesus Christ.

There are seven pipes that reach from the olive trees to the bowl. What do they represent but the *channels of communication* through which the Holy Ghost pours the oil of grace into the Church's reservoirs and individual lamps? Oil, in the Scripture, is one of the favourite symbols of the Spirit's power and presence. And how plain it is that, if any obstruction exists to the inflowing and the outflowing of the oil, the greater lamp of the Church and the lesser lamps of individual believers can no longer continue to burn and shine!

Such, then, are the outlines of this great theme—suggesting one of the finest figures and most instructive images put before us in Scripture. Here we find a brief and telling commentary on those words which the Lord Jesus Christ used, in the fifth chapter of John, with reference to John the Baptist,—" He was a burning and a shining light." In those two words, "burning" and "shining", we may find, conveyed, the major part of the whole lesson of this vision. It is our duty and privilege both to *burn* and to *shine;* and the conditions of both burning and shining are put before us in this vision of the candelabra.

How, then, am I to burn? The first necessity for my burning is that the candlestick shall be vitally connected with the olive tree. The supply of oil cannot reach the candlestick except as the pipes lead out of the trees to the bowl. What does that teach but that the first condition of my burning is that I shall be vitally linked to my Lord and Saviour as my High-Priest, and as my King? There is no possibility of my ever becoming a part of the true candlestick unless I am first of all joined with Him. When a poor sinner comes to know his sin, and to feel his guilt, and looks from his sin to his Saviour, and from his guilt to his atonement; comes to feel his alienation and finds the way of his reconciliation—that is the beginning of vital union with the only source of life or light. And when, having renounced his sin, and accepted forgiving grace, he bows at the feet of his Redeemer, and says, "Lord, command me henceforth and be my Master," he understands what it is to accept the authority of the infinite Lord, as He has understood what it was to accept the atonement of the infinite Saviour. There is the first condition of burning. You can never burn as a disciple until you first get vitally connected with Jesus Christ as Saviour and Lord.

2. The second condition of burning is that you shall receive your supply of grace through the channels of the Holy Spirit's ministry. How beautifully this vision teaches us the connection between Christ and the Spirit. When He was about to go up to take His seat on His Father's throne, He said, "It is expedient for you that I go away, for if I go not away, the Holy Spirit will not come to you; but if I depart I will send Him unto you." And Peter on the Day of Pentecost says,—"He hath shed forth,"—or "poured forth,"—"this which ye now see and hear." That is, Pentecost was the first coming to the Church at large of the abundant outflow and inflow of the oil of the Holy Spirit. But never was that Spirit given until Christ had finished the work of the High-Priest, and was prepared for the work of

the King. This figure is almost an analogy, fitting the truth at every point. For observe that Christ, as a priest, establishes the channels between the soul and God, but Christ as King pours the unceasing flow of oil through the golden pipes. When the pipes are established, the work of providing channels is done, but the work of supplying those channels with oil is never done. And so when Christ said, " It is finished," and, having died, rose from the grave on the third day, He had completed the atoning and justifying work; but His Kingly work never has been completed and never will be, until His mediatorial reign is at an end. No believer can ever burn except as he is both united to Christ and to the Holy Ghost in Christ; except as he gets the oil of grace, flowing through these appointed divine channels, from Jesus Christ, into his own heart and into his own life. And therefore a believer ought not simply to know Jesus Christ as atoning Saviour and reigning Lord, but ought to know the Holy Ghost as an indwelling power, vitally connected with Christ, as a person of the Godhead, vitally connected with the believer himself, as an indwelling presence.

3. The third condition of burning is that the wick shall reach and take up the oil. The candelabra might be connected with the olive trees, and the oil might pour through the appointed channels, but if there were no wick in the lamp, or if the wick did not reach down to the oil and take up the oil, or if there were any obstacle in the wick by which the oil's progress from the bottom to the top of it were interrupted, the lamp could not burn. And unless you have an experimental contact with Jesus Christ and the Holy Ghost, you cannot burn : and, if there is anything in your life that hinders the flowing of the Spirit into and through

you, you cannot burn. The wick that ought to flame will
flicker, and smoke, and its flame will die away, unless that
supply of oil is perpetual and actual in your life. And so the
Bible teaches us, all through, that we are to look carefully
after the individual, personal, daily communion and communication between ourselves and our Lord through the
Holy Ghost; that we are to watch over secret sin, which,
like a knot, or other defect in the wick, prevents the oil from
passing from end to end; and that we are to look after any
lack of obedience, which, like undue shortness in the wick,
prevents its reaching down, touching, and so taking up the oil.

If these are the conditions of burning, what are the
conditions of *shining?* First, that there shall be *room to
shine.* We do not take a candle and put it under a bushel,
or measure, because the measure confines the air, and
because, presently, inasmuch as oxygen is not supplied for
combustion, the light will go out. So our Lord teaches us
that, even after the Spirit of God has lighted in us the flame
of piety, and is feeding it in us by His sacred oil, we need
to get out from concealment and find a place where we shall
have room and air—room to burn, and atmosphere to feed
the combustion. Our *life* may be "Hid with Christ in
God"; but our *light* never must be hid even with Christ in
God: the source of the light a hidden life, but the light itself
a visible flame. There are many people who think that they
can live a private Christian life, as they call it, and hide their
lamp under a bushel; but if the light burns at all, it burns
dimly, it has no circumference adequate for its shining, and
no atmosphere to feed its flame; and the consequence is, if
it burns at all, it might almost as well not burn, for any
vigour that comes with the burning, or any power that comes
with the shining.

2. A second condition of shining is that there shall not only be room to shine, but that the light shall be *exalted*, lifted where the rays will have the largest range. He who tells us that our light must not be hidden under a measure, tells us also that it must be lifted on the candlestick or lamp stand. What means that, but that you should belong to the Church of Jesus Christ if you belong to Christ Himself? The Church is God's instrumentality for lifting up individual lamps on its great branches, and giving them scope for the shining of their rays. It is impossible for any believer to live as well without the fellowship of other believers as he can live with it. Now, in the Church of Christ the act of confession of Jesus is attended with the ordinance of baptism. What is that for? Not because salvation comes through such use of water, for we are not of those who believe that regeneration, in any proper sense, comes through this or any other ordinance. What, therefore, is the use of baptism? Is it not the putting of the lamp that is lighted by the Spirit in its proper place on the branch of the candlestick? It is the act of confession that Jesus Christ is my Saviour and my Lord; it is going down into the sacred waters to put on Jesus Christ, that I may come up out of those waters bearing Christ as my investiture, and thus saying to all men,—" He is my Saviour, and this is the humble act of my confession of Him as my Lord." All human history may be challenged to produce a solitary believer who has exercised the full power that ought to be and may be exercised in holy living, who has not submitted himself to the ordinances of the Church of Christ, and joined himself in humble confession to the Lord's people. In the sixtieth Psalm, fourth verse, we are told, "Thou hast given a banner to them that fear thee, that it may be displayed because of the truth." That is a

military figure to express the same idea—namely, that if you belong to the Lord's army, you ought to be ashamed not to be a standard bearer ; you should have a flag, and that flag ought to be waving and upborne in the thickest of the fight, that all men may know under whose authority you move, and in whose salvation you are made to rejoice.

3. A third condition of shining is, that the *snuffers be used on the wick*. The very act of consumption implies a charring of the wick, which is coated to-day with such charred surface because it burned and shone yesterday. And hence the same wonderful divine appointment that gave us the candlestick, ordains the golden snuffers to be used on the wick. What does that mean? What is the effect of this accumulation of burnt wick, but to make what otherwise ought to flame up fully and brightly, die down, flicker, smoke! Yes, the lamp that ought to yield flame, gives smoke ; the life that ought to be a blessing, is like a wick that is offensive both to the eyes and to the nostrils. Your life in Christ must be renewed day by day. It will not do to live on the experience of yesterday, to boast what the Lord did for you years ago, or to attempt to live by the grace He has given in the past. All that, to-day, is like a charred wick if you are depending upon it ; and it will only make your lamp burn dimly, and flicker, and smoke, and cease to be a true light. New experiences only can prepare for fresh and more luminous testimony.

One of the great errors into which disciples are prone to fall is that of dwelling upon, and telling of, wonderful experiences of the grace of God which they had perhaps ten, fifteen, or twenty years ago, while it is but too obvious to all observers that they are not enjoying very much of that sort of experience just now. That is the wick that has not had the golden snuffers applied to it! It is a blessed state of mind when one is unwilling thus to rest on any experience of the past, though it be even so recent as yesterday, but feels the need of a new experience, day by day; of having God's golden snuffers constantly applied to the wick, to remove all that which might be a false dependence, that there may be a fresh, clean, helpful and spiritual unfolding of the power and preciousness of the grace of God each day anew. Somebody asked Mr. Moody whether he had ever got "the second blessing." "Yes," said he, "but I never got any second blessing that left me to feel that I did not need a third;" and he might have added that no child of God ever had a blessing that makes a new one unnecessary, though it be the hundredth, or the thousandth blessing. Paul was one of the maturest of disciples, yet he says,— "Forgetting the things that are behind, and reaching forth unto the things which are before, I press towards the mark." I would not give a farthing for an experience of ten years ago, or of ten days ago, if that experience is not confirmed and established by the experience of to-day. If your confidence that you are converted rests only on some past transaction of your life with God, while you are not now living as a converted man or woman should live, you would better throw away all that past experience as worthless, for it may be a deceitful vision by which your eyes were deluded of the devil. There is no vision of salvation that is not misleading unless it opens the eyes to new visions of God day by day, and leads to a new life of godliness that is manifested at this very hour. Let the snuffers be diligently applied to all burnt-out wick, and let us have a flame that is ever new, brighter and brighter while life lasts.

III. Perhaps a more important lesson than any yet touched

upon, is connected with this vision of Zechariah. We have seen how we find here suggestions as to the secrets of burning and shining, but let it not be forgotten that the central lesson taught us is that all power and sufficiency are of the Holy Spirit. "Not by might, nor by power, but *by my Spirit*, saith the Lord of hosts."

If we read this vision aright, we shall learn a lesson, first about our vital connection with Jesus, as our Priest and King; secondly, a lesson about our vital connection with the Holy Spirit, as the source of daily life, and daily-renewed grace; and thirdly, about our connection with the churches of Jesus Christ. All this we have already adverted to, and let us further emphasize the fact that, in all ordinary cases, the communications of the power of the Holy Spirit come through, or in connection with, *the Church* of Jesus Christ. If any who hear me do not believe that, or think it is too strongly stated, let us turn again to God's own illustration in this vision of the candlestick. The oil flowed into the bowl through *appointed channels*, and from the bowl again through fixed channels to the individual flame. What do we mean by "means of grace"? Not that grace *necessarily* comes to us through these means; but that God has established certain fixed channels or means for the *ordinary reception* of grace. For example, in this Church of Christ certain things are exalted and magnified as they are seldom magnified in other churches. First of all, the Word of the living God. No man would be tolerated in this pulpit who did not *preach the Word* of God. Here the preaching of that Word is recognized as a foremost means of grace. It is here strenuously held that, through such preaching, grace comes to unsaved souls for salvation, and to saved souls for sanctification and edification. This is not limiting God;

as though one should say God could not reach a man who never saw a Bible or heard a sermon; but it is affirming that, for all ordinary ministries of the Spirit, the Word of God is the appointed channel. This is one of the golden pipes; and if you are to get the oil at all you must commonly get it through God's golden pipe. If you neglect the Word of God, and the preaching of the gospel, if you do not prayerfully read the Scriptures and reverently hear the preached gospel, you are not in connection with the channel of supply, and so you cannot have the abundance of oil.

This Church magnifies again the ordinances of baptism and the Lord's Supper. Why? Because baptism represents putting on Christ and burial with Him, and the Lord's Supper represents taking in Christ and living by Him; if baptism represents our entering into the Saviour as our justifier, the Lord's Supper represents His entering into us as our Sanctifier and Strengthener, the very food of our daily life. This is not saying that no unbaptized person ever was saved; or that nobody, who has not sat down at the Lord's Supper, can be made holy; but it is saying that these are among the golden pipes, through which the oil of grace flows into the hearts and lives of believers; and that he who deliberately neglects these means of grace, or wilfully despises them, obstructs the divine channels through which the oil is appointed to reach the soul.

Let us understand, however, that we can never *account for the power of God's ordinances by any mere human philosophy*. When Moses was told to lift up the brazen serpent on the pole, or cross—for that is what he lifted it up on, a banner staff which has the form of a cross,—and that whoever *looked upon it* should be healed, there was absolutely no healing power either in the brazen serpent, or in the look. All of us must concede that any such conception would be utterly absurd.

Where, then, lay the power? *In the ordinance of God*, and that is all that can be said about it. Is there any power in the mere act of going down into the waters of baptism, or in eating the bread and drinking the cup at the Lord's Supper? Of course not. Water cannot impart to you a spiritual blessing, literally washing away your sins or assuring to you justification; the bread and the cup cannot give you spiritual life and nutriment. The power lies not in these things themselves, but in the decree or ordinance of God—that is enough. Because He so ordained, we call these His ordinances. If the bitten Israelite had said, "I see no virtue in that brazen serpent, I see no good that looking at that image of brass can accomplish for me;" and if preferring to resort to human methods that seem more rational, he had got out his brass kettle and put in all the herbs he could collect and made of them a panacea by which to cure his ills, he would have died notwithstanding. There are perhaps some of you who, because you do not see how or why a look of faith at the uplifted Jesus should save you, are trying to concoct some sort of panacea in your own wisdom and strength, according to man's devices, by which to cure yourselves of the sin, and the guilt, and save yourselves from God's condemnation. There are some of you, I fear, who will die in your sins while the uplifted Christ is even to-day again set forth clearly before you as the object for your faith. Until we get over all the nonsense of attempting to philosophize on the ordinances of God, and to account for the way of the blessing, waiting to find a reason for the blessing, coming to us through these ordinances, that does not come to us outside of them—until we get over all this, and simply submit ourselves to the Lord's command, and say, " This is Thy decree, and I bow to it; this is Thine ordinance, and I obey it,"—we shall never get the blessing that ought to come, and may come to us through these divinely appointed means.

Let me add one concluding word. The strength and power of the Church, or of the individual believer, is found solely in the Holy Spirit; and, therefore, to rest on any other source of power is to lean on a bruised reed that will break, and pierce the hand that leans upon it. What constitutes the power of a church? Numbers? God would rather have seven consecrated men and women than seven thousand who are living according to the course of this world. Where lies the strength of a church? In human wealth and patronage? Sometimes these are curses instead of blessings. The power of any church is the Holy Spirit. If He be in the preacher and in the believer, and in the general body of disciples, there is no telling what wonderful things that may be done under His presidency.

Apply this truth to yourselves. You are consciously weak and feeble, now that your visible head is taken away; but, if the Spirit of Almighty God here holds full sway, you shall see the capstone laid on every enterprise of which Charles H. Spurgeon laid the corner-stone, and it shall be perfectly plain to you that, however you may be used in the building, He who has the sevenfold eyes of omniscience is the real Builder, and that therefore, from foundation-stone to capstone, it is all the work of God.

God's heart is strongly drawn out to the unsaved in this congregation. You are trying to live without Christ, and some of you are, I fear, going to die without Christ. Was there ever a time when human life seemed more uncertain than now? Remember Rev. Dr. Donald Fraser. A week ago last Monday night, having preached on the Lord's-day, he presided at the annual meeting of his congregation, apparently in his usual health; on Tuesday struck with double pneumonia, in a few days he was dead, and last Thursday was borne to burial: one week among the living with the promise of life, another week among the dead with his work on earth for ever laid down. It is an awful and august thought that, even to-day, in this congregation the seal of death is on scores of people all unseen by them—and it may be on the speaker himself. How any man can be content to live without God is a marvel. Setting aside all other considerations, it is amazing that any human being, knowing the uncertainty of life, and the immense importance of being ready for the exchange of worlds, and feeling in himself the guilt, condemnation, and downward tendency of sin, dares to live in neglect of Christ. Not to dwell on the delight of God's service, on the blessedness of being His, on the joy of being taken up into Christ and absorbed in Him, which makes even duty to be forgotten in delight—looking at the matter from the lowest point of view, how does anyone *dare to live without God?* This Bible is not true, or else there is no hope for you except in Christ Jesus. If you are not joined to Him as High-Priest and Lord, you can get neither light nor life; and, if His Holy Spirit does not supply you with the gracious oil of the Divine presence and power, there can be no flame that shines with the vitality of God, or with the power of sanctified influence. So in the name of God, I pray you, sinner and saint alike, seek vital union with Jesus; let your life be hid with Him, and let the light of your testimony burn and shine!

Sermon Four

The Eight Beatitudes; or,
The Hope of Blessedness

"And seeing the multitudes, he went up into a mountain: and when he was set, his disciples came unto him:

"And he opened his mouth, and taught them, saying,

"Blessed are the poor in spirit:
For their's is the kingdom of heaven.

"Blessed are they that mourn:
For they shall be comforted.

"Blessed are the meek:
For they shall inherit the earth.

"Blessed are they which do hunger
and thirst after righteousness:
For they shall be filled.

"Blessed are the merciful:
For they shall obtain mercy.

"Blessed are the pure in heart:
For they shall see God.

"Blessed are the peacemakers:
For they shall be called the children of God.

"Blessed are they which are persecuted
for righteousness' sake:
For their's is the kingdom of heaven."—MATT. V

THE name of "Beatitudes," or, states of blessing, has been applied to eight special benedictions pronounced in the

The Hope of Blessedness 485

opening of the so-called "sermon on the mount," and beginning this chapter.

Christ's first preaching seems to have been comprised in one very short but very important sentence, like that of John the Baptist before Him : " Repent; for the kingdom is at hand." It is not perhaps best now to discuss that most interesting topic, the "kingdom of heaven," what it means, and what are the various periods of its development, but these beatitudes teach us something of those *who belong to that kingdom*, and upon whom Christ pronounced, in these words, its highest forms of benediction.

Christ came once in the flesh, and He is coming yet again ; and each advent has a special object, as connected with the kingdom of heaven. The first coming was to make possible an empire in man and over man, by laying the foundations of that empire in individual souls. His second coming will be for the purpose of setting up that empire in glory; so that it is of vast importance that we should understand what is the character of the subjects in that kingdom, so that we may know whether we belong to the kingdom ourselves, and whether its privileges, immunities and future rewards are a part of our present and future inheritance. Hence the importance of a devout and careful study of these beatitudes. We must examine them as a whole ; we cannot take one alone, without losing a part of the lesson they jointly teach. These outlines pertain to *one* portrait. When an artist draws a picture, each line may be graceful, and masterful, but it is the union of the lines that reveals their mutual relation ; it is the combination of the various artistic delineations and even minutest touches that gives us the complete portrait. So here, though the separate outlines have each their own peculiar beauty, and grace, and show the hand of a master, it is only when we take all the lines in their combination that we get the full portrait of a true subject and citizen in the kingdom of God.

That passage of Scripture found in Luke xvii. 21, is of somewhat doubtful interpretation. It might be rendered either way—the kingdom of God is "*within* you", or "*among* you"; and, while either translation is possible and proper, it is quite possible that both meanings are right meanings. It is true that the kingdom of God is both *among us* and *within us*. The kingdom of God has never yet been set up in its visible form in this world, although people unwarrantably call the church, the kingdom. The church is not the kingdom. The kingdom is, during this dispensation, invisible. It is in the heart of man, and it is, therefore, at the same time, among men, often unrecognised. The church has many in it who belong to the kingdom, and many more who do *not* belong to the kingdom, for the limits of the church visible and of the kingdom invisible are by no means the same, or co-extensive. In this present age the kingdom is much smaller than the visible church. It has never yet been visibly set up among men; so that, being *within* every true believer, because of Christ's invisible reign in his heart, it is *among* men because of the presence among men of those who are His subjects. Disciples, in whom the kingdom is existing invisibly, are living and moving among us. What a beautiful and pathetic thought it is that, right here, in this place of worship, there are some in whom God dwells, and who represent little territories in His great celestial kingdom; and that, perhaps, the last whom we should select as prominent members of this invisible kingdom, and as most filled with God, may be the very persons who, in God's eyes, are most under the power of that kingdom which is within them.

This wonderful sermon on the mount, as it is called, is a kind of imperial discourse, delivered by the King himself, an *inaugural* address, serving as the beginning of the public utterances of the King when, as yet, He was moving among men, in disguise, as many of His disciples still move among men with but a very faint disclosure of their real character or their real fellowship with God. Of course, it was very important that, when Christ made His first public utterance with regard to the kingdom, He should lay down the foundations on which the kingdom was to be built; and those foundations, let us reverently say, are laid in all individual character which is constructed according to the will of God.

The character of the subject of the kingdom is here carefully outlined, as the first thing of importance for us to understand. He who would demonstrate that he is the true son of his father, by the exhibition of the likeness which he bears to that father, goes and stands before the father's portrait and lets all observers mark the likeness. But there is many a child on earth who does not resemble either father or mother. Every child of God, however, resembles Him; and so a divine portrait is set up before us in this Scripture gallery, that we may come and study that portrait, and then look within and see how many features are, even in their beginnings or outlines, apparent in us, and so may learn whether or not we are true subjects of the kingdom. There is no excuse for being deceived. We talk of people who are "self-deceived," and how unhappy and unfortunate it is for men to go down to the grave, perhaps, in error about themselves. But is there any fatality about thus being in error? Come into this gallery of God ; see how the Master Artist has drawn the portrait of a true child of God and subject of the kingdom, and then examine yourself by comparison. Look first without, and see the picture; then look within and discern yourself; and, if you find that the likeness is here, bless God and take courage, and seek to make the likeness more perfect. And, if you find there is no likeness, get down in penitence before God and repent of your unlikeness to Jesus, and ask Him to bestow upon you His all-transforming Spirit.

After repeated study of these eight verses, a new meaning and connection suddenly occurred to my mind which had been veiled to my eyes hitherto, and it is both a duty and delight to submit this thought to fellow disciples: that these eight particulars belong *in four pairs*, and are meant to be considered two by two; that is, there are four divisions, and each division consists of two parts, the outlines of character being in each closely joined, and having peculiar mutual relations. For instance, the poor in spirit and the mourners for sin belong together ; so do the meek and the hungry and thirsty after righteousness ; the merciful and the pure in heart; the peacemakers and the persecuted for righteousness' sake. In each case, they correspond, as do right hand and left hand in the human body, each pair bearing a relation to each other more intimate than to any others in the whole enumeration. We shall see this, if we examine the whole group more closely.

I. "Blessed are the poor in spirit." What is poverty in spirit? What is poverty in any case, according to the ordinary conception, but a *sense of need* and destitution? When poverty is most abject, the sense of need is the most overwhelming; there is a feeling of dreadful bankruptcy, not simply of having little, but of having nothing. What is poverty of spirit but that similar conviction as to spiritual need, which always begins the true Christian life? In the true history of the genuine disciple, chapter first always records the conviction that I have nothing, am nothing, and can do nothing, and have therefore need of all things! Thus the very beginning of a true life in God is poverty of spirit. I begin to see how I have, perhaps, depended upon my own righteousness which is of the law, or upon my own morality which may seem good enough before men, but is valueless in the eyes of God as a means of my justification. Thus I come to see for the first time that all my uprightness that I have been boasting of is but as worthless rags, as we read in the Old Testament, in that most remarkable sentence in Isaiah lxiv. 6, where the noun is in the plural: "all our *righteousnesses* are as filthy rags." When you have gathered together all the best works you have done, outside of God, all your boasted moralities and all your proud charities, and have clothed yourself in them, and think that you appear beautiful even in the eyes of God, suddenly your eyes are opened to see that you are covered with garments that are not only filthy but rent. They hang about you, like tattered rags that cannot even conceal your body, filthy as they are. Filth and rags! That is poverty of spirit. The Laodiceans were wretched and poor, and miserable and blind, and naked, and yet they did not know it, but they thought that they were rich, and increased in goods, and had need of nothing. The Pharisees were self-righteous moralists; they boasted of their own good works; but, if their eyes had only been anointed with the eye-salve of the Holy Spirit, they would have seen at once that this was all filth and all rags. I am poor in spirit when I come to the conclusion that, in myself, I am nothing, that all I have ever done amounts to nothing, that anything that I have ever given weighs nothing in commending me to God, and that there is no power within me which in the future can enable me to do anything that shall entitle me to the favour of God. That is poverty of spirit.

Now, it is easy to see that mourning belongs with such poverty, and naturally follows it,—in fact, follows it so closely, that it is rather its companion and fellow traveller. The mourning here referred to, is manifestly not simply the ordinary mourning of those who are in circumstances of sorrow, of affliction, of bereavement, of loss. It is *mourning for sin.* It is mourning over the felt destitution of our spiritual state, and over the iniquities that have separated between us and God; mourning over the very morality in which we have boasted, and the self-righteousness in which we have trusted; sorrow for rebellion against God, and hostility to His will; such mourning always goes, side by side, with conscious poverty of spirit.

If you would see this illustrated, you have only to go into the temple where the Pharisee and the publican met. See the Pharisee look up towards God, and hear him say, "God, I thank thee that I am not as other men are, extortioners, unjust, adulterers, or even as this publican. I fast twice in the week; I give tithes of all that I possess." This may have been all true, as he looked at it, but this man went down to his house without justification, and in a state of condemnation. His garments were rags, his white robes were filthy, though, like the Laodiceans, he did not know it. But there was a publican over yonder, standing afar off, who, in the language of the Psalms, was so troubled by his iniquities that he was not able to look up (Psalms xl. 12). He dared not lift so much as his eyes to heaven, but smote violently upon his breast, as though all the possibilities of iniquity were hidden there, and said, "God be merciful to me, the sinner"; literally, "God, meet me at the mercy-seat," or, "be propitious to me,"—for that is the meaning of the phrase "be merciful." Christ is called in the Epistle to the Hebrews our mercy-seat—translated our propitiation; and the corresponding verb is used here: "God be merciful, be favourable, to me the sinner." And *that* man went down to his house justified, because he was poor in spirit, and mourned for sin. Such is the starting-point in all holy living. That is the first sign of a subject of the kingdom. And he who has never yet come to be poor in spirit, and never known what it is to mourn for sin, though he belong to a church, and have so belonged for three-score years, does not belong to the invisible kingdom,— has never entered, or truly seen, the kingdom of God.

Let us thank God for the blessed declaration that He condescends to dwell with the humble and the contrite heart. If you can find anything more precious in the Old Testament than that is, where will it be found? He that dwelleth in the Holy place, and in whose sight the Heavens are not clean; who cannot find in any house that man ever builded for him, however magnificent, a proper dwelling place—what does He say? "To this man will I look, even to him that is poor and of a contrite spirit, and trembleth at my word." So says Isaiah (lxvi. 2), and he elsewhere declares: "I dwell in the high and holy place: with him also that is of a contrite and humble spirit" (lvii. 15). If therefore you are poor in spirit, and if you are mourning over sin, you have the two conditions that are essential to

God's in-dwelling. He will not wait till you are pure, before He dwells within you, but will dwell within you in order to *make* you pure. What He demands, as the condition of His in-dwelling, is that you shall cast out every dependence of your own in your poverty of spirit, and that you shall so mourn for the sins that have offended Him, as to put them away; and, when you get to that point of contrition,—and contrition means *ground into powder*, as though between the upper millstone of His law and the nether millstone of your conscience—God is ready to dwell with us, and from within carry on the rest of the work, and make us pure and holy.

II. The second pair of these beatitudes is: "Blessed are the meek, for they shall inherit the earth"; and "Blessed are they which do hunger and thirst after righteousness, for they shall be filled." What is meekness? Not mere mildness of temper, though it is a very common thing so to understand meekness as referred to in the Bible. It is doubtful if, in a single case, the word translated meek, in the Old or New Testament, bears that interpretation.

Meekness is *unselfishness*, self-forgetfulness or self-abandonment. Moses was not meek above any other man that ever lived on the face of the earth, if we take "meek" in the sense that he was very mild, gentle and patient. He was rather very impetuous, but was wonderfully unselfish, so much so, that he was willing to have his name blotted out of the Book of Life, and to pass out of existence himself, if that was the only price at which Israel might be saved as God's people. That is meekness, the renouncing of self-dependence and self-seeking. "The things that were gain" to Paul, those he "counted loss for Christ." He put together all that he had valued in this world, and he put all under his feet as dung, as refuse to be trodden under foot and despised for the sake of the knowledge of Jesus Christ. He became a poor man, and he remained a poor man, working at tent-making for the sake of not being burdensome in his poverty to the infant church. And that noble man went on foot over a large portion of the known world; gathered converts, organized churches, wrote epistles, spent himself day and night in the service of the Master and of the souls of men, because he was so meek, so unselfish, so self-forgetting, so self-renouncing. I suppose the peculiar meekness here referred to is the abandonment of all *self-help* in the matter of salvation.

Now, what is hungering and thirsting after righteousness? Hunger and thirst are those appetites of the human body which are the most intense and agonizing; the suffering which they cause probably exceeds any other known to man. Hungering and thirsting after righteousness, therefore, expresses, by a beautiful and very simple figure, the deepest and the most intense longing after God—after the righteousness that is in God, after justifying and sanctifying merit and beauty of character, such as are conferred upon us in Jesus Christ. Now, how naturally those two follow from what we have already considered. A man begins with poverty of spirit and the consciousness that he is nothing, and he naturally longs to be something and have something. He is willing to be something, through the merit and mediation of another, to have this poverty supplied and displaced by everlasting riches, this sinfulness displaced by everlasting righteousness; and so, in proportion as he feels poor in spirit, and mourns for sin, he both gives up all thought of self-satisfaction, and hungers and thirsts with intensest desire and longing after God and the God-like character.

This will to be like God is the very essence of hunger and thirst after Him. There is a mere vague, indefinite and lethargic feeling, which leads one to say, "I *am willing* to do so and so," when there is in fact no energy of will whatever. That word "WILL" ought always to carry with it the idea of determination, of resolve, of an energetic state of mind and a resolute sort of choice. "What *wilt* thou?" says Christ. The *will to be saved* is something more than a tame *willingness* to be saved ; it is the highest energy of faith. The *will to be sanctified* is the highest, intensest longing after holiness. The *will to be useful* is the highest prayer after service. All these imply the exercise of a vigorous, determined, fixed choice, Godward.

God says, "What *wilt thou* that I shall do unto thee?" Not the thing that you formally and indifferently pray for, but the thing that you intensely desire and will to have is your real prayer in the eyes of God. That is the voice of a hunger and thirst after God that is sure to be filled. Of course, this can never come to any soul unless there is that renunciation of self and self-dependence, which is so kindred to poverty of spirit that we can hardly draw the lines of distinction between them.

III. The next pair of beatitudes as manifestly both belong together and follow the others : " Blessed are the merciful, for they shall obtain mercy. Blessed are the pure in heart, for they shall see God."

In the first four beatitudes, *no positive acquisition of character* is presented before us. There is advance, but it is *negative* as yet. There was a disclosure of the fact that I am nothing and have nothing and can do nothing ;—poverty of spirit. There was a renouncing of self-dependence indicated by meekness. And there has been a sense of sin awakened and profound sorrow. There has been a desire that is intense after God and His holiness. But thus far there has been no radical change in the actual character, no great acquisition or new element, added. Thus far only a perception of what is defective, and of what is possible in God; but now we come to a reception of positive good, a transformation of character. There is here the dawning of love like God's. The character begins to show a change in basis, in nature, in affinity, in affection, as well as in longing. A new creation is now made manifest. What is mercifulness? It is being full of mercy. And what is mercy? It is the forgiving spirit; it is the non-retaliating spirit; it is the spirit that gives up all attempt at self-vindication, and would not return an injury for an injury, but rather good in the place of evil, and love in the place of hatred. That is mercifulness. Mercy being received by the forgiven soul, that soul comes to appreciate the beauty of mercy, and yearns to exercise toward other offenders similar grace to that which is exercised towards oneself. You see this beautifully brought out in Matthew xviii., in that parable, so familiar and so instructive. We are told (Matthew xviii. 23), of a certain king who took account of his servants. "One was brought to him that owed him 10,000 talents; but, forasmuch as he had nothing to pay, he commanded him and his wife and children, and all that he had, to be sold, and payment to be made. The servant therefore fell down and worshipped Him, saying, 'Lord, have patience with me, and I will pay thee all.' Then the lord of that servant was moved with compassion, and loosed him, and forgave him the debt. But the same servant went out, and found one of his fellow-servants, which owed him an hundred pence; and he laid hands on him, and took him by the throat, saying, ' Pay me that thou owest.' Then his fellow-servant fell down at his feet and besought him, saying, 'Have patience with me, and I will pay thee all.' And he would not, but went and cast him into prison till he should pay the debt. So when his fellow-servants saw what was done, they were very sorry, and came and told their lord all that was done. Then his lord, after that he had called him, said unto him, 'O thou wicked servant, I forgave thee all that debt, because thou desiredst me : shouldest not thou also have had compassion on thy fellow-servant, even as I had pity on thee?' And his lord was wroth, and delivered him to the tormenters, till he should pay all that was due to him. So likewise shall my heavenly Father do also unto you, if ye, from your hearts, forgive not everyone his brother their trespasses."

We introduce here the whole passage, because of its most important lesson. He that has truly received mercy will show, as the first fruits of it, a disposition to exercise mercy. And if, in your hearts, you find, after you claim to be forgiven of God, a disposition to be unforgiving towards your brother,—if, after having opened your heart, as you think, to the love of God, you feel no going out from your heart of love, even towards those who have offended, maligned, and persecuted you, stop and consider. You have never received God's mercy, unless you incline to exercise like mercy.

Let us search ourselves and judge ourselves, that we be not given over to final and fatal judgment by God Himself. There is no more dangerous symptom in a believer's soul than a retaliating, vindictive, passionate temper that heaps injury on those who have heaped injury on oneself. Some say, "I can forgive, but I cannot forget," which means no forgiveness at all. It is the sign of the old nature. How many who claim to be children of God, go through years, cherishing an insult, a slight, and, at every turn, retaliating an injury or slight upon those who, as they think, have made themselves offensive to them and injurious to their prospects! That is at least an unsanctified temper, if it be not, indeed, an unjustified heart. I would not venture to believe myself a child of God, while there is a man or woman on earth to whom I would voluntarily do a serious injury. "Blessed are the merciful, for they shall obtain mercy." If our heart is a receiving reservoir for the mercy of God, it will be a distributing reservoir, giving out mercy like unto God's. There was a man, in the city of New York, naturally of a very vindictive and passionate nature, who, during years, as himself one of the criminal class, had come into contact with the roughs of Water Street. One of the first proofs that he, who had found Christ in prison, was a true child of God was this,—that he went right back into Water Street, the very place of his haunts of crime and sin, and there began to preach the gospel of repentance and faith and love to the very people who were now his enemies. That is being merciful, and proves that one has obtained mercy and shall yet obtain greater mercy still.

"Blessed are the pure in heart, for they shall see God." Purity of heart is God's imparted holiness, extending into the inward life and spirit, and transforming a man not simply from without, but from within. Christ does not say, "Blessed are the pure in outward life"; "Blessed are the pure in speech"; but "Blessed are the pure *in heart*," where all purity begins. There was a hungering and thirsting after God in the previous pair of beatitudes. Here that hungering and thirsting after God begins to be filled, the righteousness of God taking its abode in a human soul, and transforming it into His image.

IV. We now reach the last pair: "Blessed are the peacemakers, for they shall be called the children of God. Blessed are they which are persecuted for righteousness' sake, for theirs is the kingdom of heaven."

Thus far we have seen, first, that a man recognized the deficiencies of his character, and mourned over them, and gave up all self-dependence, and hungered and thirsted after God. Then we have seen how the beginnings of the divine life appear in this man, in the renewed soul, which, having received mercy, exercises mercy. He has a God-like temper and disposition free from vindictiveness and retaliation. He is inclined to pity sinners and have compassion even upon those who have done injury to him. And then he begins also to be pure in heart,—to have the likeness of the purity of God in his own nature, in his own inmost soul.

Thus far it is *character* only that is changed. Now we have *influence* exercised. What is the peacemaker? He is a man who uses the grace that has been given him, to restore relations of amity between those that are at enmity, to bring offenders face to face with each other, and to be a medium and means of their reconciliation. Observe the words of the Lord Jesus, how carefully they are chosen. He does not say, "Blessed are the peace*keepers*," who, when there is peace already established, simply do not violate the peace. Peacekeeping is a great virtue, no doubt, and it is a great blessing for men to have a peacekeeper about, but here is something nobler: "Blessed are the peace*makers*." When there is disturbance, war, confusion, dissension; when there is a division, perhaps, among even the people of God; instead of fanning the flame of dissension, instead of driving the wedge of division farther into the midst of a congregation, peacemakers seek to smooth over difficulties, to soften down asperities. Instead of misrepresenting one another, they speak kindly and charitably; instead of magnifying people's faults, they throw the cloak of loving apology over them. Such is the work of the peacemaker—the man who sets himself to right wrongs, to reconcile those who are mutually alienated, and to restore kindly relations where amicable feeling has been disturbed. That is the peacemaker, and he is called the child of God. Why? Because God's great office, all through the ages, has been to produce reconciliation where alienation was, and to restore kindly feeling and loving fellowship where sin has entered as a wedge of terrible division. And who are they that are persecuted for righteousness' sake, but those who are willing to endure insult and injury, to have their own peace broken up while they are trying to make peace, to have other men war against them whilst they are trying to reconcile warring elements? Yet such men are loyal to God and truth; not tamely amiable, so that they are willing to compromise with wrong, and to retire from a position where firmness and inflexibility and courage are demanded of them. No, no, they will make peace, but not at the expense of purity. "The wisdom which is from above is first pure, then peaceable;" and, if they can only have peace by forsaking Christ, then they will accept conflict. "I came not to send peace but a sword," said Christ. The great Peacemaker Himself was compelled to say that the effect even of His desire and endeavour to make peace among men was to produce division, even the father being divided against the mother, and the mother against the daughter, and the brother against the sister, the foes of a man being of his own household.

You are never to make *peace* at the expense of *purity*. If there can only be peace by your retiring from a position where God means that you shall stand firm for Him,—if there can only be peace by lowering the standard and trailing the arms of Christ's warrior in the dust, then welcome war, war with the sword, and the sword to the hilt, rather than disloyalty to our Master. Love the sinner, but hate his sin. Make peace as long as you can do it without sacrificing principle, but never yield a principle even for the sake of the peace. So it is plain that these two beatitudes, again, belong together. Our Lord is now teaching us that, while we are to aim to be peacemakers, we are to be contented and cordially consent to have our own peace broken up, and to be in the midst of war perpetually, if our loyalty to Christ and to truth demands it. All peace that does not rest on righteousness is delusive and destructive of true harmony between God and man, and between man and his fellow-man.

Here then we have, in these eight lines which have been drawn by the Spirit to indicate the character of a child of God, four pairs of characteristic qualities. We begin with poverty of spirit, the consciousness of sin which begets mourning over sin. Then we renounce dependence on self, and we hunger and thirst with intense desire after God. Then, having received mercy as forgiven sinners, we exercise mercy toward sinners; and then, having been regenerated by the Spirit of God, we understand and feel and experience the quickening of holy feeling and pure desire in our hearts as the first fruits of the Spirit's work. And finally, having renounced dependence on self, we also renounce vindication of self, and we come to be peacemakers among men, while, at the same time, we resolutely stand up for God with the spirit of heroism and martyrdom, consenting to be persecuted, if need be, for righteousness' sake.

Just one word with regard to the rewards affixed to these beatitudes. "Blessed are the poor in spirit, for theirs is the kingdom of heaven." Do you feel poor in spirit? Then, you may have all the riches that are in God to make up for that poverty. "Blessed are they that mourn for sin, for they shall be comforted." Are you intensely sorry for your offences against God? You shall have all the power there is in God's grace and love to assuage the intensity of your grief over the wrong that you have done. Do you in a meek spirit give up your own self-advancement? Then you shall inherit the earth. You do not aspire to be the heir of the earth, to multiply your lands and your possessions; you rather give up all these things for the sake of Jesus Christ, if need be; but you are the very person who shall yet inherit the earth that you resign. It is not yet time for the inheritance. The meek do not inherit the earth thus far, but that time is coming when the Lord Christ comes the second time to consummate the salvation of His people. Are you hungry for righteousness? Blessed be God, you will not only have some food, but you will be filled! The intensity of your desire is fully to be supplied in the glorious riches of His gifts and graces. Have you exercised mercy? You shall find mercy as rich toward you—ten thousand times richer than the exercise of your mercy toward others. Are you pure in heart, and are you cultivating purity of heart? You shall see God. You shall see God even now and here, for purity of heart clears the eyes of every film and veil, and makes it possible for us to recognize God where the carnal mind is blind to His divine presence. Are you a peacemaker? You shall be a child of God, called such, recognized as such by the fact that you resemble Him who is the great Peacemaker. And, if you are persecuted for righteousness' sake, remember that your infinite compensation lies in the rewards that shall be distributed to martyrs when the crowns of the Last Day are given!

SERMON FIVE

The Vicarious Sufferer; or, Hope in the Cross

"Who his own self bare our sins in his own body on the tree, that we, being dead to sins, should live unto righteousness; by whose stripes ye were healed."—1 PETER ii. 24

"HE bare our sins." Round about those four words the whole system of redemption might be constructed. They tell us in language that a little child can understand, the whole mystery of the sacrifice of Christ for the sins of men. "He bare our sins." How simple are these words, and yet how sublimely full of meaning.

One cannot read or hear them without thinking of a load. Sin is represented, from the beginning of the Word of God to its close, as a heavy burden;—a burden, first of all, of conscious guilt; a burden, second, of tyrannical power and despotic control; a burden, third, of penalty. And this three-fold burden of the penalty, the power, and the guilt of sin, Jesus Christ has borne in His own body on the tree that you and I may no longer bear it. That is, in a few simple words, the doctrine of substitutionary sacrifice.

We can trace this burden bearing of the unforgiven sinner throughout the history of the race. Just as soon as Cain had committed the first murder of history, and the voice of his brother's blood cried from the ground to God for vengeance, God appeared to Cain in awful rebuke of his guilt, and the murderer said, "My punishment is greater than I can bear." It is a curious but a significant fact that the same word that is here translated "punishment" may be rendered "sin," and is so translated in the margin in some cases. Cain's sense of sin carried with it a sense of overwhelming load—guilt, and power, and penalty, all at once; and so that first sin, committed after the fall in Eden, which has a definite record in Holy Scripture, wrings out from the transgressor that confession of deep despair, "My sin is greater than I can bear."

The sin of every evildoer is greater than he can bear. If your sin were left on your head, and heart, and conscience, it would sink you to the deepest hell. You would have to bear that load through all the years of your mortal experience, and then, when you toppled from the verge of life into the great chasm of the hereafter, you would go down, down, for ever, falling under the weight of that sin into greater distance and alienation from God.

God foresaw that sin was going to be a heavier burden than any man could bear, and so He laid it on One Who is mighty to save, and Who, upon the broad shoulders of omnipotence, could sustain that burden. He put Himself beneath that awful load. He laid upon Himself not only the sins of those who shall finally be saved, but, however much unbelief may make the sacrifice of Christ unavailing in any case, there are two passages of Holy Scripture that leave no doubt that Christ assumed the load of sin and guilt, even in behalf of those who will not have Him to reign over them. In the first chapter of John and the twenty-ninth verse, when John the Baptist pointed at Jesus, he said, "Behold the Lamb of God, that beareth away the sin *of the world*." Then, in the first epistle of John, in the second chapter, we read these words: "And he is the propitiation for our sins, and not for ours only, but also for *the whole world*" (literally rendered). So there must be some sense in which the sacrifice of Christ is *sufficient* for all, though it is *efficient* only to those who believe.

Let us seek, first of all, to get into our minds and hearts this great conception, that Jesus Christ came into the world, and put Himself not only under the load of one sinner, but under the load of the accumulated guilt of the whole world; that He made a sacrifice that was so absolutely satisfactory to God that, if the whole world had believed, the whole world might have been saved. If that is not the gospel it is difficult to determine what is the meaning of such plain words as have been quoted.

In order that we may see further into the deep lesson of these four words, "He bare our sins," let us note in what sense these and similar words are used in the body of this Holy Book, by comparing Scripture with Scripture. Every book is interpreted according to the usage of language, or the way in which words are generally employed by its author; and, if you ask what these words mean which form the outlines of the body of all Christian theology, the only way to find out is to examine in what sense the Author of this book uses such words in other parts of this volume.

If we thus examine, from Genesis to Revelation, we shall find *four senses* in which the words "bearing sin," are used: First, *representation;* second, *identification;* third, *sub-*

stitution; and fourth, *satisfaction*. If we take those four conceptions,—representation—one standing as a representative before God; identification—one being made identical with those he represents; substitution—one substituted in the place or stead of others; and satisfaction—the furnishing of a satisfying atonement in behalf of others,—you have the scope of the meaning of these four words.

It may be well to take some illustrations from the blessed Word of God, to show the uses to which these words are thus put. In the twenty-eighth chapter of the Book of Exodus we shall find one of the early instances of this usage. In the thirty-eighth verse we read,—with regard to the fore-front of the mitre on which were written or engraven the words " Holiness to the Lord," and which fore-front was bound round the edge of the mitre, and occupied a place immediately in front of and above the forehead of the high-priest:—"And it" (that is, the fore-front with this inscription) " shall be upon Aaron's forehead, that Aaron may *bear the iniquity* of the holy things, which the children of Israel shall hallow in all their holy gifts; and it shall be always upon his forehead, that they may be accepted before the Lord." It is very plain that here the words, " bear the iniquity of the holy things," are used in the sense of representation. Here was the great camp of Israel. They were coming up to offer various gifts and sacrifices before the Lord, and none of those sacrifices were perfect in His eyes, for they were all offered by sinners and contaminated by the touch of their guilt and uncleanness. When Aaron put on the fore-front of the mitre, and went up before the Lord, it was as though he was declaring that he was consecrated as perfectly holy unto the service of God. He stood for the people, as representing them. He represented the offerers with their gifts; he represented the consecrated gifts with all their imperfections; but he went to plead before the Lord that they might be accepted, notwithstanding the contamination of sin and selfishness. And we see in this very plainly, someone who was far beyond Aaron our great High Priest, and who can truly claim absolute holiness to the Lord, and in whom there is no sin to be atoned for on His own part before He can atone for the sins of the people. And when our blessed Master appears as our High Priest in the presence of God, His perfection makes up for the imperfection of our holiest sacrifices and offerings, and they are accepted before the Lord for the sake of His mediation. So we get here the first notion—that which lies at the bottom—of bearing iniquity. It is representation. It suggests the High Priest, as the type of our Lord,—one man standing for others in a representative capacity, and doing for them, and in their behalf, what shall be accepted before the Lord.

II. The second thought connected with the idea of bearing sin is the idea of identification. You will find an illustration of this in the eighth chapter of the Gospel according to Matthew, and in the seventeenth verse, where we read: "Himself took our iniquities, and *bare our sicknesses.*" Here is the same verb, translated "bare" in the text—" bare our sins." St. Ambrose called the eighth chapter of Matthew, " *Scriptura miraculosa,*" or the miraculous Scripture. It follows immediately on the close of the sermon on the mount, which occupies the fifth, sixth, and seventh chapters; and this eighth chapter seems to be intended to place the sanction of divine authority and power on what Christ had spoken as God's prophet. We are told, in the close of the seventh chapter, that He taught as one "having authority, and not as the scribes." He did not refer men to the Holy Scriptures simply, but He declared, "I say unto you," as though He were, and as indeed He was, the Author of the very law, Himself. And therefore, in order that He might back up His authority for such teaching as man had never taught, by works of power such as no man had ever wrought, there are grouped together in the eighth chapter of Matthew representative cases of miraculous healing.

First, there is a leper who comes to Him and says, "Lord, if thou wilt, thou canst make me clean." And Christ put forth His hand, and touched him, and said, "I will; be thou clean." And immediately his leprosy was cleansed. Then the second miracle is wrought on the man who had the palsy, and whom Christ immediately cured, so that he rose and walked. The third miracle is performed on Simon Peter's wife's mother, who was sick of a fever. He took her hand, and the fever left her: "and she arose, and ministered to her household." Then the fourth great miracle is the casting out of the demons from those that were possessed. To the Jew, all diseases had a *typical* character. He saw in various forms of disease the curse of God, and the typical representation of the guilt and power of sin. Leprosy was, to the Jew, a walking parable of death and judgment. Palsy was, to him, a representation in type of a moral inability—the loss of power to do the will of God. Fever represented the rage and fury of contending passions and lusts; and demoniacal possession represented a human soul under the complete dominion of the devil. How wonderfully Jesus, in these four great representative miracles, demonstrated His power to cure all the diseases of sin. Have you the leprosy of guilt? He can cleanse.

Do you feel the impotence of inability? He can remove it. Have you the fever of malignant dispositions and terrible passions? He can quiet and quell that fever heat. Are you a slave of the devil? He can break your bonds.

In the midst of this chapter that contains these great miracles of healing there is a quotation from Isaiah : "Himself took our infirmities and bare our sicknesses." And if you compare the fifty-third of Isaiah you will see that sickness must here be the representative type ot iniquity, the diseases of the body representing the diseases of the soul. How did Christ take those infirmities? How did He bear those sicknesses? By identifying Himself with the sinner and the sick. How beautifully pathetic is His whole conduct! When the leper came, and, kneeling before Him, besought Him, " Lord, if Thou wilt, Thou canst make me clean," we are told that Jesus put forth His hand and *touched* him, saying, " I will; be thou clean." There was no apparent need to touch him. He had only to say, " I will ; be thou clean," and the same fiat that, in the darkness of the first creation, said " Let light be," so that light was, might have said also, " Let the leper be cleansed," and he would have been clean. But why did Christ put forth His hand and touch him? Remember that a leper, according to the law of Moses, when he went into the midst of clean people was to cry, " Unclean, unclean," and to have his head bowed down and a staff in his hand, as though to prepare the people for his approach, and to prevent anyone from possibly touching him. This leper whom Christ healed probably had not felt the touch of a clean human hand during all the days of his leprosy. Everybody shrank from him; everybody avoided him, and got out of his way when he cried and when they saw him coming.

But Jesus drew near, and put out His divine hand, and touched him, and that touch must have been almost as grateful as the word of healing. Moreover, remember this: that touch *made Jesus Christ, Himself, ceremonially unclean.* The law of Moses, as given us in the fifth chapter of Leviticus, commanded that no one should touch an unclean person or thing, and that if he did so he should himself become unclean. The touch of a leper made a man for the time being, as it were, himself a leper. Our Lord wanted to show that leper that he was identified with his sickness and disease, and so He touched him and took, as it were, the level of ceremonial uncleanness alongside of him. I do not otherwise understand that touch of Christ. It is one of the sweetest and most beautiful incidents of which we read in the gospel.

There is a story about Hindoo mothers that a kind of disease sometimes takes hold upon their children, the remedy for which is so severe that it is not safe to administer it to the child directly; but, if the mother takes it herself, it passes into her circulation, and then as she nurses the child at her breast, the medicine which she has taken, modified by the action of her own system, and imparting healing qualities to the nutritious milk with which she nourishes her babe, saves the child's life. Our Lord took upon Him our infirmities and bare our sicknesses. Like that mother identified with her child, He chose to be identified with us. Do you shrink at the thought that he became ceremonially unclean when He touched the leper? The Bible tells us that He was "*made sin for us,* though He knew no sin,"—that God counted Him as a sinner and treated Him as a sinner when He offered up His sacrificial atonement. He took the sinner's place; He was identified with the sinner, and He stooped down to the level of the sinner's guilt, that He might lift the load from the sinner's heart and conscience.

III. So we come to the third thought, *substitution*. That thought is presented very plainly in the ceremonies of the Day of Atonement, in the sixteenth chapter of Leviticus. At the twenty-first verse, we read : " And Aaron shall lay both his hands upon the head of the live goat, and confess over him all the iniquities of the children of Israel, and all their transgressions, in their sins, putting them upon the head of the goat; and the goat shall *bear upon him all their iniquities* unto a land not inhabited." It is impossible to read those words without the impression that Moses intended to represent that scapegoat, *Azazel*, or goat of "removal," as a substitute for the sinners themselves. This double sacrifice of the great day of atonement can never lose interest to a true child of God. How vivid is the picture of atoning love there set before us ! Two kids of the same age and undistinguishable from each other, one slain that by the shedding of blood remission of sin may be indicated, and the other brought alive into the presence of the Lord ; Aaron, confessing his own sins and the sins of the people, and laying both hands on the head of the live goat, and, as the Jewish rabbis tell us, pressing hard on the head of the goat to indicate the weight of sin,—that goat, by the hand of a fit man, is led away from the presence of the camp out into an uninhabited place where he can no longer hear the bleating of others of the flock from which he has been withdrawn, or the noise of the camp in the service of worship, which might draw him back. There in the desert place he wanders about, never finding his way back to the camp, and so never bringing back to the thoughts of the people the sins that have been confessed upon his head. How plain it is what John meant when he pointed to Jesus Christ, and exclaimed, "Behold the Lamb of God, that taketh away,—*beareth* away the sin of the world."

What has become of your sin, believer? It was confessed, laid heavily, on the head of Jesus Christ as God's goat of Removal, and He went away, as it were into the uninhabited place, and thus bore your sins out of your sight, and out of God's sight, and they never shall be brought back by Him, either before your eyes or before God's eyes. *You* may bring them back by your unbelief; you may take a forgiven sin, a pardoned iniquity, and bring it up before yourself, and put it between you and God, but God will never do it, and Christ will never do it, and the Holy Ghost will never do it, for those sins are buried out of God's sight as in the depths of the sea—put behind His back as no longer to be seen,—borne into the wilderness never to be brought back into the camp.

Here is God's double substitution; Christ was the slain goat and the goat, Azazel, for He represented both the expiation for sin, and its removal from before the face of God.

IV. Now once more : *satisfaction*. Where shall we find the words of the text used plainly in the sense of satisfaction? In the 53rd chapter of Isaiah; and it is impossible for a candid student of the Word of God to escape the obvious force of these words. We read, " All we like sheep have gone astray, and have turned everyone of us to his own way, and the Lord hath laid on Him the iniquity of us all;" and, again, "Surely he hath borne our griefs and carried our sorrows : He was wounded for our transgressions, He was bruised for our iniquities : the chastisement of our peace was upon Him, and with His stripes we are healed."

There are some who deny all real substitution, and say that Christ did not bear human sin except as an *example* or *martyr*. But the Word of God says, "The chastisement of our peace was upon Him;" that is to say, we had lost peace with God; we were in a condition of alienation and rebellion; and there could be no peace between God and rebels; but the chastisement that Christ endured for us restored peace between us and God. And, as though to be still more explicit, " With His stripes we are healed." The word translated " stripes " does not refer to the applying of the scourge to the back of the victim, but to the marks or wales left by the scourge. You look at Christ, and you see the marks of scourging on His back; by those stripes your healing comes. God is a just God. He does not lay your sin on Jesus, and then lay your sin on you too. If you, by faith in Christ, embracing and accepting His mediation, partake of the benefits and blessings of His death, you can look on the very wounds left on His back by the scourge, or the very wounds left in His hands and feet by the nails, and in His side by the spear, and you may say "Bless God, I am healed because He was wounded; His stripes are my healing." So Peter says in the text that He Himself " bare our sins in His own body on the tree, that we, being dead to sins, should live unto righteousness, by whose stripes ye were healed."

That sacrifice of Jesus Christ must be appropriated by faith, to be of any benefit in the salvation of a human soul. If we were left to the testimony of John, that Christ bare the sin of the whole world, we might conceive of universal salvation as the consequence of His death. But Christ Himself, the very Lamb of God, said to the Jews, "If ye believe not that I am He, ye shall die in your sins, and whither I go ye cannot come." The possibility of universal salvation is shut out from our creed by the very words of the atoning Saviour. These are not any theologian's limitations; they are bounds set on His own work by Himself. The very Redeemer, who bowed beneath the weight of human sin and sorrow to lift the intolerable load from you, says, with awful solemnity and pathos, "If ye believe not that I am He, ye shall die in your sins, and whither I go ye cannot come." Let us look back to the thought that met us at the beginning, and see what this means. Sin is a load, an awful load, an indescribable load, a load that sinks the sinner to a hopeless perdition. Jesus Christ says, "If ye believe not that I am He, ye shall die with your sins yet upon you." And what will be the consequence? You will sink, and whither He has gone you cannot come. Where has Christ gone? He has not sunk beneath, as one borne down by a burden of guilt. He has risen above. No load of sin is on Him. He ascended up on high. When the unforgiven sinner dies there can be no ascent; it must be descent. The load of sin is on him, and he gravitates toward perdition, and so it is true of him : "Whither I go ye cannot come." "I go up, ye go down. I go without a load to my Father; you go with a load to your father, the devil." Notwithstanding Christ's sacrifice, guilt, power, penalty yet lie on everyone who does not believe in and accept Him as Saviour. That is the dark and terrible side of this great subject.

How immense is the responsibility of hearing this gospel. Thousands of people gather here within the sound of these four words that tell the simple fact of a provided salvation.

It is a tremendous thought that you may hear this gospel message, and yet go down to the depths of perdition like Judas, with the sin of the rejection of Christ added to every other sin to weigh your soul down. In the thirty-third chapter of Ezekiel, it is written: "Son of man, I have set thee a watchman unto the house of Israel; therefore thou shalt hear the word at my mouth and warn them from me. If thou warn the wicked of his way to turn from it; if he do not turn from his way, he shall die in his iniquity; but thou hast delivered thy soul." He who gives you the word of warning and the word of invitation, may solemnly wash His hands clean of your blood. He has no more responsibility for the loss of your soul. The load of your sin rests heavily upon yourself. Whom will you have to bear it? Will you let Him bear it, or will you bear it yourself? If He bears it, released from the load, you rise as He rose, to the presence of the Father, justified and sanctified. If you will bear it, notwithstanding that He offers to bear it for you, you shall die in your sins, and whither He goes you cannot go.

Doubtless many of you have seen that very simple device for the instruction of children, where three crosses are represented. Over one cross are the words, "In, not on." Over another cross are the words, "On, not in." Over a third cross, "On and in." The first cross with the words, "In, not on," represents the penitent thief. Sin was in him, but it was not laid on him, for he trusted in Jesus Christ. The third cross, "On and in," represents the impenitent thief. His sin was in him, and it was also on him. But the other cross, " On, not in," represents Jesus. No sin in Him, but sin laid on Him. What was represented by the three crosses on Calvary is the picture and parable of all history. Jesus was there in the midst, the penitent and believing thief on one side, and the impenitent and scoffing thief on the other. From Christ's right hand went up a soul to Paradise; from Christ's left hand went down a soul to perdition. And it has been so all the way through the annals of the race. Christ is set forth here to-night, crucified for you. On one side there are believing souls that are going to Paradise; on the other side, unbelieving souls that are going to perdition, *for a man may go to hell from the side of a crucified Jesus.*

Sermon Six

Knowledge and Duty; or, Hope in Obedience to God

"If ye know these things, happy are ye if ye do them."
JOHN xiii. 17

THERE are certain single sentences that fell from the lips of our Lord, which embrace a whole system of truth, and this is one of those remarkable utterances, which is in itself a pearl of great price. Consider how much is involved in that one saying. Let us expand its meaning in two divisions: It teaches us that the *scope of all practice is knowledge*, and it teaches us that the *object of all knowledge is practice.* The scope of all practice is knowledge; that is to say, practice finds its horizon in knowledge. You can do only so far as you know; your practice can do no more than keep pace with knowledge. And the object or end of all knowledge is not to gratify curiosity, not even to store up information for its own sake, but to lead the way to a better, a nobler, a more serviceable life. These two divisions, suggested by the theme, furnish most ample opportunity for practical thought.

Knowing and doing make up the whole of life; but perhaps there is a deeper thought still than any that has yet been suggested. The emphasis of this saying is upon the word "happy." "*Happy* are ye if ye know these things, and, knowing them, do them." The things to which our Lord refers are, without doubt, the teaching and example of service which He has just been commending in His own person—service rendered to the least of all His disciples. He has been setting before them a parable *in action*, to define and illustrate humility—an object lesson for them to learn—that the Son of God Himself did not consider it beneath His dignity that He should take to Himself the apron of the slave, and from the ewer pour the water into the basin, and with His own hands wash the feet of His disciples ; and He says "I have set you an example that ye should do as I have done to you. Now, if ye know and understand these things, ye are happy, indeed, if ye carry out in practice that which ye know." But, while the saying may have had a special reference to what had just occurred, it is in the largest sense a universal saying; and as the stress of the whole proverb lies on the word "happy," it will be seen how important is this word. when it is remembered that, in the first place, knowledge can secure to us the highest happiness, only when it leads us to obedience ; and, in the second place, obedience itself can make us really happy, only when obedience keeps pace with our knowledge. The secret of happiness in knowing, is to have doing as the end of knowing ; and the measure of happiness in doing, is that we should never know any duty without humbly undertaking to fulfil it.

I. What was the first temptation? Careless readers of the Word of God seem to think that Eve was tempted to disobey Him by the desire after the fruit of a forbidden tree; but we cannot quite believe that, with all the delights of Paradise surrounding her, she so hungered after the taste of one more fruit, as to risk her relations of harmony with God. And if the account be read carefully it will be seen that there was quite another impulse: " When the woman saw that the tree was good for food, pleasant to the eyes, and a tree to be desired to make one wise, she took thereof, and did eat, and gave also to her husband with her; and he did eat." It is true that the fact that the tree was good for food is spoken of, and that it was pleasant to the eyes; but the greatest reason of all is that which is mentioned last of all— that it was a tree to be desired or coveted to make one wise. Satan told her that in the day in which she should eat of that fruit her eyes would be opened—that is, the eyes of her intelligence and understanding—and she would become as gods that know good and evil. That is to say, her knowledge would be increased; a new world of intelligence would open before her; she would get a new insight into mysteries, a new understanding of hidden truths. Ah, that proved too sadly the fact. The moment that she ate thereof, her eyes were opened; she did see a whole world of fact and truth, that she had not seen before. Up to that point she had known only good. From that point she knew also evil.

Thus the power of the first temptation lay in an appeal to the *appetite for knowledge*, gratified without reference to practical obedience, and in violation of the commands of God. That representative sin has been the great typical sin of the race ever since. You may think that the subtlest temptations are those which come through bodily lusts; but not so. The subtlest temptations are those which come through intellectual lusts. While appetite may ensnare one man, avarice and ambition, which are intellectual lusts, entrap a thousand. Many a man who has conquered his appetite, has been the slave of his avarice and his ambition, his greed of gold and his greed of place and power.

There is no subtler ambition than the ambition after knowledge. It seems a mean thing to be avaricious, to worship the golden calf, to think of simply hoarding treasure; but it seems a noble thing to aspire after higher knowledge, and increasing intelligence, a storing of the mind with information. And so the greatest foe that the human race has had, in the way of subtle temptation, has been the aspiration after knowledge, without due restraint upon the ways in which knowledge should be sought, the limits within which it should be sought, and the ends for which it should be sought. So I repeat that knowledge makes us truly happy only when knowledge is sought in order to practical obedience and service.

Ask yourselves now what is the object of knowing anything. What good does it do you to know? Suppose you study the human body. You ascertain the laws of respiration, how it is that the lungs act. You understand the laws of perspiration; how those wonderful little vessels that terminate in the skin discharge moisture through which they do away with a large portion of the waste or refuse of the body. You learn the mystery of circulation, how it is that the heart pulses the blood to the extremities through the arteries, and how the veins draw it back, and reinforce through the lungs the source of supply at the heart. You study the nervous system, the motor and the sensor nerves, how it is that some marvellous apparatus in the brain moves the whole body, and communicates sensations, from all parts of the body, back to the centre of life. You learn the mysteries of digestion, how it is that you take food into your body, and it is assimilated to the wants of the system. Now what is the use of all that knowledge? When does that knowledge make you the happiest? Without doubt, when it restrains your indulgence, when it leads you to take such care of this body as a temple of God, that no injury is done to its marvellous powers and capacities; so that you seek to breathe pure air, study habits of personal cleanliness, aim to invigorate the heart in its action ; so that you take care of your nervous system so that it does not fall or fail in the crises of life; and guard your digestion, so that you eat what is good for the body, and what will deposit strength and nutriment to replace the waste. The highest use of that knowledge, is to make you a stronger, a healthier, and a better man physically.

Suppose you study the laws and structure of your own mind, the powers of imagination, reason, analysis, all those marvellous faculties that go to make up the tools in this, the most marvellous chest of tools that the universe knows anything about. What is the use of this knowledge of the mind, but to get the mastery of the mind, so that, like a master workman, you can take these tools, and use them for work for God, and work for man; so that you will know how to employ your eyes, and your hands; so that you will know how to use your imagination, as a poet or an artist uses it; how to use your reason in argument, as true logic demands that the reasoning power should be used ; or how to use your powers of analysis in natural science, and in various other studies such as language and philosophy. What avails the knowledge of the mind if you do not put it in practice? The end of knowing is not simply that one may have a certain amount of intelligence or information, but that one may serve God and serve man. The highest happiness from knowledge comes when knowledge increases service. To know in order to impart, to be informed in order to inform, to be intelligent in order to instruct ignorance— that is the grandest object of knowledge. And so why do you study the workings of your own conscience? Of what good will it be to you to know that there is a moral nature within you, to see how it responds to the judgment of right and wrong, sympathizing with right, and antagonizing wrong—of what use the knowledge of this marvellous power, which we call the moral sense, if not that you should obey the conscience, and learn to be heroic in withstanding all temptations to an immoral, wicked, deceitful, treacherous, or ungodly life? Now what is the use of knowledge of God? Suppose you should know all that is knowable of God; suppose you could have your eyes opened to see the things that hitherto have been mysteries to you or concealed from you? Suppose the veil of His Temple be rent in twain from the top to the bottom, and you could look into the holiest place where God dwells, what would be the use of it? Would it make you happy? Only so far as it led you to a more devout, constant, unswerving obedience to the will of God.

This is so plain that it needs but a statement to have it appear, that the knowledge that we have is only calculated to benefit and bless us, so far as it makes us practise or do the thing that knowledge acquaints us with, as pertaining to the true purpose and performance of life.

Let us go a step further. It has already been intimated that the happiness of obeying is strictly in proportion to the knowledge used. If our obedience should keep pace with our knowledge, so as always to come up to the very limit of it, we should be perfectly happy. But so long as there is a knowledge of duty, beyond the performance of duty, there can never be real peace in the soul. And you will see that this applies both to the children of God on the one side, and to the ungodly on the other. If you seek for the causes of restlessness amongst men, whatever may be their class, their position, their character among their fellows, you will find that every restless soul is disobedient to the knowledge of duty. There is a want of harmony between practice and knowledge; and therefore I repeat with emphasis, that the happiness of knowing can be complete only so far as obedience comes up to the limit of the knowledge. " If ye know these things, happy are ye if ye do them." " He that knoweth his Lord's will and doeth it not, shall be beaten with many stripes " " Therefore to him that knoweth to do good, and doeth it not, to him it is sin." These are but the different statements of one great principle.

In amplifying and illustrating this great truth, let me give you a sentence which will carry with it its own confirmation. I would that this one sentence could be written down, where every one of us would see it every day, as we begin every day anew. It is one of the most important sentences that I have ever put in writing. It is this : "*Perfect obedience would be perfect happiness, if only we had perfect confidence in the wisdom and love of the Power we are obeying.*" The object of the revelation of God in the Holy Scripture, is that we may acquire this perfect confidence in the love and wisdom of our Heavenly Father, so that we shall, on the one hand, be impelled to perfect confidence; and, on the other hand, find in the perfect obedience perfect happiness, so that we shall be able to say, " I delight to do Thy will, O my God." That is the reason why in the ninth Psalm and the tenth verse, the Psalmist says, " They that know Thy name will put their trust in Thee." He intimates that it will be perfectly natural to trust God if we know Him. The more we know Him the more we shall know that His name is deservedly Love; that back of all His will there is infinite wisdom, and joined with His infinite wisdom is infinite affection; and, because His law is the expression of infinite wisdom and infinite love; therefore, to a true child of God who really knows his Heavenly Father, it becomes delight to do that Heavenly Father's will. And you see why his obedience will keep pace with his knowledge, because if the knowledge of God in one thing will lead him to obey, so will the knowledge of God in another thing also lead him to obey; and if he has perfect confidence in God's wisdom and goodness, in His justice and generosity, he will put all the law of God on the same basis. It is all an expression and proof of His wisdom and His love; and so we shall make no discrimination between God's commandments in our obedience, if we only know Him so truly that we trust Him fully. Perhaps it will help us all if this truth be applied in two or three departments.

In the first place, obedience, when it conforms to knowledge, and keeps pace with knowledge, brings us into *harmony with ourselves*. It is very important that a man should be in harmony with himself. It may seem a contradiction to talk about one's being in harmony with himself; but did you never see that within you there are two personalities? It is not a contradiction to speak of " I," and " myself." There is what we call a soliloquy, or a conversation with one's self. You walk along the street, and you talk with yourself, as surely as with anybody outside of yourself; and there is not one of us who does not know what this talking with himself means. There is a process which we call reflection; it is only another name for talking with one's self. You stand before a mirror and look into it. What do you see? Your exact counterpart—another self that stands behind the mirror, and your eyes look into the eyes of the reflection. Now what is reflection, as a habit of mind, but standing before the mirror of thought, and looking at yourself, and talking and communing with yourself? It is a blessed thing thus to commune with one's self, and is often attended with the greatest profit. It is of the utmost importance that you be in harmony with yourself, and especially with that part of yourself which is called the conscience. The conscience is a faculty, or a power, or a peculiarity of character, of which this is characteristic: that whenever a certain thing is approved by the judgment as right, conscience says " Do it "; whenever a thing is presented before the judgment which is pronounced to be wrong, this same conscience says " Let it alone." The judgment is not infallible: it may sometimes approve a wrong thing as right, or condemn a right thing as wrong, but the conscience will follow the judgment. Now what is it that enlightens the judgment, and helps it to discriminate between right and wrong? It is knowledge, intelligence. The more truly intelligent we become the more clear do the decisions of the judgment become. Hence we find men and women in heathen lands whose conscience approves something that your conscience sees to be wrong, because their judgment has never had the light of God thrown upon it, has never had a perfect standard of duty to correct its errors.

Knowledge, when assimilated, becomes intelligence; intelligence affords light to the judgment; and judgment in turn becomes a guide to the conscience. And, therefore, it is exceedingly important that, as far as you know what duty is, you should attempt to do it, because, as surely as you know your duty, and do it not, conscience will rebuke and chastise you, and conscience is an awful antagonist, capable of inflicting the keenest anguish, the most fearful torture. There is only one way to prevent such torture as long as you persist in doing wrong, and that is by debauching the conscience, through bribing over the judgment; convincing yourself that after all your course is not wrong; arguing against your own moral sense until you get a decision in your favour. It is sometimes possible for a time thus to silence the voice of conscience. People are constantly doing these things. Here, for instance, is a man who is indulging in intoxicating drink. He sees that it is beclouding his reason, weakening his will, destroying his *power to let alone* that which is to-day destroying more bodies and damning more souls than any other one evil in the community. But he wants to justify his indulgence. So he looks at another man and says, " That man uses intoxicating drink, and does not fall a prey to it." So, measuring himself by others, and comparing himself with others, he silences his own judgment on the subject of the wrong that he is doing himself, and compromises his own conscience. There are hundreds of so-called disciples of Christ, professedly members of His church, who are daily doing things that they know to be contrary to the voice of an enlightened judgment; and yet they try to persuade themselves that, after all, these things are not harmful, and not opposed to the will of God, because hundreds of other Christian people do the same. That is simply bribing the conscience into silence, by the false argument that *a wrong is right because of the multitude who do it,* even though everyone else, also, knows it is not the right thing.

It is important to remember that never, since the fall of man, has truth been *with the majority;* never, but always with the *minority.* Never has godly consistency been characteristic of the multitude, but always of the few. It has always been a comparatively little flock of whom holiness and saintship could be affirmed ; and, therefore, to reason from the customs of the majority to the rightness of any given course of conduct, is one of the most deceitful and dangerous methods of false reasoning. Yet this is the common anodyne with which conscience is put to sleep. I have met many a young person who is living an inconsistent life, compromising with the world, courting its favour, who is almost fatally ensnared in the meshes of gay, worldly and frivolous society, and in trying to bring such young disciple to a true life of fellowship with Jesus Christ in the separateness of a holy walk, I have been constantly met by this excuse, " I do nothing more than a great many other people do—than the officers of the church do—than the men and women who are the leaders of the congregation do." It is the same old, unsafe argument from the majority, following the multitude to do evil.

Let me repeat, that you can never be in harmony with yourself, so long as there is a single duty, understood to be such, or a single wrong, understood to be such, and yet you compromise with conscience by neglecting the duty or committing the wrong. " If ye know these things, happy are ye if ye do them." The happy saint is a man or woman who is in harmony with himself or herself, who can say, " Herein o I exercise myself, always to have a conscience void of offence toward God and towards men."

2. The second way in which happiness comes to an obedient soul is from *harmony with the truth.* All truth is a unit,

and every specific truth helps to the understanding of every other. The obedient soul comes to know more about the truth through the very means of obedience tó the truth. What a sublime philosophy that was of our Lord Jesus Christ when He said, in the 7th chapter of John, and the 17th verse, "If any man will do His will he shall know of the doctrine." Christ, who teaches us in the passage now before us, that knowledge is in order to duty, teaches us in the other just quoted, that duty helps us to higher knowledge; and there is no inconsistency in the two statements. If you know a truth, it is in order that you may do it; but if you do it, you shall know that truth better than you ever knew it before, and every other related truth beside. There is a power, in compromise with evil, to blind the eyes and dull the vision; there is a corresponding power, in obedience, to open the eyes and clear the vision. If you are in a house, where there is a little light that struggles in at the window, you can shut out that light altogether if you will, by closing the shutters; and so you can let light into a dark room by throwing the shutters wide open. Every time you compromise with a sin, or even a doubtful indulgence, you are closing the shutters and excluding God's light; every time you yield yourself to the obedience of God in that which you know to be duty, in resistance to what you know to be wrong, you open the shutters more widely, and let more light into your soul. Every time you do a right thing you get a clearer conception of right; every time you do what is wrong, you obscure your own sense of what right and wrong are. It is possible even to put out the eyes of the judgment by a persistent course of sinfulness, to sear the very eyeballs of the conscience by long habits of evil doing, so that you are given over to a reprobate mind. The harmony of truth is like the harmony of a musical instrument. You touch the keys, and you get melody. You touch the keys in chord, and you get harmony. Truth is an instrument with keys. Every act of obedience is the finger on a key evoking melody, and the more acts of obedience are multiplied, the grander is the harmony you get from the instrument. And so if you want to be happy, do whatever you know to be duty. Yield yourself immediately to every conviction of your judgment that leads you toward the right, and away from the wrong, and such unanswering obedience will impart to life a charm that no human being can understand till he has experienced its power.

"Be good, sweet maid, and let who will be clever;
Do noble things, not dream them all day long;
So making life, death, and the vast forever,
One grand sweet song."

If you want your life an anthem of praise to God, and holy service to men, strike every key on the instrument of duty, and just as soon as you know that a thing is according to the will of God, say, "By the grace of God that shall be a part of my life," and your whole life will roll a hallelujah chorus up to the throne of God.

3. I close with another suggestion, more important than anything else that has been said, and that is—that an obedient soul who makes knowledge the guide to duty, comes into *harmony with God*. This is all implied in what has been said, but there is somewhat more that needs to be added, and which I pray God to stamp upon your memories : All obedience to God, with reference to known duty, brings first a *manifestation of God to the soul*, and secondly an *intimate relationship between the soul and God*.

First, a manifestation of God to the soul. The greatest promise in the New Testament is in John, the 14th chapter and the 23rd verse : " If a man love Me, he will keep My words : and My Father will love him, and We will come unto him, and make Our abode with him." You may search the whole Bible from Genesis to the Apocalypse, and find no grander promise than that. Look at the condition—simply that a man shall so love Jesus Christ as to keep His word ; that is to say, that so far as the knowledge of the will of God comes to him in Christ, he shall yield himself up in implicit and immediate obedience. Then what will happen ? Not that he will be permitted only to come unto God, but God will come down to him, and will actually make in him His abode, manifesting Himself to him as He does not unto the world. You want an experience of God, do you ? It actually hangs on obedience. But this statement may be made without reservation—that it is impossible to commit a single act of sin against God, intelligently, without losing the divine manifestation. You may have walked for twenty years in peace, and may have had wonderful revelations of the love of God in your soul, that remind you of Paul's experiences when he was caught up to the third heaven ; but, if you recognize a temptation as put before you, and know it to be sinful to yield, and yet enter deliberately into sin, instantly the manifestation of God ceases. The revelation of God to the soul is no longer possible while you are in the midst of the commission of known sin. This is a different thing from imperfection in the performance of duty. If you see before you duty, and you humbly undertake to perform it, you may come far short of such performance of it as you would like to attain, but God will overlook your infirmity, and the imperfection of such performance ; but the moment you begin to cherish a sin or hug it to your bosom as a darling indulgence, God can have no fellowship with a soul that is complacently regarding or deliberately indulging wrong. "If I regard iniquity in my heart, the Lord will not hear me." He cannot hear me. He cannot attend to the voice of any prayer that is contaminated by voluntary continuance in known iniquity. So I repeat, there can be no manifestation of God to any soul that shuts Him out by deliberate sin. But, on the other hand, the manifestation of God may come instantaneously to a soul when sin is, by His strength, abandoned and forsaken, and the whole nature thrown open to the impression of duty, and the prayer goes up to God for grace to do that duty. And that is the reason why men who have been long in sin and under the control of horrible habits of crime, will all at once come into new light with an instantaneousness and suddenness which reminds one of the conversion of Saul on the road to Damascus; because the habit of sin is abandoned, the purpose of sin is forsaken, and there is a desire to please God in all things, and to submit and to surrender one's self entirely to the divine authority. That is, as I have said before, like suddenly throwing open the shutters of the darkened room and letting in the sunshine in its noonday splendour.

III. My closing thought is that the *intimacy of fellowship* with God depends on doing that which I know I ought to do. Here we reach the climax of the whole subject. "If ye know these things, happy are ye if ye do them." For this happiness absolutely depends on your fellowship with God.

Nothing is more common in the world to-day than for people to shrink back from intimate fellowship with the Lord, because they say to themselves, if they do not say to others, that it demands such complete surrender. They say, "If I am going to have Christ entirely for my own, I have got to give up everything else for Him." That is true, emphatically true. And some look upon it as a hardship. They think of themselves as compelled to cut off this and that indulgence, as mortifying this lust and that passion, and even restraining lawful pleasures within narrow limits, because of a desire for a higher fellowship with God. It is most amazing that such people do not see the principle that lies beneath all this. There are three degrees of association that are very familiar to us all. One is acquaintance, one is friendship, and the other is that most intimate relation into which it is possible for two human beings to come, which we call marriage. Acquaintance is commonplace; there may be thousands of people with whom we are acquainted. There are comparatively few people with whom we are in intimate friendship; and the law of God is that one man and one woman shall constitute husband and wife in that sacred relationship which is the most intimate of all, and which is the symbol of the peculiar union of Christ and His church. Now notice this fact. In acquaintance very little is surrendered and very little is enjoyed. There is an external communication; you pass people in the street, and there is a salutation; you go into their house, it may be, and occasionally spend a few moments or hours in companionship; but there is but little enjoyed as there is also very little surrendered. You come into friendship which is more intimate, where the relationship is more close, and what do you find? There must be more surrender, there must be a jealousy for that friend that you do not feel for the mere acquaintance, jealousy for his honour, his reputation, his prosperity, his family name, his external comforts. There is something that your friend has a right to demand of you as the price of friendship, and the closer the friendship the more exacting the demand. You never find fault with this, do you?

Let us go further, and notice that privilege is always in proportion to obligation, and obligation is always in proportion to privilege. The more a man gives you of his inner self, the more he demands of your inner self; the more he surrenders of his intimacy to you, the more of your intimacy does he demand in return. The more jealously he guards your reputation, the more does he exact from you in the guarding of his reputation. Is not that right? Do you find any fault with it? Is not that the privilege of friendship, that you enter into a close relationship into which the whole world does not enter? And, how is it with marriage? There is nothing else so exclusive. One woman and one man, the woman giving up her name for the man's name. giving up her home for the man's home, giving up her companionships for the man's companionships, giving up her dearest friends, if necessary, for the sake of her husband. And the husband does the same for the sake of his wife. The privilege is so exclusive that it demands an obligation correspondingly strong and exacting, and nobody ever finds fault with this exclusiveness. No virtuous man ever finds fault because he can be the husband of but one wife. To find fault with that, marks the betrayer of virtue, the victim of vice. And as the noble, virtuous man rejoices to be the husband of but one wife, so the pure and true wife rejoices to be the wife of one husband. The exclusive privilege demands a corresponding inclusive obligation.

Now see how Jesus speaks to us. He authorizes a believer to say, "My beloved is mine and I am His." Notice the singular pronoun, " My beloved is mine and I am

His "; not " *Our* Beloved is ours, and *we* are His "; but each individual soul can look up to Christ and say with the exclusiveness of peculiar privilege, " I am my Beloved's and my Beloved is mine. He is the Bridegroom and I am the bride. Therefore I can know no other Lord and Master but Himself." And if you will enter into this holiest relation with Jesus, the price of entering into that relation is an obedience that is commensurate with your knowledge and privilege. The more you covet the intimacy of Christ, the more must you submit to the exacting condition of absolute, implicit, immediate, constant, cheerful obedience and surrender.

My great desire in thus emphasizing this truth, is to help disciples to the deep and resolute determination that Christ shall have all that there is of them, and that they will have all that there is of Christ; that nothing shall stand between them and their God; that they will see nothing in the whole horizon of duty that they do not welcome in the sphere of practical obedience; that there shall be no sin that accuses them as intelligently committing it, and no obligation that shall face them as understanding its claim, and neglecting it. Once more, in the name of God, I say to you, that if you are going to have your Beloved as wholly yours, you must be wholly your Beloved's. If the bride will have the Bridegroom as her possession, the bride must be His possession. Do not think of this as a hardship. It constitutes the ecstasy of heaven. " If ye know these things, happy are ye if ye do them."

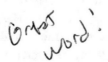

SERMON SEVEN

The Message to Sorrowing Souls; or, Hope in Trouble

"Let not your heart be troubled: ye believe in God, believe also in me.

"In my Father's house are many mansions: if it were not so, I would have told you. I go to prepare a place for you.

"And if I go and prepare a place for you, I will come again, and receive you unto myself; that where I am, there ye may be also."—JOHN XIV. 1-3

How much truth our Lord puts into a single sentence! These three verses contain the three great truths of the Christian religion,—God, Christ, and Immortality. This is a message to troubled souls; and, if we examine it carefully, we shall find that there is no form of human doubt or trouble, difficulty or perplexity, that is not met, solved and removed, in these words. I have never ministered to any congregation without preaching, at least once in every quarter of the year, a sermon to the afflicted, for in every assembly there are troubled and tried souls, to whom a special message, from time to time, is specially grateful. Let me bring to all of you, that have any kind of trouble, a divine panacea for all your ills.

I. " Believe in God." There are certain difficulties and doubts that every one of us must meet. At the very outset of our intelligent life one of the first difficulties that confronts us is the difficulty of *accounting for this creation and for ourselves.*

1. "Whence did this universe come, and whence did I come?" The answer to this class of doubts must be found in the doctrine of the existence of God, and there is no way out of these doubts to him that denies God. So our blessed Lord says to us all, with reference to this class of difficulties, " Believe in God." You see a world,—believe in a world-maker; you see design,—believe in a designer; you see an effect,—believe in a cause for that effect, and trace back every effect to its great first cause. In a personal God, the Creator of the heavens and of the earth, is the final solution of all these doubts and difficulties. It is not enough to trace back an effect to a cause because that cause may itself be an effect of another cause. You do not account for a chain by tracing back one link to another : you need to account also for the links, and must have some staple on which the first link is hung and from which it depends. And so you do not account for creation by following some present effect to its antecedent cause, because that cause itself is an effect which must be traced to something else that goes before it, and is the means of producing it. And so, through all our doubts and difficulties, we have to reach up and out until we come to a wonderful Almighty Creator, from whom the whole universe proceeds.

2. Another class of doubts that afflict us, in the nature of the case, is that which is occasioned when we see at work in this universe about us what appear to be malignant influences. We see, for instance, disease and death,

and earthquake and storm, and pestilence and famine, and a thousand forms of ill. We find not only beautiful singing birds, but birds of prey ! We find not only harmless insects, but reptiles that are poisonous and fatal in their bite and sting. We find not only sunny days, but storms and tempests, with thunder and lightning, tornadoes and cyclones; innumerable forms of what we call evil, at work in the universe. No wonder that an atheist finds himself in distress. It is an awful thing to be tossed to and fro as the mere victim of some blind chance or fate. Now, when we turn to the Word of God, we find that God says, in the 54th of Isaiah, "I have created the waster to destroy." The same hand that made the gourd that overshadowed Jonah made the worm that stung the gourd and caused it to wither. The same God that makes the sunshine makes clouds; the same God that makes the placid stream makes the stormy waves; the same God that makes the breeze fragrant with perfume of flowers makes the tornado and the cyclone. All these things come from the same creative hand. How much real relief from trouble there is to the student of the universe when he believes that all these things are working together the purpose of a mighty Creator, and that, if we could look at these things from the point of view that God occupies, we should see that there is a real good even in things that are apparently evil; we should see that, at the back of all this apparent conflict in the universe, there is a Divine plan; just as much a design in the destructive agencies as in the constructive forces; just as much a plan in the decay of a plant as in its growth; just as much a plan in that thing that seems to be hostile to our human welfare as in that which seems to be productive of our highest enjoyment; and not till we get hold of this conception that there is nothing in the experiences of man for which God is not responsible, either by way of direct decree or by way of permissive decree—not till we get to that point shall we have our doubts dissolved. I consider it is atheism and blasphemy to say that God is not responsible for His universe, and that He is not in the conduct of His whole universe. It is only when we see God sitting above the storm that we get the peace which passes understanding; it is only when we think of the thunder as His voice, and the lightning as the flash of His eye, and the wind as the breath of His nostrils, and the clouds as the dust of His feet, that we can rest in confidence that all things are working out the sublime design of a beneficent Creator.

Not only does the belief in the existence of God imply superintendence and control of all the natural forces of the universe, but it implies also that He is Ruler and Sovereign over all the affairs of men. Now, if this universe is a constructed house, so also are the historic ages. I am sorry for any man who does not believe that there is a Divine plan in human history, that this is one of the houses that God has built. It may be but the basement story that is yet built, but it will support arches and pillars above it, and the construction is going on until the domes and the pinnacles are added, and the last stone is laid with shoutings of "Grace, grace unto it." We do see in the midst of human history a great deal that demands a Divine Designer, and Planner, and Ruler behind it. This world is a kind of stage; men and women come upon the stage and transact their little parts, and then are withdrawn and we see them no more. Now if we could not believe that there is some one whose will is being executed in the activities of mankind, what an awful calamity and disaster this whole world-history would become! How all these actions of men seem as we look at them to be a mass of contradictions: we cannot thread the maze of them until we come to the centre; it is like a tangled skein that is in ten thousand or ten million knots, and no ingenuity of ours will unravel the perplexity. But as soon as you come to believe that this whole history of mankind is as thoroughly the working out of the plan of God as creation is the exhibition of His power and wisdom and goodness; when you believe that He thrusts men and women on the stage of human activity that He may use them for His will, even though they may be wicked people rebelling against His power and grace, and when He is done with them withdraws them from the stage that others may take their place,—only when we believe in the providence of God, that God's hand is in human history, and that He is moulding it and shaping it according to His will, do we find peace. And then just as in creation we see malignant powers at work which we call "*natural* forces," so in history we see malignant forces at work which we call *moral* forces. We see God's people persecuted; we see truth, virtue, purity, trodden down in the dust, and we see malignity, and violence, and rage, and hatred, and all forms of despotism triumphant. Now think of the awful condition of that man or woman who denies that in history there is a God! Such a theory makes this world move according to a blind fate, just as it makes this universe to be constructed according to a blind chance.

On the other hand, what a blessing comes to a disciple who believes in God as a Ruler and Sovereign! To my mind, the very judgment to come, which to many is only a synonym for terror, for all that which is most awful and most repulsive, has about it a glorious aspect. And why? There are ten thousand times ten thousand wrongs and evils in this world, and which never will get righted in this age. The good not only suffer persecution and oppression, but they go down to their graves sometimes as martyrs; and the wicked not only triumph for a season, but they sometimes pass to their graves in peace and leave large estates to their heirs, and they do not seem to be plagued like other men. The seventy third Psalm admits that they often seem to be overtaken by no form of calamity. But you come into the sanctuary of God and learn the end of the righteous, that it is peace, and the end of the wicked, that it is retribution and penalty; then you begin to see the scales of God's providence, uneven in this world, righting up their beam and assuming a perfect balance; but it is only so when you take that other world in view, only when you get a sight of the Divine Sovereign sitting on the Throne and with His blessed hand swaying the sceptre of all human affairs. Thus we can rejoice in the judgment to come, as a righting of the wrongs of ages. The solution to all our difficulties in human history is the Divine providence over all mankind; if God is the Creator, He is also the Ruler and the Judge.

3. Then, again, if you believe in the "Father," remember that the word "Father" expresses the antidote for ten thousand troubles. What is a father? "Like as a father pitieth his children, so the Lord pitieth them that fear Him"; like as a father chasteneth his children, so the Lord chasteneth them that He loves. All your remaining difficulties that pertain to your personal history as a child of God are solved when you think of God as your Father. For instance, there is prospective want. You have bread enough, clothing enough, in your home to-day, but you do not know but that to-morrow may bring you to destitution, to hunger and famine, to cold and nakedness, to an unsheltered, homeless

condition. But your Father says, "Seek first the kingdom of God and His righteousness, and all these things shall be added unto you." He says there is not a sparrow falls to the ground without His notice; He hears even the beasts of the field when they cry, and the very "hairs of your head are all numbered"; and He says, "Your Father knoweth that you have need of all these things; your heavenly Father knoweth how to give good gifts to them that ask Him." And, if the Fatherhood of God settles all your difficulties and perplexities about your future, why need you be concerned? Your Father will not let you hunger, your Father will not let you want, and if you simply trust Him every needful thing shall be given unto you in His good time.

II. We pass now to consider *moral and spiritual* difficulties that are solved in Jesus Christ—" Ye believe in God, *believe also in Me.*"

Here we come upon an entirely different class of troubles. For example, we do believe in God, but what kind of God is He? He is afar off, He seems to us vague, and shadowy, and distant; He is a spirit, and we cannot conceive a spirit, for we never knew anything that was intelligent and conscious that was not in a body. Thus, even when we believe in God, we cannot but ask what kind of a God is He? Down in Tahiti in the early ages, when they still had no gospel and no knowledge of Jesus Christ, they conceived of God only as some strange being in some distant sphere. They did not know very much about Him, but they thought Him connected with earthquake, and storm, and calamity, and they used to go to the graves of the dead and pray their ancestors that, if they came in contact with this distant God, they would ask Him if He would not be pleased to withhold His awful punishments and His calamities from the people of the island. That is about all they knew about God, and I am afraid it is about all that some other people know about God, though brought up in Christian lands. To them God is afar off, very vague, and very shadowy. They do not clothe Him in their minds with any definite, worthy conception. Jesus Christ came in order to tell you what kind of God you have to deal with. When Philip said, "Show us the Father, and it sufficeth us," He said, "Have I been so long time with you, and yet hast thou not known me, Philip? He that hath seen Me, hath seen the Father; and how sayest thou then, Show us the Father?" In other words, our blessed Lord was "God manifest in the flesh." Jesus says, "If you see Me, you see the Father."

John significantly says about Christ in the first verses of his gospel:—"In the beginning was the Word, and the Word was with God, and the Word was God." Now what is a word? A word is the manifestation of a thought. I have a thought in my mind; I want to communicate that thought to you; that thought takes its shape in the words I speak. You cannot see my thought, you cannot explore what is going on in my mind, but what is there, moving up and down, comes through the channels of my speech, and so travels to your ear, and from your ear to your mind; and so the thought that a moment ago was going up and down in my mind is now going up and down in your own. A word is the expression of a thought. So Christ became the Word, to take the thought out of the mind and heart of God, and translate that thought so that you could understand it; so that what was before invisible, and inaudible, and beyond the reach of your senses, comes into your mind and heart as something that was in God's, but now is in yours. Beautiful indeed is this, as an expression of what Christ is to us: you want to know God; well then, study Christ, and you will know all about Him—" He, that hath seen Me, hath seen the Father."

2. Again, you notice that you are a sinner, and have evidence in yourself that you are a sinner; you see that you commit sin very easily, and that you reach up to morality and righteousness with very great difficulty; you see that you have done many things that were wrong, and left undone many things that were right, and you are troubled about it; your conscience condemns you, you feel that there is guilt and sin, and where there is guilt and sin you know there is penalty. And now the question is, "How does God look on my sin? what is my relation to God? is there such a thing as salvation—first, from the penalty of sin; secondly, from the power of sin; and thirdly, from the presence of sin?" Now Jesus Christ comes, and he says, "Look on Me; in Me the Father is reconciling the world unto Himself; in Me is the Father preaching the doctrine of forgiveness of sin; in Me behold the Father, providing atonement for your iniquities, and offering you a full, a free, a glorious salvation."

III. There is still another class of difficulties and doubts that trouble you, and they have relation to your *ultimate condition*. "What is to be my future?" You asked a while ago, "Whence did I come?" Now you ask, "Whither shall I go? what is to be my future state? God reveals himself to me in Jesus Christ as a reconciling God: what is the effect of all this reconciliation?" Jesus says, "Look unto Me; I am the Way and the Truth and the Life; no man comes to the Father but by Me; he that comes to Me comes to the Father, and he that dwells in Me dwells in the Father, and he in whom I dwell, in him the Father also dwells."

And so we come to another great truth and thought through believing in Jesus, and that is, that you, as a redeemed man or woman, constitute a part of the bride of Jesus Christ, and that you are to be a partaker of the Divine nature ; that your sin is to be purged from you, and that you are to be wholly like unto God Himself. Now see how wonderfully this new class of doubts is satisfied by believing in God. Here is a Divine hand—first, it makes the universe ; second, it rules society ; and third, it guides, and cherishes, and nourishes, and leads every little child of God. And when we look to Jesus Christ, what do we see ? God in Jesus Christ coming down to man ; God through Jesus Christ reconciling man to Himself; and man in Jesus Christ becoming united with God. We are passing rapidly over a wonderful continent of human thought, but not too rapidly to get a glimpse of the grandeur of this conception. Let me call your attention to Jacob's Ladder. You know that our Lord virtually says in the last verse of the first chapter of the Gospel of John that He is Jacob's Ladder. He says, "Hereafter ye shall see heaven open"—just as Jacob did in the midnight vision—" and the angels of God ascending and descending upon the Son of Man." Jacob looked up and saw heaven opened, and he saw a ladder stretching from earth below to heaven above, and he saw the angels of God ascending and descending upon it. Christ says, " Hereafter ye shall see heaven open, and the angels of God ascending and descending upon the Son of Man," which shows that the Son of Man is the real ladder. A ladder is a means by which those below go up, and by which those above come down. What is Christ ? He is the ladder between God and man : in His humanity He touches the earth ; in His Divinity He touches the heaven, and on Jesus

Christ as a ladder God comes down from heaven to earth and makes Himself known to man ; on Jesus Christ as a ladder man climbs up from earth to heaven and is joined to God. Wonderful is the comprehensiveness of this short creed which Jesus Christ taught us : " Believe in God,"—that solves all the problems of creation ; " Believe in Me "—that solves all the problems of redemption. " Have you desire to know who God is ? I am God manifest in the flesh, and on me as a ladder the invisible God is descending to you. Do you want to know what your future is ? I will tell you. I am the ladder on which you will go up round by round of increasing sanctification until you stand in the perfection and the completion of the Divine image, and you are lost and absorbed in God."

We now take up the last part of this text, to which I have not adverted:—"In my Father's house are many abiding places : if it were not so, I would have told you. I go to prepare a place for you. And if I go and prepare a place for you, I will come again, and receive you unto myself ; that where I am, there may ye be also."

Here is another continent of thought, over which it does not behove us to hurry. There is quite too much misapprehension on the whole subject. In the first place, what is the Father's house ? Most people say the Father's House is heaven. I consider that a great error ; the Father's House is whatever the Father made, and that is the whole universe. Heaven is a part of it and earth is a part, and not till we get that complete conception do we understand these words. When Jesus spoke those words He was probably looking towards or referring to the Temple on Mount Moriah. There stood the central portion of the great Temple, the Court of the People, the Court of the Priests, and the Holy of Holies; and then on each side of the Temple, like wings, on the right and left were the apartments for the priests, who resided there during their periods of service. So our Lord says, "In My Father's house are many apartments for His priests and kings." "I go to prepare a place for you; and if I go and prepare a place for you, I will come again, and receive you unto myself; that where I am, there ye may be also." What wonderful thoughts come to us out of these words!

1. In the first place notice the *unity of the universe.* Here is the earth, there is heaven;—both parts of the Father's house. These are the damp dark rooms in the basement; those are the upper and beautiful rooms on the heavenward side; but it is all one house. These are the seen, and those are the unseen abodes, but all parts of one building. There may be a fog that rests on St. Paul's, but when you stand before the Cathedral you have no doubt that there is a dome above, though you do not see it. There are a great many people who mistake a fog for a denial of truth, and they do not believe anything they do not see. I am very sorry for them, but I have not time to dwell on that error. The thought to be impressed now is that all this universe, seen and unseen, is *one* universe. Here is something down here; there is something up there. Here is something we can see, and hear, and touch, and taste, and which all our senses may explore; there is something we cannot see, nor feel, nor hear, which our senses do not reach and touch; but it is just as real, only it is constituted in a different fashion, and demands a different kind of faculty to explore and appreciate it.

2. Then notice again how this wonderful truth teaches us the *dignity of being.* Being is so valuable in God's eye, that He

says to the believer, "Thou shalt never die"—you have got the security of eternity in you, and though you die, apparently, and your body is laid in the grave to go to decay, you survive, and you are transplanted like a flower from a broken pot into a celestial garden.

3. Then see again what this grand text teaches us about what we may call the *unity of life* or its *continuity*, something that is not broken. I do love to think of the Christian's life in this way, that there is no interruption to it. We say that a saint dies, but the fact is that he just goes on living; we say that he dies, but the fact is he never lived as he lives now. I knew a young man who was an infidel. He told me in conversation that he did not sympathise with my belief in God, he did not even believe in a future state. He said, "When I die I am going to dust, and that will be the end of me." He had a Christian mother, who had long prayed for him. One day he came home from his office about noon and said, "Mother, I feel fatigued; I think I will lie down till dinner is spread;" so he laid down and fell asleep. At one o'clock she spoke to him and said, "We are ready to sit down at the table," but she could not wake him. She shook him violently, but she could not rouse him. He was in a comatose state, and there was no perceptible pulse, and he sank lower and lower until his breathing also was scarcely perceptible. They sent at once for a physician, who came in, examined his pulse, listened to his heart, made a thorough examination, but said, "I can do nothing for him; you will just be compelled to leave him as he is; he may come out of it, and he may not." He went away. About five o'clock in the afternoon, as they were sitting round him, simply watching the last rays of flickering life, he opened his eyes, he looked round, he saw his mother, he stretched

out his hand and took her hand ; and he said, " Mother, what you taught me is all true ; there is a future life. I have been treading along the verge of another world, and been looking over into that other world ; mother it is all true." He shut his eyes and died. God allowed him to come back from the other world just long enough to assure that mother who had trained him in the true faith, that he saw at the last his error and abandoned his infidelity, and then he passed away.

A beautiful departure took place in Philadelphia some years ago. You have often sung in your religious meetings, "Stand up, stand up for Jesus." Do you know the origin of it? The son of Stephen H. Tyng,—that man so venerated in American history as a devout and most evangelical clergyman of the Episcopal Church—Rev. Dudley Tyng by name,—was a very beautiful character, and a very active Christian worker. One day the sleeve of his gown became entangled in a hay cutter in his barn, and instantly his arm was drawn in and cut off at the shoulder. The loss of blood was extreme, the shock of the nervous system terrible, and it was seen that he must die. He asked those he loved to sit by his bedside and see the triumph of God's grace. " I want you," said he, " to take my hand, and when I am no longer able to speak, I will press your hand to indicate to you that God is with me in my passage into the other world." When his eyes were closed, and he almost ceased to breathe, no longer able to speak, every few seconds he would press the hand he was holding and his face would light up with joy and triumph. It reminded one of a man rowing over stormy waves in the darkness of a terrible tempest. He is moving toward a shore that is beyond, and he has a flag waving in the boat to give assurance that all is right. Down goes the little boat into the trough of the sea, and you say " He is gone." But presently up comes the boat again on the crest of the wave, and the flag is flying. Down again goes the boat in the waters, and you hold your breath with anxiety ; but in a moment it comes up again on the crest of another wave, and the flag is still flying. And so, whilst that dear man passed on to the presence of the Lord, the flag of his testimony was flying, and his friends felt more like singing than weeping at his bedside. The last words he spoke were : " *Stand up for Jesus! stand up for Jesus!*" and George Duffield, D.D., took that dying expression as his text and wrote a song of triumph for the warriors of Christ.

No pastor has been at the dying bed of disciples, as many times as I have in the last thirty years, without believing in the continuity of life. Life goes right on, and when it ceases to have any sign for this world, it is only because it is lost in the glory on the other side. Death is to the believer not a *cessation* of life ; it is the *translation* of life into another sphere. Death before Christ came was as a cavern, with one opening on this side, which was closed when burial took place, by the great stone, put at the mouth of the sepulchre ; but, when Jesus went through the sepulchre to the presence of *God*, He turned the *cavern* into a *tunnel*, with an opening from the farther side and light coming in from that side, and the darkness for ever taken away. In the 23rd Psalm we read, " Yea, though I walk through the valley of the shadow of death, I will fear no evil." One of our poets has translated that into verse;

" Yea, though I walk through death's dark vale,
   Yet will I fear no ill."

Has he not mistaken the sentiment almost entirely ? The

Psalmist does not call it "*death's dark vale*," and we have no right to call it such. He calls it, "the valley of *the shadow of death*." When did you ever get a *shadow* if you did not have *sunshine?* A shadow without a light would be a curiosity. No, no ; the Psalmist knew that there is the infinite light of God in the valley of death, and so while there is shadow there, there is also sunshine, and it is because the light is intense that the shadow is deep. You walk through the shadow, but your eyes are on the light. Death is a transition from the lower rooms to the upper ones, it is going up the spiral staircase between this world and the next. It is a remarkable fact that in the New Testament, so far as I remember, it is never once said, after Christ's resurrection, that a disciple died—that is, without some qualification. Stephen "*fell asleep*." David, after he had served his own generation by the will of God, "fell on sleep, and was laid with his fathers." " Knowing that I must shortly *put off this my tabernacle*, as the Lord showed me," Peter says. Paul says, " the *time of my departure* is at hand." The figure here is taken from a vessel, that, as she leaves a dock, throws the cables off the fastenings, and opens her sails to the wind to depart for the haven. The only time where the word "dead" is used, it is with qualification :—the dead *in Christ*—the dead which die *in the Lord*. Christ abolished death and the term " death," and it is the privilege of a disciple to hold on to the continuity of life. It is our privilege, in our cemeteries, not to put up broken shafts of columns, inverted torches, and rosebuds broken off from their stems, and closed urns that indicate a quenched fire ; we ought rather to show that fire burning in glory more brightly,—to put the capital on the pillar to express completion, and to show the rosebud in the Lord's garden in fuller bloom. I am ashamed of those Christian cemeteries that exhibit on every side these miserable relics of paganism, indicating disappointment, defeat, and disaster, instead of glory, and triumph, and immortality. You may go through the six million tombs in the Catacombs, beneath the city of Rome, where the early Christians were buried, and you will not *once find, in six million inscriptions, the word " death."* " Appius lives "; " the birthday of Olympia has come." That is the way those early Christians thought of death, as a passage into immortality.

IV. But I cannot close without calling your attention to these last words : " I will come again and receive you unto Myself." What is Christ's coming again ? I have heard of some Christian people who say that Christ's coming again means *our death* ; I am very sorry for them. Throughout the whole of the Scriptures death is represented as the curse of sin. Death is the last enemy that is to be destroyed, and Jesus Christ is never represented as coming to us in death. No, no; it may please the Lord to tarry, and if death as a messenger of God comes to me in the dark guise of sorrow, and affliction, and dissolution, I must pass under the leadership of this messenger to the presence of my Lord. But *He* does not *come to us* in death ; something better than that is meant by His coming. In the 21st of John we are for ever relieved from all doubt as to what Jesus Christ's coming means. That passage shows that so far from Christ's coming meaning death, it means the *exact opposite* of death. " If I will that he tarry *till I come*, what is that to thee ? follow thou Me. Then went this saying abroad among the brethren that that disciple *should not die."* Now, if Jesus' coming means death, the saying would not have gone abroad among the disciples that He should not die. Oh, no; Christ said, "I go to prepare a place for you. And if I go and prepare a place for you, I will come again and receive you unto myself; that where I am, there ye may be also." The greatest event of history is yet to come : greater than man's creation, greater than Christ's incarnation, resurrection, ascension—is that Second Coming, which supplements and consummates them all. After Christ ascended, those bright angelic forms that stood by the disciples' side, said, " Why stand ye gazing up into heaven ? This same Jesus shall so come in like manner as ye have seen Him go into heaven." Now notice, "this same Jesus shall so come in like manner." How anybody can get anything by way of *a figure of speech* out of such plain language as that passes comprehension. " This *same* Jesus shall *so* come " —not in a different manner,—" in *like* manner as ye have seen Him *go* into heaven." The whole creation of God groans and travails in pain together, waiting for that hour of the redemption of the body, when Jesus shall so come in like manner as He was seen to go into heaven. Then our eyes shall see Him as their eyes saw Him, and then we shall be caught up together into the clouds to meet Him in the air,—a living body of disciples who look for Him and wait for His appearing ; and then those who are now sleeping in Jesus shall from their graves come forth, and join the living church caught up as the bride of Jesus Christ. That is as clear to me as any other truth in the Word of God. I am sorry to say that there were long years of my ministry during which that truth was hid from my eyes, when I was blinded to it as the Jew is blinded to the doctrine of the Messiahship of Christ as fulfilled in the New Testament. But now for the rest of my life I praise God for the privilege of giving my testimony to antidote the false testimony of previous teaching.

There are *three great events* in history—man's creation, Christ's incarnation, Christ's second coming. Between the first and the second there is a little altar of sacrifice that points back to man's fall, and onward to man's redemption in Christ ; and between Christ's incarnation and His second coming stands a little table of communion which points back to Christ on the Cross, and forward to Christ in His second coming :—" For, as often as ye eat this bread and drink this cup, ye do show the Lord's death till He come." The link between the Cross and the Crown is the Table of the Lord. Do not forget that, when you sit down at the Communion, that the bread and the cup point back to Christ's accomplished work, and forward to your accomplished salvation. Lift up your eyes. The ages are moving on, and they are bringing us closer, it may be far closer than we think, to the second advent of our Lord. Signs all round the horizon seem to indicate the speedy approach of the Master of us all in the glory of His second advent, and it behoves us to look and wait for His appearing, with our loins girded about, our lamps trimmed, and to stand in the posture of pilgrims who watch and wait for the coming Day.

SERMON EIGHT

Preservation and Presentation; or, The Hope of Consummation

"Now unto him that is able to keep you from falling, and to present you faultless before the presence of his glory with exceeding joy, to the only wise God our Saviour, be glory and majesty, dominion and power, both now and ever. Amen."— JUDE 24, 25

A PECULIAR halo of interest surrounds these verses, as forming the conclusion in the epistolary portion of the New Testament. Beyond the Epistle of Jude, nothing remains except the Apocalypse, or revelation of the future. It is as though the Holy Spirit had designed to present before us, in these words, the most important, the most encouraging, the most inspiring, hope of the entire New Testament—the hope of consummation, the consummation of hope. Moreover, there is not a single word in these two verses that has not the emphasis of a special importance: no word could be omitted here, without injuring the faultless symmetry of the passage; nor could even the order of the words be changed, without impairing the perfect beauty of this last testimony.

First of all, let us notice that *faith is a prophet*; it " shows us things to come." And faith here is seen not only pre-

The Hope of Consummation

dicting the future, but discounting the future; that is to say, bringing the future backward into the present, as a vivid and visible reality. Jude here refers to something that lies in the far future, yet it is the occasion of a rapturous doxology. The preservation of the saints and their final presentation are the subjects of these verses, and yet, although both of these blessings lie in the pathway ahead, and one of them at the very end of the age, thanks are here fervently given for them, as though they had been mercies remembered in the past or enjoyed in the present. How seldom we children of God think of praising God for blessings, yet unreceived by us, but which, being pledged to us in covenant, are as really ours as anything in the past or the time that now is. *Faith discounts the future because it counts God's promise, God's performance.* He speaks, and it is done.

Notice again the connection of the doxology with the subject, the preservation and presentation of the saints. Four words are prominent in the doxology; "glory and majesty, dominion and power." Glory and majesty are especially concerned in the presentation of the saints, for we are to be presented before the presence of His glory, and then we are to be made sharers of His majesty. "I have appointed unto you a kingdom, as My Father hath appointed unto Me, that ye may sit on twelve thrones, judging the twelve tribes of Israel." "Power and dominion" are especially connected with the preservation of the saints, and we must not lose sight of the difference in the two words used—dominion and power. "Dominion" is power in actual exercise, by way of sovereign control; it implies enemies vanquished as well as subjects governed. How is our preservation assured, but by that dominion that puts to flight the armies of the aliens with Satan at their head, and regulates all things so that they work together for the uplifting and triumphant preserving of God's saints. But " power " is something beside " dominion." The dominion of God is *over* the saint, but the " power " of God is *in* the saint, quickening his spiritual life, and enabling him to hold fast the faith once delivered to the saints. So that while " glory and majesty " have especially to do with presentation, " dominion and power " have to do with preservation.

The remaining words of this doxology, are " both now and ever." In the original language we read literally, "before all time and now and evermore." This reminds us of that love which eternally loved us, before all time ; of that power which now upholds us, and of that dominion which shall be exhibited in the ultimate triumph and final consummation of our salvation, evermore.

With these words of simple introduction, we are prepared to approach the subject more closely, and consider : first, the *preservation* ; second, the *presentation*, of the saints.

I. Preservation. " Now unto Him that is able to guard you from stumbling "—such is the force of the original. Jude must have been playing on words here. There is a beautiful correspondence in the Greek that does not appear in the English. There are two words that are very much alike—they are, indeed, composed of the same consonants and the same vowels. One of them means apostasy, or a final falling away from God ; the other means free from stumbling (αποστασια, απταιστος). The apostle, who has been writing in this whole epistle, of apostasy, says now, " God is not only able to keep you from the apostasy from which I warned you, but He is able even to keep you free from stumbling." The English supplies no two words sufficiently alike to show the beautiful resemblance in the words here used. We might venture, perhaps, to render it so as to hint this likeness :—" God is not only able to keep you free from a *fall*, but He is able to keep you free from a *fault*"; or, again, we might express it by two similar phrases :—" God is able not only to keep you from falling *from* the way, but He is able to keep you from stumbling *in* the way."

The first thought suggested here as to the preservation of the saints, is the great difference there is between the *falling of a sinner*, and the *stumbling of a saint*. When a child of God, who has chosen and pursued the good way, suddenly falls into any sin, by lack of integrity, or of fidelity, coming under the power of some strong temptation, how the world exults! Suppose the beloved pastor who, for so long preached the gospel in this tabernacle, had, during those forty years, been betrayed into any open sin,—the very thought is shocking!—the telegraphic wires would have flashed the news round the world in less than half a day, and all the infidel and godless newspapers, published throughout earth's domain, would, in double-leaded columns, have proclaimed Spurgeon's downfall! The world likes to see a godly man stumble in the way, so as to give occasion to the enemies of the Lord to blaspheme; and how quickly such enemies of the Lord avail themselves of the occasion!

Now, I maintain, on the basis of Holy Scripture, that there is a world-wide difference between the falling of a sinner, and the stumbling of a saint. The sinner habitually walks in the way of evil; the saint has deliberately chosen the way of good. When the sinner falls, he falls *in* the evil way that he is pursuing; that is, his uniform course is *secretly* sinful, but his fall involves an *outbreaking* sin. Lust has been in his heart, but it breaks out in open impurity; latent hate has been there, but it betrays him into the sin of violence; secret avarice now becomes open over-reaching or dishonesty. The sin is in accordance with the habitual life which he has been leading. On the other hand, when the child of God, who has chosen the good way, and walked in it thus far, stumbles into sin, this is *not* in accordance with his ordinary walk; and when he is recovered by the grace of God, he pursues the same path, in the same direction as before his error. There is surely a great difference between these two, which is finely expressed in the Bible, in two cases :—James says, in the 5th chapter of his Epistle, " Brethren, if any of you do err from the truth, and one bring him back." A brother is here supposed to be walking in the way of the truth, and to make a temporary deviation from that way; and someone is to go and warn him, and call his attention to the evil doing, and bring him back into the right way. Again, the Apostle Paul says, in his letter to the Galatians, 6th chapter, and 1st verse, ' Brethren, if any of you be *overtaken in a fault*, ye which are spiritual, restore such an one in the spirit of meekness." The Greek word suggests an adversary coming up from behind, and tripping up the disciple who is walking in the way of God. Some old habit of his past life pursues him, and, when he is incautious and unheeding, trips him up, so that he stumbles. Now you, says Paul, who are spiritual, go and help him up on his feet, and set him on his way again, with the comfort and the help of your sympathy and prayer.

1. Plainly, there is a great deal of difference between the falling of a sinner and the stumbling of a saint. These two differ in their *nature*. There are three conditions of soul life in this world : one is the condition of salvation; the other is the condition of damnation; and the middle is

a condition of probation. If you have made your great lasting choice of God and of holiness, your state is already a state of salvation, of present salvation. If you have made your final and fatal choice of evil and of sin, your state is already a state of damnation. It may well hush even our breathing, to consider the awfulness of this truth! What is it that makes preaching such a solemn business? I never get up thus to speak, in behalf of God, without shrinking in every fibre of my being. If there is one of you here, now, with whom the last great choice has not been made, you are still in a state of probation; and the final issue—salvation on the one hand, or damnation on the other—has not yet been settled by you. If, while I am preaching the gospel of the grace of God, at this hour, you should make your last great choice of evil, that would be damnation; and you may continue to live a score of years, but you are damned as truly as if already in hell. When the question is settled by your own final choice of evil, it is settled for ever.

> " There is a time, we know not when,
>   A point, we know not where,
> That seals the destiny of men,
>   For glory or despair!
>
> " There is a line, by us unseen,
>   That crosses every path;
> The hidden boundary between,
>   God's patience and God's wrath.
>
> " To cross that limit is to die,
>   To die as if by stealth;
> It does not pale the glowing eye,
>   Nor rob the cheek of health.
>
> " But on the forehead God has set,
>   Indelibly His mark;
> Unseen by man, for man as yet,
>   Is blind and in the dark."

Let God impress on your minds this awful thought, that to say, finally, to evil, " Be thou my good," puts you on a level with fallen angels, outside of the limit of the grace of God ; and to say to God finally, " Be Thou my God," puts you on the level of salvation, and makes that salvation a present reality. Now every sinner has fallen away from God, and he is continually falling. He is further from God, to-day, than he was when he began to fall, and will be further from God, when this service of worship is concluded, than he was when it began. But with the saint, though he falls into sin, the nature of his fall is such, that it does not affect the *ruling choice* of his soul. The things that he would, he does not, and the evil that he would not, that he does ; but, down in the centre and heart of his being, if he be truly a child of God, there is the love of God which is the love of holiness, and the choice of God which is the choice of holiness, and from every temporary deviation from the right he will surely be recovered, to assert again the power of that ruling choice.

→ 2. There is also a difference between the fall of the sinner and of the saint, in their *extent*. You go and stand at the estuary of some great river, where it enters the sea, and you notice that, when some tidal wave moves up the mouth of the river, it seems as though the whole flood of that river were moving up towards its source : yet, the fact is, that the deep current is continually moving towards the sea, and it is only at times, when the waves and the tides of the ocean flow inwards, that the current seems to be reversed, and even then it is only so on the surface. A godly man sometimes weakens in the crisis of a great temptation ; when the tidal winds and tidal waves of Satanic malice overwhelm him, and it seems as though the whole current of his being were running against God; but down beneath the superficial and temporary yielding to temptation, there is the steady, habitual, onward movement of his soul God-ward. And the limited extent of the sins of God's true people is seen the moment we carefully study them. Take David, for instance : there was the look of lust; then the crime of adultery; then the deceptive cloaking of sin; then the indirect murder of Uriah. But Nathan came to David, and told the story of the ewe lamb, and said, "Thou art the man!" and the great depths of David's heart were broken up, and in that 51st Psalm, whose lines, bathed with tears, always remind one of the dropping of the water from the ledges of a rock, we have the outburst of the penitent heart, breaking forth in one of the most pathetic penitential psalms to be found even in sacred literature. Again we see Peter, warned of Christ that he would deny him, insisting that he would not, though he should go to prison and to death; yet you hear him deny Christ, again and again, and confirm his denial with oath and cursing. Then Christ looks on him. His memory is quickened by that look ; he remembers the warning of Jesus; he goes out and weeps bitterly,— another penitential psalm in action. And, afterward, when Peter was asked what death he would die, the tradition is that he said, " Let me be crucified, for my Lord was crucified ; but let me be crucified with my head downwards, for I am not worthy to be crucified as He was."

3. Again, do not the falling of the sinner and the falling of the saint differ, not only in nature and extent, but in what may be called their *providential purpose ?*

There may be a providential purpose or design in God's permitting His people, at times, to commit sin. God is never the author of sin, but He sometimes, undoubtedly, withdraws for a time His keeping power, and allows a disciple to stumble into evil, that He may teach him lessons that he never could be taught in any other way. Moses, in Deuteronomy, compares the Lord's dealings with His people to the eagle stirring up her nest; fluttering over her young; spreading abroad her wings; taking and bearing them on her wings (Deut. xxxii. 11). How beautiful that figure is! The eagle builds her eyrie far up on the rocky heights, and when the wings of her young are beginning to grow, so that the facilities for flying are supplied them, as they are apt to be too self-indulgent and over-fond of the soft lining of a warm resting place, the mother eagle plants a thorn in the side of the nest, so that, as the little ones nestle down against the cushion of ease, they are pricked by the thorn, and so get up and begin to move around. And then, if necessary, she actually crowds them out of the nest, pushes them along towards the edge of the cliff, and sometimes even off the edge; so that, as they begin to fall, they are compelled to use their wings, fluttering and trying to sustain themselves in the air. When they tumble over and over, in unsuccessful efforts, the mother eagle, watching them, sweeps down beneath them, and spreads abroad her great wings that measure sometimes twelve feet from tip to tip, and as the little fledgling is falling to apparent destruction, she receives it upon her maternal pinions, and bears it back again to the eyrie. Does not the Lord sometimes allow His children to *fall*, because He would teach them how to *fly* ? Does He not, sometimes, let them sin, because He wants to teach them to depend on Him and so cure them of sinning? But the Lord keeps watch of His little fledgling, and, as His disciple tumbles over and over in helpless approach to destruction, He sweeps down beneath, spreads abroad His great wings, and receives the penitent believer, and bears him back again to the height of conscious fellowship with God. Peter was left to sin, in order that he might be cured of his self-confidence, and his trust in the strength of his own will. You see Peter tumbling off the edge of the cliff, falling into denial, then into other and worse denials, faster and farther, and with increasing velocity; but the prayers of Jesus Christ were beneath him. "I have prayed for *thee*, that thy faith fail not." Simon Peter fell *till he struck the prayers of Jesus*, and he could not fall any further. Yes, if we are children of God, His preserving power is round about us. We should not for a moment hold fast to God, if He did not hold fast to us. His love to us is an elastic bond of union, which bears immense strain, without breaking, and causes us to rebound, after our temporary fall into sin, back to His bosom.

4. Let us, however, notice, that our *preservation* is connected with our *perseverance*. That is surely a one-sided presentation of the " perseverance of the saints," that makes it solely dependent on a sovereign act of God. A half truth is always more dangerous than a whole error, because the devil will combine a half truth and a half lie, and he will show you the half truth side, and so you are led to accept the whole; whereas, if he showed you the side that is obviously a lie, you would turn away from it at once. Now we must be careful of half truths. See how wonderfully the Bible puts both sides of this great question. We read in the verses just preceding, " Keep yourselves in the love of God ; building up yourselves in your most holy faith ; praying in the Holy Ghost ; looking for the mercy of our Lord Jesus Christ unto eternal life," and one would think that all the truth is embraced in that one sentence,—

"*Keep yourselves.*" But two verses further on in the epistle, there is not a word about keeping yourselves :—" Now unto *Him that is able to keep you* from falling, and to present you faultless before the presence of His glory, with exceeding joy, to the only wise God our Saviour be glory." Do you keep yourselves? Yes. Does God keep you? Yes. Are the two things reconcileable? Perfectly so. "Work out your own salvation with fear and trembling, for it is God which worketh in you, both to will and to do." God will not keep you if you do not keep yourself; you will not keep yourself if God does not keep you. The two things are like right and left hands united in co-operation. God surely will not keep you, if you do not build yourselves up on your most holy faith, do not pray in the Holy Ghost, and do not look for the mercy of our Lord Jesus Christ unto eternal life; and yet, if God did not keep you, it would be impossible for you to do these things. Take the two words, "preserve" and "persevere." The same letters, whereby we spell the word "persevere," are the letters that make up the word "preserve," and the two things are as vitally connected as are the two words, etymologically.

II. Now let us turn to look, in conclusion, at the *presentation* of the saints. "Now unto Him that is able . . . to present you faultless before the presence of His glory with exceeding joy."

In monarchical countries, it has been customary, from very early times, to have a *day of presentation*, when the scions of nobility, the promising young men and young women of the kingdom, are in person presented to their Sovereign, permitted the privileges of the Court. Probably Jude drew his figure of speech from the habits and customs of countries which were imperial in their government. God is an absolute Monarch, and He has His Day of presentation; and, on that day, Christ will present the scions of His nobility before the presence of the Divine glory. But, as in an enlightened Empire no man or woman is permitted to be presented to the reigning Sovereign, on whose garments there is the taint of open immorality, or especially of disloyalty or treason, so no one will be presented on that great day of presentation except in garments of faultless purity and holiness. And so the Apostle Jude puts in the word "holy" or "faultless." We are preserved *blameless till* His coming, but we are presented *faultless at* His coming.

If there is any doctrine in the Holy Scripture that seems to me almost incredible, it is this doctrine of the faultlessness of the saints, yet it is the plain testimony of the Word. In the 5th of Ephesians, verse 27: "That He might present the church to Himself, a glorious church, not having spot or wrinkle, or any such thing; but that it should be holy, and without blemish." Then in the 1st chapter of the Epistle to the Colossians, verse 22, we read, " In the body of His flesh through death to present you holy, and umblamable, and unreprovable in His sight." Thus, taking these words together, there are eight or nine different terms used : "glorious," " spotless," "without wrinkle," " without any such thing," " holy," "without blemish," " unblamable," " unreprovable," and Jude has one more adjective, "faultless." Think of it. You, even *you*, are to be presented *faultless* before the presence of His glory. You know how wonderfully searching is the power of the sunlight. Suppose we should set a statue in a corner of a room, and put over it a veil, closing all the shutters, and darkening the house, and then admitting at one point intense sunlight;

if we gather up those rays of sunlight and, through a double convex lens, focus them on that statue, so searching is the power of the sunlight that it would seem to dissolve the veil, and show us the proportions of the statue. The presence of God's glory is so awful, that when Daniel himself, the perfect man in Babylon, was confronted with the vision of the glory, he says, " My comeliness was turned into corruption, and there remained in me no more strength." The very things that he had prided himself upon, his virtue, his morality, the excellence of his character, and the blamelessness of his life, when the glory of the Son of God beat upon him, lost their beauty, and his very *comeliness* was turned into *corruption*. And the holy man of God, John the Apostle, who leaned on the breast of Jesus at supper, when in the 1st chapter of the Apocalypse we read of his vision of the glory, tells us he "fell at his feet as dead"; and yet, astounding fact ! you and I are to be presented faultless before the presence of that same glory. Suppose your body had all been hacked up by your own hand ; with a sharp knife you had cut your arms and legs and chest, so that every part of your body was marked with the signs of your self-mutilation ; even if you survive such insane injuries to your own body, it is covered with scars. Set such a scarred body, naked, in the glare of sunlight ; how every scar stands out, showing the mark of the knife, and witnessing to the attempt at self-destruction ! Now, if there were any human medicine or surgery that could remove every such scar from that body, so that it should be perfect throughout, what would be thought of such medical or surgical treatment ? Grace is going to do with your soul just what such skill would do with your body. It will remove the last taint or scar of sin, so that even God cannot find, as it were, pimple, or freckle, not a remnant of sin, not a trace of guilt, not even a scar left by the wounds of sin on your soul, in your final, ultimate, glorious perfection. After all this labour to express this thought, there is no language to convey it; yet such is the destiny of a child of God. He will "present you faultless before the presence of His glory, with exceeding joy."

To whom does this "exceeding joy" pertain? It is generally supposed to refer to the disciples of Christ; when we read these words, we think of our own joy at being thus presented, faultless. But, whatever reference there may be to our joy, the reference is, first of all, to the joy of Christ. In the 15th of Luke, when the shepherd finds and brings back his lost sheep, he calls his friends and neighbours together, and says, "*Rejoice with me*, for I have found my sheep which I had lost." So, when the woman finds the lost piece of silver that belongs to her necklace, and restores it to its place, she calls her friends and neighbours together, and says, "*Rejoice with me*, for I have found my piece which I had lost." And our Lord adds: "*Likewise*, I say unto you, there is *joy in the presence of the angels* of God over one sinner that repenteth." We, often, carelessly read and quote Scripture. The joy here spoken of is not, primarily, the joy of the angels over a sinner that repents. It is true that they do rejoice, but then it is second-hand. The primary joy emphasized is that which is *in their presence*—the joy of the shepherd, the joy of the woman, the joy of the Father, first of all; and secondarily and sympathetically, the joy of those who are called together to *participate* in that joy. Are we not here to understand the word joy—it means *exultation*—are we not to understand it as, first of all, the joy of the Lord Christ

Himself ? His cup will be overflowing, when He shall " see of the travail of His soul, and be satisfied " ; and then, as that great infinite heart of His overflows like a full chalice, the angels will catch the excess of that overflow, and so participate in His joy.

You have doubtless been present at the unveiling of some great statue. Some artist has been selected as the sculptor, to execute some great design in stone. Then comes the day when it is to be formally presented, unveiled, before the people ; and as the flag is unwound at the signal, and the symmetrical proportions of the statue are disclosed, the shouts of the populace go up to heaven. Whose joy is greatest at such a time ? Surely the joy of the sculptor, whose work is now triumphantly completed and enthusiastically accepted. However great the joy of others, his is the crowning joy of all. The Lord Jesus Christ is bringing to completeness, the stupendous work of human redemption. Our life in Him is a hidden life, and in secret He is carrying it on until the day of consummation. Then, the souls that He has been perfecting in holiness, He will present before the presence of the infinite glory with exceeding joy ; and the light of the eternal glory, breaking upon these sculptured forms of character, will reveal not a fault. Even the omniscient eye of God will search in vain for spot, wrinkle or blemish. In that day, however intense the joy of saints, Christ's joy will be infinite, for then He shall be satisfied with the triumphs of His death, and the Father's acceptance of His redeeming work.

I pray you let this be the time when the last great choice shall be made of Jesus Christ and His salvation. You, who are yet in a state of condemnation, may pass over into a state of salvation, by simply accepting this great Redeemer as your own. Then, taking a new direction for your life, and walking henceforth in the ways of God, He is able to guard you even from stumbling; and if you should stumble, He can recover you by His grace, and you shall yet be presented without spot, blemish or wrinkle, holy, unblamable, unreprovable, faultless, before the presence of His glory. Surely this is a great gospel to preach to a lost world; and what folly and madness it is, with such a gospel preached in one's ears, to turn away from Him who holds out such a prospect of ultimate and perfect salvation, and makes such an offer of immediate and present acceptance to all who believe in the LORD JESUS CHRIST!

SERMON NINE

The Attestation of the Son of God; or, Hope Through Christ's Resurrection

"Declared to be the Son of God with power, according to the Spirit of holiness, by the resurrection from the dead."—ROMANS I. 4

THE resurrection of Christ from the dead is the basal miracle of Christianity—that is, the miracle that stands at the base of the whole system of gospel truth and fact. The declaration that He was the Son of God,—the formal, divine declaration that was, with particular power, the demonstration of his deity, made by the very Spirit of God Himself, was found in the resurrection of Christ from the dead.

There are in Christianity two miracles, that lie side by side as the base blocks in the structure : one is the *Incarnation*—God manifest in the flesh ; and the other is the *Resurrection*—Christ raised from the dead. These two miracles are so connected that Paul teaches us here that the first depends on the second—that the Incarnation rests upon the Resurrection : that is, it is proved to be a true Incarnation by the Resurrection of Christ from the dead. Christ came as a Teacher sent from God, and miracles were the seal of His authority. And so Nicodemus says in the third chapter of John, the second verse, " Master (or 'Rabbi,') we know that Thou art a teacher come from God : for no man can do these miracles that Thou doest, except God be with him." There is an instinct in our hearts which tells us that, if God does send a Teacher into the world, who shall be competent to teach even the teachers of the race, He will accredit Him, by signs unmistakable, that He is a Heaven-sent messenger. And Christ Himself appeals to miracle. For instance, in the fourteenth John, eleventh verse, He says, " Believe me for the very works' sake."—" If you cannot believe me for the sake of the words I speak, believe me for the sake of the works that I do, which set the seal of God upon my teaching."

This miracle of the resurrection is important mainly for this reason, that it establishes all the other miracles. Logicians have what they call an *a fortiori* argument—that is, an argument from the greater to the less,—" If such a greater fact be true, the lesser is credible likewise." So, if this miracle of the Resurrection be established as a veritable fact, it carries the whole argument for miracles with it, for if Christ could rise from the dead, certainly there is no other wonder-working attributed to Him that He was not capable of performing. That is the reason why this text is so very emphatic, that He was " declared to be the Son of God with power according to the Spirit of holiness by the resurrection from the dead."

To be brief and yet comprehensive, we may look first at the relations of Christ's resurrection to His own *incarnation ;* secondly, its reference or relation to our *justification ;* and thirdly its relation to our *resurrection.* It will be found in each case to be the basis, and hence the foundation of all of these.

I. First, it is the basis of Incarnation. How do we know that God was manifest in the flesh, in Jesus Christ? Most of all by Christ's rising from the dead. When Christ was appealed to, to furnish a sign that He was the Messiah, He never gave men but one sign. In the second chapter of John we are told that He was challenged by the Jews, "What sign shewest Thou, seeing that Thou doest these things?" Our Lord replied, " Destroy this temple, and in three days I will raise it up." They thought He spake of the Temple that was forty-six years in building, but He spake of the temple of His body ; so, at the very beginning of His ministry, He told the Jews that *the sign* that He was God's son was that He would rise from the grave on the third day. Then again, when, later in His ministry, He was asked for a sign, He said, in the twelfth of Matthew : " An evil and adulterous generation seeketh after a sign ; but there shall be no sign given to it but the sign of the prophet Jonah," making Jonah's being held in the belly of the great fish, and afterwards being thrown out on dry land, the sign and symbol of His own descent, as it were, into the very belly of the earth, and then being cast out by the power of God again in resurrection. Since Christ Himself gave no other sign of His being the Son of God, and the appointed Messiah, except the sign of His resurrection, everything, according to His own Word, depends on that.

There is a strange saying in the second Psalm, to which I call especial attention. In the seventh verse, Jesus Christ is represented as speaking : Jehovah has said to me, "This day have I begotten Thee." Now, if Jesus Christ were eternal, begotten of the Father before all worlds—that is, never had a proper beginning—how can it be said that Jehovah said to Him, "This day have I begotten Thee"? In the thirteenth chapter of the Acts of the Apostles and thirty-third verse, this subject is illumined by the teaching of the New Testament: "God hath fulfilled the same promise unto us in that He hath raised up Jesus again. As it is also written in the second Psalm, Thou art My Son, this day have I begotten Thee." Peter says that the reference in the second Psalm, "This day have I begotten Thee," is to the resurrection of Jesus Christ from the dead. His death is figuratively treated in Scripture as His *ceasing to be,*—as though God had, on the day of His crucifixion, lost his only begotten Son; and His resurrection is correspondingly treated in the Word of God as a *re-begetting* of Christ from the dead, as though that tomb which had never before received a human body, a sepulchre in which no man had yet been laid—that virgin tomb—had become, on the third day, a virgin womb, out of which Christ was re-born to die no more. Let us bear in mind this startling and majestic metaphor. The resurrection of Christ is held up before us, in the Scriptures, as a re-begetting of Christ, so that He became the first born or first begotten from the dead, coming out of the grave as one that is born again, or begins life anew.

How immensely important, therefore, is the resurrection of Christ. Without it we should have no infallible proof that Jesus Christ was God's first-born Son, begotten again from the dead. And so, in the sixteenth Psalm, we read, "Thou shalt not suffer Thine Holy One to see corruption." No corruption could come, even to the flesh of Christ, because that flesh was indwelt by the Holy Ghost, the Spirit of all life and power.

II. Secondly, the resurrection of Christ is the basis of our justification. In the fourth chapter of Romans and twenty-fifth verse, we are told that He "was delivered for our offences." The expression refers to the delivering up of a criminal to the sheriff or the executioner—"He was delivered up for our offences," as a malefactor, as a sinner, as one condemned; " He was raised again for our justification." And thus we are taught that there would have been no justification for a believing, penitent sinner, if Christ had not risen again from the dead. In the sixteenth chapter of John, when Christ foretold the coming of the Holy Spirit, He said, "When He is come He will convince the world of sin because they believe not on Me; of righteousness, because I go to My Father, and ye see Me no more; of judgment, because the prince of this world is judged." Let us tarry a moment to consider that convincing of "*righteousness*"—" of righteousness, because I go to My Father, and ye see Me no more."

That passage is commonly understood by a careless reader to mean that the Spirit is to convince the world of the fact of sin, and the need of righteousness, and the certainty of a judgment to come. But Christ does not say anything here about the *need* of righteousness, He says, "The Spirit shall convince the world of righteousness or justification, because I go to my Father, and ye see me no more." The thought is kindred to that in Romans iv., 25, "He was delivered for our offences, and raised for our justification." Suppose it possible for an innocent man to take the place of the guilty. Here is a man, for instance, who has committed some crime that demands his being shut up in prison for ten years; but some man, high in the State, who has served his country, like a general on the battle-field, or a great statesman in Parliament, comes forward and offers to go to prison for a time long enough to satisfy the demands of a broken law, and take the place of the malefactor. Suppose also that it were possible for the the Government to consent that there shall be such a substitution, to magnify the law and make it honourable, and satisfy the claims of general justice. So that man goes into prison, and as long as the law deems it necessary that he should remain there in order to satisfy its claims, he remains. Some day he re-appears in the street, a released man. What conclusion do you come to? That the Government is satisfied with his vicarious substitution, and that henceforth the penalty of the law over that evil-doer is done away. Now Jesus Christ consented to take the place of sinners for a sufficient time, and undergo a penalty severe enough, to satisfy Divine justice and the law. He went into the prison of the grave and remained there till the third day. Then He emerged and came forth, and appeared among men, released by God's own Spirit, and angel guards. Was not that a sign that the Divine Government was satisfied, and Divine law was expiated? The very appearance of Christ among men again was the sign that He had accomplished the righteousness that He started to work out; and so the Spirit is prepared to convince the world that there is an adequate justification for the sinner accomplished because Christ rose from the grave, went to His Father, and appeared on earth no more.

There is a possible beautiful reference to this in what Christ said to the women who met Him at the sepulchre, especially to Mary Magdelene. When she first met Him after His resurrection, she was about to embrace His person in the enthusiasm of her love, and He said, "Touch Me not, for I am not yet ascended to My Father." A little time after, the women came and held Him by the feet and worshipped Him, and He made no resistance or remonstrance. It has always been a difficulty to students of the Holy Scripture to understand why Christ should at first refuse an act of homage, which afterwards He accepted. If we look back to the great Day of Atonement, in Leviticus, we may understand it. The High Priest, when he was accomplishing the work of atonement, left the brazen altar of sacrifice, took the blood of the offering, went into the holy place, and through the holy place to the holiest of all, alone. The apostle emphasises that idea of His being alone, in the epistle to the Hebrews, "Into the holiest of all went the High Priest *alone*, once every year, with blood of atonement." For him to be touched by anybody whilst he was acting in this representative capacity was ceremonial defilement. He was not even accosted or spoken to: there was a dead silence in the camp of Israel and among the priests while this awful but significant ceremony was undergone. He went into the holy place and sprinkled the mercy-seat with the blood, and when he came out again, not in the white garments of humiliation, but in the garments of glory and beauty,—the beautiful, embroidered robes,—he saluted the people and spoke to them and was spoken to by them. I venture simply to give what has helped me greatly in the understanding of this mystery, as a possible solution of it, that Christ, after He had risen from the dead, had not yet entered into the holiest of all with the blood of atonement, formally to appear in the presence of God for us, when Mary Magdalene met Him and would have embraced Him. So He said, "Touch Me not, for I am *not yet* ascended to My Father." Then He passes, as it were, in a moment into the holiest place and presents Himself as the atoning Saviour, touches the mercy-seat with His precious blood, and, as quickly, back to earth again, and is then embraced by the worshipping women. It is at least worth thinking of, whether the interpretation of this mystery of the New Testament may not be found in the ceremonies of the Great Day of Atonement.

However this be, one thing is sure: if Jesus Christ had not risen again from the dead there could be no justification for sinners. In the fifteenth chapter of the first Epistle to the Corinthians, Christ's resurrection is not only the basis of justification, but also of the world-wide *proclamation of the Gospel.* "If Christ be not risen, your faith is vain and our preaching is vain. Ye are yet in your sins." If Christ did not rise from the dead, we have no ground for faith, and we have no hope of salvation, and, so, have no basis for preaching. This miracle of the Resurrection therefore lies at the basis of these three things : it establishes His incarnation, it makes possible our justification, and is the foundation of all preaching of a world-wide gospel.

III. Thirdly, it is likewise the basis of our Resurrection. In 1 Corinthians xv., 20 to 26, we are taught that Christ was the firstfruits of them that slept. When we read in the Old and New Testaments of those who were raised from the dead; for instance, the dead man that touched the bones of the prophet Elisha, the restoration of the son of the widow of Nain to his mother, the raising of the daughter of Jairus, and the raising of Lazarus when he had been four days dead, how are we to understand the statement that Christ was the *firstfruits* of them that slept, since there were these cases of restoration from the dead before He Himself rose ? Let us notice the difference between *resuscitation*, or being made alive again, and *resurrection*. Resurrection, Paul tells us in the sixth chapter of Romans, consists in this, "He, being raised from the dead, *dieth no more, Death hath no more dominion over him.*" The man that touched the bones of Elisha died again, so of the daughter of Jairus, and Lazarus, as well as the son of the widow of Nain ; therefore they had no proper resurrection ; they were resuscitated or restored to life again, but they were not raised from the dead in the sense that death had no more dominion over them. So Christ was the firstfruits of them that slept. He was the first human being that was ever raised from the dead nevermore to die. So He led the way in the host of those who were to be like Him, raised from the dead. " Every man in his own order, Christ the firstfruits, afterwards they that are Christ's at His coming."

Artists have sometimes overlooked this. There is a great picture you will find in many galleries, of the Crucifixion of Christ. It was first a fine painting, then reduced by the art of engraving to a first-class steel plate. It represents the three crosses, the dark heavens, the rent rocks, and, in the foreground, saints moving out of their graves and walking towards the Holy City. The unfortunate thing is that the artist overlooked the statement of Matthew, who says, "The rocks were rent, the graves were opened, and many of the bodies of the saints which slept, arose and came out of their graves *after His resurrection.*" What becomes of that picture? It is the embodiment of an error. The evangelist Matthew thinks of the rending of the rocks in connection with the earthquake, and the exposure of the graves that were in those rocks, and then he adds in a kind of parenthesis, " Many of the bodies of the saints which slept "—in those sepulchres that were rent asunder,—"arose and came out of their graves, after His resurrection ;" we are not to think that they rose before Christ. He was the firstfruits of them that slept, and saints who rose after Him were like the first sheaf laid on the altar, " on the morrow after the Sabbath," as an offering unto the Lord. So Christ's resurrection is the firstfruits of ours, for it antedates and antecedes all other resurrection.

Firstfruits were not only the first gathered out of the harvest-field, but they were a specimen, on a small scale, of the final and complete harvest. So Christ is the specimen of the resurrection. Paul says to the Philippians, " He shall change the body of our abasement that it may be fashioned like unto the body of His glory." In His forty days of resurrection life, we have some indications of what our future body shall be—substantially like His body, recognisable as identical with the body of our humiliation, but not subject to the ordinary limitations of space and time, weakness and decay. He appeared within closed doors, and disappeared instantly; He was now on earth and now in heaven, now in Judea and now in Galilee. There is an immeasurable field of research opened up before us, as to the character of the future resurrection body, which shall be glorious like His, independent, like His, of previous conditions and limitations; capable of a service that we cannot dream of now, and of enjoyments the like of which we have never experienced. His resurrection is but the foundation of ours, and furnishes the standard of ours.

All Christian peoples have had some conception of the importance of the resurrection. This very morning, in one of the great cathedrals of Europe, the resurrection of Christ has been celebrated by a beautiful and symbolic ceremony. Doves, which have been confined in cages, have been brought out in front of the great towers of the cathedral, and the doors of the cages opened, that the doves may emerge from them and mount up toward heaven. It is a symbol of the soul released from the cage of its confinement, and mounting up in resurrection glory to bask in the sunshine of God, and attain the very Heaven where He dwells.

How oftentimes we overlook the great distinction between a worldly man and a disciple. There are two Latin mottoes that I never lose sight of when I am talking on this subject. One of them represents the utmost that a man can say who has no interest in Christ, and the other represents that which a disciple can say, when he gets to the end and bound of human existence. The worldly man at most can say, *Dum spiro spero*—As long as I breathe, I hope;—but the disciple of Christ can say, *Dum expiro spero*—When I breathe out my life I still hope. Death is to a disciple the Gateway of Life.

Let me add two concluding remarks: how important it is that, in the first place, the fact of the death of Christ should be established, because otherwise there can be no true resurrection. If He did not really die, He could not really be raised from the dead. And see with what infinite pains the Word of God establishes the fact of Christ's death. First, He was crucified,—not simply bound to the Cross, as many a slave was, by ropes, but *nailed* to it by His hands and feet. That of itself would ensure death; but, to make surer still, His side was pierced with a spear, and there came out blood and water, showing that the heart was cloven in twain. If crucifixion had not caused death, the spearing of the Roman soldier would have made death sure. Then, if possible to make it still surer that Christ did not merely swoon on the cross and was taken down in an apparently lifeless state, but not really dead, He undergoes a temporary embalmment, the body is wrapped in linen with spice between the folds of the linen. This would have ensured suffocation if the breath of life had still been in the body. Then He is left in the sepulchre till the third day without food or drink or ministry of any kind. You see how fact is piled upon fact, in the statements of Scripture, making it absolutely impossible that Christ did not actually *die*. And just so is fact piled upon fact to make it impossible that we should doubt that He rose. In 1 Corinthians xv., how distinct and how definite is Paul's statement with regard to Christ's resurrection :—" He rose again the third day according to the Scriptures, He was seen of Cephas " —that is, Peter,—"then of the twelve, after that of about five hundred brethren at once, of whom the greater part remain unto this present, but some are fallen asleep. After that He was seen of James, then of all the apostles, and last of all He was seen of me also, as of one born out of due time." There are six appearances of Christ,—to Peter, to the twelve, to the five hundred, to James, to the twelve again, and last of all to Paul. If this appearance had been a mere apparition, James or Peter or Paul might have been deceived, but how can you imagine five hundred brethren at once to have seen Jesus Christ, with all their varieties of temperament, and yet such a deception or hallucination to have taken root in their minds?

And then again, notice the variety of *forms* of manifestation. For instance, in one of those appearances, "He ate and drank with them " on the shores of Galilee. Now it is impossible that an apparition should sit down at a table or a banquet board and eat and drink with other people. Then again, notice not only how He appeared over and over again, and by unmistakable signs of eating, drinking, and the like, but how He held *conversation* with them. And not only so, but we are told that for forty days He spoke to them of the things concerning the Kingdom. That is the unwritten part of the Gospel. I suppose the Acts of the Apostles embodies the teachings of Christ as to the conduct of the Kingdom, and many of the epistles do the same. That forty days' conversation with the disciples, in which He taught them the mysteries of the Kingdom, make it absolutely impossible that they should have been deceived.

And then, last of all, His *ascension*, which they beheld; and the angels which appeared after He ascended and told them the meaning of the Ascension. Here, as in the case of the death of Christ, made absolutely certain by infallible proofs, the resurrection of Christ is made absolutely certain by equally infallible proofs. And so nothing is more absolutely certain than that Jesus Christ died for our sins according to the Scriptures, and that He was raised the third day according to the Scriptures. Every Lord's-day is, therefore, in a sense an Easter Day.

There is a very beautiful hint which some find even in the very *numbers* of Scripture. We are told in the Book of the Revelation that the number of the Anti-Christ, the last great foe of God and man, is 666; 666 is a repeating decimal: it can never reach to the full number seven. May not that represent a life that never attains unto completeness, but stands for the everlasting incompleteness that never reaches to rest, as represented in the Seventh Day—the unrest of departure from God? The numerical value of the word Jesus, in the Greek represents 888. Eight is the number of victory, Christ rose on the eighth day, the victorious day, sleeping over the day of rest. In a battle where both contestants fight with equal valour and success, it is a drawn battle. Both parties refrain longer from fighting, because neither can conquer the other. There is a rest from fighting ; but if one drives the other to the wall, and annihilates the enemy's force, that is victory; so there is something beyond unrest, and that is rest, and something beyond even rest, and that is victory, and so in the very name of Christ, we have a numerical hint that He is a Victor over Sin and Death and Hell. He does not simply retire from the contest as from a drawn battle. He drives the devil to the wall, He destroys his works, and annihilates his power, and casts him into the Lake of Fire.

And so the Mighty Conqueror ascends in glory to the Father's Throne, and carries on the work of Redemption until the world is brought to the knowledge of Himself. May we all be partakers by faith in the justifying merits of His blood, and by resurrection, in the triumph of His final victory !

SERMON TEN

The Mystery of the Resurrection; or, Hope of the Rising of the Dead

"But some man will say, How are the dead raised up? and with what body do they come?"—I CORINTHIANS xv. 35

EVEN as early as the days of the apostle Paul there were sceptics who disputed the mystery of the resurrection, and the question here asked by them is a double question: First, "How are the dead raised up?"; and, second, "With what body do they come?"

This is a remarkable discourse—the longest on any one subject contained in either the Old or the New Testament. There is no objection to the resurrection which is not here covered; nothing that we need to know about the future body of the saint, to which some reference is not here made. To follow the train of thought which the apostle here indicates, will enable us to draw many helpful lessons.

Every mind, in its natural unbelief and scepticism, inquires about the resurrection. How is it possible that the dead should be raised up, and with what sort of a body are they to be raised ? These are not only questions which interest curiosity, but they have to do with our conception of the resurrection itself, and are not, therefore, vain speculations. For example, one great obstacle to the doctrine of resurrection, which men confront, is an objection not easily set aside. We discover that, when a body is buried in the grave or sepulchre, it returns to the earth ; it loses its organic form, and becomes resolved in due time, if no extraordinary influences intervene, literally into dust. Thus its substance re-enters into the composition of the soil, and, as the chemical elements of a human body are the same as the chemical elements of the earth at large, these are taken up into the life of plants, and those plants are eaten by animals, and hence these atoms come to be a part of the bodies of animals; and, as the animals as well as plants become food for mankind, these atoms may again pass into human bodies ; so that it is a literal truth that elements that once entered into bodies of persons, now departed, may come round in the wonderful economy of nature to be part of other similar bodies ; and the question arises, if these material bodies are raised again, how is it possible that a body can belong to one person when several other bodies may have contained the same atoms at different times ?

Some, in their zeal to defend what they suppose to be the doctrine of Holy Scripture have imagined that, in the last great day of the resurrection, the atmosphere will be full of flying particles of dust which, by God's direction, are seeking the bodies to which they once belonged. Years after Roger Williams, the founder of the state of Rhode Island, in America, was buried, survivors sought to exhume the body in order to give it a proper burial and erect a monument over it; but they found that an apple tree had penetrated the soil immediately over his grave, had sent its roots down to where his body had lain, and had actually taken up the material of that body into itself. The roots of the tree had entered the skull, and followed along down the line of the backbone, dividing at the hips and turning up at the feet, so that the whole body had been absorbed—taken up into the substance of this apple tree. Such a fact will show that there is a real difficulty in the doctrine of the resurrection, as it has often been construed by those who loosely and carelessly read the Holy Scripture. But you will notice that the apostle Paul distinctly says, "Thou sowest *not that body that shall be*, but bare grain; it may chance of wheat or some other grain; but *God giveth it a body as it hath pleased Him*, and to every seed His own body. So also is the resurrection of the dead." We are, therefore, under no necessity of answering the scientific objection that the atoms that we bury in the ground cannot be raised again because they have come to be part of other creations, vegetable, animal and human; for the Bible does not say that the same material atoms shall be raised again. In our bodies, at this moment, there is not a single atom that was there seven years ago, if we are to believe what we are told by the students of physiology. Every time we lift an arm, speak a word, or think a thought, there is a destruction of some atom of brawn or brain, and food and air tend to replace the atoms that are thus wasted in action, whether of thought or of muscle; so that this waste of the system is constantly replenished. Nevertheless, each of us has essentially the same body, for the change of atoms does not involve a loss of identity in the body. Why is this the same body, though there is not a single atom that is as it was ten, fifteen, twenty years ago? Because when one atom has been displaced, the other atom that has taken its place has taken exactly the same relative position in the body, and so the *type of structure* in the body is preserved. It is somewhat as though you should take out brick by brick, or stone by stone, from a building, and put another into its place, and the process should take several years. The building would remain the same although every stone and brick was thus changed, because you preserve the shape, the style, the type of the building, and these constitute its identity. A great philosopher and theologian used to illustrate this thought by holding up a penknife before his pupils. "Now," he said, "if I break one blade and have another blade put in exactly like the one I broke, it is the same knife, is it not? If the spring of the back breaks, and I have another spring put in, it is the same knife, is it not? If it is not, when did it cease to be the same knife?" In these changes of the body not only is the type of structure retained, but the new parts preserve and perpetuate the same law of association. In the text this greater theologian, speaking by the inspiration of the Holy Spirit, relieves our mind of all needless scientific difficulty by an illustration drawn from earth's harvest-field. When you put a seed in the ground, what is it that comes up from the seed? It is not the seed itself but a plant to which the seed gave rise and growth. Even if the atoms of the seed are reproduced in the plant, the plant represents a thousand times as many atoms as the seed you planted. What then is it that the seed ensures? First, that there shall be a plant growth; second, that it shall be of the like sort with the seed planted; and, third, that it shall be vitally connected with the very seed planted. If you sow barley, or rye, or Indian corn, or oats, you will not get wheat; and if you plant one kind of wheat, it will be that sort in the crop; and each stalk which comes up will be identified with the particular kernel that was planted. What is it that is to come up out of the grave in the resurrection? Not the material body that you sow, but something grander and more glorious. What, then, is it that the body which you bury assures in the resurrection? First, that another body shall come out of the grave; secondly, that it shall be of the same sort as the body buried; not flesh and blood, indeed, but the same sort of body, built on the same great type of structure; and, finally, that it shall be identically connected with the very body that you have buried; and that appears to be the doctrine of the resurrection, as here taught.

"How are the dead raised up, and with what body do they come?" All through history certain errors have crept into the Church of God about the resurrection, and they are all denied or refuted in the Holy Scripture, so that, if the Bible be taken as a guide, you will fall into none of these heresies. One of the first of these was that the resurrection is already *an accomplished fact.* Paul refers to this when, writing to Timothy, he rebukes those who say that the resurrection "is passed already, and overthrow the faith of some." If we receive the Word of God, the resurrection of the dead is *not* a past, but a future fact. Those that are now buried shall rise again, and if you and I die in Jesus Christ a glorious resurrection is before us.

In the second place, the Bible teaches that this resurrection is *not merely a spiritual resurrection.* Some say, that when a sinner becomes a believer, that is his resurrection; that, as in baptism, he is buried with Christ, so, as far as he lives unto God, he is risen with Christ. However true, that is not the whole truth, as set forth in the fifth chapter of John, from the twenty-fourth to the twenty-ninth verses, "Verily, verily, I say unto you, He that heareth My Word, and believeth on Him that sent Me, hath everlasting life, and shall not come into condemnation; but is passed from death unto life. Verily, verily, I say unto you, the hour is coming, and now is, when the dead shall hear the voice of the Son of God: and they that hear shall live. For as the Father hath life in Himself; so hath He given to the Son to have life in Himself; and hath given Him authority to execute judgment also, because He is the Son of Man." That is the *spiritual* resurrection—something that *now is*. Jesus Christ comes, by His Spirit, and preaches the word; sinners, dead and buried in the sepulchres of their iniquity, hear that word and live, and come forth in a spiritual resurrection. But that is not the only resurrection referred to in this passage. " Marvel not at this, for the hour is coming"—(before, He had said, "the hour *now is*," but here, "the hour *is coming*")—in the which, all that are in their graves shall hear His voice, and shall come forth, they that have done good unto the resurrection of life, and they that have done evil unto the resurrection of damnation." How plainly our Lord Himself makes a distinct discrimination between a present spiritual resurrection and a future bodily resurrection. He says, " Do you stumble at this spiritual resurrection? Do not marvel at this great truth, for there is a greater mystery than that. The hour is coming when they that are *in their graves* shall hear His voice and shall come forth." If, therefore, we accept the Bible as authority, then the doctrine that the resurrection is past already becomes a heresy and a lie ; and the doctrine that there is no resurrection beyond that of a dead soul raised unto life, and that the body is never to be raised, is another heresy and another lie.

In the third place, notice there are *degrees of glory* in the resurrection. If all saints are to be raised, and their bodies are to be glorious bodies like Christ's body, does God make no discrimination between the different saints that have dwelt on this earth ? If they are all to have the same glorious home, and the same glorious body, there seems to be no just consideration for difference in character, conduct, and service. The dying thief on the cross never did any work for Christ, but turned to Him in the last hour of a worse than wasted life, and was assured of Paradise. On the other hand, the apostle Paul laboured through thirty years and more of constant service, daily dying for his Lord, and he certainly ought to have a greater reward. There are so-called saints in the Church of God who are so nearly sinners that it is quite impossible for us, at times, without the greatest charity, to determine that they are saints at all ; whereas there are others so manifestly like Christ that their very faces have the likeness of the glorified Lord. " Now, do you tell me," says an unbeliever or a sceptic, "that all disciples are alike to be raised, wear a glorious body like Christ, and have equal rewards ? " The Bible answers that there are *degrees of glory* in resurrection, as star differs from star in glory. If you go out on a clear night and look up to the heavens, you will observe Sirius, the " dog-star," which is equal to a thousand suns, while the sun is equal to fifteen hundred Jupiters ; and it is shining with an exceeding bright light in the heavens, while other stars are so small that you can scarcely see them, and others you cannot see without a telescope, while some are scarcely visible even with a telescope. Star differs from star in glory; and there will be as great a difference in the *glory* of resurrection saints as there is in the *character* of living saints; some scarcely saved, and some saved abundantly; some scarcely visible in the firmament at all, and others like little suns in brightness, because of their resemblance to Christ and their self-denying service for Him. Here, then, is another error in human opinion which this discourse distinctly contradicts.

Now, with regard to the *description* of this resurrection body, wonderful things are said about it. There are *seven* features that enter into this description. First, corruption is displaced by incorruption; second, dishonour is displaced by glory; third, weakness is displaced by power; fourth, the natural is displaced by the spiritual; fifth, the mortal is displaced by the immortal; sixth, the earthly is displaced by the heavenly; and, seventh, flesh and blood give way to something that is not here described. Let us try to project our thoughts forward to the day when Christ shall come in glory, and the bodies of all His sleeping saints shall rise to meet Him in the air, and get some conception of the kind of bodies they, and we, also, if we are in Christ Jesus, are destined to have.

First, corruption gives way to incorruption. What is corruption? It is the liability to decay. You never saw a human body yet whose bloom did not fade, the light of whose eyes did not grow dim, and which did not grow weary and worn and wasted with disease; hair that did not grow gray with old age; and senses that did not fail as years passed on. The body that we are to have in the resurrection will have no elements of corruption. There can be no disease in it, no death, no fading or failing of bloom or powers or faculties or senses, but eternal undecaying youth.

Secondly, dishonour is displaced by glory. Dishonour is different from corruption; it implies *sin*. This body has been disgraced by evil lusts and carnal passions. It was meant for the temple of the Holy Ghost: it has been rather an abode of Satan, used by the spirits of evil to work evil purposes. The tongue has spoken unguardedly, unadvisedly, perhaps impurely, profanely, blasphemously; the hand has handled uncleanness, and the feet have walked in unholy ways, and the ears have listened to sounds that were debasing and corrupting, and the eye has looked with lust and evil desire. The body has thus been dishonoured by sin. It has taken part in the iniquities of the sinful soul, and has been the organ, instrument and vehicle of evil passions. All this is to give place to glory in the resurrection body. No more the eyes or ears given up to the impure suggestions and uses of Satan, nor organs and faculties desecrated to the service of evil.

Thirdly, weakness shall give place to power. We all know too well what weakness means. We undergo what we call fatigue. After we walk a certain distance, or toil a given time, the little vessels of oil that keep the joints lubricated, like the wheels and levers of a machine, begin to get dry. It becomes difficult to bend the limbs, to make any exertion, and, as we say, we are tired, fatigued, exhausted. Another form of weakness is seen in the limits placed upon the use of our strength and power. There is a bound to the sight of the eyes, and the hearing of the ears. There is a limit to strength, to the power of the arm to lift a weight or bear a burden. On all sides we are limited, can do so much and no more, can accomplish so much and nothing beyond it. In the resurrection body, weakness gives place to power. We shall know no such thing as fatigue or exhaustion. Strength will not give out. There will be no limit to the sight of the eyes and the hearing of the ears, or to the power of our service for the Lord. We shall be like the birds that mount up on wings, and, in their greatest activity, rest and repose in the very act of flight, so that, instead of being fatigued by flying, they get rest on their pinions; and so the prophet says we " shall mount up with wings as eagles; run and not be weary; walk and not faint."

Another, and fourth, particular about the resurrection body is that the natural shall give place to the spiritual. A most difficult thing this is to describe or define even to the most intelligent; but it is well to observe that these expressions, "natural" and "spiritual," scarcely convey the full force of the original, and there are no words, perhaps, that can. The original reads: the first man, or the first body, "is psychical; the second is pneumatical." The Greek called the soul *psyche*, and the spirit was known as *pneuma*. The meaning seems to be that the first body is inhabited by the soul, and adapted for the *soul;* but the second body is indwelt by, and adapted to, the redeemed *spirit*. This opens up a limitless expanse of thought. Did you ever notice that, even in the animal world, there seem to be senses of which we human beings have no knowledge? For instance, you lead a dog away fifty miles from home, blindfolded, and he will find his way back. How? By some mysterious sense which we call "scent." Nobody knows, no philosopher has ever told us, what it is. It seems to be a sense that you and I do not possess, but which is given to the lower animal creation. Suppose that there were darkness like midnight in this building, so that we could not find our way. Let a bat in here, and he will fly all around, past these columns, and though a thousand wires were strung across, he will come into contact with no obstacle whatever. He has another mysterious sense, more wonderful than vision. He will wind his way in and out, past all barriers, and among the wires, and never touch one of them. That is another peculiar sense. We call it sensitiveness to touch, but do not know what it is. The future body of risen saints may have fifty senses instead of five. More than sight, hearing, taste, touch and smell, it may have senses and powers of which we can form no adequate conception. God made this body adapted to the human life that dwells in it, and gave all the faculties and functions necessary for it while upon the earth, but he is going to give us another body, fashioned as it hath pleased him; a body not for the soul, but for the spirit; not a soul-body, but a spirit-body, with senses so much grander, larger in scope, mightier in power, that we can form no conception of them now even by the illustrations given from the animal creation.

Then we are told, fifthly, that this body is to be, not of the earth earthy, but heavenly. Or, as Paul says, in the beginning of this description, "There are bodies terrestial and bodies celestial." There is a flower that blooms in the garden : that is a terrestial body. There is a star that blossoms in the gardens of the firmament—that is a celestial body. The flowers are the stars of earth ; the stars are the flowers of heaven ; and there may be as great a difference in the glory of the resurrection body as there is between a flower and a star. One is earthy, made of earth, its composition is of dust. The other is heavenly, having no elements of dust in it, having no earthliness in it, and, as I have intimated, different in structure, different in texture, different in powers and possibilities. We have indications all through the Word of God of what the resurrection body may be. For instance, when Manoah and his wife offered their offering to the Lord, the angel that appeared to Manoah touched the cakes lying on the altar, and, as the fire rose from them, he ascended in the flame. He had a body that could be seen, and that, without doubt, could be felt, but that body could not be burnt by fire. It was not an earthly body—it was a heavenly body. And there are some indications in the Word of God that such is the character of the resurrection body, and that human beings may for a time have such a body even while on earth. For instance, when the three holy children were put into the furnace of fire by King Nebuchadnezzar, though the flame of the fire was so hot that it slew the men that took them up and cast them in, the three children walked loose in the midst of the fire, which burnt the bands that bound them, but did not interfere with the texture of their bodies. Instantaneously they were transformed, so that their bodies no longer were earthly but heavenly, so that the fire could not consume them, any more than the body of the angel that went up in the flame of Manoah's sacrifice. After the resurrection of Christ the disciples were assembled in Jerusalem, and, for fear of the Jews, shutting and bolting the doors. Christ suddenly appeared through the closed doors and stood in the midst of them, and again He vanished out of their sight. Walls could not detain Him. Doors could not shut Him in. He appeared in one moment and disappeared in another. Now, the women met Him on the road; again He was gone; now, in the midst of His disciples, and then vanishing away. A heavenly body, not an earthly body; a celestial body, not a terrestrial body. Christ was now in Judea, and the next hour, perhaps, in Gallilee; not needing to travel slowly over that long space between Judea and the lake of Capernaum, but going instantaneously where He pleased. Not only so, but it seems as if Christ was passing between heaven and earth during the forty days succeeding His resurrection, now there and now here, as He pleased. And, when the time of His Ascension came, in defiance of the law of gravity, He rose and went up. All this suggests to us the vast possibilities of the resurrection body, a body not bound by the limits of earth, but having heavenly conditions, limitations, capacities and glory.

Here, then, we have a body; no longer with corruption, but with incorruption; no longer with dishonour or sin, but with the glory of holiness; no longer with weakness and limitation and fatigue, but with the everlasting power and strength of God; no longer a mere body adapted for the temporary possession of the soul on earth, but adapted for the redeemed spirit in Paradise; no longer earthly in its elements, but heavenly in its nature and structure.

And the apostle says, sixthly, that it will be no longer mortal, but immortal. Death cannot reach that body; floods cannot drown it; fire cannot burn it; the sword cannot pierce it; no form of destruction can overtake it. It is immortal; it is undecaying; it is undying, like unto Christ's glorious body that He wears for evermore on the throne of the majesty on high.

The apostle tells us, last of all, that it is not a body of flesh and blood. Our present body is such, but flesh and blood cannot enter into the kingdom of heaven. Why? Because flesh is a tainted thing, and blood is a decaying thing. The flesh has to be replaced in its waste by new tissue, and the blood has to be replaced in its waste by new atoms and corpuscles. But there will be no flesh and blood entering into that body. What does enter into it? That is where the Bible is silent. And why? Because eye hath not seen, ear hath not heard, the heart of man hath not conceived, human language cannot express, what is to be the substance and material of that body. You can get some conception of it if you will recall the Mount of Transfiguration. While Christ was praying, He was suddenly transfigured, and His whole body became like a burning flame. Suppose that, through one of these windows, the sun or moon pours a flood of radiance. There is seen through the atmosphere what we call "sheen." Nothing else can express it; golden sheen of sunlight, silver sheen of moonlight. It is transparent, and yet visible. You can see the rays passing through the atmosphere, and yet you yourself can pass through the rays. It seems as though Christ's body, when glorified, had a very strong similarity to light. His eyes flashing as a flame of fire; His hairs shining like golden wool; His very feet burning like molten brass in a furnace; His countenance was like lightning, and His raiment like the snow which the sun shines on and transfigures to gems. It seems as though, when Christ was transfigured, the holy emotions, affections, and desires of His heart shone through a transparent body, and turned the whole into a body of sunshine. And so the Bible gives us a hint of what it cannot describe. God gives a body to His saints, as it pleases Him. No doubt it will resemble the present body, only far more beautiful; some of us would want to be far more beautiful than we have ever been here. How often, even in saints, we see deformity and ugly features of face, defective members and distorted limbs. We cannot imagine any of those things in the resurrection body; the body then will have its type of perfection, and all imperfection will be gone.

Do you not feel drawn to Jesus by the thought of resurrection life? Some of you think that you have had a hard time in this world. It is hard to get bread to eat, and raiment to put on, and coals to keep a fire with during the long and severe winter. Perhaps some of you have buried your children out of sight; some of you are widows whose husbands have been long dead, and you have been striving with your needle, or by some other form of handiwork, to keep together the little family of orphan children. You think that you have had a hard time, do you? Beloved, how will you look back upon it when the Lord gives you a body like unto His glorious body, when you no longer need to ply your needle, or work at a trade, or husband the coals for your fire, or the crust of bread to feed the hungry family, and you are no longer worried about buying clothes for your little boys or girls, and about educating them, and securing a home for them to dwell in? No more disease, no more sickness, no more dying, no more poverty, no more misery, no more weary left arms through carrying the baby, no more dropping of tears in the agonies of a night, or through the sorrows and sufferings of a worn and weary day. We shall mount up on wings like eagles, and be glorious like the sun, glowing like the sunshine, knowing no fatigue, no exhaustion, no growing old, never thinking of the possibility of a sick bed, or of a dying hour. No new-made graves there; no monuments over the dead; no weeping beside the sepulchre; no groans; no sharpness of pain; but everlasting blessedness in the presence of the Lord and the glory of His power.

And yet there are some of you who, when the dear Lord puts all the glory of this future before you, can turn aside to the beggarly elements of this world, and deliberately reject and refuse Him through whom comes the resurrection from the dead. Oh, may God touch your hearts with some holy aspirations to be one with Him in whom your soul may have an instantaneous resurrection, and in whom your body shall by-and-by have a glorious resurrection from its grave unto the holiness of fellowship and companionship with Him.

Sermon Eleven

The Christian's Inventory; or, The Hope of the Inheritance

"All things are yours; whether Paul, or Apollos, or Cephas, or the world, or life, or death, or things present, or things to come; all are yours; and ye are Christ's; and Christ is God's."—
1 Cor. III. 21—23

THERE are days in the year when merchants take account of stock. It is well sometimes for a Christian disciple likewise to stop and take an inventory of his possessions.

The Apostle Paul here gives us such an inventory, which can scarcely be apprehended without a careful study of the structure of these sentences, which furnishes another example of the genius of Hebrew poetry, as found in parallelism. And one mark of the inspired foresight of the Bible is seen in this; for, had the Hebrew poetry been, like Tennyson's odes, dependent upon metre and rhyme for its beauty, it could not have been translated into any other tongue without losing much of its charm; but when the rhyme and rhythm lie in the thought you can more readily transfer such correspondence of the thought into another language.

Here we have in the Greek a kind of short poem or

parallelism whose various parts may be arranged as in versification ; and when we thus write out these words, a new beauty is seen that could not be otherwise :—

> " All things are yours
> 'Whether Paul, or Apollos, or Cephas,
> ' Or the world,
> Or life, or death,
> Or things present,
> Or things to come,
> All are yours ;
> And ye are Christ's ;
> And Christ is God's.' "

This utterance is a kind of poetic rapture in which the Apostle discourses of the inheritance of the disciple. And, like a great many other poems, in one verse a great many things are included. If one should attempt to write a prose description of the inheritance of the saints, he might fill volumes with such a description ; but in poetry it is allowed to compact great thoughts, that might extend through volumes, into a few simple sentences.

Let us watch the working of the Apostle's mind under the guidance of the Spirit, as he wrote these words. Imagine him, perhaps sitting in a prison, or perhaps in his own hired rooms, or in the guest chamber of some friend, writing through another's hand, and led by the Spirit he dictates these words. He addresses the Corinthians, who had joyfully taken the spoiling of their goods for Christ's sake ; and he remembers how the gospel had passed by the worldly-wise, and rich, and mighty, and noble, and had taken out the refuse of the Corinthian population. They were poor originally ; but if they had had riches, they would have given them up for Christ in those days of persecution. Yet, to these very people that had nothing, and were in the eyes of the world as nothing, he bids his amanuensis write these words: "All things are yours." There cannot be anything left when you have said " All things." That is an expression that sweeps round the whole universe and takes in everything. " All things are yours." And now the thought strikes the Apostle's mind, " They will hardly understand how much that includes, unless I begin to specify," and so he adds : " Whether Paul, or Apollos, or Cephas," representing all that ministered in word and doctrine ; but that is only one department of this great possession. " Or the world." " The world " is one of the most universal terms of which we have any knowledge. It includes the whole human family; it includes the whole of human history ; it includes the whole of the habitable earth. Yet even that will not do. " Or life : " That covers the term of our existence both in this world and the hereafter ; it is all yours with all its experiences. " Or death." If there is anything that seems to have both "all seasons" and all men for its own, it is death. Only two of the human race ever escaped its all-devouring jaws—Enoch in the patriarchal era, and Elijah in the prophetic era, and yet this monster that seems to possess the whole human race is here said to be the possession of the disciple.

But even these will not exhaust the inventory. " Things present ; " these include whatsoever is and whatsoever has been, because whatsoever has been belongs to the present as the property of memory, as whatsoever is belongs to the present, as the property of actual daily experience. But all this will not suffice. " And things to come." That reaches into the illimitable ages of eternity. Paul has been trying to make specifications, to give the items in this stock-taking. But, as though discouraged with the attempt to enumerate, he has only succeeded in giving a very few of the things possessed by the disciple, but those are the most comprehensive terms possible. And,—like a man who has begun taking stock in a great manufactory, and has noted five or six great articles that one shelf contains, but, as he sees the vast accumulation of goods before him, gives up in despair in the effort to complete his work,—Paul returns to the original sentence with which he began : "All things are yours;" "I can no longer itemise your estate ; I must only epitomise it in a word, and return to the universal statement with which I began, '*All things are yours.*'" Then he adds the ground or basis of this possession. "Ye are Christ's ; and Christ is God's."

So much for the structure of the sentences. Now let us look at what they contain or suggest.

We may begin where Paul begins, with the itemised statement, and look for a few moments at what the items comprehend and represent. " Paul, and Apollos, and Cephas,"—the Aramaic name for Peter. Paul referred to himself and Apollos and Peter, partly because in the Corinthian Church there had come to be a schism or division. Some said, " I am of Paul;" others, "I of Apollos;" others said, " I belong to Peter." Paul says, "Who are these, but servants of God by whom ye believed even as the Lord gave to every man ? What difference does it make by what particular channel the grace of God comes to you ? The glory is not in the channel but in the grace."

How comprehensive is this statement ! Paul was a great evangelist, an organiser of churches, the Apostle to the Gentiles, a great writer of Epistles, having more Epistles in the New Testament than any other writer. Who was Apollos?

Apollos was an Alexandrian. He belonged to what was known as the Hellenist, or Greek, portion of the original church. He was mighty in the Scriptures of the Greek translation or Septuagint, which took its origin in Alexandria. He had not been perfectly trained as to Christian baptism, though he had received John's baptism unto repentance, until he came into contact with Priscilla and Aquila, tent-makers, who turned their own house into a kind of theological seminary or pastor's college, with one student, and they the teachers. And who is Peter? Peter was the first organiser of the Church of God, the one Apostle, to whom especially was committed the privilege of opening the door of faith, first to the Jews on the day of Pentecost, and then to the Gentile world in the palace of the Cæsars, in the house of Cornelius.

These three persons were peculiarly adapted to represent the *whole body of Christian ministers* the world over, and all time through. Paul represented the uncircumcision ; Apollos, the Greek or the Hellenist portion of the church ; and Peter, the circumcision, or the Hebrew portion ; and it was as though Paul had said, " There is not a servant of God or a minister of Jesus Christ, in this day nor in all past time or future time, who does not belong to you as the body of Christ's disciples." This is a grand thought. This pulpit held, for forty years, perhaps the greatest gospel preacher of this age, or of any age, and you had him all to yourselves in a certain sense, and many of you came to feel that Charles H. Spurgeon belonged to you. But, on the authority of Scripture we may declare that he did not belong to you exclusively, but to the whole church of Jesus Christ. He ministered in this church and you called yourselves his people ; but we might write to the new converts that have

The Hope of the Inheritance

just been formed into a Church of Christ in Japan and say: " All are yours ;" and begin with Charles Haddon Spurgeon as a representative minister of Christ. He belonged to the whole church now on earth ; he belongs to the whole church that shall yet live on earth. Why? Because he helped to furnish the Christian testimony and the Christian literature by which that church shall yet live and survive to the end of time. See how it is with Paul. Does not Paul belong to you? You never saw him ; but you take up the Epistles to the Romans, the Corinthians, the Galatians, the Ephesians, the Philippians, the Colossians, and so on through the whole body of his Epistles, and out of one of those Epistles we are now getting a new blessing for our own souls. Does not Paul belong to you? Does not Apollos belong to you? he who mightily convinced the Jews, showing from the Old Testament prophecies that Jesus was the Christ? Whosoever points out the remarkable correspondence between the old portrait of Christ drawn by prophecy in the Old Testament, and the new portrait of Him drawn by history in the New, he is verifying the Old Testament prediction, and filling up the outline of the New Testament for every believer that from that time forth should compare prophecy and history as to the Messiah. Does not Peter belong to you? Go and read his Epistles. See how he sets before us the crown jewels of the Christian in the seven precious things of those two Epistles. If you have ever got comfort out of Peter's writings in all the sermons you have heard based upon them, in all the promises you have gathered from them, do you not so far own Peter?

It is an inspiring thought that, when Jesus Christ as the Head of the church sends a minister into a pulpit, no matter where that particular pulpit may be, if that man is a true man of God, if his testimony is for Christ, if he establishes and educates disciples in the faith of the gospel, he belongs to the whole body of Christ all the ages through and all the world over. There is no monopoly in the kingdom of God. No congregation can say, " We own this man, and therefore we can circumscribe his activity because he belongs to us." A man of God is first of all Christ's servant, and the servant of the church for Jesus' sake. And so he bestows his labour wherever God calls him to labour ; he bestows that labour for a time longer or shorter where God puts him ; and when his Master calls him elsewhere, he follows the Divine leading and guiding because he is first of all the servant of Christ and not of any particular church. You own every true minister of Christ; John Knox and George Whitefield, and John Calvin, and John Wesley, and Savonarola, Chrysostom, and Augustine. There is no man in all the ages that has helped to contribute to Christian literature, to evidences of Christianity, or the exposition of the Word of God, that is not your property as believers. All these men have lived for your sakes, written for your sakes, and toiled for your edification, and the completion and fulness of your salvation.

Now look at the next item : " The world." There are three or four words in the Greek New Testament that are translated " world." One means the world-*age*, or period during which the world lasts; another means the *earth*, another means the *habitable portion* of the earth on which men dwell, and another means the *cosmos*, or the world with reference to its beauty and symmetry, order and perfection. In the majority of cases in the English New Testament where we find the word " world ", it should be translated " *age* " ; for instance, the " world to come whereof

The Hope of the Inheritance

we speak," and "the powers of the world to come," is in the original "the *age* to come" and "the powers of the *age* to come." But in this text the word used is *comos*, or created world—the world as God has made it for man. *That* is also yours. Christ says "The meek shall inherit the earth." We shall have to confess that the meek do not yet inherit the earth in the neighbourhood where we live. The earth is held by quite a different class; but the time is coming when the meek shall inherit the earth. When the Lord Jesus Christ comes to give over the kingdom to the saints of the Most High; the habitable globe, the created world in which we live,—restored to its former beauty and symmetry before the slime of the serpent was over human joys and pleasures, and before the awful earthquake of sin wrecked the fair creation of God—shall return where it belongs, to redeemed mankind. But now, meanwhile, the world really *belongs* to the saints, but there is a usurper on the throne, the prince of the power of the air, the god of this world; but he is only a usurper. When Jesus Christ in the desert strove with him in the awful temptations of those forty days, and drove him back in ignominious defeat, He wrested the sceptre out of the hands of the prince of this world, and He holds that sceptre to-day to put it into your hands when He comes, and His reward is with Him to give to every man according as his work shall be. And that is the meaning where He says to His Apostles,—" Ye which have followed Me (in the days of My humiliation), in the days of the regeneration when the Son of Man shall sit on the throne of His glory, ye shall also sit on twelve thrones." That is what He means when He says,—" If any man hath forsaken houses and lands, and father and mother, and wife and children, for the kingdom of God's sake, he shall receive manifold more in this present age, and in the age to come life everlasting."

Take the next item. "Or life, or death." Life is a very inclusive term. Think of the vastness of its meaning. A word of but four letters, yet it covers an immense territory! Life means here, as always, more than existence. Life has its dimensions: length and breadth, and depth and height. It is not enough to count the years that you live if you would measure your life. "The days of our years are three score years and ten." That is simply a line from the cradle to the grave, reaching over seventy years of length. One may broaden out his life by broadening out his sympathy, his love, by taking into the embrace of his thought and his affection things that are outside of the narrow line of self-interest. As he thinks of his neighbour; of a dying world; of the destitute and the widowed, and the orphan, and the oppressed; as he thinks of the kingdom of God in all its vast out-reachings, the little narrow line of self-interest is crossed, and the territory of life broadens out to cover a vast continent of affection and of thought. When a man begins to cultivate his own nature, when he goes down into the depths of his own soul to find out what is there of sin, and by the grace of God expel it, what is there of weakness, and by the grace of God strengthen it, and what is there of selfishness, and by the grace of God displace it; when he learns, like a man who occupies a new territory on a farm, to plough it up, and subsoil it, and enrich the ground, so that he may yet get out of his own being the utmost possible yield for himself and his family and humanity, the man is discovering the depth that is possible to life. And when he looks beyond the present and the transient and the temporal, when he casts his eyes upward to God, when he reaches up

after God, His likeness, His honour, His glory, then he is learning the height that is possible to life. And so there is a very fine poet much neglected in these days, who says,—
"We live in deeds not years, in thoughts not breaths,
In feelings, not in figures on a dial.
We should count time by heart-throbs. He most lives,
Who thinks most, feels the noblest, acts the best.
It matters not how long we live, but how."

What does our Lord mean when He says of His sheep,— "I am come that they might have life, and that they might have it *more abundantly.*" How are you going to measure your life? Not by the number of years, for you may never yet have begun to live. Your life is measured by the intensity, not the extensity of its experiences; by the high exercise of the powers that God gave you, by the depth and reality of your enjoyment, by the power and effectiveness of your service. And so life is yours, and abundantly if you will have it so.

Consider another sense in which life is yours. No man can shorten your existence, if you are a child of God, until the time of God comes. "My times are in Thy hands," says the Psalmist. "I am immortal till my work is done," said John Wesley. Your life,—God has the keeping of it; and if your life "is hid with Christ in God," even your human existence is absolutely secure under the feathers of the Almighty wings, and no dart can reach you there until God chooses.

And then, in a still grander sense than this, your spiritual life is assured in Christ. The life of which other people who are men and women of the world know nothing, is the life that you begin to know when the Spirit gives you the new birth from above. When Christ enters into your soul, when the Holy Spirit makes a temple of God of you, and when the Word of God enriches you with all knowledge and spiritual understanding; when the days of heaven come down to earth that they may surround you with the atmosphere and the fragrance of heavenly gardens,—then you have and enjoy a life of which the earthly know nothing.

And this life never ends. Your mortal existence may be cut short, as men say, prematurely, but the life that you begin in believing in Jesus Christ goes on steadily accumulating in experience, and knowledge, and joy, and capacity through endless future ages.

As was already said, if there is anything that seems to *have us* it is death, yet the Apostle says that *we have* and possess death as our own. It is a remarkable statement, but it is marvellously true. Death cannot sever the cord of life without Divine permission. If you ever think there is a malignant power in the universe that holds the sceptre of life and death, and that somehow or other God has surrendered that control, go and read the first and second chapters of the Book of Job, and see how Satan could not lay on Job even an affliction in body or estate without the Divine permission. Satan proposes, in the first place, to wreck his worldly possession and his family life, and God says, "Thou mayest do this, but touch not Job's person." Then Satan seeks to afflict Job's person with disease, and God says, "Thou mayest do this, but touch not his life." There you see the permission given that Satan should try Job by external tribulations, and even by bodily diseases, but the infinite power of God comes in and says, "Thus far shalt thou go and no farther."

But there is a nobler sense than this in which death is the possession of the disciple. Death is the refining crucible to prepare our bodies for immortality. Flesh and blood cannot enter into the Kingdom of God, and that which is corrupt cannot inherit the incorruptible. And when the body of a saint is laid in the grave it is put in the crucible of God, so that there all fleshy, mortal elements may be refined away, and that which comes out of the grave in the resurrection is only that which is incorruptible and undecaying. It is somewhat as when a silversmith puts into the crucible precious metals in their alloyed state, with all their corrupting and defiling elements, and by the power of the fire separates the elements, skims them off like scum from the top of the molten gold or silver, and pours the gold and silver into forms that mould them into bars of sterling metal. God puts the bodies of saints in the grave, and He takes out of it at the resurrection only what remains when all mortal elements are left behind.

And, moreover, until Christ comes again, death is the gateway of life eternal. When the old Latins wrote over their sepulchre, *Mors janua vitæ,*—Death the portals of life,—they did not know how true was the sentiment they were expressing. Until Christ comes it is God's decree that all disciples, entering into the glory, shall pass through the vestibule of death. There are some indeed who shall not die; Christ when He comes shall find a living Church, and saints shall be changed in a moment without the experience of death. But so long as He shall tarry, every child of God must enter through the gate of death into the glory of the hereafter. And, inasmuch as this dark vestibule is the entrance to God's palace, death is ours, for, owning the palace with God, we own the entrance way to it.

A mother felt a bee alight upon her cheek, and inflict a severe sting. Straightway after, the bee began to chase her little girl about the room, and the child was in terror lest she should also be stung. The mother said to her, "My child, you need not be afraid, for the *bee has left its sting in me.*" When death stung Jesus, he left the sting in Him, and henceforth you and I need not be afraid, for death has no sting for us: *that* has been left in the Master.

I knew very well President White, of Knox College, in America. His wife, a most precious and godly woman, fell asleep very suddenly in Jesus, and his heart was very nearly broken, when the companion of so many years had been taken from him. It was little less than a year after that time, when he was preparing a Baccalaureate sermon for the graduating class; and, sitting in his own study, in the afternoon, he took his pen and wrote the dying words of his wife, which were these: "My darling, do not weep for me. This is not dying; it is going home. I look on your face one moment; I shut my eyes, and the next moment open them on the face of Jesus." He wrote those words out in the sermon, as his concluding words to the students. Feeling somewhat fatigued, he laid down his pen, and reclined on the same pillow where his wife had died, and sweetly fell asleep in Jesus. A few moments afterwards he was found, by the members of his family, with the flush still on his cheek, and the warmth of life yet in his body, and the ink scarcely dry on the pen.

Death is yours; death shall not summon you until Christ permits; death shall refine your very body in the crucible of the grave, and death shall open the doors of the palace to let your weary feet into the place of rest.

"Things present and things to come." I have already said that those two expressions cover all that is, and has been, and shall be, all life's varied experiences of joy and sorrow, apparent adversity, and apparent prosperity. All things work together for your good if you are a child of God. You are in the heavenly system. And just as in the solar system planets revolve round the sun, and comets in their eccentric orbits dart to and fro in the midst of these other orbits but never come into collision with planets; so, if you are in God's system, even the things that seem eccentric,—out of centre, out of line, unusually exceptional,—shall all work together for your good, for you are a child of God, and an heir according to God's purpose.

Yes, the little and the great things of life all belong to you. You are called to suffer. God will see that not a single pang is inflicted that is not essential. You are called upon to give up property. God will see that you are not impoverished beyond that which is needful for the enriching of your soul. He will cut the surface roots that bind you to this world, but the tap root that unites to the rock of ages, not the mightiest tornado or cyclone can tear asunder. Do not be afraid ; trust yourself entirely to Divine care. Everything in the present life, all the sum of its experiences of apparent sorrow and apparent joy, all the history of the past that memory gleans, all the future that hope anticipates or fear apprehends, is yours, and you can safely leave it with Him. You are like a cathedral that has been building through ages; the scaffolding is round about it, obscuring its beauty and symmetry, but essential to the erection of the towering spires. But, when the whole thing is completed, the scaffolding will be torn down and burnt up, and the grand building will appear in perfection. Everything that occurs in this world is for the sake of the Church. This world itself would not stand one single hour before God if it were not for the saints. "Ye are the salt of the earth." What is the effect of salt but to preserve from destruction ?

And when God's salt is no longer in the earth, the earth will no longer be spared from the destruction that impends. ※ It is nothing but the Church that keeps the world going. The world is a great stage. An unseen Hand, behind the curtain, thrusts forward at a given time one and another actor, just like a puppet. He makes his bow, he makes his speech, he goes through his act; and then he is withdrawn, and another is pushed on. It is God's work. Life's experiences are the stage of history; and men, and women, and children, bad and good, giants in evil and giants of faith, they are all thrust on the stage by the Great God, and they go through with their parts and retire. But the Divine Hand controls it all, for his glory, for our good. Even the blasphemer that walks the earth and defies God, and defames the Scripture, and seeks to tear out the faith of disciples from their very hearts,—even the blasphemer and the infidel are somehow serving God's purpose and the purpose of the Church. You do not know how precious Jesus is to you until somebody disputes whether after all there were any Jesus or not. You do not dig so deep to find the evidences of the Holy Spirit working in your heart until somebody questions whether there be a Holy Spirit or not. You do not know how close the Bible had wrought itself into the very fibres of your being, until somebody tries to rend the Bible in pieces, or make out that after all it is nothing but a human book, full of errors and mistakes, and fallible statements, and perhaps all the more worthless because it claims to be the Word of God. Do not be afraid. God governs in this world; and the things that appear to be against you, and against the Church, are really furthering your interests, and promoting the purity, and the stability, and the final triumph of the Kingdom of God.

This is only a glance over this mighty theme: it is not possible in the age that now is, to show the Christian all his inheritances; we have to wait for the ages to come.

Now, what is the *ground of our possession ?* Three links complete the series. " All things are yours : Ye are Christ's : Christ is God's." A vast golden chain and three links. First of all, Christ inseparably bound to God, so that whatever God owns, Christ owns; secondly, the believer and Christ inseparably bound in one, so that whatever Christ owns, the believer owns. And so we have the three links : God united with the universe, the whole past, the whole present, the whole future; Christ bound to God, the believer bound to Christ ; and so the believer is, through Christ, bound to God, and bound to all God is, and all God owns. And there is the basis of your possession.

Eliezer, the steward of Damascus, when he went to win a wife for Isaac, took out the jewels that Isaac, the master, had sent with him, and displayed them before Rebekah, and said to Rebekah, " Wilt thou go and be the bride of this man?" and she said, "I will." So, I spread before you the crown jewels, but not as you see them in the Tower of London, behind platè glass and iron bars, and with all kinds of guards about, lest you should touch those priceless treasures. There are no guards here, no iron doors. These are *your* crown jewels ; and you are yet to wear them in Christ, if you are a child of God. And so we put these crown jewels before you who are believers, yes, even before those who are sinners, unbelieving, impenitent as yet, and we say,—" These belong to the Master, and they are the dowry of the Master's bride : if you will come and be espoused to this Master, you shall wear these jewels with Him."

SERMON TWELVE

The Sum of the Gospel; or, The Hope of Intercession

"Now of the things which we have spoken this is the sum: We have such an high priest, who is set on the right hand of the throne of the Majesty in the heavens."—HEBREWS viii. 1

THIS is a sort of halting place in the Epistle to the Hebrews, where Paul gathers up the threads of his previous argument and testimony, and fastens them together in one comprehensive statement: "We have such an high priest, who is set on the right hand of the throne of the Majesty in the heavens." This is, in fact, the central text in the Epistle to the Hebrews, and it presents a central and pivotal truth, as to the great scheme of redemption.

I know of no text which seems so appropriate to the close of my two years' ministry in this tabernacle. It represents the sum of the things that I have sought to speak here during the past two years, and if I were to be here forty years more, it would still represent the sum of all that I should have to say in the future. You will expect to find in it, therefore, a very large range of truth, inclusive of the most vital and precious doctrines of Holy Scripture. Let us look closely at it. We have presented before us a priest, a high priest, and one who is set down on the right hand of the throne of the Majesty in the heavens. The priest was inseparably connected with the altar and the sacrifice. The high priest was the head of the whole body of priests. There was, properly, but one high priest at any one time, and he alone had the privilege of consummating the work of atonement by going into the holiest place of all, once a year, with the blood, with which he sprinkled the mercy-seat, where he held communion with God. Then he came forth from the holiest place, and, appearing in the presence of the congregation, lifted his hands in benediction, and blessed the people.

In the high priest, accomplishing atonement, going into the holiest place, and coming forth again in the garments of glory and beauty, with hands uplifted in blessing, we have the sum and substance of all that the Word of God teaches about our blessed Saviour Jesus Christ.

There are four conspicuous truths that are indicated in this passage. Two of them have to do with the high priest, and two of them have to do with his enthronement.

With regard to the high priest, the first suggestion is that atonement has been made; the second is that intercession is going forward. And with regard to the enthronement on the right hand of God, of course that means kingship as well as priesthood. And there are two thoughts about the kingship of Christ—one is a present rule and reign, and the second is a future kingdom in glory. So, in this text, we sweep round the whole circle of the precious truth of the New Testament Scriptures.

1. The high priest stands for *atonement*. The great day of

atonement was the one occasion upon which the high priest figured in the presence of the children of Israel in the exercise of all of his great functions. He slew one of the two kids for the expiation by blood ; he confessed over the head of the other kid the sins of the people, and he sent him away into the wilderness ; and then he entered into the holy place to complete the atonement for the sins of the people by the sprinkling of the blood on the mercy-seat.

Our blessed Master has accomplished all His atoning work as High Priest. Perhaps some of you have never noticed that little word "*set*" which is found here. Like every other word which is dictated by the Spirit of God, this has a precious significance. In the temple service, as in the tabernacle service, there was no provision made for the priest's *sitting down*. He was expected to move from altar to laver, and from laver to candlestick and table of shewbread, and from these to the altar of incense. And the high priest passed all these within the veil to the mercy-seat, but there was no provision for any sitting down within the precincts of the temple. This is referred to again in this epistle, in the tenth chapter, and it is now emphasized principally that we may accustom ourselves to notice the exact language, used in the Word of God. In the 11th and 12th verses of the tenth chapter we read, " And every priest standeth daily ministering." Notice the words : " Every priest *standeth* daily ministering and offering oftentimes the same sacrifices, which can never take away sins. But this Man, after He had offered one sacrifice for sins for ever, *sat down* on the right hand of God ; from henceforth expecting " (or in a state of expectancy) " till His enemies be made His footstool." You cannot but believe and perceive that the Spirit must have guided in the use of those two words. The emphatic words are obviously these: "in the 11th verse, the word "standeth"; in the 12th verse, the words "sat down"; and in the 13th verse, the word "expecting."

Now, let us follow the high priest. He goes into the holy place,—then into the holiest place. He is there a short time with God, sprinkling the mercy-seat and offering the blood as his mute prayer of atonement. Then he turns about,. changing his garments of humiliation, the white garments of the priest, for the garments of glory and beauty that were embroidered with cherubic work; and he comes back to the people and lifts his hands, and says, "The Lord bless thee and keep thee; the Lord make His face to shine upon thee and be gracious to thee; the Lord lift up the light of His countenance upon thee and give thee peace." And thus the exercises of the great Day of Atonement were finished.

Now, on the other hand, our blessed Lord, after He had finished His sacrifice for sins, once for all, entered into the holiest place, but He has never yet come back. He took His seat within the holy place; He sat down on the right hand of the throne of God; but He is coming back, as we shall see. He sat down: that means a finished work, just as when you complete your day's labour, and, coming into your home, you take a seat and sit down among your family circle, and divest yourself of those garments which are an encumbrance to you and which have been associated with your work, and with your feet in your slippers, and your form in easy attire, you rest yourself after fatigue. Sitting down means a finished work. But, as the work of the priests was never finished, they were always standing, or walking to and fro, from altar to altar, and from place to place. But our dear Lord on the cross completed His work.

There are three cases in the New Testament in which the word "finished" is used about our blessed Master. He declares that He has finished the *words* that He has to speak to His disciples. He declares that He has finished the *work* that His Father gave Him to do. He declares on the cross that "it is *finished*"—He does not tell us what, but we understand: He has finished His atoning sufferings. And, when Jesus Christ sat down on the right hand of the throne of God, He indicated that He had no more words to speak to His people, for they are all in the New Testament, and the New Testament is now a sealed book, nothing to be added to it or subtracted from it. When He sat down at the right hand of God, it meant that He had finished all His works of mercy and charity among men, going about, in person, doing good, ministering to the sick and the poor and the distressed. And His dying cry means also that His atoning sufferings are finished, and not a pang will ever rend the Redeemer's heart again, even for the sake of the sins of men.

But His sitting down at the right hand of the throne of God means more than this. It means that He is exalted. He came down for humiliation; He went up for exaltation. He humbled Himself and became obedient unto death, even the death of the cross, and during His humiliation He had not where to lay His head. He had no such thing as a resting place; although He was never restive or restless, still He had no resting place, no place which He could call home during the time of His earthly ministry. He was without human possessions; He was hungry, and thirsty, and weary, and faint, subject to the infirmities to which we are subject. But now, as He was once humbled, He is exalted, and exalted far above all beings and above all heavens.

The argument of this Epistle to the Hebrews up to this point is an argument about the infinite exaltation of Christ. For instance, the Hebrews thought a great deal of Abraham, the father of the faithful, but Abraham had no resting place; he was a pilgrim, a stranger, going about from place to place, and dwelling in tents. And so Christ is infinitely exalted above Abraham, for He has a sure and eternal dwelling place in the very temple of God above. They thought a great deal of Moses, who was the legislator of the children of Israel, and there is a phrase which occurs in the New Testament: "The Scribes and Pharisees sit in Moses' seat." Moses did have a seat. It was the seat of a judge; it was the seat of a lawgiver; it was the seat of one who controlled temporarily, as a sovereign. But Christ's seat is far above Moses' seat, for Moses was but a servant, and Christ is a Son. Moses was not an original lawgiver; he constructed his code of laws according to the divine pattern showed him in the mount. But Christ is the original lawgiver. He did not merely announce the law of the Sabbath, as something dictated to Him from above, but He Himself was the Lord of the Sabbath and the lawgiver of the Sabbath; and therefore He could administer the law, or even change the law if He should so please. Christ was exalted above even angels, for the angels themselves are nothing but servants, and Christ is a Son in His own house, commanding the universal homage of all the obedient angelic creation. The apostle begins this epistle with the argument that Christ is made so much better than the angels, as He hath by inheritance obtained a more excellent name than they. And then, once more, Christ is seated, as one who is in the expectation of final and glorious triumph when His enemies shall be made His footstool. How beautiful this figure is ! It suggests one sitting down without a footstool or a resting place for his feet. The expectant King is on His Father's throne, but the footstool has not yet been brought upon which He shall rest His feet. But that footstool is to be brought, and it is to be found in the very necks of enemies who have refused to submit themselves to His dominion; and when it is ready, He shall mount upon it to His *own throne!* It is, therefore, a prophecy of His coming triumph in His final exaltation as King, no longer on His Father's throne, but on His own.

The thoughts presented thus far have probably been more or less familiar, and so we pass on to speak of the other aspect of Christ's exaltation. We are told in this passage that He is the Mediator of a better covenant, which is established upon better promises. See the 6th verse : "But now hath He obtained a more excellent ministry, by how much also He is the Mediator of a better covenant, which was established upon better promises." That is one of the most interesting statements to be found in the Word of God. Few of us have any intelligent conception of what that phrase means, " the Mediator of a better covenant." We are told of the blood of the everlasting covenant ; and in this Epistle to the Hebrews, at the twelfth chapter, of the blood of sprinkling—the blood of the Mediator of this new covenant, which speaketh better things than the blood of Abel. There are two covenants in history. One was a covenant of law, but this is a covenant of grace. A covenant is a contract in which two parties mutually agree that each shall do a certain thing; and, unless each party fulfils the conditions, the covenant becomes void. For instance, if I should make an agreement in writing, that I would purchase a certain field of you for £500, that is a covenant. Now that

The Hope of Intercession

covenant depends for its ratification, first, upon my possession of the ground; and, secondly, upon your possession of the price. If I pay the money, and do not have the ground, the covenant is void. If you give the ground, and I do not pay the money, the covenant is void. Now, the old covenant was something like this: God promised certain privileges and blessings to His ancient people, on condition that they should fulfil certain obligations and duties to Him, but they continued not in their covenant; that is, they made void the provisions of the covenant by their own unfaithfulness and disobedience. And so we are told in this passage of Scripture that, as they continued not in this covenant, God regarded them not. (See the ninth verse.) Now, He tells them that He is going to make a new covenant, and let us notice what it is. "For this is the covenant that I will make with the house of Israel after those days, saith the Lord; I will put My laws into their mind, and write them in their hearts: and I will be to them a God, and they shall be to Me a people: And they shall not teach every man his neighbour, and every man his brother, saying, Know the Lord: for all shall know Me, from the least to the greatest. For I will be merciful to their unrighteousness, and their sins and their iniquities will I remember no more." You see, the old covenant was one that God made directly with men. There was no mediator of that covenant except Moses, and he was a mediator only in the sense of conveying to the children of Israel the terms that God prescribed as to their fidelity and loyalty. They broke their part of the covenant; they departed from God; they wanted to go back into Egypt. They broke His laws; they withheld sacrifices; they forsook His ordinances; they neglected even the seal that was on the covenant, the rite of circumcision, and failed to keep the passover. They became an apostate people. God sent them into captivity, and He annulled the old covenant. Now, what does He say? "I will make a new covenant." What is it? Not a law written upon tables of stone, for those very tables might be broken; not a covenant conditioned on human obedience, which is not a safe thing for God to trust to; but an unconditional covenant, a covenant made not with man, but with Christ Jesus as man's representative, who is faithful to Him that appointed Him, in all things, and never fails to fulfil all conditions. So God makes a covenant with Jesus Christ concerning believing children who were then, or should afterwards be born, believe, and be born anew. And Christ keeps His word and fulfils His part, and so there is no possibility of failure in this new covenant.

Now, when we read of this "Mediator of a better covenant, established upon better promises," what does this mean? That, when you come and trust yourself to the keeping of Jesus Christ, God's new covenant does not become void upon your lapses into sin, upon your backslidings, upon your going down into fits of depression and prayerlessness and temporary alienation from God. Not at all. No, He looks at Jesus Christ who is the Mediator, not merely as declaring to you the terms of the covenant, but as standing in the presence of God as your substitute and representative; so that when you look at your infirmity and frailty, when you see how far you have departed from God, even in holy acts, how little heart you have had in His worship, how little sincerity in His service, how little punctuality and fidelity in sacred duties; when you look back over your whole life, and say, "Wretched man that I am, who shall deliver me from the body of this death!

Who shall save me from these sins against my Saviour that I daily commit," God replies to you, "I do not look upon *you* at all; I do not condition My new covenant upon your fidelity or unfaithfulness. My covenant stands sure, for it is made not with you, a frail and fallible human being, but with My own Son, your perfect and all-sufficient Saviour." This precious Mediator of the new covenant does not simply become the channel through which the knowledge of the covenant comes to you, as Moses was with the children of Israel; but He takes your place in heaven, and there, seated on the right hand of the throne of the Majesty in the heavens, He represents redeemed humanity. He represents every believing man and woman and child in all the ages of the past, and present, and future; and, behind His perfection, all their imperfection is hidden. Is not that a great deal better than the old covenant—this new covenant of grace? And what a strengthening and helping thing this is to a child of God who understands it! How a disciple will bless God, who learns this great truth, that is hidden from so many minds. You need not be looking at yourself; you need not be looking at your sins and your failures and your want of fidelity. Keep your eyes fixed on your Master and Lord, and think of Him as the Mediator, and think of God as looking upon Him as your substitute and representative, who bare your sins past, and present, and future, in His own precious body on the tree. And while you are to seek with all your might, depending on grace, to be holy, do not be discouraged and think of the covenant as null and void, because now and then you fall back into sin, or into temptation, or because you dishonour and reproach your Master by neglect of duty, but think of God as keeping covenant with Christ for you, even unto the end.

3. Now, a word with regard to the *kingship* of Christ. "Set on the right hand of the throne of the Majesty in the heavens." See how words are piled up there to express this glorious idea. " On the right hand "—the place of power and favour—" of the throne of the Majesty in the heavens." The inspired writer can say nothing more than that. If anything means the right of kingship, that does. Exaltation above Abraham, above Moses, above Aaron and the whole circle of the priesthood, above even angels, so that they all fall at His feet in profoundest homage! What does that mean? It means that He is your Master and Lord, as well as Saviour and Mediator. It means that at present He is by His spirit ruling over His church, and reigning in the hearts of the believing and sanctified children of God. It means that your life, as a disciple, is in His hands, and that He is laying out the plan of it, that His will compasses the whole range of your activity; and, if you submit yourself thoroughly to Jesus, while you are working out to the end your own salvation with fear and trembling, He is working in you to will and to do of His good pleasure, so that your will is His will, and your work is His work ; and you need not think of the feebleness of your own endeavours, nor look at the imperfection of your own service, but remember that He knows how to use even the broken, frail, earthen vessels to convey to men the excellency of His power and of His grace.

You, who are believing children of God, having accepted Christ as your Saviour, and depended upon His high priesthood for your salvation, will you not now accept Him as your enthroned and reigning King, and just bow yourselves before the Mastership of Christ, and say, " Henceforth, Jesus, thou shalt rule in me, and reign over me, even to the end"? He is set down on the right hand of the Majesty in the heavens, and He asks your absolute submission; He wants your perfect self-surrender; He wants to control you. How we would rejoice if we could apprehend what this control means. There are so many of us who profess to be children of God who, after all, have no real sense of the *ruling of Christ* in our lives. We think that we are left more or less to ourselves. Here is a tempted soul that says, "What shall I do? Here is an awful temptation before me, and I do not feel the power to resist it. I feel as though I must give way before it. What shall I do?" Such despairing soul has not the slightest conception of the mighty power of a ruling Christ. His being seated on the right hand of God means that all the power of omnipotence is at His disposal, and that, as your Mediator before God, He represents you before God and represents God to you; that is to say, He is both God's apostle and man's high priest; He at once represents God to you, and represents you to God, and as your sins are represented in His atoning work, and as your service is represented in His perfect service, so the power and wisdom and goodness of God are all pledged in that Mediator, to your benefit and blessing.

What is a mediator? One who comes between two parties; who is the channel for the communication of the lower with the higher, and the higher with the lower. Christ, as the Mediator of the better covenant, represents the lower, that is man, before God; He represents the higher, that is God, before man. And, just as He will take your sins and show God that they are all atoned for in His finished work, so He will take God's power and show you that that power is absolutely sufficient for you in your struggles with sin and your endeavours to overcome evil. If you could only get possession of that thought—that Christ is your Mediator, that He is your King; that He is there on the right hand of the throne of God, with all the omnipotence of God at *His* disposal, and to put that omnipotence at *your* disposal, you would be jubilant in Jesus Christ. You would say, " Sin shall not have dominion over me. I am God's child."

How often we waver between sin and holiness, between the will of God and the will of the devil, and it seems as though the will of the devil must carry the day! How little do we understand that Jesus Christ " was manifested that He might destroy the works of the devil." Let every child of God not only accept Jesus Christ as having done something for him eighteen hundred years ago on the cross, having then died for him; but as having risen and as living for him, as not only the justifier, but the sanctifier, as not a dead Christ but a living Christ, as a real Christ, as a real King, Master, Saviour, Sovereign, and Lord. You cannot be overcome of sin; I say it boldly: you cannot be overcome of sin except as you lose sight of Christ, lose hold upon Him, and so lose your grip upon omnipotence. By believing prayer you can lay your hand on the very hand that holds the sceptre of the universe, and command the omnipotence of God to assist you. That is what you can do. Faith will lay hold of Christ as a reality, and bring Christ down to interpose to save you from perils, from sins, from dangers, from disasters, in your spiritual life.

4. But there is another blessed and glorious thought. Jesus is a *coming* King. He is now set down on the right hand of the throne of God, but He is coming from God's right hand to ascend His own throne. He is coming in power, in majesty and in glory, to consummate your salvation. In

Adolph Saphir's great book on the "Divine Unity of the Scripture" is a very original and a most refreshing view of this truth. In the sixth chapter of the Gospel according to St. John, there are two miracles recorded, and within the compass of one chapter, as though they had an intimate connection one with the other. The first miracle is the feeding of the five thousand with the few barley loaves, and the second miracle is the appearing of Christ to the disciples when they were rowing on a stormy sea, so that the ship immediately was at the land whither they went. Now, look at the suggestions of those two miracles. Those hungry people in the wilderness represent the world hungering for food, and never satisfied until Christ feeds that hunger. The disciples have Christ in the midst of them. They bring their five loaves and their two fishes to Christ. He blesses the loaves and the fishes, and breaks them, and distributes them, and the disciples carry them to the multitude, and everybody is fed and everybody is filled, and they take up twelve baskets of fragments after all have eaten. What does that mean? It means Christ co-working with all true disciples and evangelists and preachers of the Word, enabling them to take the five barley loaves of this precious gospel, which is despised by men and does not come up to the standard of human philosophy and learning and culture, and which men think, after all, is very poor diet for philosophers and sages. It represents these disciples taking the Word of God, the simple message of salvation, which was foolishness to the Greek and a stumbling-block to the Jew, and with it feeding all believing souls the world over. And to-day the miracle is going on. You are feeding in the name of Christ upon some of the barley loaves and fishes, and if you will open your mouth wide and receive the food you shall be filled; and yet,

after we have thus distributed, there shall be baskets of
fragments, enough, if this whole city would but come and
hear the Word of God, to fill every poor soul in London and
in the world.
 Now look at the other miracle. What is that? The
world is represented by a restless and tossing sea. It is not
now hunger: it is unrest: it is opposition to God. The
ship in the midst of the sea is the poor little church of
disciples tossed on the stormy waters, Satan commanding
the winds and waves to blow and beat upon it, and seeking
to destroy it utterly. Christ is away on the mountain-top,
communing with the Father. He is not with the disciples.
He is out of their sight, and they toil in rowing, but the
ship does not make any progress. The unrest of the world
continues; the hostility of the world abides. The world
opposes Christ, just as much as it ever did. Though some
people seem to think that the world is growing better, the
carnal heart hates Him as it always hated Him, and if He
were on the earth to-day the world would be just as ready
to crucify Him as it was in the days of His flesh. The
disciples who are hoping to convert the world keep pulling
away at their oars, but they cannot still the sea, and they
cannot bring the vessel nearer to the shore. All they can
do is to keep the vessel from sinking. But in the fourth
watch of the night Jesus comes to them as they are toiling
in rowing, and immediately the ship is at the land whither
it goes. The sea becomes stilled when He appears, and
straightway the church reaches her heavenly harbour. Do
you not see the significance of those two miracles? The
first, the world in its hunger coming to Christ, and getting
the loaves and the fishes, and being filled in the ministry of
the word; and the second, the world in its unrest and its

hostility to Christ beating away against the little ship of the church and trying to swamp it and destroy it and sink it; and all that disciples can do is to keep the ship afloat. We cannot still these waves; we cannot give peace instead of this unrest; we cannot abate this hostility of the world. But, just as soon as Jesus comes, now on the mountain communing with the Father—just as soon as He comes, there will be peace. The world will be brought to a new state, and the church will be at the shore whither it seeks to go.

"Now of the things that we have spoken this is the sum." We have a high priest who once accomplished a perfect atonement for us; who, having finished His words for our instruction, and finished His works of charity and mercy on earth, finished His atoning suffering, and said, "It is finished"; then through the rent veil passed into the holiest place, and took His seat on the right hand of the throne of the Majesty on high, ruling over His people, reigning in their hearts. He, being the Mediator of a new covenant established upon better promises, representing His people before God, and making their service perfect because His own service is identified with it, representing God to His people in bringing down the mighty power of God to control them in their sinful propensities and carnal desires, buoys them up with patience, and gives them encouragement and hope and joy and the assurance of His divine presence. And there He sits. He has no footstool yet, but the day is coming shortly when He shall bruise Satan under His feet and under your feet, and then His enemies shall be made His footstool. And, while the church is rowing against wind and tide, and trying to get nearer heaven, and making little or no progress, He is watching us from the mountain-top where He communes with the

Father; and in the fourth watch of the night, when the crisis is greatest, when the danger is most extreme, when the darkness is most desperate and the distress of the church is the most overwhelming, He will suddenly appear, and we shall see Him in the very midst of the sea, walking on the sea in the Majesty of God; and immediately when He comes into the ship it will be at the land. It will touch the millennial shore, and all the dangers and disasters of church life will be past.

Who does not want such a Saviour? I am sure that if I had not long ago accepted Him as my Saviour, I should accept Him now. He grows upon me. The glory of this Christ, the perfection of His divine majesty, of His mediation, the grace and the strength that He bestows upon the children of men, grows upon me. What He was and what He is and what He is to be grows upon me. I feel that my past is made sure, for He has atoned for my sin. I feel that my present is made sure, for I have offered my heart as His dwelling-place, and asked Him to reign over me. I feel that my future is sure, for He ever liveth to make intercession for me and to save to the uttermost all that come unto God by Him. The mystery is that any sinner can hear this gospel and turn away from it. However poor the preacher, this is a great gospel. No words can represent it, but it is magnificent, it is majestic. And I cannot understand how the multitudes can come and crowd this Tabernacle, and hundreds and thousands of them go away untouched by this gospel, caring neither for what Christ meant when He said, "It is finished," nor for what Christ means when He says, "I am the Mediator of a better covenant," nor for what Christ is ready to do when He says, "I am the ever-living Intercessor," nor for what Christ is coming to do when, as the returning King, He shall withdraw the veil within which He disappeared, and, in garments of glory and beauty, come forth to lift His pierced hands in benediction. It is hard to understand the indifference of people to this gospel. Perhaps it is just as well that I should cease to preach it, here, and give way to someone who, with more power of persuasion, can preach it after me. But I tell you, it is a solemn and awful thing, to hear such a gospel preached, and yet to turn away from the finished atonement, from the complete mediation, from the everlasting intercession, of Him who is the present Saviour and the coming King!

Great Sermons by Great Pulpiteers

J. D. JONES
The Apostles of Jesus
ISBN 0-8254-2971-4   144 pp.   (pb)

CLARENCE E. MACARTNEY
Chariots of Fire
ISBN 0-8254-3274-x   160 pp.   (pb)

The Faith Once Delivered
ISBN 0-8254-3281-4   144 pp.   (pb)

Great Women of the Bible
ISBN 0-8254-3268-5   160 pp.   (pb)

The Greatest Questions of the
Bible and of Life
ISBN 0-8254-3273-1   160 pp.   (pb)

The Greatest Texts of the Bible
ISBN 0-8254-3266-9   160 pp.   (pb)

The Greatest Words in the Bible
and in Human Speech
ISBN 0-8254-3271-5   144 pp.   (pb)

He Chose Twelve
ISBN 0-8254-3270-7   144 pp.   (pb)

The Parables of the
Old Testament
ISBN 0-8254-3278-2   160 pp.   (pb)

Parallel Lives of the Old and
New Testaments
ISBN 0-8254-3280-4   128 pp.   (pb)

Prayers of the Old Testament
ISBN 0-8254-3279-0   128 pp.   (pb)

Paul the Man: His Life and Work
ISBN 0-8254-3269-3   176 pp.   (pb)

Strange Texts but Grand Truths
ISBN 0-8254-3272-3   144 pp.   (pb)

Twelve Great Questions About
Christ
ISBN 0-8254-3267-7   152 pp.   (pb)

GEORGE H. MORRISON
Highways of the Heart
ISBN 0-8254-3290-1   200 pp.   (pb)

The Weaving of Glory
ISBN 0-8254-3291-x   208 pp.   (pb)

Wind on the Heath
ISBN 0-8254-3289-8   192 pp.   (pb)

The Wings of the Morning
ISBN 0-8254-3288-x   192 pp.   (pb)

CHARLES HADDON SPURGEON
Spurgeon's Sermons
on Angels
ISBN 0-8254-3690-7   160 pp.   (pb)

Spurgeon's Sermons for Christmas and Easter
ISBN 0-8254-3689-3   160 pp.   (pb)

*Spurgeon's Sermons on the
Cross of Christ*
ISBN 0-8254-3687-7   160 pp.   (pb)

*Spurgeon's Sermons on Family
and Home*
ISBN 0-8254-3688-5   160 pp.   (pb)

*Spurgeon's Sermons on New
Testament Men, Book One*
ISBN 0-8254-3783-0   160 pp.   (pb)

*Spurgeon's Sermons on New
Testament Miracles*
ISBN 0-8254-3784-9   160 pp.   (pb)

*Spurgeon's Sermons on New
Testament Women, Book One*
ISBN 0-8254-3782-2   160 pp.   (pb)

*Spurgeon's Sermons on Old
Testament Men, Book One*
ISBN 0-8254-3772-5   160 pp.   (pb)

*Spurgeon's Sermons on Old
Testament Men, Book Two*
ISBN 0-8254-3789-x   160 pp.   (pb)

*Spurgeon's Sermons on Old
Testament Women, Book One*
ISBN 0-8254-3781-4   160 pp.   (pb)

*Spurgeon's Sermons on Old
Testament Women, Book Two*
ISBN 0-8254-3790-3   160 pp.   (pb)

*Spurgeon's Sermons on the
Parables of Christ*
ISBN 0-8254-3785-7   160 pp.   (pb)

*Spurgeon's Sermons
on Prayer*
ISBN 0-8254-3691-5   160 pp.   (pb)

*Spurgeon's Sermons on the
Resurrection*
ISBN 0-8254-3686-9   160 pp.   (pb)

*Spurgeon's Sermons on
Soulwinning*
ISBN 0-8254-3787-3   160 pp.   (pb)

*Spurgeon's Sermons on Special
Days and Occasions*
ISBN 0-8254-3786-5   160 pp.   (pb)

Available from Christian bookstores, or

P. O. Box 2607 • Grand Rapids, MI 49501-2607